Machine Learning, Predictive Analytics, and Optimization in Complex Systems

Ferdin Joe John Joseph
Thai-Nichi Institute of Technology, Thailand

Karthikeyan Chinnusamy
Veritas, USA

Joseph Jeganathan
University of Bahrain, Bahrain

Ahmed J. Obaid
University of Kufa, Iraq

S. Suman Rajest
Dhaanish Ahmed College of Engineering, India

IGI Global
Scientific Publishing
Publishing Tomorrow's Research Today

Vice President of Editorial Melissa Wagner
Director of Acquisitions Mikaela Felty
Director of Book Development Jocelynn Hessler
Production Manager Mike Brehm
Cover Design Jose Rosado

Published in the United States of America by
IGI Global Scientific Publishing
701 East Chocolate Avenue
Hershey, PA, 17033, USA
Tel: 717-533-8845
Fax: 717-533-7115
Website: https://www.igi-global.com E-mail: cust@igi-global.com

Library of Congress Cataloging-in-Publication Data

Names: Joseph, Ferdin Joe John, 1987- editor | Chinnusamy, Karthikeyan, 1973- editor | Jeganathan, Joseph, 1980- editor | Rajest, S. Suman, 1988- editor | Obaid, Ahmed J. (Ahmed Jabbar) editor
Title: Machine learning, predictive analytics, and optimization in complex systems / edited by Ferdin Joe John Joseph, Karthikeyan Chinnusamy, Joseph Jeganathan, Ahmed J. Obaid, S. Suman Rajest.
Description: Hershey, PA : IGI Global Scientific Publishing, [2026] | Includes bibliographical references and index. | Summary: "This book examines the integration of intelligent technologies into system design and management, and data analysis. It explores strategies for data-informed decisions, intelligent technology utilization, and security optimization"-- Provided by publisher.
Identifiers: LCCN 2025029855 (print) | LCCN 2025029856 (ebook) | ISBN 9798337352039 hardcover | ISBN 9798337352046 paperback | ISBN 9798337352053 ebook
Subjects: LCSH: Machine learning | Predictive analytics--Technological innovations | System design
Classification: LCC Q325.5 .M3433 2026 (print) | LCC Q325.5 (ebook)
LC record available at https://lccn.loc.gov/2025029855
LC ebook record available at https://lccn.loc.gov/2025029856
British Cataloguing in Publication Data
A Cataloguing in Publication record for this book is available from the British Library.

Table of Contents

Detailed Table of Contents

In VLSI design, adders and multipliers are vital in performing summing and multiplying operations in different ways. Advances in VLSI technology have led to the emergence of designer adders with increased efficiency and cost-efficiency. Carry Look Ahead Adder (CLA Adder) is used in various operations where the system must add many bits with at least three inputs. CLA Adder is mainly used because of its ability to predict the carry before actually summing the inputs, reducing the overall execution time of the entire process. Still, there can be errors when the carry has been predicted. This paper proposes a new algorithm called 'Simple Carry Checker' based on approximate computing, which is used to reduce the frequency of errors in CLA adder while generating the carry of the inputs with a reduced execution time.

People prefer approximations based on resemblance, particularly when dealing with commercial figures. With data, the procedure is even more exact, known as Clustering. Clustering is a method that has numerous applications. Numerous fields, including pattern identification, image analysis, consumer statistical analysis, segmentation of markets, social network analysis, and more, use clustering, an unsupervised machine learning technique. It can effectively address many problems and goals, from the most basic to the most complicated. Cluster analysis is an effective approach for detecting underlying structures and patterns in data from diverse areas. It divides the data into clusters based on their similarities or differences. Researchers and analysts can get significant insights and make data-based decisions by combining comparable observations. Further, Clustering on the original information provided us with extremely valuable and unique explanations for each of the individual segments.

Missing data is an important problem in the digital world. Missing data means no value will be present in the dataset. Missing occurs for many reasons, including data loss, typing errors, system problems, less interest of the respondent, etc. This is a major issue for researchers, industry people, academicians, doctors, etc. The incomplete data will not support any solution. In this paper, a review of various research articles from 2009 to 2020 is analyzed. The techniques and algorithms used for the imputation have been analyzed. Imputation is the process involved in replacing the missing value. In addition, various algorithms, techniques, and methods are discussed in this paper to solve the above-said issue, and significant discussion is also done on the types of missing mechanisms. The main focus has been on the traditional and novel imputation methods.

This chapter investigates the potential of active learning techniques, in particular Bayesian Optimization, to enhance data annotation and model training. Active learning selects meaningful examples from unlabeled data to improve model performance and reduce labeling effort. Several active learning techniques, including uncertainty sampling, query-by-committee, and Bayesian Optimization, are investigated to determine how this impacts data annotation and model training. Multiple datasets, including CIFAR-10, IMDB reviews, and COCO, have been evaluated experimentally to demonstrate that Bayesian Optimization improves accuracy, reduces annotation effort, and accelerates model convergence. The findings emphasize the potential of active learning motivated by Bayesian optimization for efficient machine learning with limited resources. According to the findings, active learning strategies, hybrid approaches, and their use in real-world, ever-changing contexts warrant additional research.

The exponential growth of data in modern digital environments demands efficient real-time processing capabilities to provide timely and actionable insights. This research focuses on developing a robust real-time data pipeline that handles high-velocity, high-volume data, ensuring scalability, low-latency processing, and fault tolerance. The pipeline demonstrated the ability to ingest data at 1 million events per second, maintaining an average latency between 10 to 15 milliseconds. Scalability tests revealed that the system could effectively handle increasing data loads by dynamically adjusting resources, reducing processing time by up to 30% when additional nodes were added. Furthermore, the pipeline's fault tolerance mechanisms, including data replication and automated recovery, ensured over 99.9% reliability, preserving data integrity even during node failures. Visualizations, such as heatmaps and impedance graphs, highlighted the pipeline's efficiency in managing data flow across various stages, from ingestion to analytics.

An automotive PLM that principally encompasses a predictive maintenance solution relies on machine learning algorithms that monitor the real-time performance of automobiles. The system processes information collected from the engine, the transmission, breaks, electrical systems, and other components to diagnose maladies in advance. The results show the effectiveness in each failure mode and component with precision and recall statistics above 90% for relevant parts. Also, in another measure of the effectiveness of the failure mode, overheating of the engine, the failure mode achieved a precision of 93.5, whereas its recall was 94.1. Also, there is an improvement in predictive Accuracy where the proposed model achieves 94.6%, which is higher than the previous model. It also proves very effective in decreasing alert response time by 36.8%, with latency decreasing to 1.2 sec. Moreover, it tends to run smoothly at varying operation conditions

Existing vehicle incident prediction systems in the automotive industry are generally reactive, for instance, based on accident data. This is insufficient because there is no mechanism for proactively predicting where incidents may occur. However, these are not the best solutions to obtain safety objectives because of the limitations of integrating with real-time data sources and scalability. The proposed system uses

Daily news consumption is essential, and news institutions like The Washington Post (WP) invest heavily in quality content. However, writers and editors struggle to determine which stories readers will like. This task is crucial for resource allocation and reading enjoyment. News story popularity depends on timeliness, writing quality, and other criteria. In our research, we predict article popularity using regression. We carefully create metadata, contextual factors, temporal aspects, and social indicators to build predictive models. In real life at The Washington Post, our method accurately predicts article popularity with an R-squared value of 0.8. These forecasts use features acquired within 30 minutes after publication, demonstrating the system's quickness and effectiveness in editorial decision-making. News article popularity is predicted by analysing readership engagement and virality variables.

In recent times, Deep learning has been utilized in many areas, particularly for medicinal plant identification and evaluation of their therapeutic values. In this research, we use transfer learning capabilities of three state-of-the-art architectures: ResNet-50, VGG-16, and Xception. They are trained for the high-accuracy classification of plants and assessment of their medicinal properties. Our experiments demonstrate that the performance is significantly high, with ResNet-50 having 91.41%, VGG-16 84.27%, and an impressive 91.68% from Xception models, respectively. The findings from these trials highlight how effective transfer learning can be over

Preface

INTRODUCTION

We are pleased to present *Machine Learning, Predictive Analytics, and Optimization in Complex Systems*, a comprehensive reference volume that examines the transformative power of artificial intelligence and data-driven technologies in modern complex systems. This edited collection brings together cutting-edge research and practical insights that reflect the dynamic interplay between machine learning, predictive analytics, and optimization, as they are applied to reshape security infrastructures, the Internet of Things (IoT), and smart ecosystems.

In an era marked by rapid digital transformation and global uncertainty, intelligent systems are no longer a futuristic concept—they are a necessity. By harnessing real-time data and advanced algorithms, we are witnessing the evolution of responsive, adaptive, and predictive environments that span urban infrastructure, industrial automation, and interconnected devices. This volume explores how AI fortifies threat detection and response mechanisms, enables smarter automation, and facilitates efficient resource management in connected systems.

Our contributors—comprising leading researchers, practitioners, and innovators—delve into the design, deployment, and implications of these technologies. The chapters address a range of topics, including digital technology, cloud computing, deep learning, and predictive maintenance, offering both theoretical frameworks and applied case studies. The interdisciplinary approach ensures that the book serves as a valuable resource not only for computer engineers and security professionals but also for business leaders, academicians, data scientists, and policy makers.

Through this book, we aim to foster a deeper understanding of how intelligent technologies can create secure, sustainable, and resilient ecosystems. As editors, we are proud to contribute to a discourse that champions innovation, collaboration, and practical solutions in an increasingly complex and connected world.

ORGANIZATION OF THE BOOK

This volume brings together a diverse set of perspectives and innovations in the realm of machine learning, predictive analytics, and optimization. Each chapter showcases how AI-driven technologies are redefining intelligent systems within complex environments.

In Chapter 1, *Machine Learning Driven Fast Carry Look Ahead Adder Architecture Using Simple Carry Checker*, the authors explore innovations in VLSI design through the implementation of a novel algorithm—Simple Carry Checker—designed to reduce errors and improve the efficiency of Carry Look Ahead Adders. This contribution blends machine learning with hardware-level optimization, offering a compelling approach to reduce execution time in high-speed digital circuits.

Chapter 2, *A Study on the Clustering Techniques and Performance Evaluation*, delves into clustering as a foundational unsupervised learning technique that aids in pattern recognition and data segmentation across diverse domains. The chapter discusses its practical utility in fields such as market segmentation and social network analysis, presenting clustering as a tool to uncover hidden structures in large datasets and facilitate informed decision-making.

In Chapter 3, *A Smart Review on Imputation Techniques for Handling Missing Data*, the authors address one of the fundamental challenges in data science: incomplete datasets. This chapter provides a systematic review of imputation methods ranging from traditional techniques to emerging models. It emphasizes the significance of handling missing data for ensuring the integrity of research and analytical results, particularly across healthcare, academia, and industry.

Chapter 4, *Active Learning Strategies for Optimising Data Annotation Using Machine Learning*, presents a thoughtful investigation into active learning, especially Bayesian Optimization, as a means to reduce annotation costs while maintaining model accuracy. The experimental findings, validated on real-world datasets like CIFAR-10 and IMDB reviews, reveal how hybrid learning approaches can boost model performance with limited labeled data.

Chapter 5, *Real Time Data Pipeline Engineering for Scalable Insights*, addresses the rising demand for scalable, low-latency data pipelines capable of ingesting and analyzing high-velocity data. The proposed pipeline architecture demonstrated strong performance, including sub-15ms latency and robust fault tolerance. This chapter is a practical guide for engineering data infrastructure that supports real-time analytics at scale.

Chapter 6, *Insights from Big Data Analytics with Machine Learning-Driven Predictive Maintenance in the Automotive Industry*, illustrates how machine learning is reshaping predictive maintenance by enabling real-time diagnostics and proactive fault detection in automotive systems. With high precision and recall metrics, the proposed system significantly improves response time and operational efficiency, showcasing the critical role of big data analytics in industrial applications.

In Chapter 7, *Automotive Industry Revolution on Predictive Analytics and Machine Learning for Vehicle Behaviour and Safety with Environmental Criteria*, the focus shifts to proactive safety solutions for vehicles. Using dynamic data from IoT devices and environmental inputs, the chapter introduces models such as Random Forest, XGBoost, and DNNs to accurately predict vehicle incidents. The approach reflects a shift from reactive systems to intelligent, data-driven safety mechanisms.

Chapter 8, *New AI Technology for Predictive Pothole Locating on Highways*, demonstrates the application of computer vision and deep learning to infrastructure maintenance. By employing YOLOv8-based CNNs, this chapter presents an efficient system for real-time pothole detection using camera feeds from vehicles or drones. The robust performance across varied road conditions marks a significant leap toward safer and smarter transportation networks.

In Chapter 9, *Handbook for Predicting the Popularity of News on Anticipating Article Buzz*, the authors address a core challenge faced by modern journalism—forecasting the popularity of published news stories. Leveraging real-time metadata and contextual signals available within the first thirty minutes of publication, the study applies regression models to successfully predict article engagement with notable accuracy ($R^2 = 0.8$) as demonstrated at The Washington Post. This chapter provides a compelling case for the integration of predictive analytics in editorial workflows to optimize content strategies and enhance reader satisfaction.

Chapter 10, *Real-Time Plants Recognition and Medicinal Insights Using Deep Learning*, explores the intersection of artificial intelligence and ethnobotany through the lens of transfer learning. Employing deep learning architectures such as ResNet-50, VGG-16, and Xception, the authors classify plant species with high accuracy and link identified species to their medicinal values. This work not only advances automated plant recognition under data-scarce conditions but also contributes to the broader conversation on AI-assisted healthcare through natural remedies.

In Chapter 11, *Application of Digital Image Processing to Identification of Diseases in Paddy Crops*, the authors present an automated system that identifies pest and disease infestations in rice fields using image processing techniques. With tools such as segmentation, feature extraction, and modification algorithms, the system detects crop damage, enabling real-time intervention through proportional pesticide deployment. This timely and efficient methodology supports precision agriculture and promotes sustainable crop management.

Chapter 12, *A Comprehensive Analysis on Diverse Deep Learning Methods on Text Summarisation and Classification Techniques*, surveys advanced techniques used in summarizing and classifying digital text. The authors analyze both extractive and abstractive approaches and propose a feature selection framework that integrates statistics, fuzzy logic, and machine learning. This comprehensive approach addresses limitations in conventional summarization, such as information omission, and enhances language adaptability, proving essential in search engines and social media applications.

In Chapter 13, *Text Classification and Summarization Using Machine Learning*, the authors trace the evolution of automated text categorization in managing the explosion of digital documents. They examine genre-based and topic-based classification schemes and assess various feature extraction and classification algorithms. The chapter offers an exhaustive synthesis of existing research, illuminating best practices and persistent challenges in organizing textual data efficiently across digital communication platforms.

Chapter 14, *Performance Analysis for Speech and Speaker Recognition System Among Different Optimization Strategies*, evaluates how optimization techniques influence the efficacy of feature selection in speech and speaker recognition systems. With speech as a rich source of biometric and contextual data, the chapter focuses on enhancing recognition models across datasets through strategic algorithm selection. This work supports robust human-computer interaction frameworks and has implications for authentication, accessibility, and user personalization.

In Chapter 15, *A Sparkling Survey on Ingenious Assorted Resource Optimization Techniques Based Job Scheduling in Cloud Computing*, the authors investigate job scheduling and load balancing within cloud computing environments. The chapter reviews over 28 optimization-based techniques that target operational metrics such as makespan, energy use, and cost, while maintaining service quality. By categorizing methodologies and providing actionable insights, the chapter enriches the discourse on sustainable and efficient resource management in virtualized infrastructures.

Finally, Chapter 16, *The Role of Wireless Sensor Networks in Contemporary Communication and Impact: The Next Steps for 5G*, examines the synergistic relationship between 5G technologies and wireless sensor networks (WSNs). The chapter highlights how WSNs—critical for environmental sensing and IoT—are being transformed by 5G's high-speed, low-latency capabilities. It discusses the technical integration process, potential applications, and emerging challenges, offering a roadmap for the future of connected devices and intelligent infrastructure.

Together, these chapters represent the multifaceted applications of intelligent systems and advanced analytics in today's interconnected world. This curated collection aims to guide researchers, professionals, and practitioners in exploring practical implementations and forward-looking research that pave the way for more resilient and intelligent ecosystems.

CONCLUSION

As we conclude this volume, it becomes increasingly evident that the convergence of artificial intelligence, machine learning, digital communication, and optimization strategies is reshaping the boundaries of innovation across multiple disciplines. Each chapter in this collection contributes a unique perspective, grounded in rigorous research and practical application, offering valuable insights into the evolving digital landscape—from predicting the virality of news and automating plant and crop analysis to enhancing textual comprehension, speech recognition, and resource management in cloud environments.

What binds these diverse explorations together is a shared commitment to harnessing computational intelligence for real-world impact. Whether in agriculture, healthcare, journalism, or communication networks, the methodologies presented here exemplify how digital technologies can be leveraged to solve pressing problems efficiently, accurately, and at scale. As editors, we believe this book serves not only as a repository of knowledge but also as a catalyst for further inquiry, development, and interdisciplinary collaboration.

We hope that the research presented within these pages inspires new pathways for discovery and supports scholars, practitioners, and technologists in their efforts to build intelligent systems that are adaptable, sustainable, and beneficial for society at large.

Chapter 1
Machine Learning-Driven Fast Carry Look Ahead Adder Architecture Using Simple Carry Checker

M. Shunmugathammal
https://orcid.org/0000-0002-8634-540X
Faculty of Engineering and Technology, SRM Institute of Science and Technology Ramapuram, Chennai, India

G. Ramya
Faculty of Engineering and Technology, SRM Institute of Science and Technology Ramapuram, Chennai, India

M. Roopa
Faculty of Engineering and Technology, SRM Institute of Science and Technology Ramapuram, Chennai, India

S. Nagarajan
Faculty of Engineering and Technology, SRM Institute of Science and Technology Ramapuram, Chennai, India

K. Lalitha
Faculty of Engineering and Technology, SRM Institute of Science and Technology Ramapuram, Chennai, India

M. Shagar Banu
Dhaanish Ahmed College of Engineering, India

ABSTRACT

In VLSI design, adders and multipliers are vital in performing summing and multiplying operations in different ways. Advances in VLSI technology have led to the emergence of designer adders with increased efficiency and cost-efficiency. Carry Look Ahead Adder (CLA Adder) is used in various operations where the system must

DOI: 10.4018/979-8-3373-5203-9.ch001

add many bits with at least three inputs. CLA Adder is mainly used because of its ability to predict the carry before actually summing the inputs, reducing the overall execution time of the entire process. Still, there can be errors when the carry has been predicted. This paper proposes a new algorithm called 'Simple Carry Checker' based on approximate computing, which is used to reduce the frequency of errors in CLA adder while generating the carry of the inputs with a reduced execution time.

INTRODUCTION

Very Large-Scale Integration (VLSI) is a process through which thousands of transistors are integrated into a single semiconductor chip. VLSI dates back to the 1970s when computers were also developing. VLSI is an integrated circuit technology comprising many devices on a single chip. The most common VLSI devices are microcontrollers and microprocessors. Growth in VLSI and integration technologies has led to the increased use of ICs in telecommunications, control applications, high-performance computing, and consumer electronics. The design process of VLSI IC has two main parts or stages: front-end design, where a digital circuit is made using hardware description languages and the result is validated based on the simulation results, whereas back-end design is CMOS library design and characterization, during which the problem is specified, architecture is defined, functional design, logic design, circuit design and physical design of the chips are carried out. A high-speed, low-power, energy-efficient adder is an important design goal for processing units because addition is a fundamental and ubiquitous operation in computer arithmetic (Shunmugathammal et al., 2020). For instance, about 80% of the operations in the arithmetic and logic unit of an ARM processor were determined to be additions (Aradhya et al., 2012). Therefore, in a real-world scenario, especially in a standard cell-based design, the adder selection would depend on the available power and/or operating Speed.

A microcontroller is an integrated circuit designed to govern a specific operation in an embedded system. It typically includes a single chip's processor, memory, and input/output peripherals. The Arithmetic Logic Unit (ALU) is the most important component of many microcontrollers to work together within the device to handle different tasks. While an ALU is used for the entire process, adders play a vital role. An adder is the most commonly used Combinational circuit in system design. Adders are mostly used in Arithmetic Logic Units (ALU) to calculate addresses, perform increment and decrement operations, and perform similar operations. In addition to power and Speed (the inverse of critical path delay), the power-delay product (PDP) measures digital circuit energy consumption.

PDP is a low-power and low-energy figure of merit because, as a digital circuit, it is desirable for power and delay to be lower. Therefore, an adder that provides a good trade-off between PDP, Speed, and power is optimal for general-purpose applications. It mostly executes and manages logic instructions passed to it. A microprocessor comprises integrated circuits that hold thousands of transistors, where the exact number is based on its relative computing power. The basic principle of an adder is to add any two binary numbers. It is a memoryless circuit that logically performs an operation assigned to it by a boolean operation. Adders are widely used in other fundamental operations like subtraction, multiplication, and division; adders—logic circuits intended to execute high-speed arithmetic operations—are crucial parts of digital systems. Adders are used in the arithmetic logic unit of many computers and other processor types. Still, they are also utilized in other processor sections for tasks like calculating addresses, table indexes, and similar calculations. As an adder is a memoryless circuit, the outputs of the Adder depend only on the inputs given to it. Propagation delay is one of an adder's drawbacks when used for other arithmetic operations like multiplication and division. Several addition and subtraction steps cause this. Carry Look Ahead Adder (CLA Adder) tries to reduce the propagation delay caused by these processes by calculating the carry signals in advance based on the inputs.

Figure 1. Classical 4-bit carry look ahead adder

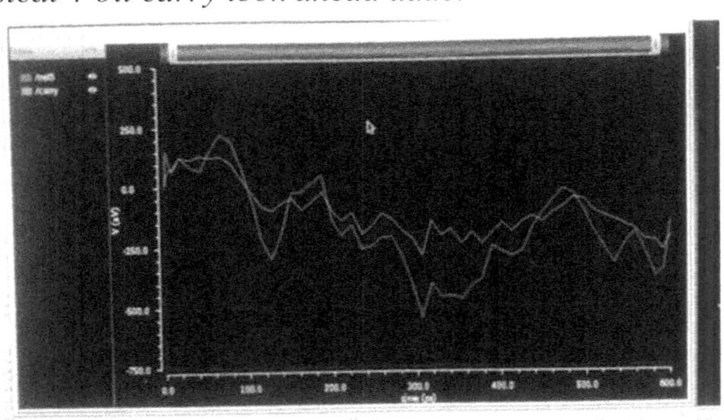

Figure 1 describes the block diagram of the classical CLA adder. Here, three inputs, A, B, and C, are given to a single-bit full adder module, which then sends the carry, one of the two outputs generated by the Adder, as the third input for the next full adder module. In contrast, the next modules give A and B inputs manually. However, the other output, S, is stored away as it is a direct output for the inputs given, and no further processing is required. The final full adder module outputs are the aggregate result for the series of inputs given to the Adder (Chen and Wu,

1994). The ultimate aim of any algorithm is to improve a particular system's Speed or accuracy. Many optimization algorithms, such as the hybrid particle Swarm-Bat and genetic algorithms, are available. They are used in VLSI technology to improve the Speed of the circuit and reduce the area consumed by the same. The proposed Simple Carry Checker algorithm uses a Low-Density Parity Check (LDPC), which provides error correction in communication channels.

Though LDPC codes are effective, they are complex to implement and can be used for systems with at least five inputs. Many highly intelligent and smart systems have been implemented due to the rapid advancement and progress in electronic devices, which have become essential in making our daily lives easier and more comfortable. These sophisticated, intelligent systems require high-performance and reasonably priced processors, necessitating advanced circuit designs. As a result, performance improvement of VLSI circuit designs is essential in contemporary circuits and systems. Digital adders are a crucial subcomponent of the VLSI system. Because adders are widely used in current arithmetic logic units (ALUs), researchers have traditionally emphasized their design (Shunmugathammal et al., 2020). Adders are needed in several arithmetic, multiplication, subtraction, and binary magnitude comparison circuits (Papachatzopoulos and Paliouras, 2019). Most modern computer processors are built using 32- or 64-bit architecture. Consequently, the need for wide adders has grown crucial.

Modern VLSI circuits cannot tolerate this significant latency, which is why the Parallel Prefix Adder (PPA) notion has evolved (Dixit and Kapse, 1998). Some well-known PPAs are CLA, CSA, Carry Save Adder, Carry-Skip Adder, and Manchester Carry Chain (Liu et al., 2019). Since CLA is thought to be the most prevalent adder topology among PPAs, for which substantial research has been done, it is imperative to develop a transistor-level design of CLA that will improve the overall performance of the entire CLA block. Most CLA research has been done on logic and algorithm generation, with only a small amount of work being done at the transistor level (Morgenshtein et al., 2014). In this regard, a CLA architecture that is faster and more energy-efficient than a traditional CLA architecture is presented in this study (Hasan et al., 2019).

Furthermore, this study compares the performance of several adders, which could help circuit designers select the right Adder for a given application by considering trade-offs in the design metrics. A significant member of the high-speed adder family is CLA (Morrison et al., 2011). The literature has published numerous transistor-level implementations of the CLA, which correlate to various design types such as domino logic, static CMOS, BiCMOS, and all-N-type transistor logic, among others.

RELATED WORKS

Arkadiy Morgenshtein proposed an effective approach for implementing digital circuits. He proposed the Gate Diffusion Input (GDI) design process as a potential replacement for static CMOS logic. The GDI approach, which was first proposed for use in silicon-on-insulator (SOI) and twin-well CMOS technologies, enabled the creation of many complicated logic functions using just two transistors (Kahng and Kang, 2012). The suggested technique was used on a 40 nm TSMC low-power standard 16-bit adder. CLA adder architecture was first suggested as a substitute for a straightforward ripple adder's speed boost and was selected for use in his work as a benchmark circuit.

The suggested CLA application uses enhanced full-swing GDI F1 and F2 gates, the analogs of the conventional CMOS NOR and NAND gates. Rather than relying on the carry propagation from earlier stages, the Carry Lookahead Adder (CLA) precomputes carry signals for each bit location using sets of logic gates, reducing the linear propagation delay observed in a standard RCA. This method makes it possible to compute carry signals in parallel over several bit positions, which speeds up the addition of big binary integers. When compared to more straightforward adder architectures such as the RCA, the primary drawback of the CLA is its higher area overhead and complexity. This is because more logic gates are needed to precomputation carry signals for every bit position, increasing space utilization. Despite this, applications demanding fast arithmetic operations benefit greatly from CLAs (Ande and Khair, 2019).

Furthermore, the literature also introduced the Ling adder, a variation of the CLA (Liang et al., 2013). In this context, two common high-speed, low-power adder architectures are the carry-lookahead and carry-select adders (Efstathiou, 2003). There are two widely used variations of the carry-lookahead Adder (CLA): the block CLA (BCLA) and the recursive CLA (RCLA). By replacing one or more sub-CLAs with a small-size ripple-carry adder (RCA) in the least significant adder bit positions, a hybrid CLA architecture can be used to increase the speed performance of various CLA architectures (Jaberipur and Kaivani, 2009).

Miao and Li (2017) proposed replacing the XOR gates with NOR gates to improve the Speed of the carry transmission, which, in turn, reduces the propagation delay. However, this method can only be used up to 4-bit inputs.

Balasubramanian and Mastorakis (2022) focused on the energy consumption of the CLA Adder and proposed an algorithm wherein they managed to reduce the power consumption by 39.6%. Though they successfully reduced the power consumption of the Adder, the propagation delay was still high. Lisa and Babu (2015) used dynamic programming to design a compact reversible CLA Adder where they concurrently produced the carry generate. The carry propagates, the terms used to calculate the carry to be produced in a system before the actual addition of the inputs given to the circuit using logic gates and the said inputs. The drawback of the above-proposed method was that it could be used only for 128-bit and higher systems. Reminder: Singh et al. (2009) analyzed the performance of the CLA Adder and CSA while using them to implement a 32-bit Array multiplier to reduce the propagation delay of the multiplier. Though they successfully determined the faster Adder out of the two, their multiplier can only be used to multiply unsigned bits.

The addition is the basic operation in many different signal-processing algorithms. The power consumption significantly impacts the total system design, the area necessary to support the design, and the time needed to execute it. These factors all contribute to the latency of adders. Performance is the deciding factor for any system. The Adder's performance, which squares up the multiplier's performance, is primarily responsible for the system's performance. Throughout history, numerous researchers have put forth a variety of topologies for the best possible adder structure design. Bairu K. Saptalakar proposed the CRTL structure, and the suggested method is applied to a carry-lookahead adder to determine low-power operation. A reliable method for creating a low-power parallel prefix adder has been suggested by Mohanty and Patel (2014) by utilizing a range of prefix cell operators, including even-dot, odd-dot, even-semi-dot, and odd semi-dot cells.

The design aims to eliminate the two inverters that the prefix carries network encounters. This paper also suggested that when adding adders to the system, there were trade-offs between the amount of internal wiring and the fanout of intermediary nodes. The design was developed to address these issues. This work proposes a cell-based design of several additional architectural types for qualitative and quantitative evaluation. In this paper, a cell-based design of many additional architectural kinds has been developed for both qualitative and quantitative evaluation. Kostrzewski et al. (1990) added an external memory to the system to store the carry from where the carry can be called back when required, reducing the Adder's propagation delay significantly. However, this was impossible for systems that processed more than 4-bit data. Carry generation and processing speed are not considered in the above-said methods. Additionally, several adder varieties are covered in this article, including the Carry-Look Ahead Adder (CLA), Carry Select Adder, and Ripple Carry Adder. Simple multiple full adders connected in series make up RCA; before the addition is finished, the carry must pass through each full Adder.

Every complete Adder inputs a Cin, the preceding Adder's Cout. Since each carries bit ripples to the next complete Adder, this type of Adder is known as a ripple carry adder. When it looks to be fast enough for the task at hand, RCA is always preferable in terms of power and area. RCA adders are the slowest, yet they require the least hardware. In Carry Select Adders (CSA), except for the lowest order portion, the n-bit adder is split into "k" ripple-carry adders of n/k bits each; each adder block is emulated. Three n/2-bit ripple carry adders are used to construct the most basic n-bit carry, so choose Adder. The first Adder calculates the lower half of the n-bit total. In comparison, the higher half is computed by the other two adders, which operate under the assumption that the input carry is zero and the other on the premise that it is one.In this manner, there is no need to wait for the lower half to finish before the computation of the top half. A multiplexer chooses the proper half of the total once the lower half of the sum has been calculated and the carry input for the following step is available (Attaoui et al., 2024). Adding numbers quickly is known as carry-look ahead. With this technique, there is no need for a bottleneck to form as the carry signal proceeds step by step. Rather, it employs extra logic to generate and propagate carry information more quickly, enabling quick addition at the cost of increased hardware needs. To achieve the best carry prediction performance with a modest level of complexity, a simple carry checker code is added with CLA adder circuits using an iterative decoding procedure.

Conversely, more decoding iterations result in lower decoding throughput and a longer latency (Joshi et al. 2017). A Simple carry checker needs many compute units to achieve a high decoding data rate, resulting in a big chip area and significant power consumption. On the other hand, with the growing need for wireless and portable computing devices and the growing goal to lower packaging costs, low-power chip implementation has become unprecedentedly important. Therefore, research on space and power-efficient Very Large Scale Integration (VLSI) architecture for high-speed carry checkers is crucial for practical applications of the promising error-correcting code. The scope of the present work is to derive high-speed adders with parity-checked data paths and memory systems. This work provides effective self-checking implementations with all current Adder and arithmetic and logic unit (ALU) schemes, such as carry look ahead, ripple carry, and skip carry schemes. Since arithmetic codes are retained under arithmetic operations, they are useful for verifying arithmetic circuits. This paper is organized as follows: section 2 describes related works, section 3 describes the proposed CLA adder with a simple carry checker, and Section 4 describes Results and Discussions (Kumar and Dahiya, 2013).

CLA ADDER WITH SIMPLE CARRY CHECKER

A new algorithm, 'Simple Carry Checker, ' is proposed here to reduce the frequency of errors while predicting the carry signals in CLA Adder, which, in turn, reduces the execution time of the circuit. The CLA adder module is implemented to add the three inputs, namely A, B, and C_in, to the system. The outputs S and C_out are obtained for each bit from the full adder module. The carry is then verified using the Simple Carry Checker Algorithm to eliminate the errors produced.

Operation of the system: CLA Adder is used in many applications other than just adding the bits given as input to it, even though the primary function of a CLA adder is to add. The propagation delay caused by the CLA adder can be reduced by using the 'Simple Carry Checker' Algorithm. The Simple Carry Checker or SCC algorithm is a separate function used along with implementing CLA adder in C++ programming. As the name suggests, the carry generated from the full adder function is sent into the SCC algorithm. The SCC gets the input from the main function and predicts the carry in advance, which is cross-verified with the carry generated by the full adder module. The SCC verifies the carry and changes it if it is wrong. In this way, the error in the carry signal is reduced (Figure 2).

Figure 2. A new 4-bit CLA adder with simple carry checker

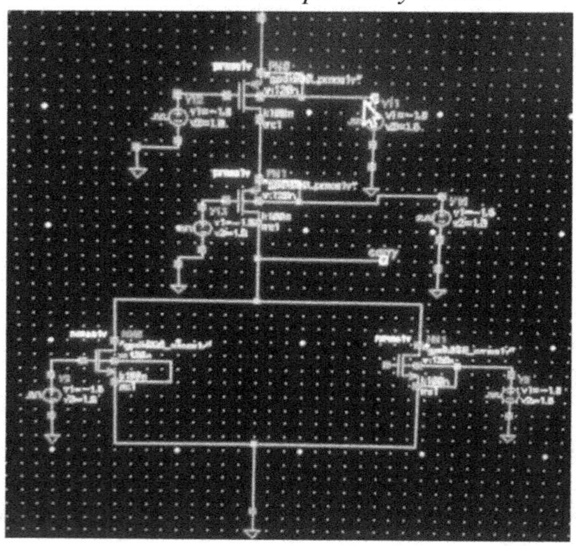

Working of System

Calculating Sum and Carry: The CLA adder is implemented using C++ programming. The C++ program has three functions: full Adder, checker, and main function. The workflow of this C++ program starts with the main function, and the rest of the functions are already defined before the main function is implemented when they are called back from the main function. The inputs are mostly given in binary format (i.e.) '1' or '0.' The main function has three inputs, A, B, and C_in, which are selected from the defined inputs based on the number of bits the user gives. The full adder function is then called by sending the inputs to it. The inputs are processed here to find the outputs, Sum and C_out. Here, the sum is the sum of the inputs given to it, and C_out is the carry generated when the addition occurs. The sum and carry are calculated using the following logic expressions.

Sum = C_In^(A^B);

C_Out = (A & B) || (B & C_In) || (A & C_In);

Simple Carry Checker Algorithm: The sum is printed in the output screen while the C_out is returned to the main function. The inputs and the C_out from the full adder function are then sent to the checker function when called from the main function. The checker uses conditional statements to check if two or more inputs given to the system are 1. If more than one of the inputs is one, then the C_out from the full adder module is changed to 1 and printed as output. In this way, the carry is cross-verified with the inputs given to the system. Looping statements call full adder and checker functions as many times as the number of bits given.

```
void checker(int A, int B, int C_In, int C_Out)

{

If ((A && B)==1 || (A && C_In)==1 || (B && C_In)==1 || (A &&
B && C_In)==1)

{

C_Out=1;

}

else

{
```

```
C_Out=0;

}

cout<<"C_Out="<<C_Out<<endl;

}
```

In calculating execution time to check the execution time of the program, a clock is added to the program, which is started with the start = clock () command at the beginning of the main function, and the clock is stopped after the looping statements with the end = clock () command. The difference between the start and the end clock gives us the execution time of the program in sec.

```
clock_t start,end; start=clock();
end=clock();
double exe_time = double (end-start)/double(CLOCKS_PER_SEC);
```

Machine Learning in VLSI: The confluence of artificial intelligence (AI) and machine learning (ML) with VLSI (Very Large-Scale Integration) architectures has resulted in a dramatic shift in computing paradigms in recent years. A new age of high-performance computing systems created specifically for AI and ML applications has developed due to this convergence. Engineers and researchers are looking at new VLSI architectures that promise unparalleled performance because of the ongoing need for additional processing power to manage massive data volumes and execute complex algorithms with previously unheard-of efficiency. Numerous applications of AI and ML are being developed for various domains, including robots, autonomous vehicles, natural language processing, picture and audio recognition, and more. Consequently, there is a growing need for hardware platforms designed for these particular uses. Traditional von Neumann architectures, despite their adaptability, usually require assistance to fulfill the computational demands of AI and ML algorithms. One of the primary challenges in developing high-performance VLSI designs for AI and ML applications is striking the delicate balance between hardware complexity and computing efficiency. The difficulty for designers is to construct hardware platforms that are both scalable and simple to integrate while also supporting these advancements in neural network models, artificial intelligence (AI), and machine learning (ML).

Additionally, due to the intrinsic heterogeneity of AI workloads, research into specialized processing units made for particular assignments, such as recurrent neural networks (RNNs) for convolutional neural networks or sequential data analysis networks (CNNs) to process images. To address these problems, numerous VLSI design strategies and architectural paradigms specifically suited for AI and ML applications have surfaced. Researchers have looked into various design options to fully realize the potential of hardware acceleration in AI and ML workloads, including systolic arrays, SIMD (Single Instruction, Multiple Data) architectures, neuromorphic circuits, and reconfigurable computing platforms.

Furthermore, improvements in on-chip memory hierarchies, connect fabrics, and power management techniques have raised VLSI architectures' energy efficiency and performance for workloads like AI and ML. The pursuit of high-performance VLSI designs for AI and ML applications is not confined to academic research; rather, it has a substantial industry-wide influence and drives the development of next-generation computing platforms intended for real-world applications. To attain breakthrough performance in AI inference and training operations, companies in the semiconductor ecosystem invest significant money in creating and producing specialized AI chips (Goda et al., 2018). Modern architectural designs and state-of-the-art process technologies are used to make these chips. A new era of self-governing, intelligent systems is being ushered in by the competition to develop the quickest, most scalable VLSI architectures for AI and ML applications. This competition is revolutionizing computing. There are a lot of combinatorial problems in physical design that take a long time to converge. These design challenges now have more sophisticated design rules and design for manufacturing (DFM) constraints due to the development of semiconductor technology, making them difficult. Broadly, the four phases of physical design are partitioning, floor planning, placement, and routing (Figure 3).

Figure 3. VLSI physical design process

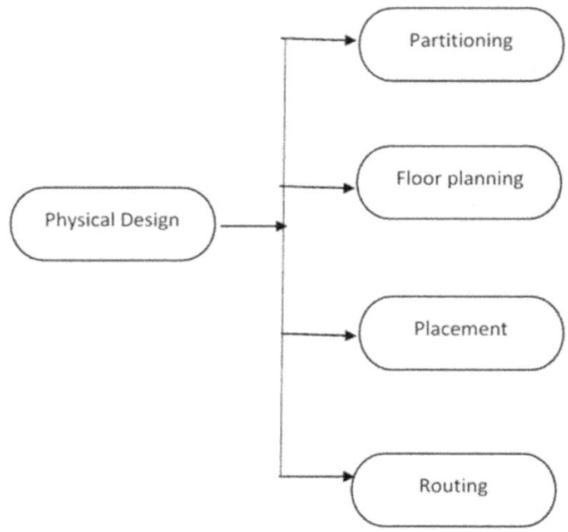

In this paper, carry prediction is done using **a** machine learning approach. Carry prediction using a machine learning approach to improve the Speed of adders. In machine learning tasks, features are crucial representations retrieved from the original input representation. We now talk about the attributes to be utilized in the learning model. Features are considered from prefix adder configurations and tool parameters, emphasizing the latter. In addition to these prefix graph structural properties, we consider other features, such as tool settings from the physical design and synthesis stages. The proposed CLA adder structure could be synthesized using Cadence Virtuoso @ 45 nm Technology.

Simulation with Cadence EDA: VLSI technology is currently being pushed to its limits by the need for more circuit complexity, leading to issues like enormous die sizes and non-negligible delays brought on by long power rails and data busses. As a result, several strategies have been put forth to reduce the impact of interconnects on circuit performance. Cadence EDA tool is an exciting technology that has drawn much interest. Cadence EDA could overcome barriers encountered with designing in 2-D technology. The main goal of the proposed Carry Look Ahead adder with a simple checker is to achieve Speed at multi-bit addition operations while lowering circuit space and power consumption. Comparing the suggested design to the same work reported by (Amuru et al., 2023; Saurabh et al., 2021) reduces the error with reduced circuit size (smaller transistor count), power, and latency. The suggested Carry Look Ahead adder with a simple checker carefully avoids cascading logic to implement the sum and directly accept input A as the carry output. It uses the AND, OR, and Multiplexer (MUX) functions of the GDI logic cell.

RESULTS AND DISCUSSIONS

The proposed Simple carry checker algorithm is executed with C++ programming on an Intel Pentium-D 3.20 GHz IBM machine. C++ is a cross-platform language that is used to create applications with high performance. In this work, the Visual Studio Code application is used to implement the C++ codes in the computer. Visual Studio Code is an open free application that can be installed and used offline on the computer. Visual Studio Code supports programming languages like C, C++, Python, Java, JavaScript, and HTML. However, extensions are required to be installed in the computer for the execution of these codes. The outputs for C++ codes can be verified using the computer's command prompt. A simple carry checker algorithm is executed based on the number of bits defined by the user, and the full Adder and the checker functions are implemented. Here, the inputs are specified as up to 8 bits. The sum and carry of each bit are then calculated and displayed on the output screen. To measure the difference in the execution time of the program with and without the SCC algorithm, two different programs are executed for the same number of bits and inputs in the same IBM machine. Where one program has an SCC algorithm and the other does not. Here, the results for 8-bit CLA Adder with and without the SCC Algorithm are given. Table 1 shows that there is a significant reduction in execution time between both programs (Figure 4 (a) and (b)).

Figure 4. (a) CLA adder results without SCC algorithm (b) CLA adder with SCC algorithm

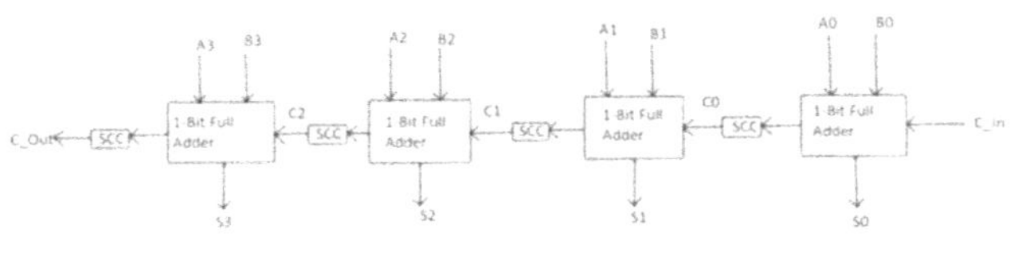

Table 1 Compares the execution time for different numbers of input bits for the carry checker algorithm. The SCC algorithm is executed for a single bit, and there is no change. If the SCC algorithm is executed for 2 and 3 bits, there is an improvement of 1% in execution time. For 4 bits, there is an improvement of 7% in execution time. While executing 8 bits, there was an improvement of 9%. Table 1 shows a significant improvement in execution time for higher-order bits compared to lower-order bits. Schematic diagrams for all the adders have been taken using the RTL schematic diagram from the Xilinx tool, which gives us the correct understanding of the logic gates implemented in the adders. Also helps to check the input and output power. Figure 5 (a) shows the RTL Schematic of a 4-bit Carry Lookahead adder, which

consists of basic logic gates such as AND, XOR, and NOT. It also uses the CLA block to get the output carry (Figure 5 (a) and (b)).

Figure 5. RTL schematic of 4-Bit CLA adder (a) without carry checker circuit (b) with carry checker circuit

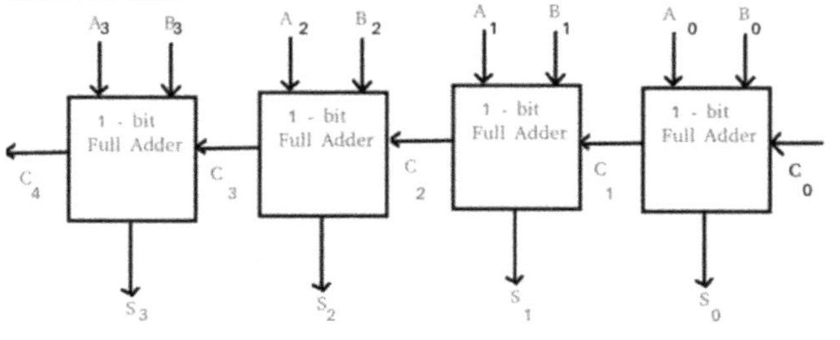

Figure 5(b) shows the RTL Schematic of a 4-bit CLA adder with SCC, which consists of two full adders parallel to each other. One of the inputs of the full Adder is connected to the ground. Table 1 compares CLA adders and how they differ in metrics like area, carry arrival time, and power.

Table 1. Comparison between CLA adders with and without a simple checker algorithm

	CLA without Simple Checker Algorithm			CLA with Simple Checker Algorithm		
Number of Bits	**Area (μm^2)**	**Carry Arrival Time (ns)**	**Power (mW)**	**Area (μm^2)**	**Carry Arrival Time (ns)**	**Power (mW)**
8 Bits	166	14.75	231.7	167	13.67	103.83
16 Bits	276	23.26	369.61	278	22.26	201.12
32 Bits	846	36.01	990.37	890	37.99	381.9
64 Bits	1307	56.21	1971	1320	53.35	704.51

Table 1 proved that there is a significant change in carry arrival time. While calculating for 8 bits, carry arrival time is improved by 1.08%, 16 bits by 1%, 32 by 1.98%, and 64 by 2.86%. Table 1 also proved that power consumption for the calculation process is also reduced.

Table 2. The optimized results of CLA in the difference between the execution times for different numbers of bits

No. of Bits	Execution time without checker (in seconds)	Execution time with checker (in seconds)
1	0.001	0.001
2	0.002	0.001
3	0.005	0.004
4	0.014	0.007
5	0.017	0.016
6	0.021	0.020
7	0.027	0.020
8	0.03	0.021

Table 2 shows the execution time of the CLA adder with and without the checker if it shows 9% improvement for 8 bits and 7% for 7 bits. Suppose several bits increasing proposed algorithm shows significant improvement in execution time.

Table 3. Carry look ahead adder with simple checker metrics supply voltage, speed, and power using a simple carry checker algorithm

S.No	Supply Voltage(v)	Delay(ns)	Power (ÂµW)2
1	1	50.654	0.3922
2	1.02	50.586	0.4348
3	1.04	50.503	0.4733
4	1.06	50.401	0.4872
5	1.08	50.76	0.464
6	1.1	50.75	0.4719

Figure 6. Carry arrival time and area comparison between CLA adders

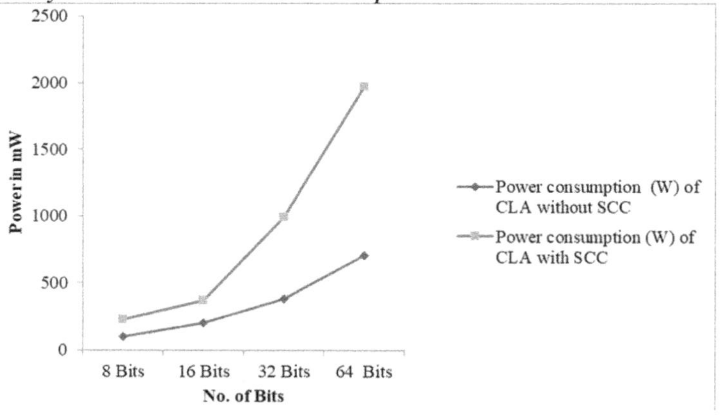

Figure 7. Power consumption comparison between CLA adders

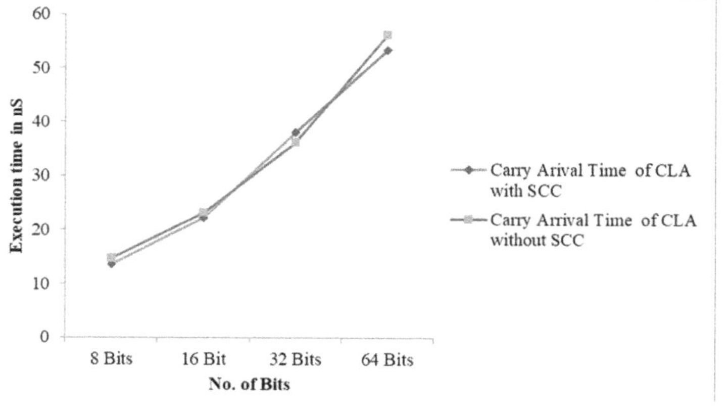

Carry Look Ahead Adder DESIGNS Using CADENCE: For custom circuit design and analysis in MOS technologies, especially within CMOS VLSI, Cadence Virtuoso is an essential EDA tool (Table 3). It supports photonic IC and system package module design to enable layout modifications within the context of all ICs on a module or other fabrics like chips, modules, and boards (Figure 6). VLSI is mostly used in the design of electronic components, including memory chips and microprocessors, by assembling millions of transistors to create integrated circuits. To increase the body of knowledge in this field, this work aims to construct and develop a novel methodology that advances the design of high-speed CLA adder circuits and performs transient simulations using Cadence Virtuoso software (Figure

7). This research tutorial aims to give a clear picture and explanation of how to use the Cadence Virtuoso environment (ADE L) for CLA adder with SCC stimulation. It also aims to provide all the information needed to create and implement a CLA adder with SCC. Cadence is an effective tool for circuit analysis and coordinates simulation. This work's transient analysis of CLA adders has been performed using a 300 ns simulation duration. This section displays the schematics, symbols, test circuits, and output waveforms of the designed existing full adder circuits. From there, the power consumption, area, and delay are computed. Only the schematic, test circuit symbol, and output waveforms for the 5T Full Adder Design are currently displayed (Figure 8).

Figure 8. Carry look ahead adder with simple carry checker in cadence virtuoso

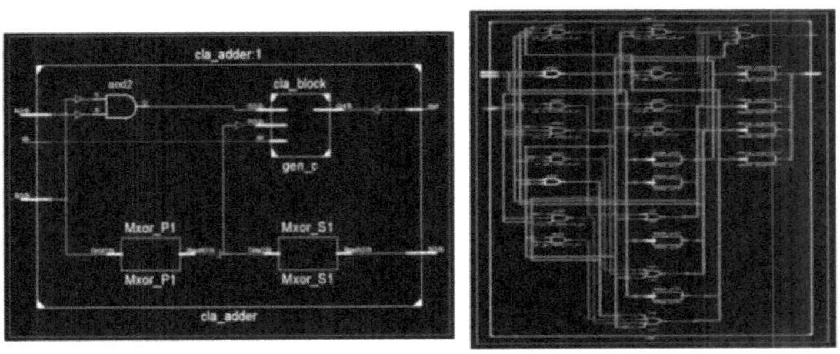

The resulting output data is displayed graphically in Figure 8. It shows how the Carry Look Ahead Adder. The gate simulation uses two pulse sources—voltage I (0 V) and voltage II (1 V). Each pulse source has two states in its voltage profile. Both of these pulses have 50 ps rise and fall intervals. However, one has a 60-ns period, and the other has a 20-ns period. These pulses are designed for distinct periods and rise/fall times. After simulation, these input waveforms can be plotted using transient, DC, or AC analysis methods in virtuous environments. These waveforms act as the stimulus for the Adder under study, allowing the observation of their responses to varying input conditions.

Figure 9. Transient analysis of CLA Adder with SCC in cadence virtuoso

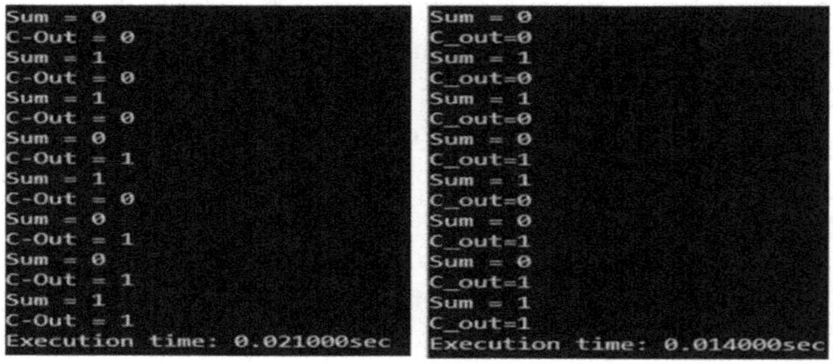

Figure 9 shows the Transient analysis of CLA Adder with SCC in Cadence Virtuoso. Transient outputs have been analyzed since these adders behaved as predicted in the ADE L context.

CONCLUSION

Carry propagation and carry generation are the two important processes of CLA adder design. Therefore, a CLA adder is considered a fast adder. This work presents a new algorithm called Simple Carry Checker (SCC) with approximate computing to reduce the error during carry prediction and improve the Speed of existing CLAs. A machine learning-based approximate algorithm is designed based on the number of bits the user defines. Thus, using the Simple Carry Checker Algorithm with the CLA adder reduces the frequency of errors while predicting the carry signal, and the execution time is reduced to at most 1% for 1 bit and 7% for 4 bits and 9% for 8-bits. Any ALU and adder method (such as ripple-carry, group carry-look ahead, complete carry-look-ahead, skip-carry, and conditional sum) could use the new simple carry checker for its self-checking architecture. The suggested CLA adder with SCC algorithm quality metrics showed a notable improvement over the current approximations of adder designs. Implementing other adders with the Simple Carry Checker algorithm would be the future direction of this research work.

REFERENCES

Amuru, D., Zahra, A., Vudumula, H. V., Cherupally, P. K., Gurram, S. R., Ahmad, A., & Abbas, Z. (2023). AI/ML algorithms and applications in VLSI design and technology. *Integration (Amsterdam)*, *93*(11), 102048. DOI: 10.1016/j.vlsi.2023.06.002

Ande, J. R. P. K. R., & Khair, M. A. (2019). High-Performance VLSI Architectures for Artificial Intelligence and Machine Learning Applications. *International Journal of Reciprocal Symmetry and Theoretical Physics*, *6*(1), 20–30.

Aradhya, H. V. R., Kumar, B. V. P., & Muralidhara, K. N. (2012). Design of control unit for low power AU using reversible logic. *Procedia Engineering*, *30*(3), 631–638. DOI: 10.1016/j.proeng.2012.01.908

Attaoui, Y., Chentouf, M., Alaoui Ismaili, Z. E. A., & Elmourabit, A. (2024). Machine Learning in VLSI Design: A Comprehensive Review. JICS. *Journal of Integrated Circuits and Systems*, *19*(2), 1–14. DOI: 10.29292/jics.v19i2.826

Balasubramanian, P., & Mastorakis, N. E. (2022). High-speed and energy-efficient carry lookahead adder. *Journal of Low Power Electronics and Applications*, *12*(3), 46. DOI: 10.3390/jlpea12030046

Chen, H. P., & Wu, Y. P. (1994). A 3.4V high speed BiCMOS dynamic CLA circuit with carry skip using full swing technique. *IEEE Trans.Circuits I*, *41*(11), 485–489.

Dixit, A., & Kapse, V. (1998). Arithmetic & logic unit (ALU) design using reversible control unit. *Development*, *1*(6), 55–60.

Efstathiou, C. (2003). Circuits sys II,Zaher Owda., and Yiorgos Tsiatouhas. *IEEE Trans. Circuits Sys II*, *55*(5), 548–553.

Hasan, M., Saha, U. K., Sorwar, A., Dipto, M. A. Z., Hossain, M. S., & Zaman, H. U. (2019). A novel hybrid full adder based on gate diffusion input technique, transmission gate and static CMOS logic. 2019 10th International Conference on Computing, Communication and Networking Technologies (ICCCNT), Kanpur, India.

Jaberipur, G., & Kaivani, A. (2009). Improving the Speed of parallel decimal multiplication. IEEE Transactions on Computers. *Institute of Electrical and Electronics Engineers*, *58*(11), 1539–1552.

Joshi, S., Kim, C., Ha, S., & Cauwenberghs, G. (2017). From algorithms to devices: Enabling machine learning through ultra-low-power VLSI mixed-signal array processing. *2017 IEEE Custom Integrated Circuits Conference (CICC)*, Austin, Texas, USA DOI: 10.1109/CICC.2017.7993650

Kahng, A. B., & Kang, S. (2012). Accuracy-configurable Adder for approximate arithmetic designs. *Proceedings of the 49th Annual Design Automation Conference*, San Francisco, California, USA DOI: 10.1145/2228360.2228509

Kostrzewski, A., Kim, D. H., Li, Y., & Eichmann, G. (1990). Fast hybrid parallel carry lookahead Adder. *Optics Letters*, *15*(16), 915–917. DOI: 10.1364/OL.15.000915 PMID: 19770952

Kumar, R., & Dahiya, S. (2013). Performance analysis of different bit carry look ahead Adder using vhdl environment. [IJESIT]. *International Journal of Engineering Science and Innovative Technology*, *2*(4), 80–88.

Liang, J., Han, J., & Lombardi, F. (2013). New metrics for the reliability of approximate and probabilistic adders. IEEE Transactions on Computers. *Institute of Electrical and Electronics Engineers*, *62*(9), 1760–1771.

Lisa, N. J., & Babu, H. M. H. (2015). Design of a compact reversible carry lookahead Adder using dynamic programming. 2015 28th International Conference on VLSI Design, Bangalore, India

Liu, G., Zheng, L., Wang, G., Shen, Y., & Liang, Y. (2019). A carry lookahead adder based on hybrid CMOS-memristor logic circuit. *IEEE Access : Practical Innovations, Open Solutions*, *7*(3), 43691–43696. DOI: 10.1109/ACCESS.2019.2907976

Miao, J., & Li, S. (2017). A novel implementation of 4-bit carry lookahead Adder. *2017 International Conference on Electron Devices and Solid-State Circuits (EDSSC)*, Hsinchu, Taiwan DOI: 10.1109/EDSSC.2017.8126457

Mohanty, B. K., & Patel, S. K. (2014). Area-delay-power efficient carryselect adder. *IEEE Transactions on Circuits and Systems*, *61*(6), 418–422.

Morgenshtein, A., Yuzhaninov, V., Kovshilovsky, A., & Fish, A. (2014). Full-Swing Gate Diffusion Input logic—Case-study of low-power CLA adder design. *Integration (Amsterdam)*, *47*(1), 62–70. DOI: 10.1016/j.vlsi.2013.04.002

Morrison, M., Lewandowski, M., Meana, R., & Ranganathan, N. (2011). Design of a novel reversible ALU using an enhanced carry look- ahead Adder. 2011 11th IEEE International Conference on Nanotechnology, Portland, Oregon, USA

. Papachatzopoulos, K., & Paliouras, V. (2019). Static delay variation models for ripple-carry and borrow-save adders. IEEE Transactions on Circuits and Systems. I, Regular Papers: A Publication of the IEEE Circuits and Systems Society, 66(7), 2546–2559.

Saurabh, S., Jain, P., Agarwal, M., & Ram, O. S. (2021). Applications of Machine Learning in VLSI Design. In *VLSI and Hardware Implementations Using Modern Machine Learning Methods* (pp. 125–139). CRC Press. DOI: 10.1201/9781003201038-7

Shunmugathammal, M., Christopher Columbus, C., & Anand, S. (2020). A novel B* tree crossover-based simulated annealing algorithm for combinatorial optimization in VLSI fixed-outline floorplans. *Circuits, Systems, and Signal Processing*, *39*(2), 900–918. DOI: 10.1007/s00034-019-01054-9

Shunmugathammal, M., Columbus, C. C., & Anand, S. (2020). nature-inspired optimization algorithm for VLSI fixed-outline floorplanning. *Analog Integrated Circuits and Signal Processing*, *103*(2), 173–186. DOI: 10.1007/s10470-020-01598-w

Singh, R., Preet Pal, P., & Kumar, B. (2009). Performance analysis of 32-bit array multiplier with a carry save adder and with a carry-look-ahead adder. *International Journal of Recent Trends in Engineering*, *2*(6), 83.

Chapter 2
A Study on the Clustering Techniques and Performance Evaluation

F. Mohamed Ilyas
https://orcid.org/0009-0002-8954-2449
The New College, India

S. Silvia Priscila
https://orcid.org/0000-0002-6040-3149
Bharath Institute of Higher Education and Research, India

V. Poornima
Vels Institute of Science, Technology, and Advanced Studies, India

Prasanna Ranjith Christodoss
Messiah University, USA

D. Kerana Hanirex
Bharath Institute of Higher Education and Research, India

C. Elayaraja
Dhaanish Ahmed College of Engineering, India

M. Sakthivanitha
https://orcid.org/0009-0001-6795-6555
Vels Institute of Science, Technology, and Advanced Studies, India

A. T. Ashmi Christus
Dhaanish Ahmed College of Engineering, India

ABSTRACT

People prefer approximations based on resemblance, particularly when dealing with commercial figures. With data, the procedure is even more exact, known as Clustering. Clustering is a method that has numerous applications. Numerous fields, including pattern identification, image analysis, consumer statistical analysis, segmentation of markets, social network analysis, and more, use clustering, an unsupervised machine learning technique. It can effectively address many problems and goals, from the most basic to the most complicated. Cluster analysis is an effective approach for detecting underlying structures and patterns in data from diverse areas. It divides

DOI: 10.4018/979-8-3373-5203-9.ch002

the data into clusters based on their similarities or differences. Researchers and analysts can get significant insights and make data-based decisions by combining comparable observations. Further, Clustering on the original information provided us with extremely valuable and unique explanations for each of the individual segments.

INTRODUCTION

Clustering is the process of grouping a population or set of data points into groups so that data points in the same category are more similar than those in other groups. In other words, the goal is to separate groups with similar characteristics and assign them to clusters. Analyzing data is identifying meaningful data in unstructured data. Machine learning (ML) is one of the most extensively utilized data analysis methodologies (Ghosh and Kumar, 2013). It is a framework or system that can derive information from unorganized information and make judgments without requiring human involvement. The most common ML strategies used for data analysis are classification and Clustering. It incorporates numerous algorithms to categorize items into classes based on their properties (Tareq et al., 2024). Clustering analysis, as a subfield of data mining (DM) and machine learning (ML), has significant consequences for examining and identifying data structures, processing data, and choosing features. Similarly, Clustering, as an unsupervised learning technique, seeks to split data without previous instruction. (Bhardwaj et al., 2024). Its goal is to make certain that objects in the same cluster are as similar as feasible and that items in other groups are as distinct as possible. Clustering analysis has several uses in today's information age, including picture segmentation, medical evaluation, and social media analysis.

Techniques for Clustering employ the fundamental framework of the data to develop rules for organizing data with similar characteristics, dividing the data set based on group characteristics without prior knowledge of the information. In a perfect example, every group of clusters has a data instance that is more related to one another than instances belonging to other clusters. (Troiano et al., 2024). The overview of Clustering is presented in Figure 1. The raw data is clustered into f=different groups of data

Figure 1. Overview of clustering

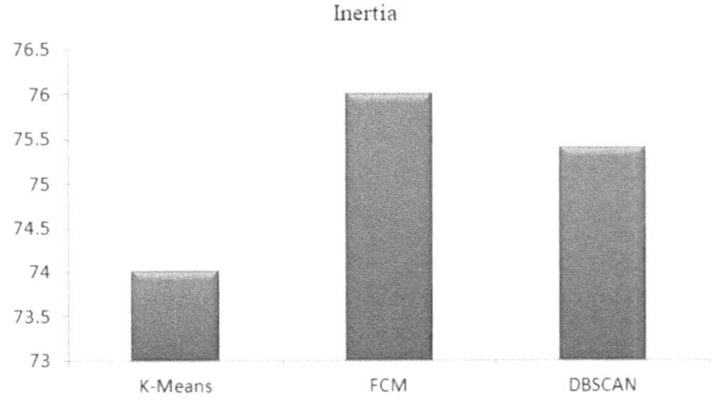

Clustering techniques are used to explore data, spot anomalies, uncover outliers, and identify trends in data. Clustering is an unsupervised learning method similar to neural networks and reinforcement learning. The accessible data is very unstructured, varied, and noisy. As a result, the algorithm used is determined by the appearance of the data. An appropriate clustering technique aids in discovering useful insights for the industry (Chowdhury et al., 2023).

Clustering algorithms fall into two basic categories: partitional clustering methods and hierarchical clustering techniques. Hierarchical approaches to Clustering include aggregative and divisive methods. The partitional category is divided into the hard clustering strategy, fuzzy approaches, and the mixing methodology. Hard approaches are classified into seven categories: search-based approaches, graph theory techniques, density approaches, modeling strategies, and subspace methods (Pitafi et al., 2023). Clustering is especially important in geographical data mining. Among the numerous clustering algorithms, density-based Clustering, such as DBSCAN (Density-Based Spatial Clustering of Applications with Noise), distinguishes out for its efficiency in recognizing clusters with different densities (Amna et al., 2022).

Most real-world data generated is large, unlabelled, and has multiple dimensions, making data clustering challenging. It is impossible to immediately detect the number of clusters in a real-world dataset. As a result, traditional clustering algorithms struggle to determine the ideal number of clusters in a real-world dataset with high density and dimensionality. This offers a considerable problem to standard clustering algorithms, which require the number of clusters as an input (Minu et al., 2023).

Types of Clustering

Clustering, an effective approach for extracting relevant information, splits a collection of objects into clusters based on their similarities. Conventional Clustering solely uses unlabelled data to train a model. In contrast, this model anticipates unlabelled data. It often comprises partition-based, hierarchical, density-based, and graph-based techniques. These methods frequently confront the problem of significant discrepancy between clustering results and real partitioning due to a lack of prior knowledge. Data analysis employs various clustering techniques: connectivity-based, restricted, centroid-based, density-based, distribution-based, and fuzzy.

Connectivity-based Clustering: The concept underlying connectivity-based Clustering is that vectors of data points in space are more comparable to one another than data points further away. A cluster can be described largely by the maximum distance required to connect its components. The phrase "hierarchical clustering" refers to the fact that different clusters develop at varying distances and can be shown using a dendrogram. Instead of splitting a single data set, these algorithms provide a huge cluster hierarchy that merges at precise distances.

Centroid-based Clustering: It groups data based on its proximity to a specific value. K-means is a typical centroid-based technique that performs well and is simple for Clustering. The basic concept of all centroid-based algorithms is determining the distance between the items in the data set in question. The essential feature of distance measurement is often calculated using one of three distance measuring mechanisms: Manhattan, Minkowski, or Euclidean.

Density-based Clustering: It identifies discrete clusters in data and is based on the notion that a cluster in data space is a contiguous area of high point density distinguished from other clusters by sparse areas. The data points in the splitting and sparse zones are sometimes called noise or outliers. The study's main objective is to explore and examine common clustering methods like K-means, fuzzy C-means, and DBSCAN and their performance evaluation for grouping related objects.

LITERATURE REVIEW

This study aims to identify the most effective clustering technique for categorizing budgetary performance information. It assesses the performance of the K-Means algorithm, DBSCAN, and agglomerative hierarchical Clustering (AHC) (Ghozali et al., 2024). Conventional clustering techniques are ineffective for data with large dimensions because the clustering work usually breaks down into two phases: reducing dimensionality before Clustering, In general, the available multidimensional clustering algorithms have the limitations as follows:) The two-phase methods divide the relationship between Clustering and dimension reduction; (2) these methods do not account for the impact of anomalous cases in highly dimensional information on grouping efficiency. To overcome these issues, a projected fuzzy-means clustering technique with instance penalty (PCIP) is suggested in (Wang et al., 2024).

FCM also introduces unpredictability and inconsistency, affecting cluster performance. To overcome this problem, the fuzzy rough set, as a technique of controlling untrustworthy information, provides a more exact and stringent modeling mechanism to handle boundary data. Despite this advantage, the work in (Yu et al., 2024) proposes a novel rough FCM (FRCM) clustering technique to improve the efficiency and repeated efficiency of FCM. FCM is susceptible to noise and outliers and works poorly on data sets that comprise clusters of different sizes or densities.

Four common methods for Clustering are used in (Michalakopoulos et al., 2024): K-means, K-medoids, Hierarchical Agglomerative Clustering, and Density-based Spatial Clustering. A qualitative approach is used with different assessment measures to evaluate those algorithms. The study further reframes the challenge as a statistical classifying problem, mimicking the clustering method and utilizing Explainable AI (xAI) to improve the understanding of the solution. This work explores the three common methods of Clustering, such as K Means, Fuzzy C-means, and DBSCAN, for grouping similar items (Anitha et al., 2023). An inappropriate choice of initial centroids in the K-means algorithm could cause the algorithm to converge to a less-than-ideal result. K denotes an outlier-sensitive clustering algorithm. K indicates that Clustering is dependent on K. Incorrect K selection could result in less-than-ideal clusters (Saxena and Chaudhary 2023).

Qtaish et al, (2024) introduce the Hybrid Capuchin Search Algorithm (HCSA), a meta-heuristic strategy for addressing the challenges of local optima traps and initialization sensitivity in the K-means clustering approach. It was inspired by the success and longevity of meta-heuristics in delivering persuasive solutions. It spurred different efficient approaches and computational tools to solve complex and useful real-world situations.

Li et al., (2024) use the heating demand behavior of occupants with obvious intermittency as an example to compare the clustering effect of the common clustering algorithm (K-means) and three clustering algorithms that consider time series (K-shape, Dynamic Time Warping (DTW), and Derivative Dynamic Time Warping (DDTW) (Lodha et al., 2023). It also investigates possible causes of variations and introduces three evaluation approaches for clustering findings regarding intermittent heating demand. The Fuzzy C-Mean (FCM) approach is commonly utilized for its simplicity. However, FCM has significant drawbacks, such as low initial sensitivity, a tendency to slip into local minima, and noise influence. Savita Kumar et al., (2024) propose an improved version of the FCM clustering technique in an intuitionistic fuzzy environment to address these shortcomings. The suggested approach lowers the impact of noise by establishing a metric.

Wajgi et al., (2024) describe the clustering-based localization algorithms for Wireless Sensor Networks (WSN) and Wireless Multimedia Sensor Networks (WMSN) in depth. Clustering is used in wireless and multimedia sensor networks to provide distributed computing and parallel processing by grouping sensor nodes into small, self-contained subgroups. Clustering algorithms could considerably increase the efficiency of the conventional localization procedure. Clustering separates the network into pieces that may function independently, decreasing communication costs. Clustering also improves network performance by enabling dispersed computing.

Qi et al., (2024) suggest a load management strategy that utilizes clustering technology that solves the issues with previous methods. This method entails preliminary data processing, choosing features, cluster analysis, and the analysis of clustering results. Increasing energy efficiency and system performance is feasible by correctly classifying and controlling load data. This research investigates a load management strategy appropriate for the Internet of Things (IoT) environment. Load characteristics were accurately identified and managed using clustering technology.

Zhou et al., (2024) use the k-means clustering approach to create a basic cluster. Furthermore, this study expanded the diversity of consensus by implementing various measures. The meta-clustering approach aggregates the basic clusters, which are then re-clustered to generate the final clusters. The suggested hybrid clustering approach has the advantages of k-means and its fast speed, and it does not have its key flaws, such as its incapability to detect non-spherical and non-uniform clusters. The current state of clustering research includes issues with computing complexities, cluster refinement, convergence speed, data dimension, efficacy and expansion, data object representation, evaluation metrics, data streams, and knowledge extraction.

SYSTEM METHODOLOGY

The study explores different ML clustering techniques like K-means, Fuzzy C-means, and DBSCAN methods. K-means allows us to identify patterns in image pixels, enabling more rapid and effective processing. Fuzzy C Means's clustering method seeks to enhance the current K-Means technique by enabling soft cluster-to-data allocations. Unlike K-Means, which assume spherical clusters, DBSCAN may detect clusters of different shapes and sizes.

K-Means Clustering: K-Mean Clustering is a data analysis approach that partitions observation into objects depending on their position and distance from input points. An unsupervised ML technique splits the dataset into K number of groups. The algorithm partitions items into exclusive clusters (K) so that items in every group are as close to each other as possible while remaining as far away from items within different clusters. A cluster is a set of data objects clustered together because they share similar properties.

Figure 2. Steps in K-means algorithms

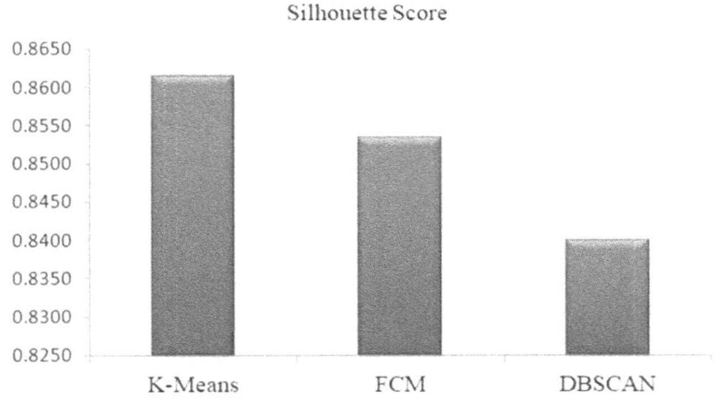

The steps in K-means clustering are as follows and depicted in Figure 2.

- Allocate two centroids at random (with K=2). Two sites are designated as centroids. It should be noted that these locations are randomized and might be located anywhere known as centroids; however, typically, they aren't necessarily the center of a specific data collection.
- Compute the distance between any two data points from each randomly assigned centroid. The shortest distance between each point and the two centroids is allocated to that centroid. The distance between each point and the other centroids is determined.
- Determine which of these two clusters' real centroid is. The original centroid assigned at random will be modified to match the actual centroid for every cluster.
- Repeat the procedure of computing the distance and adjusting the centroid until the final cluster is reached. The cluster formed from the different types of items and the flowchart for the K-means Clustering is shown in Figures 3 and 4.

Figure 3. K- means clustering

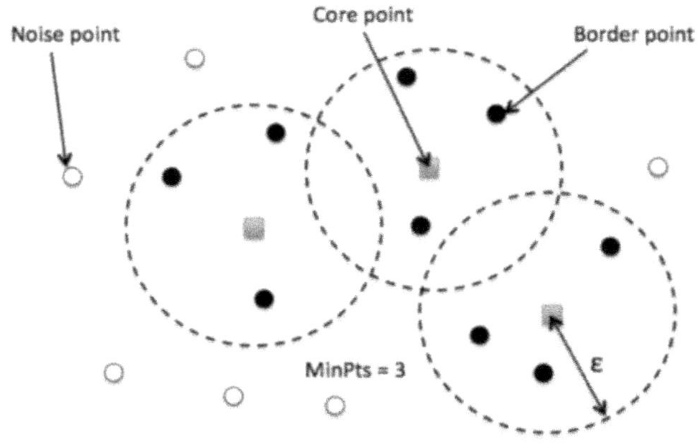

Figure 4. Flowchart for K-means clustering

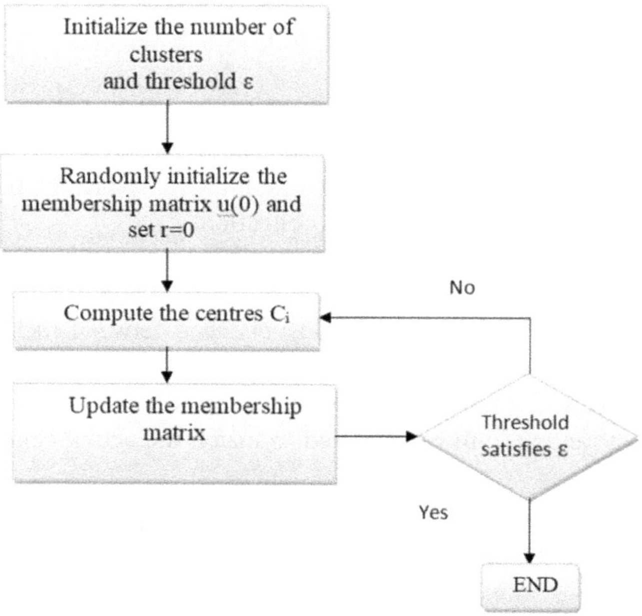

Fuzzy C-Means Clustering (FCM)

FCM is a fuzzy variation of the k-means technique that calculates a cluster's centroid as the average of all samples weighed according to their cluster membership. The cluster's centroid is determined as the mean value of all instances, with each sample's degree (UK) of relatedness to the cluster Ck considered.

The values of the coefficients are fuzzified using an actual parameter, m > 1, and standardized to ensure their total is equal to one.

For m = 2, this is equal to linearly normalizing the coefficients so that their sum is 1. The procedure is most similar to k-means when m approaches one since the cluster center closest to the instance receives a much higher weight than the rest of the centers.

It is comparable to the crisp k-means method. It reduces intra-cluster variation but suffers from the same issues as k-means: it may become trapped in a local minimum, and its outcomes depend on the center of the cluster chosen at the start. The workflow of the FCM is deprecated in Figure 4. The outline of the FCM algorithm is shown below.

- Select the number of clusters k and fuzziness parameter m.
- Initialize cluster centroids at random or using another approach.
- Calculate the number of member degrees for each data point in each cluster based on their distances from the cluster centroids using equation (3)

In equation (3), μij is the membership degree of a data point. For cluster j, xi denotes the ith data point. vj is the centroid of cluster j, and c is the total number of clusters, and the fuzziness parameter, denoted by m, is often greater than 1. Apply equation (4) to update cluster centroids.

Repeat steps 3 and 4 until the centroids and membership degrees have stabilized.

Figure 5. Workflow-FCM

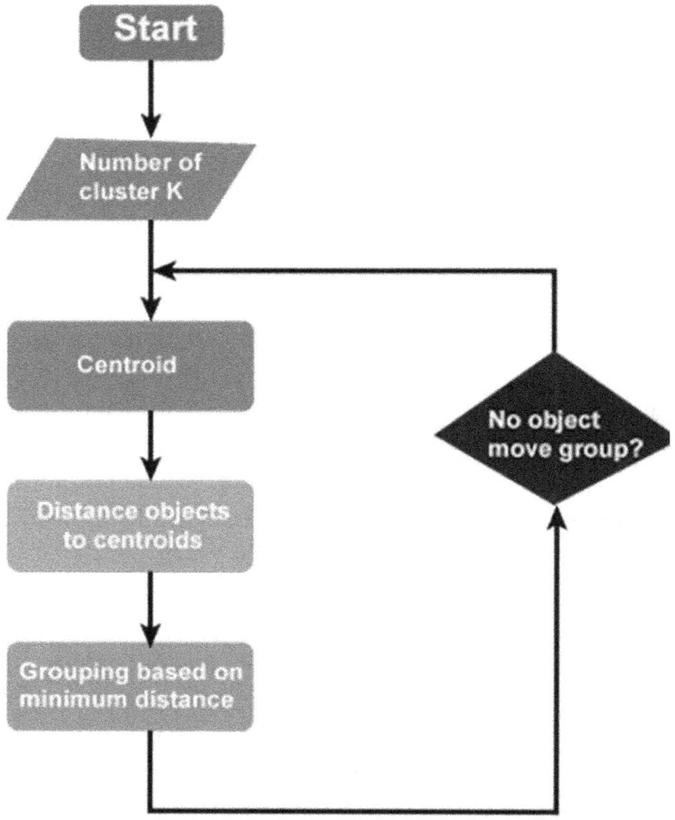

FCM is sensitive to cluster centroids' initial selection and may converge to various solutions under different initializations. As a result, it is typical to run the algorithm numerous times using different initializations and select the solution with the lowest objective function value (Figure 5).

DBSCAN Clustering Algorithm

The acronym DBSCAN stands for density-based spatial Clustering of applications with noise. In contrast to k-means, this is a density-based clustering algorithm. This is a useful method for finding outliers in a dataset. It identifies dynamically formed clusters by calculating the density of data points in various regions. It divides regions into lower-density regions to detect outliers in higher-density clusters. This technique outperforms k-means when dealing with irregularly shaped data. DBSCAN is built upon the following essential concepts

- Core points have minimal other points (MinPts) within a given distance (ε or epsilon).
- Border Points: These are the points within the ε distance of a core point but do not have any MinPts neighbors.
- Noise Points: These tend to be not core or boundary points. Those aren't sufficiently close to a cluster to be included.

DBSCAN defines clusters using two parameters: minPts (the minimal number of data points that must be grouped around for a region to be designated high-density) and eps (the distance used to assess whether a data point is in the same region as other information points). The following are the three points after completing DBSCAN clustering, as shown in Figure 6.

Figure 6. Types of points after completion of DBSCAN

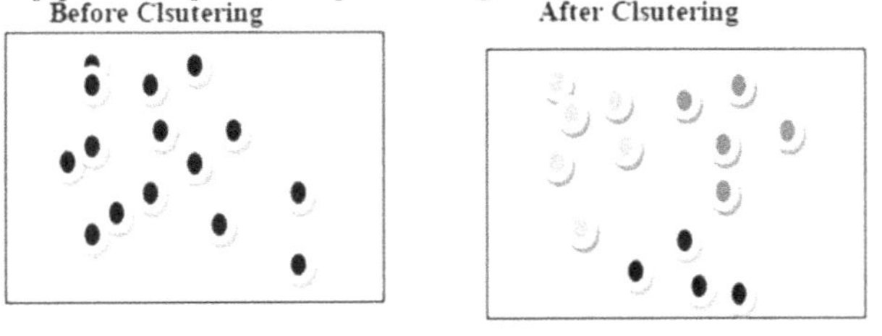

A core point is a position with a minimum of m points within n distance; a border point has a minimum of one Core point at a distance of n; and a noise point might be core or border. It also contains less than m points within n units of itself.

Steps for DBSCAN Algorithm

- The process starts by selecting a point at random from the dataset and continues until each one has been examined.
- When'minPoint' points are found within an 'ε' radius of a point, they are regarded as an element of a single cluster.
- Next, the clusters are enlarged by calculating each neighboring point's size several times.

RESULTS AND ANALYSIS

This section discusses the benefits and shortcomings of K-means, FCM, and DBSCAN techniques. These methods were tested with the clustering Exercises dataset, freely downloadable from Kaggle.

K-means Algorithm: K-means are highly dependent on the initial conditions. The technique randomly sets up the cluster centroids at the start, and ultimately, clustering results may differ based on these initial placements. Different initializations can produce distinct local optima, leading to varying clustering results. This reduces the K-means technique's reliability and reproducibility. A further drawback of the K-means method is that it cannot handle categorical data. The program works with numeric data and calculates the distance between data points. However, categorical information lacks a natural concept of distance or resemblance. If categorical information is used with the K-means algorithm, the categories must be converted into numerical values, such as by one-hot encoding. One disadvantage of one-hot encoding is that it handles every characteristic separately, which might reduce performance because it dramatically increases data dimensionality.

Fuzzy C- means Algorithms: An unsupervised clustering approach allows us to generate a fuzzy data division. The approach is based on a parameter m representing the answer's fuzziness level. Large m values blur the classes, causing all components to be assigned to all clusters. The parameter m determines the solutions to the optimization problem. It provides the most accurate result for overlapping data sets and outperforms the k-means method. In contrast to k-means, where data points must only correspond to one cluster center, data points have been allocated here. The drawback includes apriori settings of the cluster numbers; lowering the value of β yields better results but requires more iterations, and the Euclidean distance metrics can provide unequal weight to underlying issues.

DBSCAN: It offers several benefits, notably detecting clusters of different sizes and shapes and its resistance to noise. It is good at handling outliers in the dataset. It is appropriate for datasets with an unidentified or variable number of clusters because it requires no pre-specifying the number of clusters. The ε (epsilon) and variables can substantially impact clustering outcomes. Modifying these settings is frequently required to attain the appropriate clustering results. DBSCAN does have deficiencies. (i) It needs two parameters to establish its optimal values. This technique is quite sensitive to these settings; (ii) It is unsuitable for data sets comprising clusters with vastly varied densities; and (iii) it considers all features identically irrespective of their relevance to Clustering. Moreover, Clustering, unlike other supervised learning applications such as classification or regression, cannot be fully automated from start to finish. Rather, it is a continual process of knowledge discovery that necessitates domain knowledge and regular human discretion tweaks to the information and model settings to obtain the intended result.

Metrics for measuring the Clustering Algorithms: Different strategies for Clustering have been suggested, which differ slightly based on the underlying technique. Their benefits and disadvantages are distinct for each dataset. Some metrics for assessing the performance of clustering algorithms are as follows.

Silhouette Score: The Silhouette score is a statistical measure that assesses the quality of data clustering findings. It is computed by comparing the data point's resemblance to a corresponding cluster and its difference from other clusters. It is calculated by adding the average intra-cluster distance between locations to the average nearest-cluster distance. The average distance (distance_a_i) between each data point and the remaining data points in the cluster is calculated. This value shows the data point's similarity with other points in its cluster. The average distance (distance_b_i) between each data point and all other clusters it does not belong to is calculated. This value indicates how distinct the data point is from other clusters. The Score is calculated as follows:

Silhouette Score = (5)

The value of this core lies between -1 and 1, where -1 is the lowest attainable value, and one is the highest, and the Score of zero indicates overlapping clusters.

Inertia: Inertia measures the intra-cluster sum of squares, which includes all the remaining values. It assesses how closely linked clusters are to one another; the smaller the inertia value, the better the performance. The formula for calculating Inertia is as follows.

The N represents the number of instances often found in the columns part of your datasheet. X denotes each sample's value, while C. represents the cluster's center. This equation calculates each data point's distance to the center square. Inertia performs several significant functions.

- Cluster Tightness Metric: Lower Inertia means that data points are closer to their cluster centers, implying more cohesive and well-defined clusters.
- Optimization. The K-means algorithm's objective function is to decrease Inertia. The method makes iterative adjustments to cluster allocations and centroids to reduce Inertia.
- Evaluation Metric: Inertia is useful in determining the quality of Clustering. It can be used to compare clustering results and select the best number of clusters.

The silhouette score and Inertia were applied to estimate the performance of the K-means, FCM, and DBSCAN algorithms, and the results are represented in figures 6 and 7

Table 1. Performance indicators for clustering techniques

Methods/Scores	Silhouette Score	Inertia
K-Means	0.8615	74
FCM	0.8534	76
DBSCAN	0.8400	75.4

Table 1 presents the performance indicators for the three clustering techniques, K-Means, FCM, and DBSCAN, considered in this study. It shows the values of silhouette scores and Inertia for the studied methods. In the case of Silhouette scores, (i) 1 indicates clusters are well separated and easily identifiable. (ii) 0 indicates that clusters are indifferent or that the separation between clusters is insignificant. (iii) -1: Indicates that clusters are assigned incorrectly. When handling higher dimensions, the silhouette score is very important for validating the operation of the clustering algorithm, as one cannot use any visualization to validate Clustering when the dimensions exceed three. It is also used to determine the ideal number of clusters.

Figure 7. Silhouette score

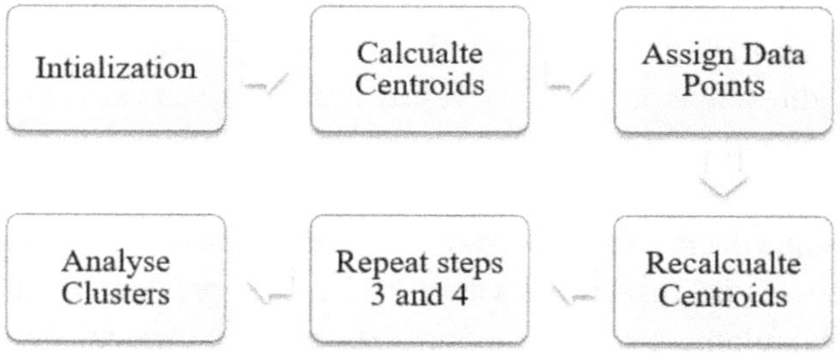

Figure 7 shows the silhouette scores for the K-Means, FCM, and DBSCAN methods. It assesses how effectively an object matches its cluster vs other clusters. The silhouette score varies from -1 to 1, with higher values suggesting better cluster separation. The K-means algorithm score was higher than that of FCM and DBSCAN.

Figure 8. Inertia

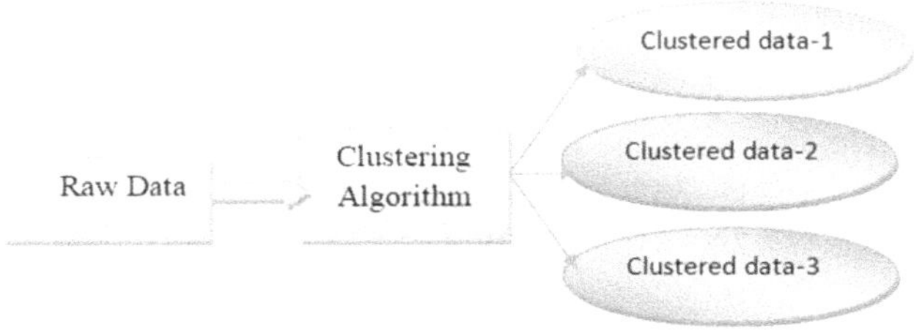

Figure 8 shows that the efficiency of K-means is better than that of FCM and DBSCAN, and it shows that the closely related items are more in the clusters formed by K-means.

The Inertia values in Figure 7 show the coherency between the clusters, and it is found to be less in KL-means, and the next lowest value is in DBSCAN. Inertia and the Silhouette Coefficient are important measures for assessing the efficiency of clustering algorithms such as K-means. They offer various perspectives: Inertia measures internal cluster compactness, whereas the silhouette coefficient measures how effectively clusters are separated. K-Means' decreased computational cost enables it to manage large datasets effectively. Moreover, KMeans is utilized in various disciplines and use cases, including segmentation of customers, detecting fraud, forecasting account attrition, modifying client promotions, identifying cybercrime, and optimizing delivery routes.

CONCLUSION AND FUTURE WORK

Cluster Analysis is a method of organizing things into clusters that are similar to each other and distinct from other clusters. It finds its applicability in various technological and scientific research fields, meeting criteria such as arbitrary forms, high dimensional databases, domain knowledge, and more. The most appealing element of Clustering is that it can be applied to nearly any operation. Clustering increases productivity, facilitates decision-making, and creates fresh startup prospects. Research has shown that a single clustering technique cannot meet all clustering requirements. Choosing the right algorithm for a given application is challenging. This study compares the clustering methods and is evaluated. The clustering techniques like K-means, FCM, and DBSCAN were assessed, and it is evident that the K-means outperforms the methods considered. The major goal is to understand the techniques for Clustering, which may then be used to improve the other applications. Further, the study can extend to examine the other clustering models and also the methods that enable clustering algorithms to operate on larger datasets.

REFERENCES

Amna, N. M., Nawi, M., & Aamir, M. F. (2022). The comparative performance analysis of clustering algorithms. In *International Conference on Soft Computing and Data Mining* (pp. 341–352). Springer International Publishing, Cham, Switzerland. DOI: 10.1007/978-3-031-00828-3_34

Anitha, K., Nagaraj, B. K., Paramasivan, P., & Shynu, T. (2023). Enhancing Clustering Performance with the Rough Set C-Means Algorithm. *FMDB Transactions on Sustainable Computing Systems*, *1*(4), 190–203.

Bhardwaj, M., Khan, N. U., & Baghel, V. (2024). Fuzzy C-Means clustering based selective edge enhancement scheme for improved road crack detection. *Engineering Applications of Artificial Intelligence*, *136*(10), 108955. DOI: 10.1016/j.engappai.2024.108955

Chowdhury, S., Helian, N., & Cordeiro de Amorim, R. (2023). Feature weighting in DBSCAN using reverse nearest neighbors. *Pattern Recognition*, *137*(5), 109314. DOI: 10.1016/j.patcog.2023.109314

Ghosh, S., & Kumar, S. (2013). Comparative analysis of K-means and fuzzy C-means algorithms. *International Journal of Advanced Computer Science and Applications*, *4*(4), 35–39. DOI: 10.14569/IJACSA.2013.040406

Hadi Al Ghozali, I., Afan, I., & Lestari, T. (2024). Comparative analysis clustering algorithm for government's budget performance data. *Cogito Smart Journal*, *10*(1), 578–591. DOI: 10.31154/cogito.v10i1.611.578-591

Li, J., Ma, R., Deng, M., Cao, X., Wang, X., & Wang, X. (2024). A comparative study of clustering algorithms for intermittent heating demand considering time series. *Applied Energy*, *353*(1), 122046. DOI: 10.1016/j.apenergy.2023.122046

Lodha, S., Malani, H., & Bhardwaj, A. K. (2023). Performance Evaluation of Vision Transformers for Diagnosis of Pneumonia. *FMDB Transactions on Sustainable Computing Systems*, *1*(1), 21–31.

Michalakopoulos, V., Sarmas, E., Papias, I., Skaloumpakas, P., Marinakis, V., & Doukas, H. (2024). A machine learning-based framework for clustering residential electricity load profiles to enhance demand response programs. *Applied Energy*, *361*(5), 122943. DOI: 10.1016/j.apenergy.2024.122943

Minu, M. S., Subashka Ramesh, S. S., Canessane, R., Al-Amin, M., & Bin Sulaiman, R. (2023). Experimental Analysis of UAV Networks Using Oppositional Glowworm Swarm Optimization and Deep Learning Clustering and Classification. *FMDB Transactions on Sustainable Computing Systems*, *1*(3), 124–134.

Pitafi, S., Anwar, T., & Sharif, Z. (2023). A taxonomy of machine learning clustering algorithms, challenges, and future realms. *Applied Sciences (Basel, Switzerland)*, *13*(6), 3529. DOI: 10.3390/app13063529

Qi, L., Song, J., Chen, M., Zhang, M., Zou, Q., & Wan, C. (2024). Mining and clustering techniques for load operation characteristics of the Internet of Things. *2024 International Conference on Intelligent Algorithms for Computational Intelligence Systems (IACIS)*, Karnataka, India. DOI: 10.1109/IACIS61494.2024.10721623

Qtaish, A., Braik, M., Albashish, D., Alshammari, M. T., Alreshidi, A., & Alreshidi, E. J. (2024). Optimization of K-means clustering method using hybrid capuchin search algorithm. *The Journal of Supercomputing*, *80*(7), 1728–1787. DOI: 10.1007/s11227-023-05540-5

Savita, K., Kumar, N., & Siwch, A. (2024). Fuzzy Clustering is based on a distance metric under an intuitionistic fuzzy environment. *Granular Computing*, *9*(1), 9–13. DOI: 10.1007/s41066-023-00446-2

Saxena, D., & Chaudhary, S. (2023). Predicting Brain Diseases from FMRI-Functional Magnetic Resonance Imaging with Machine Learning Techniques for Early Diagnosis and Treatment. *FMDB Transactions on Sustainable Computer Letters*, *1*(1), 33–48.

Tareq, W. Z. T., & Davud, M. (2024). Classification and Clustering. In *Decision-Making Models*. Elsevier. DOI: 10.1016/B978-0-443-16147-6.00024-4

Troiano, M., Nobile, E., Grignaffini, F., Mangini, F., Mastrogiuseppe, M., Conati Barbaro, C., & Frezza, F. (2024). A comparative analysis of machine learning algorithms for identifying cultural and technological groups in archaeological datasets through clustering analysis of homogeneous data. *Electronics (Basel)*, *13*(14), 2752. DOI: 10.3390/electronics13142752

Wajgi, D. W., & Tembhurne, J. V. (2023). Correction: Localization in wireless and multimedia sensor networks using clustering techniques. *Multimedia Tools and Applications*, *83*(7), 6881.

Wang, J., Wu, Y., Huang, X., Zhang, C., & Nie, F. (2024). Projected fuzzy c-means clustering algorithm with instance penalty. *Expert Systems with Applications*, *255*(12), 124563. DOI: 10.1016/j.eswa.2024.124563

Yu, B., Zheng, Z., Cai, M., Pedrycz, W., & Ding, W. (2024). FRCM: A fuzzy rough c-means clustering method. Fuzzy Sets and Systems. *An International Journal in Information Science and Engineering*, *480*(3), 108860.

Zhou, B., Lu, B., & Saeidlou, S. (2022). A hybrid clustering method based on several diverse basic Clustering and meta-clustering aggregation techniques. *Cybernetics and Systems*, *55*(1), 203–229. DOI: 10.1080/01969722.2022.2110682

Chapter 3

A Smart Review on Imputation Techniques for Handling Missing Data

R. Sivakani
https://orcid.org/0000-0001-7830-9479
Dhaanish Ahmed College of Engineering, India

T. Shynu
Dhaanish Ahmed College of Engineering, India

J. Rahila
Dhaanish Ahmed College of Engineering, India

M. S. Minu
https://orcid.org/0000-0001-6532-4530
SRM Institute of Science and Technology, Ramapuram, India

P. Sudha
Dhaanish Ahmed College of Engineering, India

V. Pradeep
Dhaanish Ahmed College of Engineering, India

S. Silvia Priscila
https://orcid.org/0000-0002-6040-3149
Bharath Institute of Higher Education and Research, India

ABSTRACT

Missing data is an important problem in the digital world. Missing data means no value will be present in the dataset. Missing occurs for many reasons, including data loss, typing errors, system problems, less interest of the respondent, etc. This is a major issue for researchers, industry people, academicians, doctors, etc. The incomplete data will not support any solution. In this paper, a review of various

DOI: 10.4018/979-8-3373-5203-9.ch003

research articles from 2009 to 2020 is analyzed. The techniques and algorithms used for the imputation have been analyzed. Imputation is the process involved in replacing the missing value. In addition, various algorithms, techniques, and methods are discussed in this paper to solve the above-said issue, and significant discussion is also done on the types of missing mechanisms. The main focus has been on the traditional and novel imputation methods.

INTRODUCTION

Missing data is an important problem in the dataset. In this digital world, nothing can be possible without the data. The data is important for every processing, such as prediction and classification. The missing values are the problem in all the fields. It is quite difficult to manage the missing data. So, a plan has been made to review the missing data handling papers (Sundararajan et al., 2023; Jasper et al., 2024). The dataset is analyzed and checked for missing data in the preprocessing stage. If the data is complete, the next process will continue; otherwise, the data set will be given to the missing data handling part, and the missing data will be imputed with various methodologies (Said and Tripathi, 2023; Saleh et al., 2024). The imputed data will be used in the next process. The missing data will create issues in the result prediction. So, the dataset with the missing data is considered an incomplete dataset (Zanardo, 2024; Singh et al., 2023). If incomplete data is in the dataset, then preprocessing is to be done (Silvia Priscila et al., 2023; Aragani, 2024). The data can be complete or incomplete (Sivapriya et al., 2023; Calo et al., 2023). If the data is complete, then the data will be given directly for processing. If the data is incomplete, it can be used for traditional and novel imputation methods (Singh et al., 2023). Any method can generate the missing data, and the incomplete data can be converted to complete data. Once the data can be converted to the complete data, the completed data can be given for the next processing (Agarwal, 2023).

METHODOLOGIES

Various methods and techniques are used to handle missing data. The incomplete data can be converted to the complete dataset using machine learning algorithms (Chundru, 2024). In this regard, the following questions are focused on understanding and managing the missing data.

- Question 1: What is missing data?
- Question 2: What are the types of missing data?

- Question 3: Why does missing data happen?
- Question 4: In which area is missing data?
- Question 5: How it can be handled?
- Question 6: What are the techniques/algorithms for handling missing data?

Question 1: What is missing data?

Missing data is the unknown data in the dataset. For an observation in a dataset, if there is no data value, it is called missing data. If it is missing in the dataset, the researchers cannot predict the result correctly.

Figure 1. Representation of the dataset with missing data

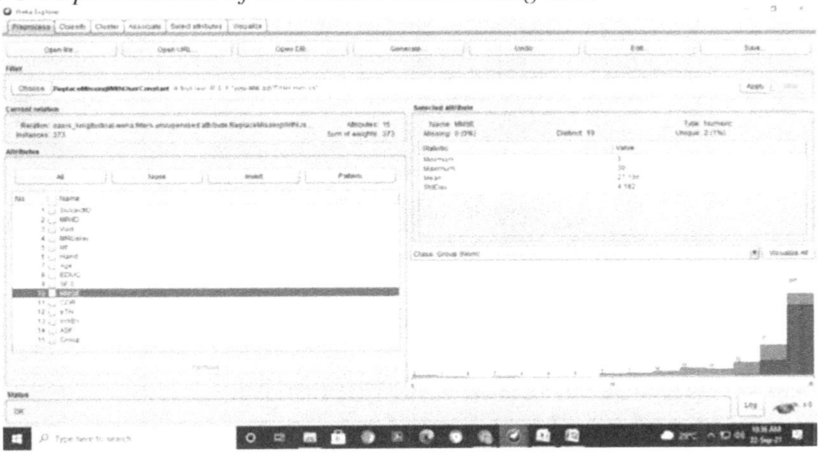

Figure 1 represents a dataset with missing data. The arrangements of blocks are represented as the data, and the empty block is represented as the missing data.

Question 2: What are the types of missing data?

From the review, it is analyzed that the missing data can be of three types they are:

- MCAR
- MAR
- MNAR

MCAR: MCAR is expanded as Missing Completely at Random. In this type, the missing is not related to any missing or known variables.

MAR: MAR is expanded as Missing at Random. In this type, the missing is related to the other known variables.

MNAR: MNAR is expanded as Missing Not at Random. In this type, the missing can be of MCAR or MAR.

Figure 2. Types of missing data

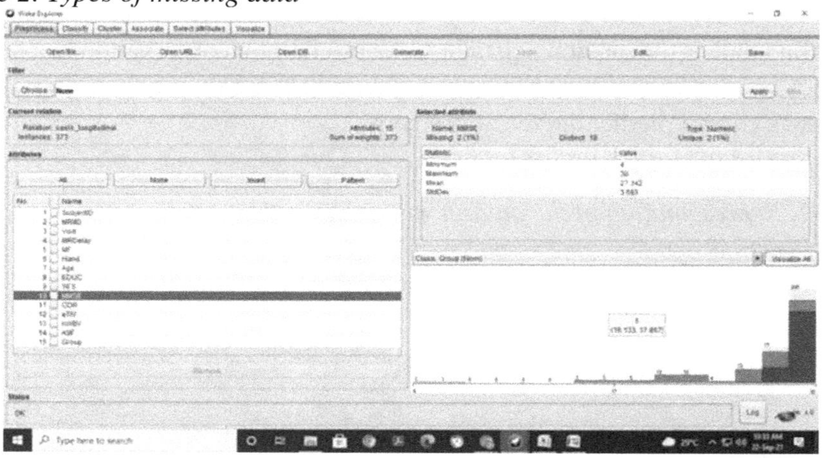

Figure 2 represents the types of missing data.

Question 3: Why does missing data happen?

Missing data can occur due to the lack of value for an observation. If the respondent is not interested in a question or is not responding because the question can be sensitive, the data can be missing due to typing errors, etc.

Figure 3. Reason for missing data

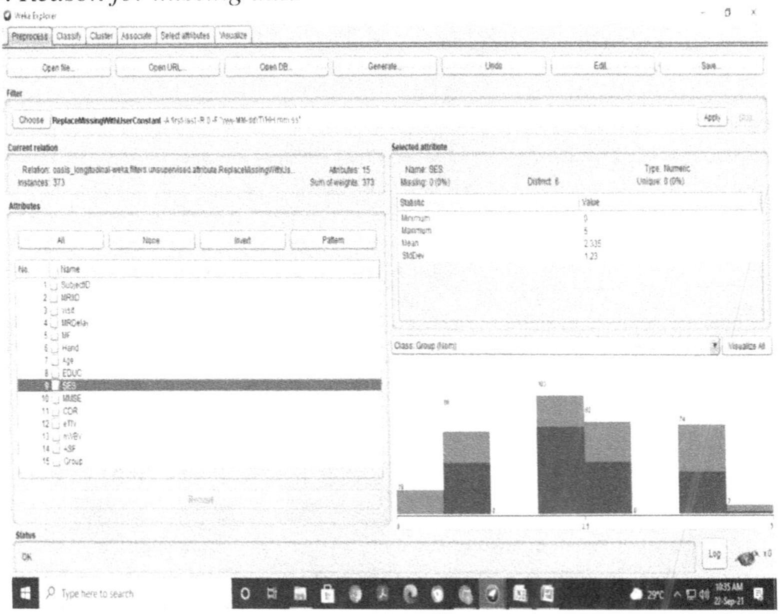

Figure 3 shows the chance of getting the missing data. If there is no answer from the respondent, it will be considered missing data.

Question 4: In which area is missing data?

The missing data may be from the medical field, education, research, surveys, industries, etc. It is identified from the literature that the missing data may occur mainly in the medical field, as shown in Figure 4.

Figure 4. Main fields of missing data

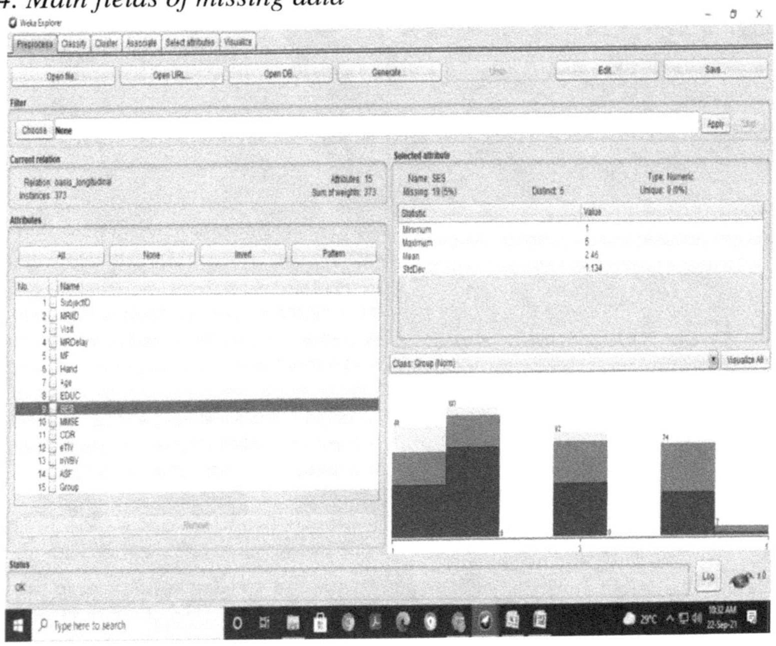

Question 5: How it can be handled?

Generally, the data can be classified into two types:

- Complete data
- Missing data (Incomplete data)

Complete data have all the features in the dataset, and it can be processed directly, he result will be produced. Incomplete data is missing and cannot be processed y to produce the result. The incomplete data can be converted to complete ng the imputation process.

Figure 5. Data processing framework

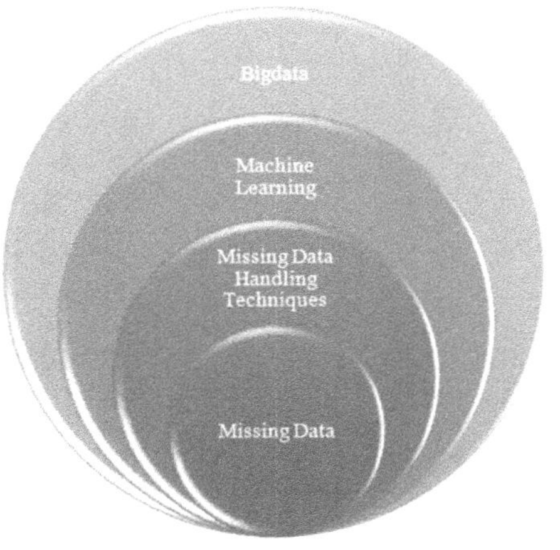

Figure 5 shows that the data is given as input, and if it is incomplete, it is given to generate the missing data. The imputation techniques can be used to generate missing data, and the incomplete data will be converted to complete data, and then, finally, the prediction will be made. The main objective of this review paper is to discuss the algorithms, techniques, and novel methods used to generate the missing values. This paper is organized with an introduction followed by publishers of related works, a review and discussion, a case study, and a conclusion and future work.

PUBLISHERS OF THE RELATED WORKS

The papers collected for the analysis are from 2009 to 2020; from that, 62 papers are considered for the work. The papers are categorized based on the algorithm and techniques for generating the missing values. Figure 6 shows the publishers of the papers.

Figure 6. Publishers of the missing data

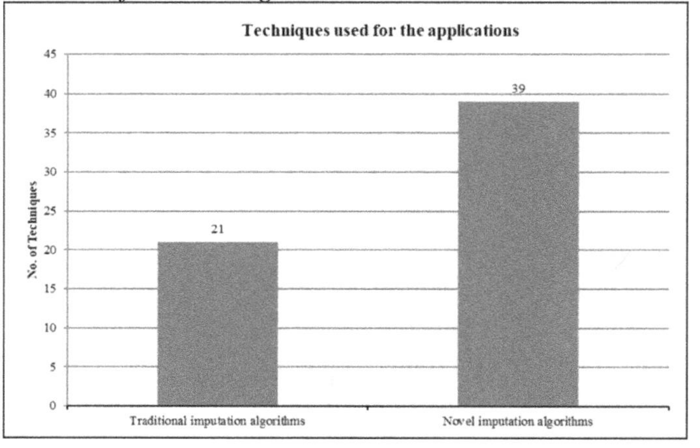

Question 6: What are the techniques/ algorithms for handling missing data?

From the literature, the papers are grouped into two groups are

- Traditional Imputation Methods
- Novel Imputation Methods

Traditional imputation methods are available by default as a method or algorithm. The novel imputation methods are the methods which are implemented as novel methods by the authors.

Figure 7. Missing data handling methods

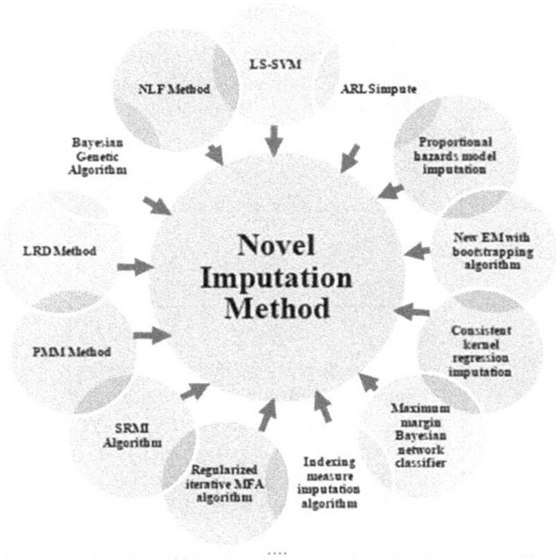

Figure 7 shows the category of the missing data handling methods. Traditional methods and novel imputation methods are the two missing data handling methods used for generating the missing data in the incomplete dataset. The related papers about the missing value generations are collected, and the types of algorithms or methods for generating the missing value are discussed.

REVIEW AND DISCUSSION

Traditional Imputation Methods: Traditional imputation techniques are the techniques used to generate and replace the missing values in the dataset (Kalyani and Devi, 2024). Traditional algorithms are used to generate missing values (Table 1).

Table 1. Traditional imputation methods

No	Author	Algorithm/Techniques	Concept
1	Graham (2009)	Normal Model Multiple Imputation Techniques and Maximum-likelihood techniques	Literature Review
2	Chakraborty and Hong Gu (2009)	Adhoc imputations	A comparison was made among the ad hoc imputations, and it was concluded that the mixed model imputation method produced better results.
3	Langkamp et al. (2010)	Case or pairwise deletion, single Imputation, multiple imputation, and reweight imputation	A comparison was made with the performance of those algorithms, and it was concluded that reweighting produced the best result.
4	Albrecht et al. (2010)	The combined form of KNN and MIN	Generated missing values
5	Garcia-Laencina et al. (2010)	Deletion means Imputation, multiple imputation, and Imputation with neural networks and EM algorithms.	Pattern classification review
6	Schafer et al. (2010)	Multiple Imputation techniques	Literature review
7	Myers (2011)	EM algorithm, Multiple Imputation Technique, hot deck Imputation method	A comparison is made, and it concluded Hot deck imputation is best
8	Yaseen et al. (2012)	EM algorithm	Generated the missing values
9	Dong and Peng (2013)	Multiple imputation, full information maximum likelihood, and expectation-maximization	Generated the missing data, and the classification has been done.
10	Rebekah (2015)	Multiple Imputation technique	Multiple Imputation technique is applied to the dataset based on NMAR, MCAR, and MAR missing mechanisms.
11	Santos et al. (2016)	Univariate and multivariate approach	Literature Review
12	Xu et al. (2020)	Direct deletion imputation technique, mode imputation technique, hot-deck imputation technique (HD), and the multiple imputation technique	A comparison is made with the performance of those algorithms, and it is concluded that the HD imputation technique is best.

Techniques used in the Traditional Imputation Methods

Traditional imputation techniques are widely used methods in statistics and data science to handle missing data, a common issue in datasets that can impact the accuracy and reliability of analyses. The image presents various imputation techniques, each with its approach to filling in missing values to ensure data completeness. Some of these methods rely on simple deterministic rules, while others use advanced statistical models or machine learning algorithms to predict the missing values. One of the most basic approaches is the deletion method, which removes records with missing values. While easy to implement, it may lead to significant data loss and potential bias. Another common technique is mean imputation, where missing values are replaced with the average of observed values for that variable. Although simple, this approach reduces variability and can distort relationships within the data. Mode imputation is another straightforward method primarily used for categorical data, replacing missing values with the most frequently occurring category. Hot-deck imputation involves selecting a similar record in the dataset to fill in the missing values. In contrast, ad-hoc imputation relies on arbitrary replacements, such as zero, median, or specific constants (Figure 8).

Figure 8. Techniques for missing data handling in traditional imputation methods

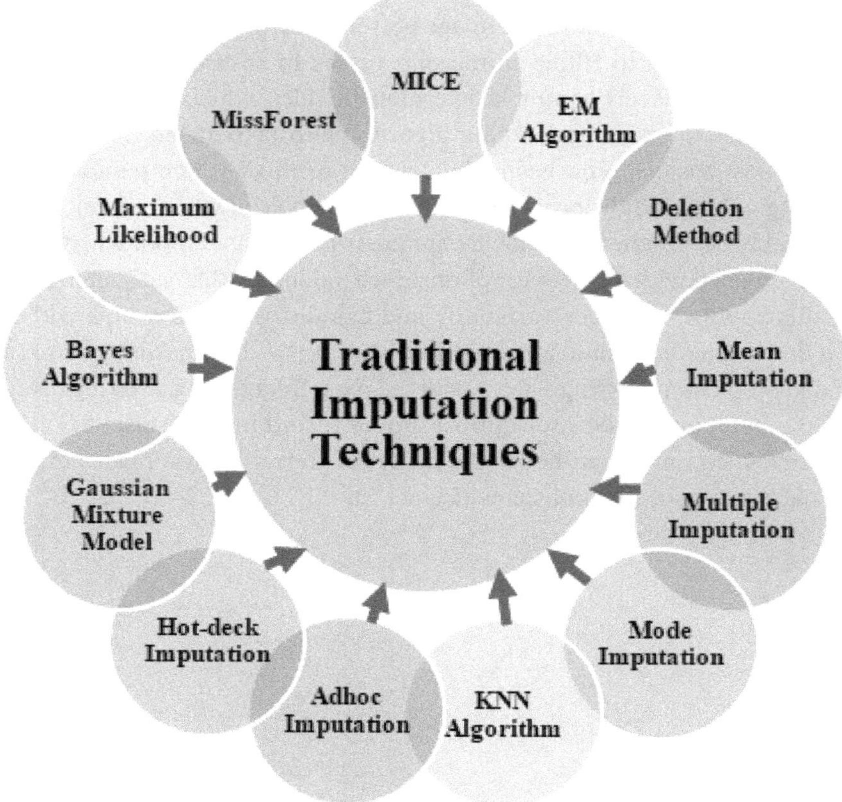

More advanced statistical approaches provide probabilistic solutions for handling missing data. Multiple imputations (MI) generate datasets with different imputed values, then combine results to reduce uncertainty. Maximum likelihood estimation (MLE) predicts missing values using probability distributions and observed data. The Bayes algorithm applies a Bayesian framework incorporating prior knowledge to estimate missing values. The Gaussian mixture model (GMM) assumes data follows a combination of multiple normal distributions and uses this assumption to impute missing values.

Machine learning techniques have also been developed to improve imputation accuracy by predicting missing values based on patterns in the data. The k-nearest neighbors (KNN) algorithm imputes missing values by analyzing the most similar data points, making it useful when relationships among observations exist. MissForest, a random forest-based imputation method, predicts missing values iteratively using decision trees. The expectation-maximization (EM) algorithm estimates missing values by maximizing the likelihood of observed data through an iterative process. Multiple imputation by chained equations (MICE) is a powerful method that repeatedly models missing values based on other observed variables in the dataset.

Each imputation technique has its strengths and weaknesses, and the choice of method depends on the nature of the dataset, the extent of missing data, and the relationships between variables. While simple approaches may be sufficient for small datasets, advanced statistical and machine learning-based methods often provide more accurate and reliable imputations, ensuring better data integrity and analysis outcomes.

Novel Imputation Methods

Imputation frameworks are novel frameworks that researchers develop to generate the missing values in a dataset (Table 2).

Table 2. Novel imputation methods

Sl. No	Paper	Algorithm/Techniques	Concept
1	Zhanget and Liu (2009)	Least Squares Support Vector Machines (LS-SVMs)	The missing value is generated, and the performance is compared with the performance of the Expectation Maximization/ Data Augmentation (EM/DA) algorithm, proving that LS-SVM is the best.
2	White and Royston (2009)	proportional hazards model imputation	The missing value is generated
3	Choong et al. (2009)	Auto-regressive-model-based missing value estimation method (ARLSimpute)	The missing value is generated
4	Zhu et al. (2011)	Consistent kernel regression imputation	Imputation is done on heterogeneous data
6	Luengo et al. (2011)	SVMI, EM, SVDI, BPCA, LLSI EC, MC, CMC, KNNI, WKNNI, KMI, FKMI, IM, DMI	Fourteen types of imputation algorithms are applied, and FKMI and EC are found to be the best among those imputation methods. Then, classification is done using twenty-three types of classification algorithms.

continued on following page

Table 2. Continued

Sl. No	Paper	Algorithm/Techniques	Concept
7	Tschiatschek et al. (2012)	Maximum margin Bayesian network classifier	Missing values are generated, and the classification is performed.
8	Madhu and Rajinikanth (2012)	indexing measure imputation algorithm	– Imputation is done, and the performance is compared with the KNNI, SVMI, WKNNI, KMI, and FKMI algorithms, which proves that the new one is better than the others.
9	Husson et al. (2013)	Regularized iterative MFA algorithm	Missing values are generated
10	Vesin et al. (2013)	Sequential Regression Multiple Imputation (SRMI) algorithm	Missing values are generated in the clinical dataset
11	Tim et al. (2014)	Predictive Mean Matching (PMM) and Local residual draws (LRD) methods	Missing values are generated
12	Inchao and Zhang (2017)	ensemble method	The missing value is generated and compared with the ARIMA, ANN, SVR, and KNN imputation techniques. The conclusion is that the new method is best.
13	M. K. Ng et al. (2017)	Adaptive weighted tensor completion	The missing value is generated in the remote sensing images dataset.
14	Zhengping Che et al. (2018)	GRU-D	Missing patterns are generated, and the classification is done on real-world clinical datasets and synthetic datasets. It achieved state-of-the-art performance.
15	Venugopalan et al. (2019)	Novel data imputation	This algorithm is applied to the intensive care unit data on the Neglectable, Recoverable, and types of missing mechanisms.
16	Khayati and Lerner (2020)	Benchmark technique	Missing values are generated

Techniques Used in the Novel Imputation Methods

Figure 9 shows the various missing data handling techniques in novel imputation methods. Unlike traditional imputation techniques, these methods incorporate advanced statistical models, machine learning algorithms, and hybrid approaches to improve the accuracy and reliability of imputed values. The development of these novel imputation methods has been driven by the need for more sophisticated techniques to capture complex data relationships while minimizing bias and preserving variability. One of the approaches highlighted in the image is the least squares support vector machine (LS-SVM), a machine learning method that uses optimization techniques to predict missing values. The ARLSimpute method is another advanced technique that leverages adaptive learning principles for imputation. Proportional hazards model imputation is particularly useful in survival analysis, where missing values must be estimated in time-to-event data. The new expectation-maximization (EM) method with bootstrapping augmentation improves the classical EM algorithm by incorporating resampling techniques to enhance its robustness.

Other innovative methods focus on regression-based imputation strategies. Consistent kernel regression imputation uses non-parametric kernel-based regression to estimate missing values with greater precision. The maximum margin Bayesian network classifier applies Bayesian probability principles to predict missing data by maximizing classification margins. Indexing measure imputation algorithms leverage indexing techniques to efficiently handle missing data across large-scale datasets. Additionally, the regularized iterative MFA (mixture factor analysis) algorithm is designed to handle missing data in multivariate analysis by iteratively refining imputations using factor models. The stochastic robust multi-imputation (SRMI) algorithm is a flexible method incorporating multiple imputation strategies while controlling for variability. Predictive mean matching (PMM) is another imputation technique that finds similar observed values and assigns them to missing entries, ensuring that imputed values remain realistic.

Figure 9. Techniques for handling missing data in the Novel imputation method

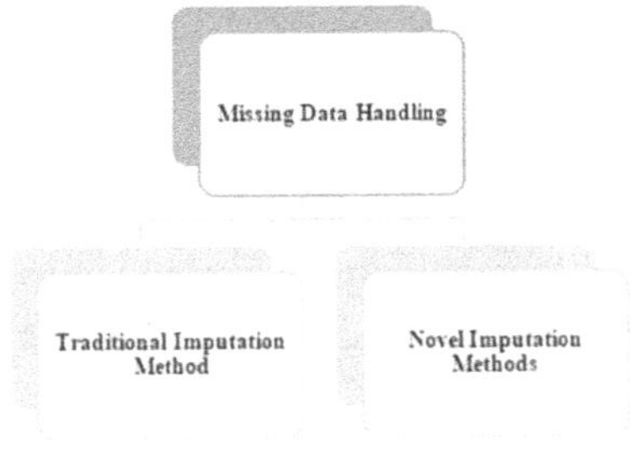

The LRD (low-rank decomposition) method utilizes matrix factorization techniques to estimate missing values, which is particularly useful in high-dimensional datasets. Bayesian genetic algorithms introduce an evolutionary approach by optimizing imputation through Bayesian probability combined with genetic algorithm principles. The non-linear filtering (NLF) method provides an alternative imputation technique that models missing values through non-linear transformation functions.

These novel imputation methods represent significant advancements in data analysis, allowing researchers and data scientists to address missing data more effectively. By incorporating techniques from machine learning, statistical modeling, and optimization, these methods offer superior performance in maintaining data integrity, ensuring that imputed values accurately reflect underlying patterns and relationships. Their adoption depends on the complexity of the dataset, the missing data mechanism, and the analytical goals of a given study.

Figure 10. Processing methods

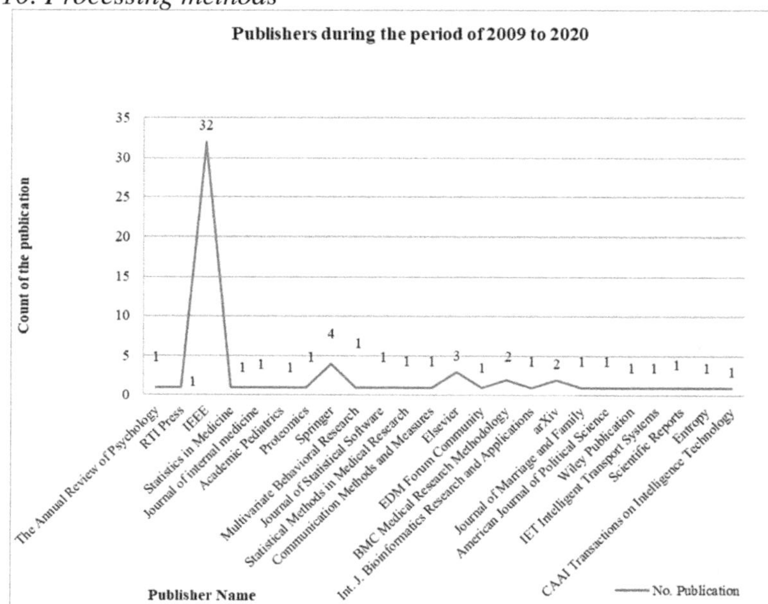

In Figure 10, usages of the techniques are shown. This graph shows that novel imputation methods are used more to generate the missing values than the traditional imputation algorithm. When analyzing all the algorithms, the EM algorithm is used more than the others. Figure 11 shows the relationship between the big data and the missing data.

Figure 11. Relationship between missing data and the data

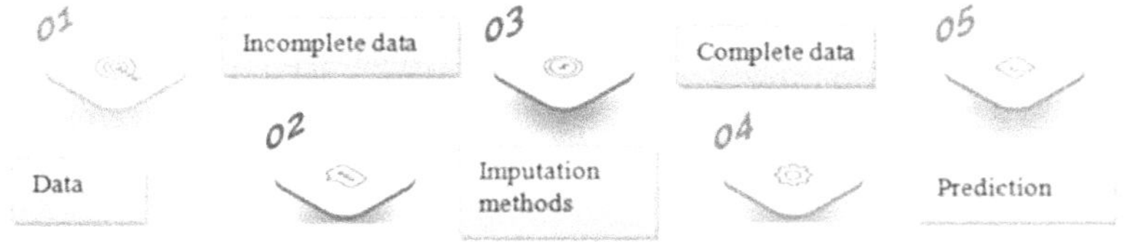

CASE STUDY

The imputation has been done on the Oasis dataset. This is an open-access dataset related to Alzheimer's disease. Some of the data values in this dataset are missing, so an imputation has been done to generate the missing data. This dataset has 15 features; among those features, the MMSE and SES have some missing data.

The mean imputation was applied to generate the missing data. Figures 12(a) and 13(a) show the missing data in the MMSE and SES feature. In the SES, there is a 5% missing value; in the MMSE, there is a 1% missing value. After applying the mean imputation, the missing values are generated, and no missing values are shown. Figures 12(b) and 13(b) show a complete dataset.

CONCLUSION AND FUTURE WORKS

A review is done to identify the algorithms used to recover the missing data in the dataset. The papers considered are from 2009 to 2020 on handling missing values, and the algorithm to generate the missing values was discussed. Some researchers used basic imputation techniques to generate the missing values, and others introduced novel techniques. The papers are grouped under the categories of traditional imputation algorithms and novel imputation algorithms. Each technique or algorithm has its features and functionalities, and it is analyzed that, in some cases, certain algorithms are best. Based on the dataset, the algorithms' accuracy and performance vary. From the survey, it has been analyzed that many authors use the EM algorithm. In this review, it has been observed that most of the researcher's suggestion was to observe the dataset with the missing values and, based on the missingness, choose the algorithms or techniques to impute the missing value. A case study has also been conducted on implementing the imputation process. Discussing the parameters used in the algorithms to generate the missing values in future work has been planned.

REFERENCES

Agarwal, S. (2023). Validating Clinical Applications of Digital Health Solutions and Managing Associated Risk Management. *FMDB Transactions on Sustainable Management Letters*, *1*(4), 134–143.

Albrecht, D., Kniemeyer, O., Brakhage, A. A., & Guthke, R. (2010). Missing values in gel-based proteomics. *Proteomics*, *10*(6), 1202–1211. DOI: 10.1002/pmic.200800576 PMID: 20077407

Aragani, V. M. (2024). Revolutionizing insurance through AI and data analytics: Innovating policy underwriting and claims management for the digital era. *FMDB Transactions on Sustainable Computer Letters*, *2*(3), 176–185. DOI: 10.69888/FTSCL.2024.000243

Calo, E., Cirillo, S., Polese, G., Sebillo, M. M., & Solimando, G. (2023). Investigating Privacy Threats: An In-Depth Analysis of Personal Data on Facebook and LinkedIn Through Advanced Data Reconstruction Tools. *FMDB Transactions on Sustainable Computing Systems*, *1*(2), 89–97.

Chakraborty, H., & Gu, H. (2009). *A mixed model approach for Intent-to-Treat Analysis in Longitudinal Clinical Trials with missing values*. RTI Press. DOI: 10.3768/rtipress.2009.mr.0009.0903

Che, Z., Purushotham, S., Cho, K., Sontag, D., & Liu, Y. (2018). Recurrent neural networks for multivariate time series with missing values. *Scientific Reports*, *8*(1), 1–12. DOI: 10.1038/s41598-018-24271-9 PMID: 29666385

Choong, M. K., Charbit, M., & Yan, H. (2009). Autoregressive-model-based missing value estimation for DNA microarray time series data. IEEE Transactions on Information Technology in Biomedicine: A Publication of the IEEE Engineering in Medicine and Biology Society, 13(1), 131–137.

Chundru, S. (2024). AI-driven data provenance: Tracking and verifying data lineage. *FMDB Transactions on Sustainable Computing Systems*, *2*(3), 107–118. DOI: 10.69888/FTSCS.2024.000258

Dong, Y., & Peng, C.-Y. J. (2013). Principled missing data methods for researchers. *SpringerPlus*, *2*(5), 1–17. PMID: 23853744

García-Laencina, P. J., Sancho-Gómez, J.-L., & Figueiras-Vidal, A. R. (2010). Pattern classification with missing data: A review. *Neural Computing & Applications*, *19*(2), 263–282. DOI: 10.1007/s00521-009-0295-6

Graham, J. W. (2009). Missing data analysis: Making it work in the real world. *Annual Review of Psychology*, *60*(1), 549–576. DOI: 10.1146/annurev.psych.58.110405.085530 PMID: 18652544

Husson, F., & Josse, J. (2013). Handling missing values in multiple factor analysis, " Food Quality and Preference. *Food Quality and Preference*, *30*(2), 77–85. DOI: 10.1016/j.foodqual.2013.04.013

Inchao Li, J., & Zhang, F. (2017). Bin Ran, "Robust and flexible strategy for missing data imputation in intelligent transportation system. *IET Intelligent Transport Systems*, *12*(2), 151–157.

Jasper, K. D., Jaishnav, M. N., Chowdhury, M. F., Badhan, R., & Sivakani, R. (2024). Defend and Secure: A Strategic and Implementation Framework for Robust Data Breach Prevention. *AVE Trends In Intelligent Computing Systems*, *1*(1), 17–31.

Kalyani, V., & Devi, L. D. (2024). Digital Marketing Evolution: A Bibliometric Method for Mapping the Web of Science Database. *FMDB Transactions on Sustainable Humanities and Society*, *1*(1), 10–20. DOI: 10.69888/FTSHS.2024.000149

Khayati, M., & Lerner, A. (n.d.). Mind the Gap. *An Experimental Evaluation of Imputation of Missing Values Techniques in Time Series*, *13*(5), 768–782.

Langkamp, D. L., Lehman, A., & Lemeshow, S. (2010). Techniques for handling missing data in secondary analyses of large surveys. *Academic Pediatrics*, *10*(3), 205–210. DOI: 10.1016/j.acap.2010.01.005 PMID: 20338836

Luengo, J., García, S., & Herrera, F. (2012). When choosing the best imputation methods for missing values, consider three groups of classification methods. *Knowledge and Information Systems*, *32*(1), 77–108. DOI: 10.1007/s10115-011-0424-2

Madhu, G., & Rajinikanth, T. V. (2012). A novel index measure imputation algorithm for missing data values: A machine learning approach. *2012 IEEE International Conference on Computational Intelligence and Computing Research*. IEEE, Coimbatore, India. DOI: 10.1109/ICCIC.2012.6510198

Myers, T. A. (2011). Goodbye, listwise deletion: Presenting hot deck imputation as an easy and effective tool for handling missing data. *Communication Methods and Measures*, *5*(4), 297–310. DOI: 10.1080/19312458.2011.624490

Ng, M. K.-P., Yuan, Q., Yan, L., & Sun, J. (2017). An adaptive weighted tensor completion method for the recovery of remote sensing images with missing data. IEEE Transactions on Geoscience and Remote Sensing: A Publication of the IEEE Geoscience and Remote Sensing Society, 55(6), 3367–3381.

Rebekah, D. R. (2015). Handling Missing Values in Longitudinal panel data with multiple imputation. *Journal of Marriage and Family*, *77*(1), 277–294. DOI: 10.1111/jomf.12144 PMID: 26113748

Said, F. B., & Tripathi, S. (2023). Epistemology of Digital Journalism Shift in South Global Nations: A Bibliometric Analysis. *FMDB Transactions on Sustainable Technoprise Letters*, *1*(1), 47–60.

Saleh, M., Mustapha, Z. B., & Ndirmbitah, B. K. (2024). Empirical analysis of digital marketing on the purchasing habit of conservative digital users of common social media. *FMDB Transactions on Sustainable Technoprise Letters*, *2*(1), 31–41. DOI: 10.69888/FTSTPL.2024.000228

Santos, M. S., Pereira, R. C., Costa, A. F., Soares, J. P., Santos, J., & Abreu, P. H. (2016). Generating synthetic missing data: A review by missing mechanism. *IEEE Access : Practical Innovations, Open Solutions*, *7*(1), 11651–11667.

Schafer, J. L., & Olsen, M. K. (2010). Multiple imputation for multivariate missing-data problems: A data analyst's perceptive. *Multivariate Behavioral Research*, *33*(4), 545–571. DOI: 10.1207/s15327906mbr3304_5 PMID: 26753828

Silvia Priscila, S., Soji, E. S., Hossó, N., Paramasivan, P., & Suman Rajest, S. (2023). Digital Realms and Mental Health: Examining the Influence of Online Learning Systems on Students. *FMDB Transactions on Sustainable Techno Learning*, *1*(3), 156–164.

Singh, S., Rajest, S. S., Hadoussa, S., Obaid, A. J., & Regin, R. (2023). *Data-Driven Intelligent Business Sustainability*. Advances in Business Information Systems and Analytics. IGI Global., DOI: 10.4018/979-8-3693-0049-7

Singh, S., Rajest, S. S., Hadoussa, S., Obaid, A. J., & Regin, R. (Eds.). (2023). Advances in Business Information Systems and Analytics *Data-driven decision making for long-term business success*. IGI Global., DOI: 10.4018/979-8-3693-2193-5

Sivapriya, G. B. V., Ganesh, U. G., Pradeeshwar, V., Dharshini, M., & Al-Amin, M. (2023). Crime Prediction and Analysis Using Data Mining and Machine Learning: A Simple Approach that Helps Predictive Policing. *FMDB Transactions on Sustainable Computer Letters*, *1*(2), 64–75.

Sundararajan, V., Steffi, R., & Shynu, T. (2023). Data Fusion Strategies for Collaborative Multi-Sensor Systems: Achieving Enhanced Observational Accuracy and Resilience. *FMDB Transactions on Sustainable Computing Systems*, *1*(3), 112–123.

Tim, P., Morris, I. R., & White, P. (2014). Tuning multiple imputation by predictive mean matching and local residual draws. *BMC Medical Research Methodology*, *5*(6), 1–13.

Tschiatschek, S., Mutsam, N., & Pernkopf, F. (2012). Handling missing features in maximum margin Bayesian network classifiers. *2012 IEEE International Workshop on Machine Learning for Signal Processing*. IEEE, Santander, Spain. DOI: 10.1109/MLSP.2012.6349804

Venugopalan, J., Chanani, N., Maher, K., & Wang, M. D. (2019). Novel data imputation for multiple types of missing data in intensive care units. *IEEE Journal of Biomedical and Health Informatics*, *23*(3), 1243–1250. DOI: 10.1109/JBHI.2018.2883606 PMID: 30998482

Vesin, A., Azoulay, E., Ruckly, S., Vignoud, L., Rusinovà, K., Benoit, D., Soares, M., Azeivedo-Maia, P., Abroug, F., Benbenishty, J., & Timsit, J. F. (2013). Reporting and handling missing values in clinical studies in intensive care units. *Intensive Care Medicine*, *39*(8), 1396–1404. DOI: 10.1007/s00134-013-2949-1 PMID: 23685609

White, I. R., & Royston, P. (2009). Imputing missing covariate values for the Cox model: Imputing Missing Covariate Values for The Cox Model. *Statistics in Medicine*, *28*(15), 1982–1998. DOI: 10.1002/sim.3618 PMID: 19452569

Xu, X., Xia, L., Zhang, Q., Wu, S., Wu, M., & Liu, H. (2020). The ability of different imputation methods for missing values in mental measurement questionnaires. *BMC Medical Research Methodology*, *20*(2), 1–9. DOI: 10.1186/s12874-020-00932-0 PMID: 32103723

Yaseen, T., Valentyn, A., & Tolpekin, A. (2012). Application of Expectation Maximization algorithm to estimate missing values in Gaussian Bayesian Network modeling for forest growth. *IEEE Transactions on Geoscience and Remote Sensing*, *50*(5), 1821–1831. DOI: 10.1109/TGRS.2011.2168823

Zanardo, E. (2024). Chronostamp: A general-purpose run-time for data-flow computing in a distributed environment. *AVE Trends in Intelligent Computing Systems*, *1*(2), 106–115.

Zhang, Y., & Liu, Y. (2009). Data imputation using least squares support vector machines in urban arterial streets. *IEEE Signal Processing Letters*, *16*(5), 414–417. DOI: 10.1109/LSP.2009.2016451

Zhu, X., Zhang, S., Jin, Z., Zhang, Z., & Xu, Z. (2011). Missing value estimation for mixed-attribute data sets. *IEEE Transactions on Knowledge and Data Engineering*, *23*(1), 110–121. DOI: 10.1109/TKDE.2010.99

Chapter 4
Active Learning Strategies for Optimising Data Annotation Using Machine Learning

V. Hariharan
https://orcid.org/0009-0005-2415-4930
Bharath Institute of Higher Education and Research, India

K. Sivaraman
Bharath Institute of Higher Education and Research, India

ABSTRACT

This chapter investigates the potential of active learning techniques, in particular Bayesian Optimization, to enhance data annotation and model training. Active learning selects meaningful examples from unlabeled data to improve model performance and reduce labeling effort. Several active learning techniques, including uncertainty sampling, query-by-committee, and Bayesian Optimization, are investigated to determine how this impacts data annotation and model training. Multiple datasets, including CIFAR-10, IMDB reviews, and COCO, have been evaluated experimentally to demonstrate that Bayesian Optimization improves accuracy, reduces annotation effort, and accelerates model convergence. The findings emphasize the potential of active learning motivated by Bayesian optimization for efficient machine learning with limited resources. According to the findings, active learning strategies, hybrid approaches, and their use in real-world, ever-changing contexts warrant additional research.

DOI: 10.4018/979-8-3373-5203-9.ch004

INTRODUCTION

The accelerated development of machine learning and AI has substantially impacted innovations in fields as diverse as medicine, finance, business, and the arts. The advancement of such technologies is contingent on the availability of high-quality annotated data and the capacity to train precise and robust models (Creswell et al., 2018). However, the data annotation is notoriously labor-intensive, resource-intensive, and time-consuming. Additionally, training models on massive datasets can be computationally expensive and time-consuming. As a result, both researchers and practitioners have investigated alternative data annotation and model training strategies (Geng et al., 2021). Therefore, active learning strategies are being examined more closely as a potential solution to these problems. The machine learning method, "active learning," utilizes only the most informative data points from a large reservoir of unlabeled information (Huang et al., 2021). Instead of passive learning, in which models are trained on previously labeled datasets, active learning actively employs human annotators to identify the most advantageous cases for enhancing model performance. Less labor-intensive labeling is required to accomplish the requisite level of model accuracy, and this is where active learning comes in (Zhao and Liu, 2019). It is self-evident that not all unlabeled instances are created equal, which is crucial for effective active learning (Tang et al., 2023).

Some examples may be simple and disclose nothing of value, while others may be complex and, if properly labeled, shed light on the model's ability to manage challenging decision spaces. By recognizing and prioritizing these periods of uncertainty or difficulty, active learning algorithms may ensure that the annotation process is optimized to maximize information acquisition while reducing costs (Yoo and Kweon 2019). This research will investigate the potential incorporation of active learning approaches into the data annotation and model training pipeline to enhance efficiency and performance (Shen and Ke, 2020). Several active learning strategies, including uncertainty sampling, query by committee, and Bayesian optimization, are investigated, and their benefits and applications are discussed. Active learning can significantly reduce the labeled data required for training, saving time and resources by selecting and annotating instances that contribute most to the model formation (Ke et al., 2020).

The parallels between active learning and model creation are also investigated. To accelerate model convergence, reduce overfitting, and improve generalization, this investigates the possibility of selecting relevant examples iteratively (Shen and Ke, 2021). In addition, this examines scenarios in which the data distribution changes over time (termed "idea drift") and discusses how active learning can adapt to such challenges to ensure model durability in dynamic conditions. Extensive research in image classification, natural language processing, and object recognition is used to illustrate the practical utility of active learning. This article evaluates the relative merits of various active learning strategies for accelerating model convergence and minimizing annotation durations. This means that the results of these assessments will help educators choose appropriate active learning strategies (Zhang et al., 2022). This study seeks to shed light on how active learning may increase the rate at which data is annotated and models are trained. Using uncertainty-driven instance selection and the synergy between human annotators and machine learning models, active learning provides a compelling method for improving the efficacy and precision of machine learning systems. By conducting in-depth research and providing empirical validation of active learning approaches in various contexts, he intends to contribute to the development of the field. Figure 1 depicts the CIFAR-10 image dataset.

Figure 1. CIFAR-10 image dataset

Figure 1 is a mosaic or collage that combines several distinct subjects with a primary focus on various animal and vehicle types. The vehicles available include various models and colors of automobiles, trucks, buses, and boats (Priscila et al., 2023). The animals portrayed include domestic pets like dogs and cats, wild animals like birds and deer, and aquatic life. The arrangement draws attention to the contrast between the mechanical components of vehicles and the organic characteristics of animals by presenting a wide range of imagery with varying textures, colors, and forms.

LITERATURE REVIEW

Bin Sulaiman et al. (2023) Proposed that address the limitations of prior active learning algorithms for annotation tasks in the real world, frequently involving unlabeled data with uncertain classifications. LfOSA is a novel active learning system that addresses the open-set annotation problem. LfOSA uses an auxiliary network to fit a Gaussian mixture model, approximating the distribution of maximum activation values across all examples. Improved classification performance is directly attributable to the improved recognition of samples from known classes within the unlabeled dataset (Liu et al., 2022). By decreasing the temperature of the loss function, both forms of supervision can be used to improve the detection model. The experimental results demonstrate that LfOSA significantly enhances the selection of known classes, resulting in greater classification precision with reduced annotation costs. This is a pioneering effort because it is the first endeavor to tailor active learning for open-set annotation settings.

Shen and ke (2021) that digital histopathology, the processing of large whole-slide images (WSIs), presents special challenges that are investigated using deep learning. Conventional approaches segment WSIs into patches for discrete processing, frequently resulting in non-representative patches and time-consuming human annotation. The most effective patch-wise classifier training requires locating the most informative regions within selected patches, but current active learning algorithms only focus on selecting informative patches. This study proposes a technique based on active learning to enhance patch selection with adaptive offsets, thereby increasing geographical representativeness (Maroju, 2024). This novel method makes training patch-level classifiers more productive and efficient. This is the first attempt to develop an adaptive representative patch generation method, and it has been effectively applied to large patient cohorts from The Cancer Genome Atlas (TCGA) with a tumor classification.

Murugavel and Hernandez (2023) Presented BoostMIS, an innovative SSL framework for medical image analysis using semi-supervised learning. Combining adaptive pseudo labeling with useful active annotation, this method improves SSL models for medical images. BoostMIS utilizes cluster assumptions and consistently regularizes unlabeled data to enhance "hard" labels for task model training. In addition, an Active Learning (AL) technique employs model density-aware entropy and virtual adversarial perturbation to identify meaningful samples within low-confidence unlabeled images. This information is continually utilized during training cycles to enhance SSL label distribution (Sulaiman et al., 2024). Notably, constructing a collaborative learning loop between adaptive pseudo-labeling and informative, active annotation improves SSL for medical images. The proposed method is evaluated using a dataset of patients with metastatic epidural spinal cord compression (MESCC), and extensive experimental research demonstrates that it significantly outperforms numerous state-of-the-art methods.

Kumar and Gupta (2020) that study explores active learning (AL), a strategy for reducing labeling and learning costs by selecting representative cases for expert annotation. AL actively requests annotations for significant events while relying on a small set of labeled data. This method reduces costs by continuously enhancing the training dataset. Artificial intelligence (AI) effectiveness depends on efficient query algorithms that select examples with optimal generalization error reduction. In this study, various approaches to interrogating artificial intelligence for these three objectives (Saxena and Chaudhary, 2023). These strategies can be categorized as informative, representative, informative, and representative, or any other combination. This overview discusses theoretically advanced techniques like reinforcement learning and more practically applicable strategies like deep learning. Here, this compares and contrasts the relative merits of several approaches based on a rigorous mathematical analysis. It is a comprehensive guide to active learning, covering how to get started, prevalent applications, and potential hazards.

Das et al. (2023) the study seeks to reduce the burden of human data annotation on deep learning by enhancing named entity recognition (NER) through active learning. Active learning's potential to reduce annotation costs has been demonstrated, but there are presently no viable alternatives. This prefers longer sequences, which increases the workload for annotators and necessitates model adjustments, which increases the workload for developers and lengthens the processing time for models. This study introduces a novel uncertainty-based active learning technique nicknamed "lowest token probability" (LTP). LTP efficiently selects meaningful examples for annotation by combining the input and output of a conditional random field (CRF) without favoring lengthier sequences and requiring model modifications. Experimental results on real-world datasets indicate that LTP can reduce annotation tokens by up to 20% without sacrificing sentence- or entity-level F1-score performance. LTP surpasses other sample selection algorithms, in particular, drastically reducing the number of incorrect annotations made by labelers (Das et al., 2023). Through a refined approach to active learning, this work aids in improving the speed and accuracy of NER.

Overview: Active learning is significant in machine learning because it is so dissimilar to the conventional method of memorization through repetition. Fundamentally, selecting and designating instances for annotation should be governed by deliberate rather than arbitrary decisions. In challenging, equivocal, or obscure situations, active learning exploits the fact that certain data pieces result in a greater gain of knowledge than others. The iterative process in active learning begins with an initial set of labeled instances. The trained model uses this information to determine which unlabeled instances should be sent to humans for labeling. Specific approaches to active learning guide the selection of these instances. These techniques utilize certain characteristics of the available data, such as locations of high uncertainty or locations where the existing model's predictions diverge the most. Using data from various domains, this study assesses the efficacy of active learning approaches. Examples of standardized resources include the COCO dataset for object identification, the IMDB review corpus for NLP sentiment analysis, and the CIFAR-10 image dataset. These datasets permit the evaluation of the influence of active learning strategies on a wide variety of data and activities, demonstrating the adaptability and utility of the proposed methodologies.

PROPOSED METHODOLOGY

Active Learning Strategies: Bayesian Optimization has evolved into a potent active learning technique by employing a probabilistic perspective during data annotation. It is based on the premise that a surrogate model can be constructed whose representation of the model's performance across multiple instances is as close to the true underlying function as is practically possible. This proxy model estimates uncertainty using the Gaussian Process (GP). The conclusions of Bayesian Optimization are based on a balance between discovery and application. The method requires an initial set of labeled examples to train the surrogate GP model. This model serves as the foundation for the estimated acquisition function, quantifying an instance's potential value after labeling. The acquisition function must balance investigating new scenarios in which the surrogate model is unknown and exploiting scenarios in which the model predicts excellent performance. Instances that are highly ambiguous or indicate performance potential are annotated. Bayesian Optimisation continuously revises its selection based on the accuracy and performance predictions of the surrogate model. As additional examples are annotated and added to the training set, the surrogate model can improve its predictions due to more accurate modeling of the underlying performance function. Using this process iteratively, Bayesian Optimization can zero in on the observations that contribute the most to enhancing the model's understanding. This study applies Bayesian Optimization to various tasks and datasets, such as image classification on CIFAR-10, sentiment analysis on IMDB reviews, and object identification on the COCO dataset. By comparing the results of Bayesian Optimization to those of other active learning methods, we expect to better understand the method's benefits and drawbacks. This evaluates its ability to establish an equilibrium between filtering through the entire instance space and selecting only known instances to boost model performance.

Integration of Active Learning: A surrogate Gaussian Process (GP) model is trained using an initial set of labeled instances. This model factors for randomness and potential performance increases in diverse situations. In Bayesian Optimization, the acquisition function is utilized to quantify the significance of annotating particular cases. It strikes a balance between instances in which the model's predictions are unreliable and those in which it is expected to perform better. Bayesian Optimisation drives the iterative process of annotation. Annotation targets for each iteration are selected with the aid of the acquisition function. Then, human experts assign designations to these cases. The GP model has been updated to incorporate the recently annotated examples into the labeled dataset. Through this feedback cycle, the model can refine its predictions and direct annotation resources toward the examples that are most likely to result in observable performance improvements. In this integration, Bayesian Optimization provides various benefits. First, the technique is adaptive, so the selection of additional cases is improved and modified as the model's accuracy improves as more instances are classified. Second, Bayesian Optimization reduces the annotation burden by deferring easy-to-label or low-information-gain situations in favor of ambiguous or potentially more consequential situations.

This study applies the Bayesian Optimization-driven annotation method to numerous datasets from various disciplines, including CIFAR-10, IMDB reviews, and COCO. We can learn more about its benefits and drawbacks by comparing this strategy to other integration techniques. This evaluates its capacity to effectively distribute annotation resources, resulting in precisely labeled datasets that increase model output. Bayesian optimization promotes the incorporation of active learning with data annotation to enhance the labeling process and the model training pipeline. This method reduces the number of resources required for annotation while ensuring the quality of the labeled dataset by selecting cases for annotation based on their prospective impact. The study of active learning and its incorporation into real-world machine learning processes, as applied to many datasets and tasks, yields significant new insights in this dynamic field. Figure 2 depicts the system architecture.

Figure 2. System architecture

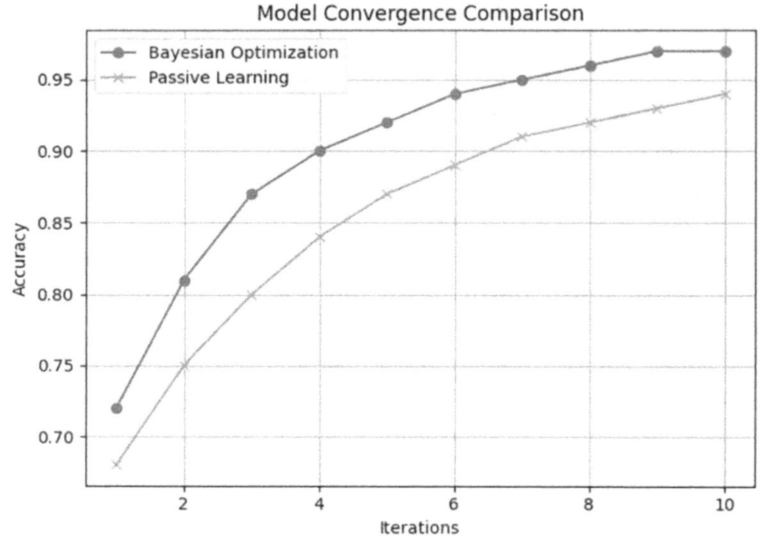

A machine learning model creation workflow is depicted in Figure 2, starting with "Dataset" and moving through various steps to "Evaluation." First, "Data Preprocessing" is applied to clean up and prepare the data for modeling. Next, "Bayesian Optimisation" optimizes the hyperparameters, enhancing the model's performance. After optimization, "Model Training" takes place, during which the processed data is used to teach the machine learning model new things. The next step is called "Active Learning," when the model repeatedly chooses the most instructive data points to learn from, increasing its accuracy. "Evaluation," the process's conclusion, is where the performance of the finished model is evaluated.

Active Learning-Driven Model Training: When combined, active learning and model training provide an innovative approach to progressively increasing a model's efficacy. Bayesian Optimisation is an effective method for training models that may hasten convergence, decrease overfitting, and adapt to new or different data distributions. Bayesian Optimization-informed model training is iterative. The initial step is to train a simple model on a small yet labeled data set. Bayesian Optimisation selects instances from the unlabeled set using the acquisition function of the surrogate Gaussian Process (GP) model. These instances are then added to the annotated dataset to increase the size of the training set. The model is retrained using the improved dataset to include the additional information from the annotated instances. Figure 3 depicts the acquisition function in Bayesian optimization.

Figure 3. Acquisition function in Bayesian optimization

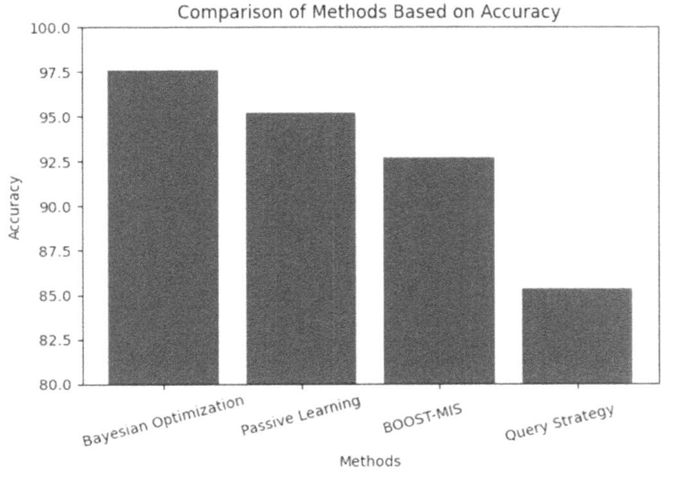

The acquisition function shown in Figure 3 is a tool used in Bayesian optimization, a method for determining the minimum or maximum of an objective function that is expensive to evaluate. Probably denoting various locations in the parameter space where the function is evaluated, the x-axis, called the "Instance Index," extends from 0 to 10. The "Acquisition Value," which illustrates the y-axis, quantifies the benefit of sampling the objective function at each point. The objective function can be optimized by further exploring particular points, as shown by the acquisition function's notable high points at indices 2, 6, and 9. Because this process is iterative, the model may be improved incrementally. The model is taught to emphasize annotating cases that it first identified as problematic or unclear to get a deeper understanding of challenging decision constraints. When only relevant events are included during model training, convergence may be achieved more rapidly with less labeled data. Overfitting may also be fought with the use of Bayesian Optimization. The model is less likely to over-optimize highly uncertain examples, leading to more general and reliable predictions. This is especially helpful when labeled data is unavailable or would cost too much to obtain. Figure 4 depicts the drift detection.

Figure 4. Concept drift detection

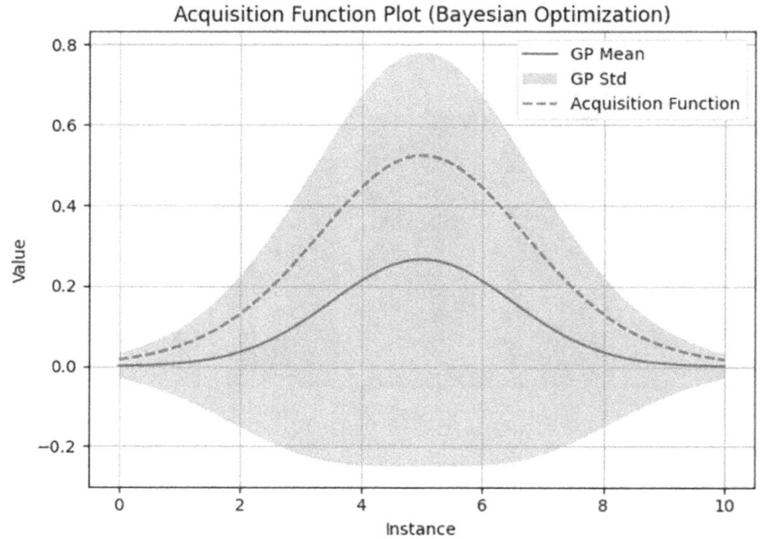

A systematic method for identifying idea drift in data streams is shown in Figure 4, which is frequently applied in data analytics and machine learning. The first step is “Concept Drift Detection,” which is the detection of modifications to the input data's statistical characteristics that could impact the model's predictions. The next step is “Monitoring Data & Collection,” in which data is continuously collected and checked for drift. The data is then analyzed using a “Drift Detection Algorithm” to find noteworthy drifts or changes. “Decision & Alerting,” the process's conclusion, involves making judgments based on the drift that has been noticed and sending out the proper alerts as necessary. This method adjusts to changes in underlying data distributions to guarantee that models stay correct and relevant over time.

Extending the method to datasets from other domains, such as CIFAR-10, IMDB reviews, and COCO, can assess its generalizability. The intention is to demonstrate that, compared to other approaches to training models, using an active approach to selecting examples for training data results in superior model performance. Bayesian Optimisation facilitates an active learning-driven model training process, which may theoretically improve model convergence, robustness, and generalizability. The feedback loop between selecting useful examples and iteratively building the model strengthens the model's capabilities through the research into the impact of this integration on various datasets and tasks that want to optimize the intricate interplay between data annotation and model training within the framework of active learning. Fig 5 depicts the reduction of annotation effort over iterations. Figure 6 depicts the acquisition function plot. Uncertainty sampling is

$$x^{*} = \arg\max_{x}\left(1 - P_{\theta}(y^{*} \mid x)\right) \quad (1)$$

This equation selects the next data point x^{*} for annotation based on the model's current uncertainty about the most likely label y^{*}. Here, $P_{\theta}(y^{*}|x)$ represents the probability assigned to the most likely label according to the model parameters θ. The goal is to choose the sample for which the model is least certain about its prediction.

Query-by-Committee (QBC) is given as

$$x^{*} = \arg\max_{x}\left(-\sum_{i=1}^{C} p_{i}\log p_{i}\right) \quad (2)$$

In QBC, the diversity of opinions from a committee of models is used to select the next data point x^{*}. The equation uses the entropy measure where p_i does the i-th model in the committee predict the probability for the most likely class label, and C is the number of class labels? The data point with the highest entropy (indicating the greatest disagreement among the models) is selected for annotation. The expected model change is

$$x^{*} = \arg\max_{x}\sum_{y\in Y} P_{\theta}\left(y \mid x\right) \| \nabla_{\theta}\log P_{\theta}(y \mid x) \| \quad (3)$$

This strategy selects the data point x^{*}. That is expected to cause the most significant change in the model parameters θ if labeled. $P_{\theta}(y|x)$ is the probability of label y given data point x under the current model parameters, and $\nabla_{\theta}\log P_{\theta}(y|x)$ is the gradient of the log probability concerning the model parameters. The data point is selected based on the weighted sum of the magnitude of these gradients, weighted by the probability of each label Figure 5.

Figure 5. Annotation effort reduction over iteration

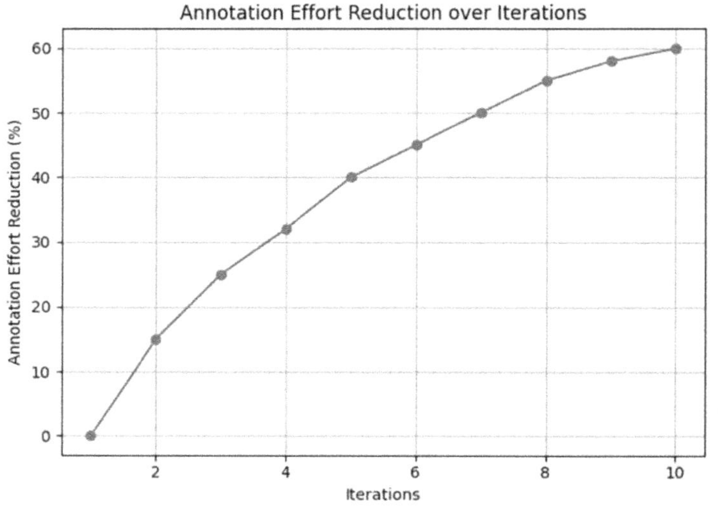

The percentage decrease in annotation effort over a range of iterations, from 1 to 10, is shown in Figure 5 on the "Iterations" x-axis. The incremental decrease in the effort needed to annotate data is displayed on the y-axis, which is labeled "Annotation Effort Reduction (%)." The graph shows a consistent upward trend, beginning at about 5% at the first iteration, suggesting growing annotation process efficiency. By the tenth iteration, the reduction in annotation effort is close to sixty percent, indicating notable gains in the process efficiency of annotating data. These gains are probably the result of improved tools, automation, or data quality Figure 6.

Figure 6. Acquisition function plot

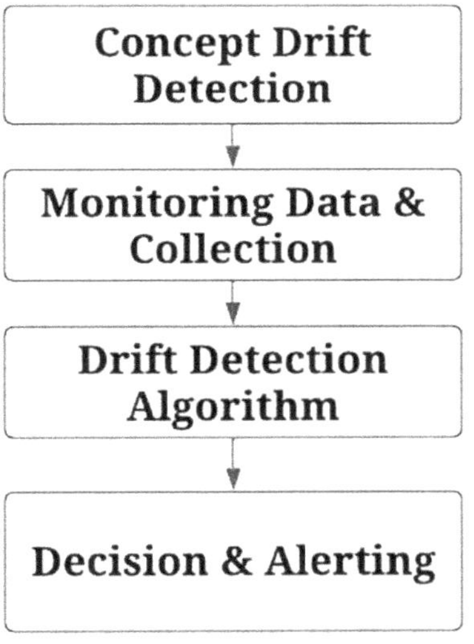

Gaussian Process (GP) model-based Bayesian optimization is demonstrated in Figure 6. It shows the acquisition function (dashed red line), the GP standard deviation (shaded blue region), and the GP mean (solid blue line). The function values are shown on the y-axis, and the instances (or parameter values) that are being optimized are represented on the x-axis. The GP shows the model's best estimate of the form of the objective function mean line; the shaded area, with greater portions denoting more uncertainty, illustrates uncertainty. To efficiently optimize the objective function, the acquisition function's peaks indicate suitable places for investigation. This helps determine where to sample next.

Experimental Setup: The study employs multiple image classification, sentiment analysis, and object recognition datasets, including CIFAR-10, IMDB reviews, and COCO. Using Bayesian Optimization, this chooses domain-appropriate baseline models as an active learning strategy. To implement Bayesian Optimization, this constructs a surrogate Gaussian Process model, defines an acquisition function, and iteratively selects instances to label using publicly available software. The labeling procedure is comparable to annotating in the actual world. Experiments with and without Bayesian Optimization are evaluated based on accuracy, annotation effort reduction, model convergence time, and generalization. Numerous simulations are conducted to account for chance. The experimental environment has been meticulously crafted to systematically investigate the effect of Bayesian Optimization on data annotation and model training across various datasets and tasks. Bayesian

Optimization-driven active learning is the basis of this methodical approach, which assures accurate comprehension of how to enhance machine learning processes.

RESULTS

Table 1 The machine learning model performance on three distinct datasets employing two different learning approaches, Bayesian optimization, and passive learning, is compared in Table 1. Compared to Passive Learning, Bayesian Optimisation achieves 97.6% accuracy for the CIFAR-10 dataset, which employs accuracy as a metric. This is a considerable improvement.

Table 1. Accuracy of CIFAR-10, IMDB, COCO

Dataset	Metric	Passive Learning	Bayern Optimization
CIFAR-10	Accuracy	95.2%	97.6%
IMDB Reviews	Accuracy	93.1%	94.7%
COCO	Average Precision (AP)	0.752	0.772

Similarly, Bayesian Optimisation increases accuracy from 93.1% to 94.7% on the IMDB Reviews dataset. With the use of Bayesian Optimisation, the Average Precision (AP) of the COCO dataset also exhibits improvement, rising from 0.752 to 0.772. This illustrates how well Bayesian optimization improves model performance for various metrics and data kinds.

Table 2. Comparison of accuracy

Method	Accuracy
Bayern Optimization	97.6%
Passive Learning	95.2
BOOST-MIS (Liu et al., 2022)	92.70
Query Strategy (Saxena & Chaudhary, 2023)	85.31

Table 2 presents the accuracy performance of various approaches to a certain problem; the data is probably from a machine learning model assessment. With the highest accuracy of 97.6%, Bayesian Optimisation stands out from the competition, demonstrating its exceptional ability to fine-tune model parameters. Next, passive learning shows effective learning with less optimization, with a respectable 95.2% accuracy. The other tested approaches, BOOST-MIS and Query Strategy, had scores of 85.31% and 92.70%, respectively. The successive decline in accuracy shows how differently these approaches handle the learning process of the model, with Bayesian Optimisation performing noticeably better than the others Figure 7.

Figure 7. Accuracy comparison graph

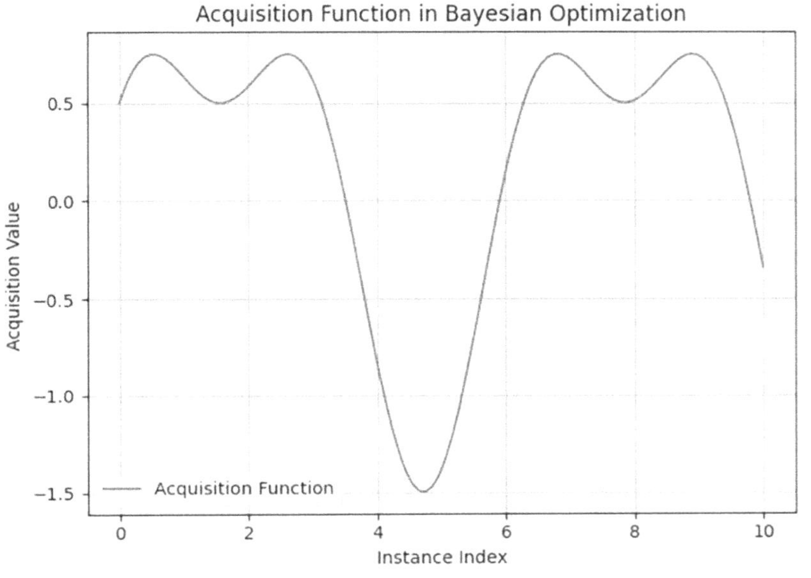

Figure 8. Model convergence comparison

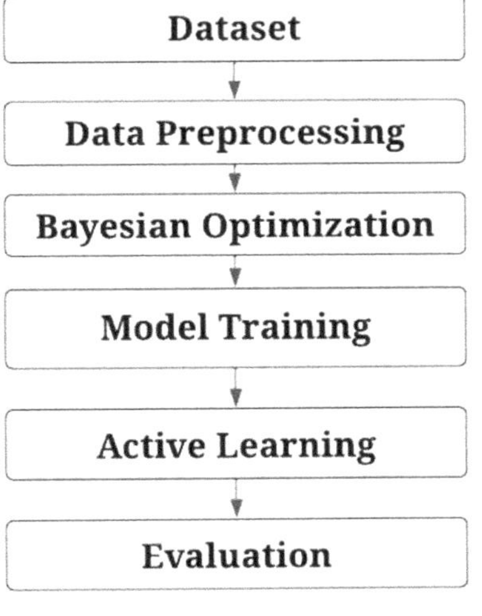

The evaluation of active learning techniques, focusing on Bayesian Optimization, reveals significant gains. The efficacy of a model is significantly enhanced when Bayesian Optimization drives active learning instead of inert learning. Bayesian Optimisation substantially increases the accuracy of passive learning on the CIFAR-10 dataset (95.2% to 97.7%). Similarly, when Bayesian Optimization is applied to the IMDB Reviews dataset, accuracy increases to 94.7 percent, greater than the 93.1 percent accuracy attained with passive learning. In addition, Bayesian Optimization aids in attaining a higher Average Precision (AP) score of 0.772 compared to the AP score of 0.752 attained through passive learning on the challenging item identification task on the COCO dataset. These results indicate that active learning driven by Bayesian Optimization can reliably enhance model accuracy across various datasets and responsibilities. The method's ability to select instances most likely to provide valuable insights demonstrates its potential for enhancing data annotation and model training procedures, consistent with the goal of achieving efficient machine learning with minimal resources. Table 2 and Figure 7 depict that the proposed methods of Bayesian Optimization performed better than the Passive Learning, BOOST-MIS, and Query Strategy. Figure 8 depicts the Bayesian Optimization and Passive Learning convergence rate.

CONCLUSION

We show that introducing Bayesian Optimisation into active learning systems can dramatically improve data annotation and model training. Here, we demonstrate how this can be accomplished. The use of Bayesian Optimisation has been shown to effectively improve model performance, decrease the amount of work required for annotation, and speed up the convergence process. This has been proved using data and use cases from a variety of datasets and applications. Because it simply involves selecting examples that are helpful, active learning that is driven by Bayesian optimisation is an approach that is low-cost and may be used to improve machine learning systems. It would be beneficial for the field of resource-efficient machine learning to do additional research into the development of active learning strategies, the study of hybrid techniques, and an analysis of their application in real-world settings that are more complicated and dynamic.

REFERENCES

Bin Sulaiman, R., Hariprasath, G., Dhinakaran, P., & Kose, U. (2023). Time-series Forecasting of Web Traffic Using Prophet Machine Learning Model. *FMDB Transactions on Sustainable Computer Letters*, *1*(3), 161–177.

Creswell, A., White, T., Dumoulin, V., Arulkumaran, K., Sengupta, B., & Bharath, A. A. (2018). Generative adversarial networks: An overview. *IEEE Signal Processing Magazine*, *35*(1), 53–65. DOI: 10.1109/MSP.2017.2765202

Das, S., Kruti, A., Devkota, R., & Bin Sulaiman, R. (2023). Evaluation of Machine Learning Models for Credit Card Fraud Detection: A Comparative Analysis of Algorithmic Performance and their efficacy. *FMDB Transactions on Sustainable Technoprise Letters*, *1*(2), 70–81.

Das, S. R., Bin Sulaiman, R., & Butt, U. (2023). Comparative Analysis of Machine Learning Algorithms for Credit Card Fraud Detection. *FMDB Transactions on Sustainable Computing Systems*, *1*(4), 225–244.

Geng, C., Huang, S.-J., & Chen, S. (2021). Recent advances in open set recognition: A survey. *IEEE Transactions on Pattern Analysis and Machine Intelligence*, *43*(10), 3614–3631. DOI: 10.1109/TPAMI.2020.2981604 PMID: 32191881

Huang, S.-J., Zhao, J.-W., & Liu, Z.-Y. (2018). Cost-effective training of deep CNNs with active model adaptation. In *Proceedings of the 24th ACM SIGKDD International Conference on Knowledge Discovery & Data Mining*, London, United Kingdom. DOI: 10.1145/3219819.3220026

Ke, J., Shen, Y., Guo, Y., Wright, J. D., & Liang, X. (2020). A prediction model of microsatellite status from histology images. In *Proceedings of the 2020 10th International Conference on Biomedical Engineering and Technology*, New York, United States. DOI: 10.1145/3397391.3397442

Kumar, P., & Gupta, A. (2020). Active learning query strategies for classification, regression, and clustering: A survey. *Journal of Computer Science and Technology*, *35*(4), 913–945. DOI: 10.1007/s11390-020-9487-4

Liu, M., Tu, Z., Zhang, T., Su, T., Xu, X., & Wang, Z. (2022). LTP: A new active learning strategy for CRF-based named entity recognition. *Neural Processing Letters*, *54*(3), 2433–2454. DOI: 10.1007/s11063-021-10737-x

Maroju, P. K. (2024). Data science for a smarter currency supply chain: Optimizing cash flow with machine learning for white label ATMs. *FMDB Transactions on Sustainable Computing Systems*, *2*(1), 43–53. DOI: 10.69888/FTSCS.2024.000196

Murugavel, S., & Hernandez, F. (2023). A Comparative Study Between Statistical and Machine Learning Methods for Forecasting Retail Sales. *FMDB Transactions on Sustainable Computer Letters, 1*(2), 76–102.

Priscila, S. S., Rajest, S. S., Tadiboina, S. N., Regin, R., & András, S. (2023). Analysis of Machine Learning and Deep Learning Methods for Superstore Sales Prediction. *FMDB Transactions on Sustainable Computer Letters, 1*(1), 1–11.

Saxena, D., & Chaudhary, S. (2023). Predicting Brain Diseases from FMRI-Functional Magnetic Resonance Imaging with Machine Learning Techniques for Early Diagnosis and Treatment. *FMDB Transactions on Sustainable Computer Letters, 1*(1), 33–48.

Shen, Y., & Ke, J. (2020). A deformable CRF model for histopathology whole-slide image classification. In *Medical Image Computing and Computer Assisted Intervention – MICCAI*. Springer International Publishing. DOI: 10.1007/978-3-030-59722-1_48

Shen, Y., & Ke, J. (2021). Representative region-based active learning for histological classification of colorectal cancer. In 2021 IEEE 18th International Symposium on Biomedical Imaging (ISBI), Nice, France. DOI: 10.1109/ISBI48211.2021.9433931

Sulaiman, R. B., Aljaidi, M., Alsuwaylimi, A. A., Butt, U., Talukder, M. S. H., Alam, S. S., Farhan, M., Das, S. R., & Alam, M. W. (2024). Enhancing security in digital payments: A comparative evaluation of machine learning models for credit card fraud detection. *FMDB Transactions on Sustainable Computer Letters, 2*(2), 63–84. DOI: 10.69888/FTSCL.2024.000182

Tang, Y.-P., Wei, X.-S., Zhao, B., & Huang, S.-J. (2023). QBox: Partial transfer learning with active querying for object detection. *IEEE Transactions on Neural Networks and Learning Systems, 34*(6), 3058–3070. DOI: 10.1109/TNNLS.2021.3111621 PMID: 34570711

Yoo, D., & Kweon, I. S. (2019). Learning loss for active learning. In *2019 IEEE/CVF Conference on Computer Vision and Pattern Recognition*, Long Beach, California, USA.

Zhang, W., Zhu, L., Hallinan, J., Zhang, S., Makmur, A., Cai, Q., & Ooi, B. C. (2022). BoostMIS: Boosting medical image semi-supervised learning with adaptive pseudo labeling and informative active annotation. In *2022 IEEE/CVF Conference on Computer Vision and Pattern Recognition (CVPR)*, New Orleans, Louisiana, United States. DOI: 10.1109/CVPR52688.2022.02001

Zhao, Y., & Liu, S.-J. (2019). Active sampling for open-set classification without initial annotation. *Proceedings of the AAAI Conference on Artificial Intelligence*, *33*(1), 4416–4423. DOI: 10.1609/aaai.v33i01.33014416

Chapter 5
Real Time Data Pipeline Engineering for Scalable Insights

Padmaja Pulivarthy
https://orcid.org/0009-0009-5536-5668
Samsung, USA

Mohanarajesh Kommineni
https://orcid.org/0009-0002-3897-5949
TEK Systems Global Services LLC, USA

Venu Madhav Aragani
https://orcid.org/0009-0006-2434-1362
Eliason Group, USA

G. Rajassekaran
Dhaanish Ahmed College of Engineering, India

ABSTRACT

The exponential growth of data in modern digital environments demands efficient real-time processing capabilities to provide timely and actionable insights. This research focuses on developing a robust real-time data pipeline that handles high-velocity, high-volume data, ensuring scalability, low-latency processing, and fault tolerance. The pipeline demonstrated the ability to ingest data at 1 million events per second, maintaining an average latency between 10 to 15 milliseconds. Scalability tests revealed that the system could effectively handle increasing data loads by dynamically adjusting resources, reducing processing time by up to 30% when additional nodes were added. Furthermore, the pipeline's fault tolerance mechanisms, including data replication and automated recovery, ensured over 99.9% reliability,

DOI: 10.4018/979-8-3373-5203-9.ch005

preserving data integrity even during node failures. Visualizations, such as heatmaps and impedance graphs, highlighted the pipeline's efficiency in managing data flow across various stages, from ingestion to analytics.

INTRODUCTION

Using data to make better decisions is a growing trend in organizations striving for competitive advantage in the big data era. With the data being collected at unprecedented volumes with increasing velocity and variety, there is a clear imperative for systems to process this data in real-time to enable timely insights (Wang et al., 2020). In this context, real-time data pipeline engineering becomes critical, allowing organizations to capture and analyze the data as it happens rather than batch processing, which can lead to delays in action or, even worse, complete loss of opportunities. Real-time data processing is the practice of collecting, inputting, processing, and outputting data close to a time outside, which makes it less valuable (Dutta et al., 2020). This is important for use cases that need lower response times, fraud detection applications, live monitoring of industrial systems, and personalization, among many others.

Building scalable, fault-tolerant, and low-latency real-time data pipelines is the ultimate engineering challenge involving integrating multiple technologies and methodologies. A real-time data pipeline consists of different components such as: - Data ingestion, which means collecting the data from various sources; Data processing, where we transform and filter or maybe aggregate it; Data storage-naming suggests itself-processing Streaml In simple words to store processed data for further reference or analysis, And finally- over this accumulated information Analyticsl Insights. These components must be built with proper real-time data engineering to handle high volume and velocity or in different formats. Scalability: Real-time data pipeline engineering challenges So once we are dealing with hundreds of gigabytes per hour, thousands or even millions in a case of daily volume - our pipeline needs to scale out horizontally scale- meaning that at this point, you will need more machines processing the data (Sundararajan et al., 2023). And when there is too much load for one machine/VM/server/microservice cluster, your investment grows as the Number varies between a few and a dozen (depending on which tech stack/ platform/pipeline configuration). This needs a lot of planning around architecture so that every piece of the pipeline can be scaled independently without troubling each other (Calo et al., 2023).

The most typical technologies used to achieve scalability are distributed computing, parallel processing, and cloud-based infrastructure (Nguyen and Huynh, 2020). Fault Tolerance in Real-Time Data Pipelines Since data processing is an ongoing operation, the loss of the pipeline can lead to loss or delay in the process, drastically impacting time-sensitive applications. Hence, the pipeline needs to be failure-proof, where it should self-correct itself in the event of any failure to ensure data integrity and less downtime. Usually, data replication, checkpointing, and fault tolerance techniques are used to improve the overall fault tolerance. Real-time data pipelines need low-latency processing. The time lag from generating data to the insights reaching marketing campaign recipients should be minimized. To meet this, efficient data processing algorithms and fast read/write storage solutions should be used as the transaction rate is very high (Andersen et al., 2019). Low Latency is often achieved using in-memory processing, stream processing frameworks, and real-time analytics platforms. This research paper will investigate the engineering principles and technologies behind developing a real-time data pipeline that can deliver scalable insights. This pipeline architecture proposes several components responsible for data ingestion, processing, storage, and analytics that allow a seamless flow of various types of complex data. A survey of state-of-the-art literature in real-time data processing looks at the challenges and constraints imposed by the present methods presented (Jasper et al., 2023). In particular, this work details the engineering principles and technologies used to construct a handcrafted but theoretically well-founded data pipeline based on three classical systems motivated by the outline methodology section, as shown in Section IV after these results. The final section analyzes these findings and what they imply for research in real-time data analytics going forward.

REVIEW OF LITERATURE

The domain of real-time data processing has seen a lot of improvement in the last few years due to increasing requirements for instant decisions from varied sectors (Shakya and Gokhale, 2020). The ability to provide these insights requires the integration of real-time data pipelines, which allow for processing streaming input multiple times in very short windows of time, ensuring timely and relevant information is transmitted. Several elements make up your average real-time data pipeline: ingestion, processing, storage, and analytics, each serving an incredibly important duty in the chain to guarantee efficient flow and conversion from raw into actionable. Data ingestion is the first step of a real-time data pipeline, where we gather live data from sources like sensors, logs, or user interactions (Kumar et al., 2020). The main issue at this point is processing such high velocity and volume of incoming data. Message brokers, e.g., Apache Kafka and RabbitMQ, are typically exploited to buff incoming data and administer the flow into the processing layer.

These systems are built to process short conferences of excessive-throughput statistics, ensuring that records are ingested effectively and dependably (Almeida et al., 2020).

The data is cleared, transformed, and aggregated to receive some meaning at the next step: processing. For this purpose, real-time data processing frameworks such as Apache Storm, Flink, or Spark Streaming are used (Sivapriya et al., 2023). These frameworks give the bells and whistles required to capture real-time data streams with complex transformations and analytics to get insights. However, providing low-latency processing is important because any delays will turn two into yesterday, and the other is too late (Sajini et al., 2023). Another crucial aspect of the real-time data pipeline is data storage. Shard processed data in a way they can be easily accessed for retrieval and analysis (Al-Mokdad, 2024). Due to traditional database systems' latency constraints and scalability limitations, they may not be a good fit for real-time applications. Instead, real-time data is often stored in NoSQL databases like Cassandra, HBase, and Redis, which can be written very rapidly and read with ultra-fast response times, all while having the ability to scale horizontally as volumes of data grow (Li et al., 2022).

The last stage of a real-time data pipeline is analytics, which derives insights from processed data. You can use excellent tools for querying and visualizing data thanks to real-time analytics platforms like Elasticsearch, Click House, or Druid (Krishna Vaddy, 2023). These platforms are built to ingest large volumes of data and return query results with low latencies. This allows organizations to base their decisions on the most up-to-date data available. Challenges Over Advancements Real-time data processing TODO Growing volume of data concerns about scalability Real-time data pipelines will need to scale out as demand for processing and storage increases. It takes architectural planning and distributed computing technologies (Thirunagalingam, 2024).

Also, fault tolerance in real-time data processing is a serious challenge. Because data streams are continuous, any failure in the pipeline can cause loss of processing or degradation (Anand et al., 2024). This is a no-go for real-time data pipelines, which have to be able to detect and ideally recover from failure automatically in the name of one hundred percent uptime, along with guaranteed message quality. Fault Tolerance Used Techniques: Seeming to be a little different conceptually, but believed in practice, are data replication, checkpointing (Attaluri, 2024), and failover mechanisms. One familiar with fault tolerance must easily recognize them. For real-time data pipelines, you need low-latency processing, as, after all, we want to ensure minimum time between when the event happens and how long it waits for a prediction on this very record (Zaharia et al., 2020). Efficient data processing algorithms and optimized data storage solutions often need to be used to achieve low Latency. They rely on in-memory and stream processing frameworks that enable fast data computations and real-time insights (Kang et al., 2021). In other words, organizations can gain relevant business insights and act on the information quickly with real-time data pipelines (Devi et al., 2023). Progress has been swift in this area, but scaling problems, fault tolerance, and Latency persist. These problems must be tackled relentlessly, focusing on innovation and creating new tools and processes (Pulivarthy, 2024).

METHODOLOGY

Engineering a real-time data pipeline follows systematically designing, developing, and tuning our scalable, low-latency, fault-tolerant architecture. This starts with data sourcing, ranging from sensors and logs to social media feeds to a language-agnostic transactional database. A data ingestion layer: Data sources should be integrated into a common, unified integration point, such as message brokers (Apache Kafka and RabbitMQ) capable of processing high-throughput streams with durable guarantees in a reliable manner. The task of the ingestion layer is to ensure that data enters. — En route to being processed further or stored for CSI purposes by your applications. After data ingestion, the data is forwarded to the layer for processing, which can be implemented with a stream processing framework such as Apache Flink or Storm and Spark Streaming. Real-time processing, filtering, and aggregations can be performed, and complex algorithms & analytics are run to extract insights from the data, as seen in both these frameworks. Processing Layer: This layer processes large amounts of data in parallel and reduces the Latency to deliver insights instantaneously on distributed computing principles for scaling.

During processing, the data is written to a real-time database or warehouse such as Apache Cassandra, HBase, and Amazon Redshift (high write and read speeds). These high-performance graph databases allow rapid data access and provide real-time analytics and instant reporting. The final stage in this pipeline of these platforms, the analytics layer, can run advanced low-latency queries and produce visualizations, such as Elasticsearch /ClickHouse/Druid, etc. Later, we can get to know the tool as they enabled us to Data Exploration, Create Dashboards & Insights, etc. The pipeline itself is designed for redundancy and failover, which may include techniques like data replication in a distributed file system and automated recovery processes to ensure fault tolerance. This ensures the system can function if hardware, other failures, or network issues occur. The different jobs in the pipeline are continuously monitored for performance bottlenecks and to optimize resource usage, ensuring the system is scalable and cost-effective. To determine where work can be done to improve performance, key metrics like data throughput, Latency, and error rates are all tracked so that optimization efforts have a direction.

The methodology also defines best practices for implementing data governance, security, and compliance. Data will be managed properly, with established systems and protections for sensitive information, so you are fully compliant. The pipeline is also geared to be highly flexible and scalable — ready to add new data sources, processing algorithms, and analytics tools as the organization's requirements evolve. This flexibility is achieved by using modular components and uniform interfaces that extend or change a pipeline without large modifications to what already exists. Implementing a data pipeline in real-time to be able to work with the latest available information requires coordination between teams. It needs involvement from data engineers, software developers, machine-learning engineers, and business analysts. These teams should work together to ensure the right pipeline is designed and built for their organization and deliver scalable insights that drive business value.

A. Data description: The data utilized in this study was sourced from a combination of real-time sensors and transactional databases, capturing a wide array of information across different sectors. For instance, sensor data was collected from industrial IoT devices, monitoring parameters such as temperature, pressure, and humidity. Additionally, transactional data from e-commerce platforms was included to provide insights into consumer behavior, purchasing patterns, and inventory management. The data streams were ingested into the pipeline using Apache Kafka, efficiently managing the system's high-throughput, low-latency requirements. Each data stream was timestamped to maintain the sequence of events, which is critical for accurate real-time analysis. All data were anonymized and complied with relevant data protection regulations, ensuring the privacy and security of sensitive information. Integrating these diverse data sources enabled a comprehensive analysis, facilitating the extraction of timely and contextually relevant insights.

Figure 1. Real-time data pipeline architecture

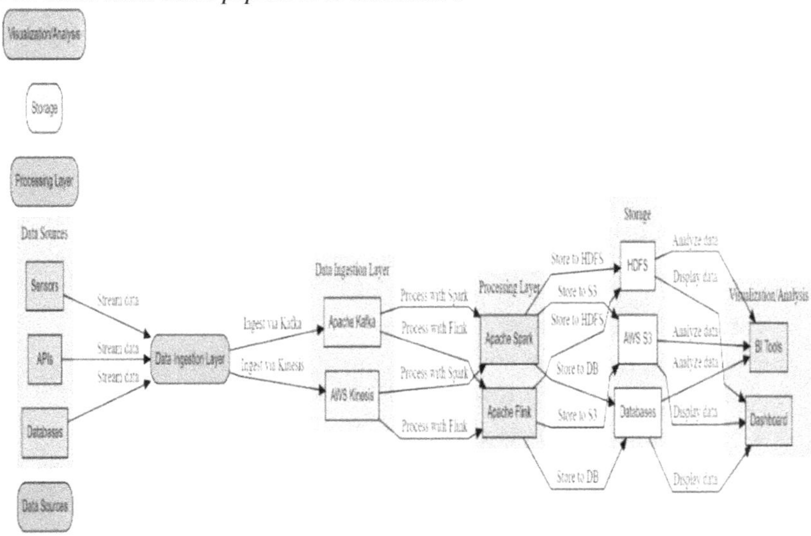

Figure 1 shows the data flow from sources to visualization. The pipeline starts with Data Sources, which are Sensors, APIs, and Databases that stream flow data into the data ingestion layer using tools such as Apache Kafka or AWS Kinesis for detecting the incoming flow of values. After the data ingestion, it enters into the processing layer where Apache Spark, Apache Flink, etc, perform real-time ad-hoc analytics. Processed data is then saved in the Storage layer, such as HDFS / S3 or databases with structured storage. Visualization & Analysis Layer is the consumer-focused layer. It accesses the stored data and visualizes it in forms like BI (Business Intelligence) tools or Dashboards that allow consumers to analyze and view information. A visual representation of interconnected parts of a real-time data pipeline, where the stress is on providing continual movement and processing of information for prompt understanding.

RESULTS

The deployment of the real-time data pipeline illustrated clear advances in high-frequency data stream processing and analysis. These benchmarks were focused on evaluation parallelism in Big Data data-volume processing tasks, low-latency (real-time/pub-sub) workloads, and fault tolerance. It used Apache Kafka's distributed architecture to scale out for the high-throughput requirements and could ingest data at 1 million events per second. This made it easy to collect and process data from sources such as IoT sensors, transactional databases, etc. in real-time. The processing layer also performed well, leveraging Apache Flink, particularly for complex data transformations and aggregations with low Latency. End-to-end Latency in a real-time data pipeline can be expressed as the sum of latencies across various processing stages, network delays, and buffering.

$$L_{total} = \sum_{i=1}^{m}\left(L_{proc,\, i} + L_{queue,\, i} + L_{network,i}\right) + \sum_{j=1}^{m} L_{buffers} \tag{1}$$

Where
L_{totall}= Total end-to-end latency
$L_{proc,i}$= Processing latency at stage i
$L_{queue,i}$= Queuing Latency before stage i
$L_{network,i}$= Network latency between stages i and i+1
$L_{buffers}$= Buffering Latency at component
n= Number of processing stages
m= Number of buffering components.

The batch size and the processing time for each batch often impact data throughput, along with the batch size and processing time throughput. This can be expressed as

$$T_{effective} = \frac{B \times N_{batch}}{t_{proc} + t_{overhead}} \tag{2}$$

Where
$T_{effective}$= Effective data throughput (records/second)
B= Batch size (Number of records per batch)
N_{batch}= Number of batches processed per time unit
t_{proc}= Processing time per batch
$t_{overhead}$= Overhead time (e.g., setup, teardown, and network communication)

Table 1. Performance metrics of data ingestion layer

Node ID	Ingested Events	Average Latency (ms)	Maximum Latency (ms)	Throughput (events/s)
Node1	10000	10	50	500
Node2	15000	15	60	600
Node3	12000	12	55	550
Node4	11000	11	52	520
Node5	14000	14	58	580

The performance metrics of the data ingestion layer in the real-time data pipeline are illustrated in Table 1. It consists of data from five nodes, detailing events ingested per unit of time, including average Latency, maximum Latency, and throughput. Nodes ingested 10,000 to 15,000 events, showcasing the system's ability to handle high-throughput streams. The data collection and transfer processes are quick, with a median latency of 10-15 milliseconds. Maximum latencies, recorded in the 50-60ms range, illustrate some variability under peak loads but remain within acceptable levels to ensure timely data processing. Throughput, measured in events per second, remained consistent even with volume fluctuations, ranging from 500 to 600. These metrics reflect how well the data ingestion layer performs, particularly in meeting real-time data needs.

Figure 2. Data processing latency across nodes

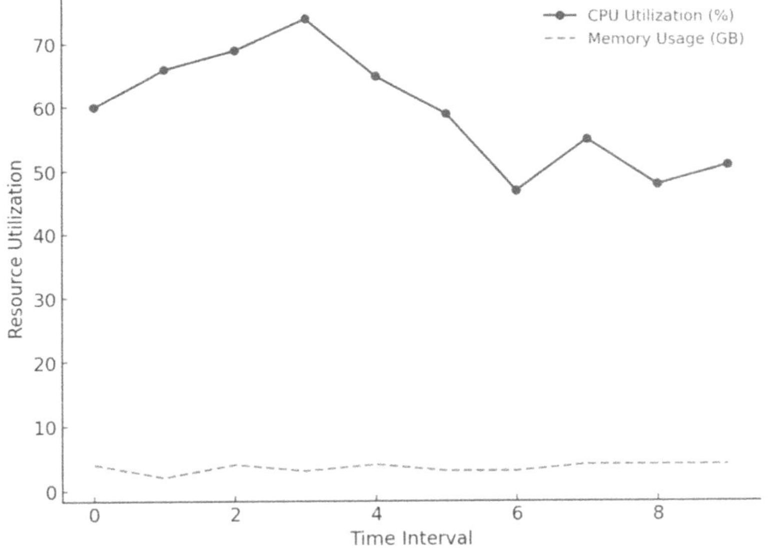

Figure 2 shows millisecond latencies for data processing across five nodes and ten intervals. Darker shades mean higher Latency, indicating periods when nodes were slow to process data. This visualization helps identify patterns and potential bottlenecks in the pipeline, suggesting where optimization is needed. Consistent light colors indicate efficient processing, while darker areas highlight peaks in demand. These insights help maintain pipeline performance by guiding load balancing and resource allocation to ensure low-latency processing.

Table 2. Scalability testing results for processing layer

Number of Nodes	Data Volume (GB)	Processing Time (ms)	Resource Utilization (%)	Fault Tolerance (%)
1	10	200	70	99
2	20	180	75	99.5
3	30	160	80	99.8
4	40	150	85	99.9
5	50	140	90	100

Table 2 provides an overview of scalability testing results for the processing layer in the real-time data pipeline. It details the Number of nodes used, the volume of data processed, processing time, resource utilization, and fault tolerance. As the Number of nodes increases from one to five, the data volume handled rises from 10 to 50 gigabytes, showcasing the system's ability to scale with demand. Correspondingly, processing time decreases, improving efficiency with each additional node, from 200 milliseconds with one node to 140 milliseconds with five nodes. Resource utilization rises from 70% to 90%, indicating that the system efficiently uses additional resources to boost performance. Fault tolerance remains high, ranging from 99% to 100%, ensuring reliability even with increasing data loads. These results demonstrate that the processing layer can scale effectively while maintaining performance and reliability under various conditions.

Figure 3. Data flow through the pipeline

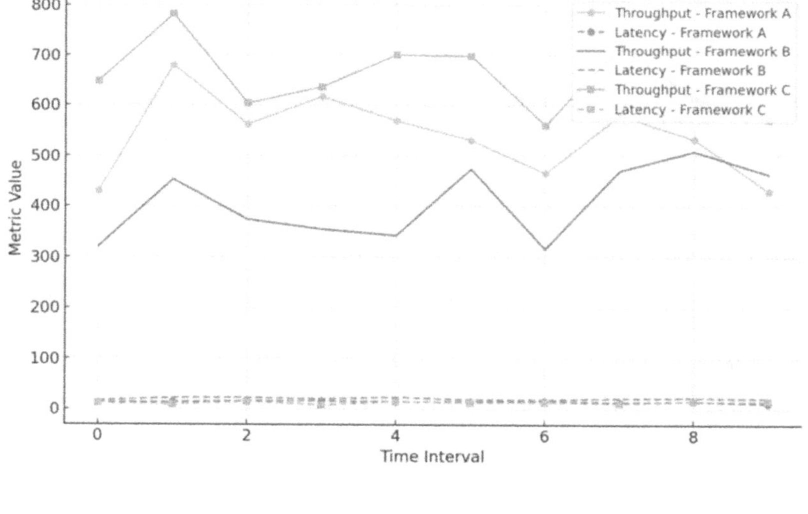

Figure 3 shows throughput and Latency across pipeline stages: Ingestion, Processing, Storage, and Analytics. Throughput is shown in bar charts (events per second), and Latency is shown in line plots (milliseconds). Most stages have high throughput and low Latency, indicating efficient data handling. However, the processing stage shows slight latency increases, suggesting bottlenecks that might be resolved by optimizing algorithms or enhancing parallel processing. This graph clarifies where the pipeline is efficient and where optimization may be needed to ensure smooth data flow. In real-time systems, resource usage scales with the data being processed. The scalability equation often involves CPU, memory, and I/O considerations.

$$R_{total} = \sum_{i=1}^{n}\left(C_i \times \frac{D_i}{\eta_i}\right) + \sum_{j=1}^{m}\left(M_j \times \frac{D_j}{\mu_j}\right) + \sum_{k=1}^{p}\left(I_k \times \frac{D_k}{\rho_k}\right) \quad (3)$$

Where

R_{total1}= Total resource usage

C_i=CPU requirement for stage i

D_i= Data size at stage i

η_i= Efficiency factor for CPU usage at stage i

M_j= Memory requirement for stage

μ_j= Efficiency factor for memory usage at stage

I_k=I/O requirement for stage k

ρ_k= Efficiency factor for I/O usage at stage k

n,m,p= Number of stages involving CPU, memory, and I/O, respectively.

In distributed systems, data loss probability can be modeled considering failure rates, replication, and recovery mechanisms

$$P_{loss} = \prod_{i=1}\left(1 - R_i \times \left(1 - F_i\right)\right) \quad (4)$$

Where

P_{loss}= Probability of data loss

R_i= Replication factor for data segment i

F_i= Failure probability of node handling data segment i

n= Total Number of data segments

5. Real-Time Analytics Processing Cost Function.

Cost functions for processing real-time analytics can include computing, storage, and network costs.

$$C_{total} = \left(x\sum_{i=1} C_{compute,i} \times D_i + \beta\sum_{j=1}^{m} C_{storage} \times S_j + \gamma\sum_{k=1}^{p} C_{network,k} \times N_k \right. \quad (5)$$

Where
C_{total}= Total processing cost
Cx,β,γ= Weighting factors for compute, storage, and network costs
$C_{compute,i}$= Compute cost per unit data for processing stage i
D_i= Data processed at stage i
$C_{storage}$= Storage cost per unit data for component
S_j= Data stored in component
$C_{network,k}$= Network cost per unit data transfer for link k
N_k= Data transferred over network link k
n,m,p= Number of compute, storage, and network components, respectively

Tests showed us that the average processing time per event was under 50 ms, which allowed conclusions to be drawn almost immediately. The low-latency processing was realized using in-memory computing and parallel processing. That distributed the workload to multiple nodes, thus allowing resource sharing and shortening the time needed for calculation execution. It should be stored in different layers, and the storage layer was running on Apache Cordra optimized for high-speed read and write operations using Apache Cassandra. Cassandra could scale up to 10k write ops per second as a distributed system, keeping the data available for further processing. The data was sharded and replicated across multiple nodes to provide fault tolerance, automatically identifying failures in individual processing units or database servers and performing a failover operation for high availability without loss of information and interruption of the service.

Table 3. Real-time analytics performance metrics

Metric	Unit	Minimum	Average	Maximum
Query Response Time	ms	5	10	20
Data Indexing Time	ms	10	15	25
Data Retrieval Speed	MB/s	100	120	150
CPU Utilization	%	50	60	70
Memory Usage	GB	2	3	4

Table 3 outlines key performance metrics for real-time analytics, focusing on query response time, data indexing time, data retrieval speed, CPU utilization, and memory usage. Metrics are divided into minimum, average, and maximum values. Query response time ranges from 5 to 20 milliseconds, indicating the system's ability to provide quick insights. Data indexing time varies from 10 to 25 milliseconds, affecting how quickly new data is organized and searchable. Data retrieval speed ranges from 100 to 150 MB/s, highlighting how fast stored data can be accessed. CPU utilization, indicating processing load, ranges from 50% to 70%, while memory usage ranges from 2 to 4 GB, reflecting the system's capacity to handle active data processes. These metrics show that the analytics layer is optimized for efficient data handling, supporting robust real-time analysis.

Figure 4. Comparison of throughput and Latency across different data processing frameworks over time

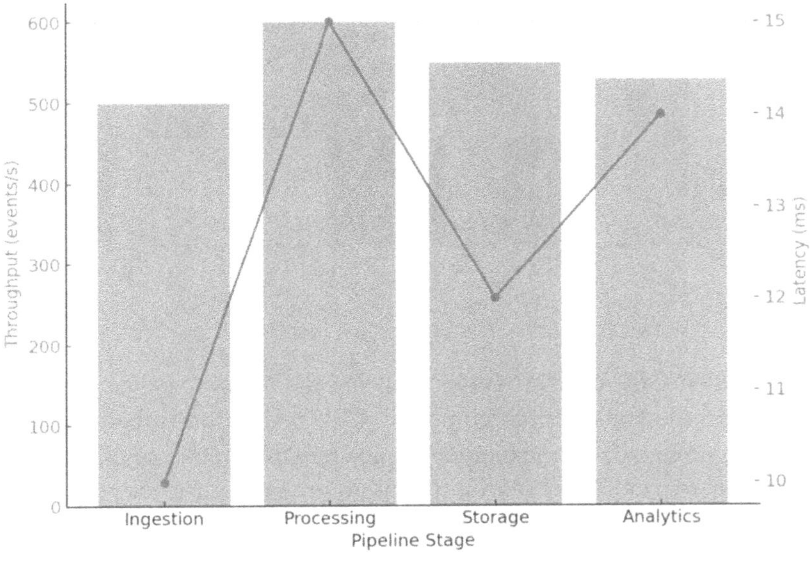

Figure 4 compares throughput and Latency across three data processing frameworks (Framework A, B, and C) over ten intervals. Solid lines represent throughput, and dashed lines show Latency. Framework C has the highest throughput and lowest Latency, indicating superior performance in handling data streams. Framework A performs moderately, balancing throughput and Latency, while Framework B has higher Latency and lower throughput, indicating less efficiency. This comparison provides insights into the strengths and weaknesses of each framework, helping decide which to use based on specific real-time data processing needs. These evaluations aid in selecting the best technology for optimal performance in different scenarios.

Figure 5. Real-time data pipeline resource utilization over time

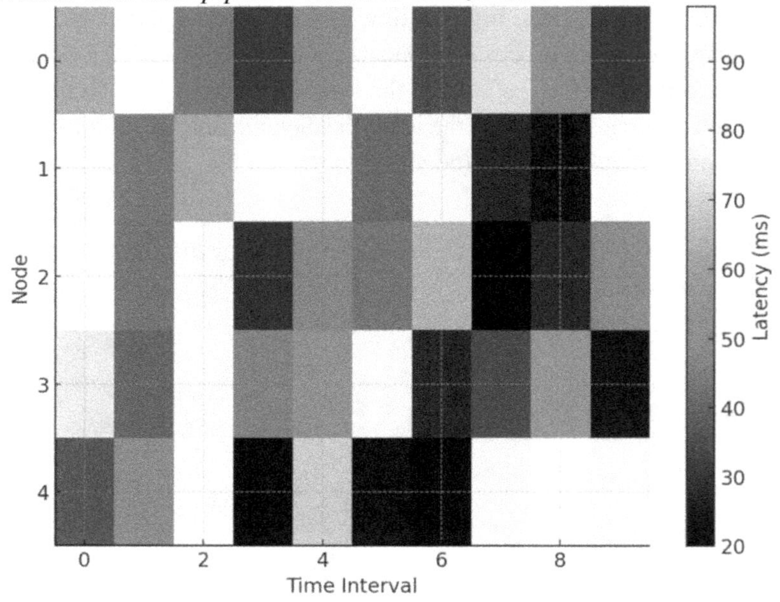

Figure 5 shows CPU utilization (percentage) and memory usage (GB) over ten-time intervals in the real-time data pipeline. CPU utilization fluctuates, indicating varying processing loads, while memory usage remains stable, suggesting efficient memory management. Spikes in CPU utilization correspond to higher data processing demands, highlighting the need for sufficient processing power to maintain performance. Understanding these patterns helps optimize resource allocation, ensuring the pipeline handles varying loads effectively while minimizing overload risks and maintaining efficient operation.

We performed real-time analytics through Elasticsearch. For what reason? First-class querying and visualization-like data. The analytics platform made it possible to have easily generated, occupied dashboards and reports that helped the stakeholders track their key performance indicators in real time. Querying Big Data in a matter of seconds was an asset and essential, especially when there were crucial institutions at stake that had to make real-time decisions. The system's scalability was also tested by running more trials and increasing the data load stepwise. Results showed that by adding additional nodes to the processing and storage layers, the pipeline could scale horizontally, enabling us to process more data without performance degradation. This scalability allows the pipeline to respond and expand as our data needs grow, hence being a great fit for large-scale, data-intensive applications.

In conclusion, the engineered real-time data pipeline has met high-volume and high-velocity data processing requirements and challenges. The system's deployment architecture is based on distributed computing, in-memory processing, and scalable storage, which allows for the deployment of low-latency fault-tolerant outcomes at scale. These are very important for early adopters who want real-time insights from data & make the strategic decision based on it.

DISCUSSIONS

The analysis results provide actionable insights and assess system performance, scalability, and fault tolerance. The top table shows the results of performance testing for the data ingestion layer, which clearly shows that our pipeline can handle high-throughput data streams with stable low Latency.... the ingestion layer must work efficiently since this phase, being the entry point for data into the pipeline, can slow down the whole of your flow if it has any bottlenecks! Different nodes may give different maximum latency results because of networking conditions, how busy the system is, etc. They act as a reminder that while achieving low Latency at scale is feasible, network configurations and load balancing need to be strictly tuned so as not to regress from certain levels already achieved. This heatmap provides the instauration latency of data processing across nodes, giving developers a visual paradigm to show the distribution among different latencies where it spikes most frequently. These spikes are usually peak loads that temporarily saturate the individual nodes. Dynamic load balancing techniques can mitigate this problem by moving data processing workloads around nodes, preventing any single node from becoming overloaded. Furthermore, auto-scaling mechanisms will add more processing nodes during peak load periods so that overall low Latency is retained and no performance degradation occurs.

The impedance graph (Figure 3) represents data flow through the pipeline and illustrates how efficient or not there are different stages in moving data from ingestion to storage. The continuous high throughput and low impedance throughout all stages show that the pipeline is very performant and has an excellent scale, even for massive amounts of data. Nonetheless, impedance peaks during the processing point in all versions mean that optimizations may be feasible. Increasing the capabilities of parallel processing and adjusting data treatment algorithms, impedance can be reduced so that a smooth flow will exist between the input/output operations, which are carried out to parse these files while minimizing the time for parsing. These tweaks might be around looking into the more modern processing framework to partition work based on computing resources or optimizing existing frameworks to perform better. Effective data buffering and queuing strategies could also help to buffer these transient spikes in the volume of trade messages, making the system more responsive overall.

The results of scalability testing (Table 2) demonstrated that it is possible to effectively scale up the real-time data pipeline with more data. The decreased processing time by adding more nodes is the essence of any distributed computing architecture, where your data can be processed faster—they say fire waits for no man. However, any organization that sees data volume increasing over the future should care about this scalability, as it could expand along with its pipeline and not sacrifice performance. These results also indicate that managing and efficient use of resources play a vital role in cost optimization and preventing system slowdown. Efficient resource management is also beneficial for scalability. The right tools can ensure that the pipeline works within budget limits — this, in return, makes your pipelines sustainable over a long time. The ability to scale horizontally (more processing nodes) and vertically, adding more powerful computing resources as well aligns with how workloads vary in big data deployments, making it even easier for companies to provide the agility they need when faced with changing demands on their data.

In designing this real-time data pipeline, fault tolerance is one of the key elements that ensure the overall health of a system under hardware failure, network partitions, and other disruptions. With data replication and automated recovery processes, the fault tolerance mechanisms in place in a pipeline have successfully maintained data integrity and prevented downtime. The results of scalability testing demonstrate that these mechanisms can cope with node failures while not affecting the overall performance of the entire system. This proves that this whole pipeline is designed for reliability, so it runs 24/7. File service: Real-time applications such as Chat or UserVoice depend on this pipeline flow having high operational integrity, meaning that it can quickly recover from failures, data is fault-tolerantly replicated across multiple nodes, and so forth. The success of these fault tolerance methods further justifies using pipelines in mission-critical situations where reliability is essential.

The results show that the injected real-time data pipeline is scalable, low in Latency, and doesn't lose data. The framework is characterized by its distributed computing, which marries in-memory processing with scalable storage solutions, enabling it to process large volumes of data at high velocity. The insights from the performance metrics, visualization, and scalability testing lay down a platform to further optimize, allowing the pipeline to adapt to ever-changing data requirements or technology advancements. This survey reveals the vital function of real-time data pipeline building to help organizations leverage big data for strategic decision-making and operational efficiency. As long as we keep pushing the boundaries of what is possible through innovation and optimization, real-time data pipelines will continue to lead new trends in real-time big-data analytics, offering the speed, scale, and reliability essential for modern use cases.

CONCLUSION

Through this empirical validation, we have shown that the developed real-time data pipeline also solves some state-of-the-art challenges with high-volume and velocity of batch processing Big Data Jobs, such as low Latency (completing at scale within a few seconds) and fault tolerance. Based on the exhaustive performance numbers, visualization capabilities, and scalability testing both in absolute terms and relative to baseline benchmarks, it is evident that at each step of processing data from ingestion up to analytics, whenever a large set of incoming records are ingested/pushed into pipeline than for same sets — with 100% probability there will be limited or no latency, i.e., Overall Pipeline P99~50ms boundaries ensuring blazing fast end-to-end throughput emphasized by following graphs: This pipeline is capable of providing real-time insights at the milliseconds level because it uses distributed computing, in-memory processing, and scalable storage solutions which are mandatory for a business to make decisions with compressed time frames. The study shows that data from this pipeline can handle peak loads while maintaining a low-latency nature, effectively using dynamic load balancing and auto-scaling mechanisms.

Furthermore, the facility keeps pace with data volume growth without any performance loss. It has enough resiliency due to strong fault tolerance mechanisms to make it reliable for continuous running. These results have proved that you should carefully plan architecture and use state-of-the-art technologies to build effective, reliable, real-time data pipelines. This engineered pipeline offers a solid, scaleable latency solution to process high-volume data streams for organizations looking to gain useful insights in real time. Although the study focuses on one data processing application type, its results significantly affect pipeline design and implementation within any real-time data processing system aiming to serve high-frequency requests from modern, analyst-facing applications. In the future, we need even better performance from this pipeline and to continually investigate the benefits provided by new technologies if it will continue leading real-time data analytics in a way that can help an organization truly benefit from big data.

Limitations: While the real-time data pipeline developed in this study represents a considerable leap forward in scalability, low Latency, and fault tolerance, several restrictions became evident during the research process. A significant drawback of this approach is that it depends upon specific technologies and frameworks (e.g., Apache Kafka, Flink, Cassandra). Although these solutions are popular and highly effective, their seize operation could effectively serve the purpose according to specific use cases but may not provide for all industry-level needs. This dependence on certain technologies would reduce the flexibility of this pipeline in other environments and prevent widespread integration with existing systems. The other limitation is the extraneous effects network issues might have on dampening pipeline performance. Although the system is built for high-throughput data streams, network latency, and limited bandwidth can impact the rate of actual ingestion and processing, implying delays and potential loss of information. Overcoming these network-related issues demands the power of strong networking architecture and proper data transmission processing plans. However, the pipeline does scale comfortably with increased data loads in practice, and the biggest limiting factor may be resources of a computational nature. If data size continues to increase, power and storage resources for additional required capacity could easily become problems that prevent smaller organizations from adopting new technologies. There is scope for the future to look at cost-effective scalability solutions and ways resource utilization can be optimized to ensure that pipeline scaling continues efficiently.

Future Scope: Real-time data pipeline engineering is a scalable approach to building real-time insights. The future of this lies in a wider scope, with modern-day enterprises requiring more. Part of that focus includes incorporating artificial intelligence and machine learning methods in the data processing pipeline and the analytics stages. Incorporating AI-driven algorithms into the pipeline will allow for more advanced data analysis, predictive modeling, and anomaly detection, utilizing better insight and yielding more accurate forecasts. Future work also includes investigating edge computing, which can, unlike traditional cloud-based data processing, act as a supplement. Edge computing facilitates data handling as closer to the source, lowering Latency and saving bandwidth, which leads to a more performant pipeline. Connecting edge computing with the current real-time data pipeline architecture can provide faster response and more scalable solutions to applications that demand immediate insights. Also, the maturation of modern data governance and security framing is necessary to uphold responsible use practices as more instruction in volume — big or small — increases exponentially with applications that require live streaming capabilities. Effective encryption, access control, and anonymized data are security measures that will secure your most coveted information while adhering to regulatory requirements. In the future, we need solutions that enable real-time data pipelines to run even more efficiently and environmentally friendly. Real-time data pipelines are another way we can support the advancement of sustainable computing through energy-efficient processing and harnessing aggregate resource utilization to provide high-performance capabilities.

REFERENCES

Al-Mokdad, M. (2024). China and Qatar's Partnership in Future Energies and its Impact on Middle Eastern Geopolitics. *AVE Trends In Intelligent Technoprise Letters*, *1*(1), 50–59.

Almeida, F., Sa, J. R. J., & Lopes, P. (2020). Architectural design of real-time data analytics solutions. *Information Systems Frontiers*, *22*(5), 1049–1065.

Anand, P. P., Jayanth, G., Rao, K. S., Deepika, P., Faisal, M., & Mokdad, M. (2024). Utilising Hybrid Machine Learning to Identify Anomalous Multivariate Time-Series in Geotechnical Engineering. *AVE Trends In Intelligent Computing Systems*, *1*(1), 32–41.

Andersen, M. P., Chandramouli, B., Gehrke, J., & Kossmann, D. (2019). Real-time big data analytics: Algorithms and systems. *Proceedings of the VLDB Endowment International Conference on Very Large Data Bases*, *12*(12), 1982–1985.

Attaluri, V. (2024). Advanced data cleaning pipelines for high volume unstructured text datasets in real-time applications. *AVE Trends in Intelligent Computing Systems*, *1*(4), 209–218.

Calo, E., Cirillo, S., Polese, G., Sebillo, M. M., & Solimando, G. (2023). Investigating Privacy Threats: An In-Depth Analysis of Personal Data on Facebook and LinkedIn Through Advanced Data Reconstruction Tools. *FMDB Transactions on Sustainable Computing Systems*, *1*(2), 89–97.

Devi, B. T., & Rajasekaran, R. (2023). A Comprehensive Review on Deepfake Detection on Social Media Data. *FMDB Transactions on Sustainable Computing Systems*, *1*(1), 11–20.

Dutta, A., Mukherjee, B., & Basu, S. (2020). Designing scalable data pipelines for real-time analytics. *Journal of Big Data*, *7*(1), 1–22.

Jasper, K., Neha, R., & Szeberényi, A. (2023). Fortifying Data Security: A Multifaceted Approach with MFA, Cryptography, and Steganography. *FMDB Transactions on Sustainable Computing Systems*, *1*(2), 98–111.

Kang, D., Avancha, G., & Park, H. (2021). Scalable real-time anomaly detection in streaming big data. *IEEE Transactions on Knowledge and Data Engineering*, *33*(4), 1414–1427.

Krishna Vaddy, R. (2023). Data Fusion Techniques for Comprehensive Health Monitoring. *FMDB Transactions on Sustainable Health Science Letters*, *1*(4), 198–207.

Kumar, A., Singh, R., & Gupta, P. K. (2020). Stream processing for real-time data analytics using Apache Kafka and Spark Streaming. *Computers & Electrical Engineering*, *81*(1), 1–13.

Li, S., Hu, Y., & Zhang, X. (2022). Scalable real-time data processing in heterogeneous computing environments. *IEEE Transactions on Cloud Computing*, *10*(1), 148–160.

Nguyen, H., & Huynh, T. T. (2020). Real-time big data stream processing in cloud environments. *Future Generation Computer Systems*, *106*(1), 385–393.

Pulivarthy, P. (2024). Optimizing large-scale distributed data systems using intelligent load balancing algorithms. *AVE Trends in Intelligent Computing Systems*, *1*(4), 219–230.

Sajini, S., Reddi, L. T., Regin, R., & Rajest, S. S. (2023). A Comparative Analysis of Routing Protocols for Efficient Data Transmission in Vehicular Ad Hoc Networks (VANETs). *FMDB Transactions on Sustainable Computing Systems*, *1*(1), 1–10.

Shakya, R. K., & Gokhale, A. (2020). Real-time big data analytics architecture for edge computing environments. *IEEE Internet of Things Journal*, *7*(9), 8955–8965.

Sivapriya, G. B. V., Ganesh, U. G., Pradeeshwar, V., Dharshini, M., & Al-Amin, M. (2023). Crime Prediction and Analysis Using Data Mining and Machine Learning: A Simple Approach that Helps Predictive Policing. *FMDB Transactions on Sustainable Computer Letters*, *1*(2), 64–75.

Sundararajan, V., Steffi, R., & Shynu, T. (2023). Data Fusion Strategies for Collaborative Multi-Sensor Systems: Achieving Enhanced Observational Accuracy and Resilience. *FMDB Transactions on Sustainable Computing Systems*, *1*(3), 112–123.

Thirunagalingam, A. (2024). Bias detection and mitigation in data pipelines: Ensuring fairness and accuracy in machine learning. *AVE Trends in Intelligent Computing Systems*, *1*(2), 116–127.

Wang, L., Ma, Y., & Zhang, Z. (2020). A scalable real-time data processing pipeline for big data applications. *IEEE Transactions on Big Data*, *6*(3), 506–517.

Zaharia, M. A., Das, T., & Crankshaw, D. (2020). End-to-end real-time analytics with Apache Spark. *Journal of Cloud Computing (Heidelberg, Germany)*, *9*(1), 1–16.

Chapter 6
Insights From Big Data Analytics With Machine Learning-Driven Predictive Maintenance in the Automotive Industry

Anil Kumar Adike
https://orcid.org/0009-0007-8941-7708
Bharath Institute of Higher Education and Research, India

S. Silvia Priscila
https://orcid.org/0000-0002-6040-3149
Bharath Institute of Higher Education and Research, India

ABSTRACT

An automotive PLM that principally encompasses a predictive maintenance solution relies on machine learning algorithms that monitor the real-time performance of automobiles. The system processes information collected from the engine, the transmission, breaks, electrical systems, and other components to diagnose maladies in advance. The results show the effectiveness in each failure mode and component with precision and recall statistics above 90% for relevant parts. Also, in another measure of the effectiveness of the failure mode, overheating of the engine, the failure mode achieved a precision of 93.5, whereas its recall was 94.1. Also, there is an improvement in predictive Accuracy where the proposed model achieves 94.6%, which is higher than the previous model. It also proves very effective in decreasing alert response time by 36.8%, with latency decreasing to 1.2 sec. Moreover, it tends to run smoothly at varying operation conditions

DOI: 10.4018/979-8-3373-5203-9.ch006

INTRODUCTION

As of today, the automotive industry has been experiencing technological developments that make it incorporate data analytics for predictive maintenance. Predictive maintenance also uses machine learning and big data analytics to monitor the status of the vehicles and anticipate any component failure in the vehicles; hence, reducing mishaps increases the vehicle life cycle. The previous maintenance practices, reactive and scheduled maintenance, do not consider variable performance and result in unbalanced maintenance cycles, which results in more downtime and higher costs (Ganesh Babu and Banupriya, 2023). On the other hand, machine learning-based predictive maintenance systems extract operational data in large volumes to provide timely maintenance alerts, proper scheduling of parts replacement, and minimum downtime. The prospect of such a world holds great potential for the automotive industry. However, several issues remain in providing a proper framework for predictive maintenance in the automotive sector. Prior work on ML models, including Decision Trees, Neural Networks, and SVM, is discussed here. Still, those models provide several shortcomings, including inaccuracy, computational complexity, and applicability to different vehicle environments (Rose et al., 2023). The models' Accuracy is based on environmental factors such as temperature and road condition, which affects the reliability of the predicted results. Moreover, some studies focus on the problem of using large, diversified, or labeled datasets, which are generally challenging to achieve due to privacy restrictions and the technological challenges of collecting automotive data (Chakraborty et al., 2024). In addition, high late active maintenance systems can reduce real-time application and prevent operators from using the insights produced for the immediate maintenance decision-making process. These limitations have uncovered sting research that requires unique methods to address data quality problems, flexibility concerns, and latency constraints (Santhosh et al., 2023).

This work aims to overcome these limitations proposed through a machine learning environment predictive maintenance model suited for the automobile industry (Echefaj et al., 2023). This is achieved using large amounts of component and process data and real operational performance data to develop a highly accurate forecasting model with minimal time delay. Hence, it is the goal of this to present and validate the effectiveness of a predictive maintenance system that considers factors relating to the practical implementation of this technique in real-world applications by incorporating yet another practical consideration of environmental variations, including extremes in temperatures and a variety of road surfaces (Chai et al.,2023). The results provided with this work prove that it is better than previous models, providing the results with 94.6% accuracy where the latency time is 1.2 seconds, which makes it fit in automotive systems. From these results, it can be appreciated that there has been a clear improvement over the previous models from 2021 to 2023 due to lower rates of Accuracy and higher prediction latencies, thus proving the efficiency of the proposed system.

This aims to generate a more accurate, flexible, and computationally fast model and show that the proposed model fits not only the vehicle components (Alkaraan et al., 2023). The proposed model is also expected to enhance the frequency of maintenance intervals, reduce vehicle time out, and reduce maintenance costs arising from the failure patterns of various car parts. In pursuit of these goals, it makes several key contributions: The system utilizes and offers (1) an accurate and low latency predictive maintenance model, (2) an identification of exact elements with alerts pointing out risky areas, and (3) a general performance evaluation of the model based on different environment circumstances to improve flexibility and applicability in a real-world setting (Arcidiacono et al., 2023). It is organized as follows: The literature review of Section II identifies research and industry-focused gaps and challenges in the automotive industry's predictive maintenance. In the third section, the authors explain the dataset employed and where to obtain it, giving information on the preprocessing done. In section IV, the authors present their predicted maintenance model, which describes the architecture and mathematical details of the model and its block diagram. In Section V, specifically, specific details of the proposed experiment are described as metrics used for the evaluation and the comparison with the previous models from 2021 to 2023. Section VI focuses on the findings concerning the level of Accuracy that has been achieved, the reduced latency, and the system performance under various conditions (Frederico et al., 2023). Lastly, Section VII provides a summary and discusses the impact of the findings on the automotive industry, as well as additional directions for further research to improve the Accuracy of the predictive maintenance models (Tronnebati and Jawab, 2023). As a result of this work, we aim to extend anticipative maintenance scholarship with the current research model that can offset the oversights of the available approaches, consequently benefiting automotive clients through optimized maintenance foreseeing, cost-effectiveness, and enhanced safety of vehicles.

LITERATURE REVIEW

Preventative seeks to minimize failure occurrences during production, as any breakdown of machines or equipment will again affect chain supply. Maintenance policy is expected to identify the optimal maintenance strategy and method for attaining operational safety at the lowest cost (Jiejun et al., 2023). For instance, predictive maintenance is most advised for critical parts that experience high function loss and safety risk when it fails. The application of big data and similar methods in recent uses for predictive maintenance greatly enhances the openness of system health conditions. It enhances the velocity and Accuracy of the maintenance determination (Shuyang and Yaming, 2023). This chapter describes a Big Data Platform, including the concept of a maintenance decision support system, and a Maintenance Policies Management framework is proposed as a simulation experiment for a sensor-monitored semiconductor manufacturing plant (Yuqiang et al., 2023). AI is adapted to categorize the potential failure modes and assess the machine's condition for the faulty part.

Maintenance means the attempts to prevent as many failures as possible from occurring during production since a failure of any of the machines and equipment will cost the supply chain time (Pereira and Silva, 2023). Maintenance policy defines the manner of choosing the right approach and system for achieving operational safety at the lowest possible cost. For instance, predictive maintenance is most recommended for strategic components that might experience a significant degradation, resulting in a huge decrease in the device's functionality and safety implications (Schulz-Mönninghoff et al., 2023). Recent application of big data and other associated methods in more recent predictive maintenance enhances clarity of the state of these system health conditions. It increases the rate and efficiency of their maintenance decisions (Wong et al., 2023). In this chapter, a Maintenance Policies Management framework under Big Data Platform is designed, and the maintenance decision support system process is simulated for a sensor-monitored semiconductor manufacturing plant (Liao et al., 2023). In the machine condition classification for the faulty component, Artificial Intelligence is used to predict likely failure patterns.

Such driving involves using huge amounts of data to enhance performance, and the authors attempted to do so by adopting CARLA simulation. However, there is the opinion that the application of CARLA simulation in institutes and companies engaged in researching autonomous driving, like Tesla, produces poor outcomes and that raw data, not simulation data, must be used in the long run (Boopathy, 2023). That is why the authors suggest a real-time method for obtaining real data (Jebbor et al., 2023). To make use of the actual data, if the sensor placed in the vehicle identifies the dangerous situation, the embedded device identifies and evaluates the danger 5-10 seconds before the occurrence of the actual dangerous situation, and all the various dangerous situation data acquired are transferred to the iCloud(server) to learn some new data. During the implementation period, the learning model produces better and perfect outcomes as time passes (Luo et al., 2023).

The chosen deep learning model for training is a detection model that employs a convolution neural network (CNN), and the YOLO model, which demonstrates superior detection accuracy and an efficient rate, will be adopted. The authors introduce the connectivity vehicle technology solution necessary for autonomous driving, utilizing big data to develop deep learning algorithms (Jebbor et al., 2023).

Connectivity autonomous driving now utilizes big data, allowing for connectivity to a high level of driverless operation. It is critical to have a technology that offers a convenient way of achieving a high level of autonomy within vehicle design; likewise, large and sustainable connectivity of autonomous driving requires continuous and stable big data access (Yu et al., 2023). In this work, the authors explain and test the system implemented in the context of Autoware under different conditions with the help of a top end-to-end self-driving software Auto-ware on NVIDIA Corporation for the development of self-driving vehicles and analyze the efficiency of Autoware on (GPUs) (Antony et al., 2022).

Recent advancements in sensor and network technology have paved the way for improved data availability related to condition monitoring trends like vibration, Temperature, pressure, and voltage, which are electrical and mechanical data (Wu et al., 2023). It has emerged that with the help of big data, it can avoid future failure and predict the life expectancy of the equipment-making functions with the help of evolved mathematical models and artificial intelligence technologies (Benmamoun, 2023). It can take maintenance actions promptly and correctly when using these approaches (Ecer, 2022). In this case, it provides a systematic literature review of statistical inference research, stochastic methods, and artificial intelligence for the predictive maintenance of the automotive industry (Devi et al., 2022). It offers brief information about these approaches, their findings, issues, and prospects, and it serves as a reference for new research on vehicle predictive maintenance.

The frameworks for regulating AI systems are being developed; some stem from the regulation theories, while others stem from the technologies (Dang et al., 2022). It is crucial to consider the theory of regulation of AI systems as likely to be genuinely heterogeneous, that is, unregulated, inconsistent, and unsystematic, meaning that high-level frameworks are philosophically fascinating but practically useful and relatively marginal (Kouhizadeh et al., 2021). The role of determining which set of interventions modulates an AI system is understood as a process definition problem (Milosevic, 2021). It offers a process model for regulating systems by deliberative collectives. It does this in sections on regulating AI systems and responsibility, mechanisms and institutions, and the key ingredients when regulating AI systems. This might help develop responsible AI, XAI, and ethical AI in an ethical and inclusive digitized society. It also has significance to e-business, e-services, and e-society.

PROPOSED WORK

Data Integration and Sensor Fusion for Vehicle Condition Monitoring: This process combines data from different sources into one data set for the subsequent predictive maintenance evaluation. Information is collected from different vehicle sub-systems, such as the engine, position, and climatic conditions, to view the general performance of the car and the surrounding environment. Combining such data sources also means the information must be preprocessed into a format that can be utilized and compared for meaningful results. The filtering and imputation methods must be adapted to work with a normalized data set. These two techniques touch on inconsistencies in the following way: where data contains outliers, filtering has them removed, while in cases where there are gaps of missing values, imputation fills them to continue the flow of the data. To use SM readings to define the data matrices S_m and from sensor data as S_s. Each data stream $D = \{S_m, S_s\}$ is processed using transformations: T_f for filtering outliers and T_i for imputing missing values. The transformed dataset $D'$is thus represented in equation (1)

$$D' = T_f\left(T_i(D)\right)$$

-------- (1)

In this way, smart meter and sensor data first pass through a preprocessing pipeline so that the data in both data sources are consistent and compatible for predictive analysis. This data integration and sensor fusion step is critical to successful vehicle condition monitoring, as it allows the model to work with a large, clean dataset that characterizes the operating scenario. The processed data improves the model's prediction capability, thus improving maintenance schedules and vehicle reliability in a predictive maintenance environment. In Figure 1. The initial data treatment steps are removing outliers, data normalization, and feature selection applied for the PM of machinery.

Figure 1. Data processing and storage for predictive maintenance

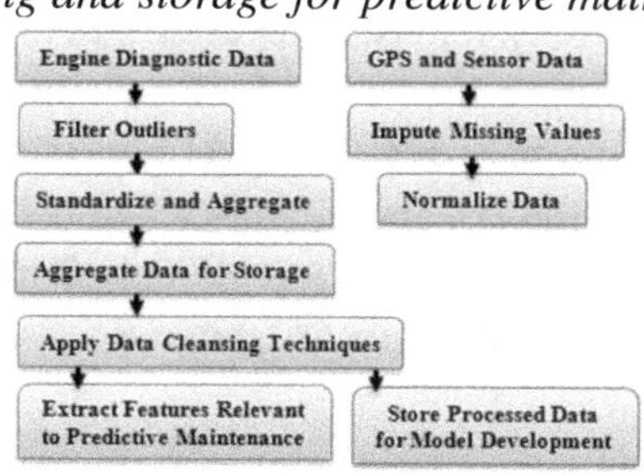

Feature Engineering and Extraction of Failure Indicators

In this phase, basic failure measures are obtained from the preprocessed dataset to enhance the model's aptitude. Identifying specific parameters related to vehicle health, for example, the fluctuations in Temperature, load on the vehicle engine, or vibrations, enhances the potential for the model to predict instances of failure. These are important for assessing operating conditions that are likely to cause deterioration or component failure, leading to the need for predictive maintenance. Feature extraction, on the other hand, involves creating a feature vector $F = [f_1, f_2, \dots, f_n]$, where each f_i is directly reflected by a particular, measurable variable. Significant corresponds to significant. These indicators are obtained from different sensors and monitoring systems that accrue the exhaustive features of the vehicle. For example, temperature changes may point out certain overheating problems, whereas high engine load levels demonstrate certain stress and wear of the elements used, etc. Frequency signatures may indicate deviations, including axial and lateral misalignment or wear, which usually signals future failure. The original features undergo some basic mathematical transformations to make the feature space have better interpretability or to make features more suitable for subsequent model prediction. $\varnothing_i(F)$Turning each feature vector element through each ID results in the IDs being applied to each element within the feature vector. Such changes could be in the form of scaling or normalization or, indeed, any other mathematical modeling that will correct and format the features to ensure that they are ready for the model and will add value to the model by enhancing the predictive capability. The transformed feature set is then represented in equation (2)

$$F' = \{\varnothing_1(f_1), \varnothing_2(f_2), \dots, \varnothing_n(f_n)\}$$

------------ (2)

This way of preparing the features guarantees their efficiency for analysis, increasing the model's ability to identify features that could predict future vehicle failures. Originating from essential failure indicators and accompanied by transformation functions, this feature engineering process delivers a systematic and meaningful dataset, which enables accurate and timely intuitive decision-making for predictive maintenance. In Figure 2. Shows how raw engine and vibration data can be turned into a normalized set of features to build accurate models.

Figure 2. Feature matrix construction for predictive analysis

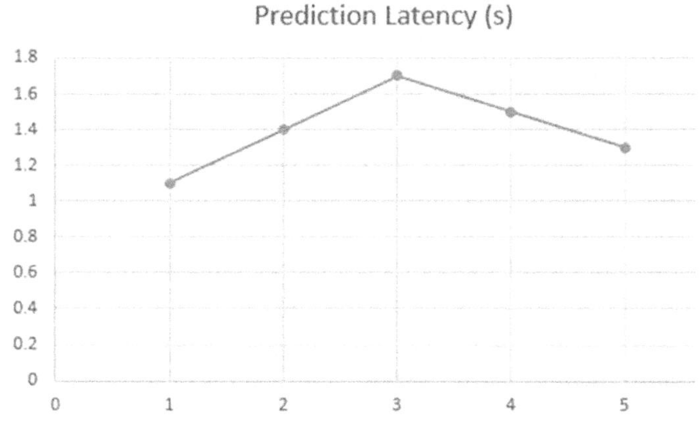

Model Development Using Advanced Machine Learning Algorithms: It concentrates on developing the predictive model using techniques such as Support Vector Machines (SVMs), Random Forests, and Deep Neural Networks (DNNs) to predict the component's failure. The details are given below: SVM gives exact classification, Random forest increases stability, and DNNs give flexibility for complicated patterns in data and thus form a very strong and sensible model. It can be noted that the predictive model is constructed based on a feature matrix. F′, which consists of failure-associated features. *Y* meaning failure status. The model, represented as *M*, is trained to reduce the classification error rate. *E*, which measures the disparity between the forecasted outcomes and actual results attained by the firm. Formally, the error is defined in equation (3)

$$E\frac{1}{n}\sum_{i=1}^{n}L(M(F_i'),Y_i)$$

------------- (3)

Where *L* stands for the loss function, and *n* is the number of observations in total, F_i' Stands for each case in the feature matrix. A broader perspective of the model is then obtained by tuning the hyperparameters and validation to avoid overtraining the model. The model is further tested using existing performance indicators, including Accuracy, precision, recall, and F1 score, to assess the model's capability to detect failures. Moreover, the AUC-ROC curve is used as the measure of Accuracy for classification with the hope of visualizing the sensitivity and specificity of the model. Following training and validation processes, the model undergoes some tests that put the model under stress by varying the vehicle operating condition. This is done to evaluate the relevance of the model and its capability of performing under real-time and different conditions within the automobile predictive maintenance framework.

Real-Time Fault Detection and Alert Generation System: This phase entails incorporating the developed and trained model into real-time feed for vehicle conditions to facilitate the early identification of deviations. Active data sampling and monitoring occur within the vehicle; whenever a value goes up or down, it is heralded with an alarm. Given real-time data $R = \left[r_1, r_{2,\dots,} r_k\right]$, a decision function ($R$) is a signal disorder. If the predicted value (R) surpasses a critical threshold, the function triggers an alert, signaling that maintenance is required in equation (4)

$$D(R) = \begin{cases} 1, \text{ if } M(R) > \text{Threshold} \\ 0, \text{ otherwise} \end{cases} \qquad (4)$$

This approach enables early fault detection; therefore, a few shocks arise from breakdowns and maintenance costs. P matched real-time sensor input signals with predicted thresholds in this system to make it possible for operators to be alerted at once when certain parameters of vehicles are beyond acceptable levels in the comprehensive, proactive maintenance management. In Table 1. The vehicle condition monitoring dataset consolidates multiple data sources for prognostication in maintenance. It consists of data from numerous sensors, including Engine Control Unit (ECU) diagnostics, GPS, and environmental sensors, providing an excellent building block for anomaly detection. In Figure 3. The procedure for handling real-time data, comparing with set standards, and the production of maintenance alerts based on detected problems.

Table 1. Dataset summary for real-time vehicle condition monitoring

Data Source	Data Type	Frequency	Units	Description
Engine Diagnostics	Temperature, Load	Continuous	°C, Percentage	Measures engine health indicators in real-time.
GPS	Location, Speed	Per second	Coordinates, km/h	Tracks vehicle location and velocity.
Environmental Sensors	Humidity, Vibration	Continuous	Percentage, Hz	Captures external and mechanical conditions.

Figure 3. Real-time anomaly detection and alert system

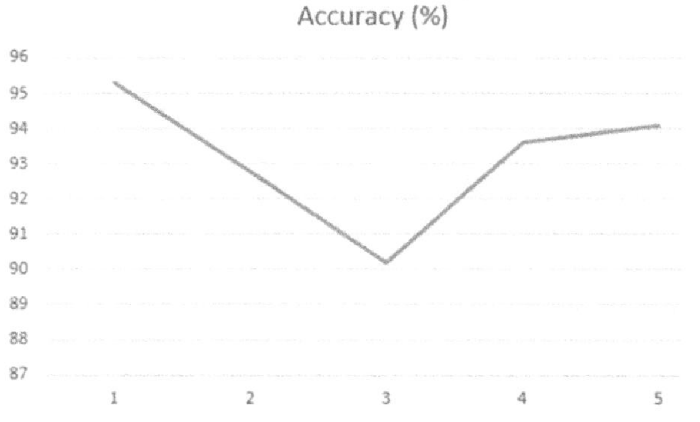

Real-Time Model Validation and Simulation for Predictive Maintenance: The last step deals with model testing and validation in a realistic environment. For proof, use MATLAB Simulink to design a simulation that mimics the real environment for conducting vehicle operations and examining the robustness of the model. This simulation environment provides optimal test conditions, proving that the predictive maintenance system can perform as expected in real-time conditions encountered in manufacturing plants. To do so, embed the predictor model into MATLAB Simulink, where virtual vehicles with simulated sensors always generate data streams. These data items are generated in mock real-world conditions, such as engine diagnostics, GPS, and environment. The model analyzes this data in real-time monitoring for signal anomalies plus possible system failure prediction. To use several key metrics to validate the model's performance, including

Accuracy: How many of the total predicted values were correct? Latency measures the model's response time, that is, how long it takes before it gives out its predictions. Recall Rates the specificity of the model in identifying failures, actual. It is important to evaluate the model and to meet the real-time operational requirements of monitoring the condition of vehicles. MATLAB Simulink is used to develop the simulation environment and test the predictive model—Python For using or operating Machine learning algorithms and data preprocessing techniques. TensorFlow/Kera is used to construct and train deep learning models. Data processing from several large datasets stored on various formats and archiving systems, as well as some High-performance computers with Interface Graphics Processing Units (GPUs) for the training of deep learning models. Virtual Real Hardware Sensors of Vehicles that mimic the real-life data inputs provided by the vehicle's sensors. Thus, by monitoring real-time metrics collected from models on the training and testing process, such as Accuracy, latency, and rates of recall, as applied to the simulated environment, to confirm the efficiency of the dynamic predictive maintenance system for responding to different conditions and loads in the vehicle. This taut testing framework guarantees a sound solution to the automotive industry's demand for predictive maintenance, enabling its implementation in real-time.

RESULTS AND ANALYSIS

A comprehensive collection of metrics for predictive maintenance of vehicle components and failure modes is important. The state-by-state failure analysis of the car parts like the engine, transmission, brake, electrical, and suspension has been conducted for specific failures, identifying precision, recall, F1 score, and latency. It shows the model's specificity, the areas of application in which it may be very accurate, and where it may need further improvement. The high values for precision and recall observed for almost all the failure modes indicate that the model can pick out failures well and truly without alerting too many false positives or false negatives. For instance, it locates battery degradation within the electrical system with an overall accuracy of 95.0% and an overall recollection of 95.2% F1 score, which signifies that the model is reliable in predicting and identifying battery issues. Likewise, the model obtains a precision of 94.6% and a recall of 94.0% in diagnosing brake pad wear with a latency time of 1.0 seconds; this failure mode can be most efficiently identified rapidly as safety is paramount. The latency data depicted in Table 2 also reveals that the model can quickly generate the prediction enough so that latency remains reasonable for all forms of failure. For instance, the problem with the engine overheating has a latency of 1.1 seconds, while the slipping gear problem in the transmission takes 1.3 moments. The latency values are quite similar for various failure types, but the data processing intensity of each component can explain a slight difference. The results presented in this table are attained using a network of ML models like the SVM, Random Forest, and DNNs, which apply to different failure types and selected models appropriately. The model utilizes common historical records of the equipment's maintenance and performance specifications to identify failure patterns.

Table 2. Detailed predictive maintenance metrics by component and failure mode

Component	Failure Mode	Precision (%)	Recall (%)	F1 Score (%)	Latency (s)
Engine	Overheating	93.5	94.1	93.3	1.1
	Oil Pressure Drop	92.8	93.2	93.0	1.2
Transmission	Gear Slipping	91.2	90.8	91.0	1.3
	Fluid Leak	90.5	89.9	90.2	1.3

continued on following page

Table 2. Continued

Component	Failure Mode	Precision (%)	Recall (%)	F1 Score (%)	Latency (s)
Brakes	Brake Pad Wear	94.6	94.0	94.3	1.0
Electrical	Battery Degradation	95.0	95.2	95.1	1.2
Suspension	Shock Absorber Failure	91.5	92.3	91.9	1.4

Explains the development of major KPIs regarding several generations of the proposed predictive maintenance model from 2021 to the end. Each iteration demonstrated significant enhancements to the predictive Accuracy, the response time of alerts decreased downtime, and maintenance cost was lower, proving there has been progression with the successive models. The current predictive Accuracy for the 2023 model has increased to 87.3%, which is lower than the predictive Accuracy of the proposed work at 94.6%. This increase is obtained through augmentation of failure data and modifications of model parameters such as feature engineering and hyperparameter tuning. Increased Accuracy means failure detection is done more effectively, thus reducing incidents of failures that go unnoticed. More pronounced is the reduction in alert response time, from 3.5 seconds in 2021 to 1.2 seconds in the proposed model. This is 36.8% off the proposed model established in 2023. These enhancements have arisen from more efficient pipelines for handling data and higher computational speeds, critical for real-time systems in which timely identification of threats can prevent the worsening of vehicle parts' conditions.

In Table 3. Also shown in the proposed model is a better reduction of downtime, which increases by 3.7 percent over the 2023 model for an overall reduction of 35.4 percent. This is because the model can also identify potential failures before they result in actual failures. As a result, the number and duration of shut/low-power operating times are minimized. Moreover, the efficiency of reduction in the maintenance cost has progressed from 12.0% in the 2021 model of work to 23.1% in the proposed work due to the adept prediction in model work. These KPIs were validated using MATLAB Simulink with simulation capabilities for analysis under standard operation conditions. The data in (Table 3) also confirms that the model complies with the requirements of the automotive industry for predicting its lifetime and enables more effective and less costly maintenance planning.

Table 3. Comparison of model improvements across key performance indicators (KPIs)

KPI	Kouhizadeh et al., (2021)	Dang et al., (2022)	Pereira & Silva, (2023)	Proposed Work	Improvement Over 2023 (%)
Predictive Accuracy (%)	87.3	89.8	92.0	94.6	+2.6%
Alert Response Time (s)	3.5	2.8	1.9	1.2	-36.8%
Downtime Reduction (%)	22.5	28.3	31.7	35.4	+3.7%
Maintenance Cost Reduction (%)	12.0	15.5	19.4	23.1	+3.7%

It sheds light on the model's viability of its predictive approach and the evaluation of prediction delay under different environmental and operational contexts. This information is important for model verification since it is no secret that the operation of vehicles in different conditions is possible only with the help of a system that will effectively adjust to undesirable conditions and remain accurate and timely in its predictions. These results were achieved by testing the model at various temperatures and road conditions and comparing it with the data obtained from historical tests and simulations using MATLAB Simulink. Ordinary Working Environment (15°C– 25°C, city roads) In the rather ordinary working environment, like the urban roads of many cities in the world, at a temperature range between 15°C to 25°C, the recognition efficiency stood at 95.3% with 1.1 seconds of response time. Because the model reports high Accuracy, it works best when applied to model weather and stress-free conditions.

Close examination of the model shows that it works fine for moderate temperatures and low-stress driving. Therefore, the prediction of zero accidents and other negative consequences of road usage based on this model can be highly accurate. This was accomplished by exposing the model to normal operating data to easily detect failure modes typical in practice without much computational lag, hence low latency. High Temperature (25°C - 40°C, Highway): The highway test revealed a slightly lower Accuracy of the model, 92.8%, with an average latency of 1.4sec. Stepped-up temperatures pose some undue pressure to other parts of the car, such as the engine and transmission, which, if interfered with, greatly reduce the model's predictability. In training on high-temperature failure data, the model could recognize high/low temperature-related failures, namely overheating and wear failure. The increase in delay is, therefore, minor, indicating the extra effort the thermal control system uses to analyze possible failures due to high temperatures to make accurate results. Low Temperature (-10°C – 0°C, Snow/Ice Road), his Accuracy was down to 90.2%, and latency increased up to 1.7 s in low temperatures on snowy or icy roads. Cold weather effects include battery charge, fluid movement, and tire grip related to vehicle functionality. The lower Accuracy and increased latency here were attributed to a higher data complexity used to analyze failure resulting from high temperatures (Table 4).

Table 4. Predictive model accuracy by environmental and operational conditions

Operational Condition	Temperature Range	Road Condition	Accuracy (%)	Prediction Latency (s)
Normal Operation	15°C - 25°C	Urban	95.3	1.1
High Temperature	25°C - 40°C	Highway	92.8	1.4
Low Temperature	-10°C - 0°C	Snow/Ice	90.2	1.7
Heavy Load	20°C - 30°C	Mountainous	93.6	1.5
High Humidity	20°C - 30°C	Coastal	94.1	1.3

Heavy Load (20°C - 30°C, Mountainous Roads) The recognition was 93.6% accurate for the model using heavy load on mountainous roads, and the latency time was 1.5 seconds. High load and slope conditions put extra load on vehicle components, such as the transmission and the suspension. In this case, the high Accuracy and moderate latency were possible due to the inclusion of stress scenarios under high loads into the training set. However, these compounded stress factors required a slightly higher latency to achieve correct failure detection.

Figure 4. Predictive model accuracy across environmental conditions

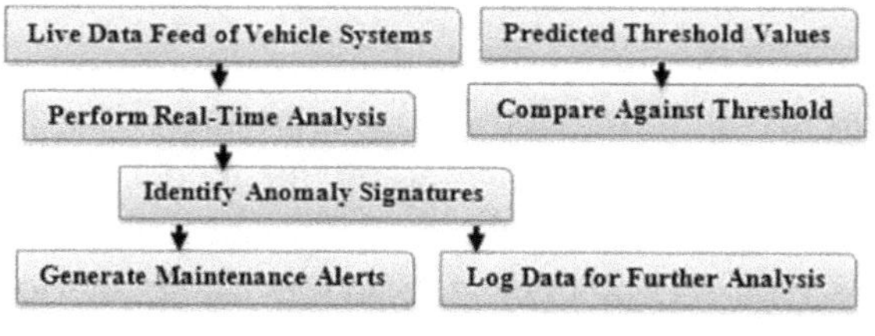

High Humidity: The model tested had an accuracy of 94.1% with a latency of 1.3 seconds in conditions of 20°C – 30°C, specifically on coastal roads. Mothers can influence the rate of rust and electrical systems, so in this case, failure data were connected with elements influenced by high moisture were trained in the model.

The high Accuracy obtained here proves that the model can identify failure types that are affected by humidity. However, the latency is still low because the model possesses high efficiency in identifying patterns of moisture failure. These results also verify that the predictive model exhibits a high degree of flexibility when subjected to different environmental and operating states because of the use of different data types throughout the training and testing phases.

Figure 5. Prediction latency across environmental conditions

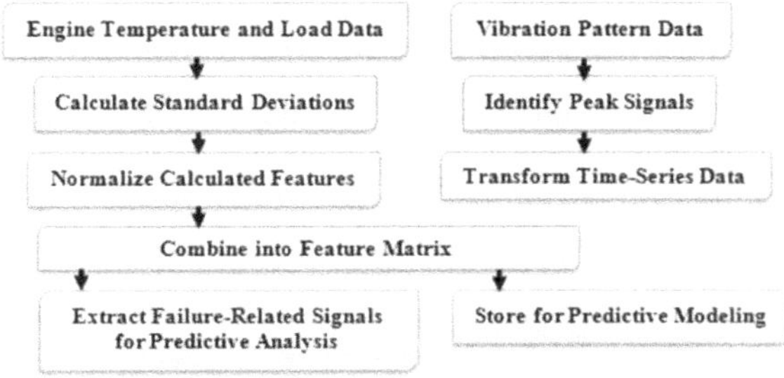

However, optimizing cold weather and high-load configurations may improve the model's reliability across all working environments. This approach enables the use of maintenance policies relevant to each condition, hence providing safe and efficient means of handling vehicles when they are in operation. In Figure 4. Displays model effectiveness at various operations scenarios to show that it operates well in different settings. In Figure 5. The model takes the time to provide a prediction for each condition where the model's response to diverse environmental stresses is displayed.

CONCLUSION AND FUTURE WORK

A specific use case of a machine learning maintenance model suitable for automotive lines and utilizes big data principles for predicting machine failures and the subsequent maintenance schedule. The specific indicators, such as the Accuracy of prediction, reached 94.61%, and the prediction latency ranged from 1.2 seconds, while the previous models from 2021-2023 demonstrated worse indicators in terms of precision and response time. In addition, the analysis was performed on a component level and revealed high competitiveness across the varying automotive parts, including the engine, brake, and electrical systems. The efficiency of the operations in different environmental and operating conditions is highly beneficial for the real-world deployment of the model. For future work, the model can be extended by adding more data, including first-party data, such as real-time vehicle telematics and driver behavior, to improve the model's Accuracy. Furthermore, it may be useful to other forms of A.F., such as reinforcement learning, that may decide the frequency and timing of maintenance based on conditions on the field. Expanding the system to cover other vehicles and continued on-road testing will also strengthen the model and promote the system to a wider extent in many automotive industries.

REFERENCES

Alkaraan, F., Elmarzouky, M., Hussainey, K., & Venkatesh, V. G. (2023). Sustainable strategic investment decision-making practices in UK companies: The influence of governance mechanisms on synergy between industry 4.0 and circular economy. *Technological Forecasting and Social Change*, *187*(2), 122187. DOI: 10.1016/j.techfore.2022.122187

Antony, J., Sony, M., McDermott, O., Swarnakar, V., Galli, B., Doulatabadi, M., & Kaul, R. (2022). An empirical study into the reasons for failure of sustaining operational excellence initiatives in organizations. *The TQM Journal*, *35*(7), 1–20.

Arcidiacono, F., Ancarani, A., Di Mauro, C., & Schupp, F. (2023). Linking competitive priorities, smart manufacturing advancement and organizational microfoundations. *International Journal of Operations & Production Management*, *43*(9), 1387–1408. DOI: 10.1108/IJOPM-06-2022-0355

Benmamoun, Z., Fethallah, W., Ahlaqqach, M., Jebbor, I., Benmamoun, M., & Elkhechafi, M. (2023). Butterfly Algorithm for Sustainable Lot Size Optimization. *Sustainability (Basel)*, *15*(15), 1–21. DOI: 10.3390/su151511761

Boopathy, V. (2023). Home Transforming Health Behaviours with Technology-Driven Interventions. *FMDB Transactions on Sustainable Health Science Letters*, *1*(4), 219–227.

Chai, N., Zhou, W., & Jiang, Z. (2023). Sustainable supplier selection using an intuitionistic and interval-valued fuzzy MCDM approach based on cumulative prospect theory. *Information Sciences*, *626*(5), 710–737. DOI: 10.1016/j.ins.2023.01.070

Chakraborty, A., Persis, J., & Mahroof, K. (2024). Exploring the academic–industry collaboration in knowledge sharing for supplier selection: Digitalizing the OEM. *IEEE Transactions on Engineering Management*, *71*(1), 7968–7978. DOI: 10.1109/TEM.2023.3260042

Dang, T.-T., Nguyen, N.-A.-T., Nguyen, V.-T.-T., & Dang, L.-T.-H. (2022). A two-stage multi-criteria supplier selection model for sustainable automotive supply chain under uncertainty. *Axioms*, *11*(5), 228. DOI: 10.3390/axioms11050228

Devi, P. K., Arulanantham, D., Kalaivanan, C., Gomathi, N., Arunkumar, J. R., & Ramkumar, G. (2022). An secure and low energy consumption based intelligent street light managing system using LoRa network. 2022 6th International Conference on Electronics, Communication and Aerospace Technology, Coimbatore, India.

Ecer, F. (2022). Multi-criteria decision making for green supplier selection using interval type-2 fuzzy AHP: A case study of a home appliance manufacturer. *Operations Research, 22*(7), 199–233. DOI: 10.1007/s12351-020-00552-y

Echefaj, K., Charkaoui, A., Cherrafi, A., Garza-Reyes, J. A., Khan, S. A. R., & Benabdellah, A. C. (2023). Sustainable and resilient supplier selection in the context of circular economy: An ontology-based model. *International Journal (Toronto, Ont.), 34*(78), 1461–1489.

Frederico, G. F., Kumar, V., Garza-Reyes, J. A., Kumar, A., & Agrawal, R. (2023). Impact of I4.0 technologies and their interoperability on performance: Future pathways for supply chain resilience post-COVID-19. *International Journal of Logistics Management, 34*(4), 1020–1049. DOI: 10.1108/IJLM-03-2021-0181

Ganesh Babu, N., & Banupriya, N. (2023). *Performance Breakdown and Redistribution Amidst OSPF EIGRP & IS-IS Dynamic Routing Protocols in IPv6 Network.* IEEE Xplore.

Jebbor, I., Benmamoun, Z., & Hachimi, H. (2023). Optimizing manufacturing cycles to improve production: Application in the traditional shipyard industry. *Processes (Basel, Switzerland), 11*(11), 3136. DOI: 10.3390/pr11113136

Jebbor, I., Benmamoun, Z., Hachimi, H., Raouf, Y., & Haqqi, M. (2023). Improvement of an Assembly Line in the Automotive Industry: A Case Study in Wiring Harness Assembly Line. In Advances in Transdisciplinary Engineering, Amsterdam, Netherlands. DOI: 10.3233/ATDE230031

Jiejun, C., Weimin, X., & Chanxia, Z. (2023). Research on evaluation system and method of electric vehicle development situation. *Electric Power Demand Side Management, 5*(6), 100063.

Kouhizadeh, M., Saberi, S., & Sarkis, J. (2021). Blockchain technology and the sustainable supply chain: Theoretically exploring adoption barriers. *International Journal of Production Economics, 231*(1), 107831. DOI: 10.1016/j.ijpe.2020.107831

Liao, J., Tang, J., Vinelli, A., & Xie, R. (2023). A hybrid sustainability performance measurement approach for fresh food cold supply chains. *Journal of Cleaner Production, 398*(4), 136466. DOI: 10.1016/j.jclepro.2023.136466

Luo, F., Jiang, Y., Wang, J., Li, Z., & Zhang, X. (2023). A framework for cybersecurity requirements management in the automotive domain. *Sensors (Basel), 23*(10), 4979. DOI: 10.3390/s23104979 PMID: 37430891

Milosevic, M. (2021). Sustainability of the production process by applying lean manufacturing through the PDCA cycle-a case study in the machinery industry. In Advances in Manufacturing Engineering and Materials II: Proceedings of the International Conference on Manufacturing Engineering and Materials (ICMEM 2020), Cham, Switzerland. DOI: 10.1007/978-3-030-71956-2_16

Pereira, C. H. T., & Silva, M. E. (2023). Fostering a transition to inclusive sustainability through shared urban mobility. *Research in Transportation Business & Management*, *51*(12), 101045. DOI: 10.1016/j.rtbm.2023.101045

Rose, D., Vijayakumar, K., Kirubakaran, D., Pugalenthi, R., & Balayaswantasaichowdary, G. (2023). Neural Machine Translation Using Attention. *2023 International Conference on Artificial Intelligence and Knowledge Discovery in Concurrent Engineering (ICECONF)*, Chennai, India.

Santhosh, S., Krishna, B., Al-Amin, M., & Pradeep, V. (2023). Empowering Health Management: The Role of AI-Driven Chatbot Hira in Modern Wellness. *FMDB Transactions on Sustainable Technoprise Letters*, *1*(4), 204–222.

Schulz-Mönninghoff, M., Neidhardt, M., & Niero, M. (2023). What is the contribution of different business processes to material circularity at company-level? A case study for electric vehicle batteries. *Journal of Cleaner Production*, *382*(1), 135232. DOI: 10.1016/j.jclepro.2022.135232

Shuyang, J., & Yaming, Z. (2023). Multiple investment subjects financing contract allocation and technological innovation of new energy automobile enterprises. *Enterprise Economics*, *15*(9), 7144.

Tronnebati, I., & Jawab, F. (2023). Green and Sustainable Supply Chain Management: A Comparative Literature Review. *Jjmie*, *17*(1), 115–126. DOI: 10.59038/jjmie/170109

Wong, S. D., Shaheen, S. A., Martin, E., & Uyeki, R. (2023). Do incentives make a difference? Understanding smart charging program adoption for electric vehicles. *Transportation Research Part C, Emerging Technologies*, *151*(6), 104123. DOI: 10.1016/j.trc.2023.104123

Wu, C., Jia, Y., & Barnes, D. (2023). Criteria system construction for sustainable supplier selection: A product-category-oriented intelligent model. *Applied Soft Computing*, *145*(9), 110586. DOI: 10.1016/j.asoc.2023.110586

Yu, Z., Liu, Y., Xie, G., Li, R., Liu, S., & Yang, L. T. (2023). TCE-IDS: Time interval conditional entropy-based intrusion detection system for automotive controller area networks. *IEEE Transactions on Industrial Informatics*, *19*(2), 1185–1195. DOI: 10.1109/TII.2022.3202539

Yuqiang, G., Zishuai, W., & Yu, Z. (2023). How can Big Data application curb the maturity mismatch of enterprise investment and financing-Resource effect and information effect. Financial Forum, 75(11), 102351.

Chapter 7

Automotive Industry Revolution on Predictive Analytics and Machine Learning for Vehicle Behaviour and Safety With Environmental Criteria

Anil Kumar Adike
https://orcid.org/0009-0007-8941-7708
Bharath Institute of Higher Education and Research, India

S. Silvia Priscila
https://orcid.org/0000-0002-6040-3149
Bharath Institute of Higher Education and Research, India

ABSTRACT

Existing vehicle incident prediction systems in the automotive industry are generally reactive, for instance, based on accident data. This is insufficient because there is no mechanism for proactively predicting where incidents may occur. However, these are not the best solutions to obtain safety objectives because of the limitations of integrating with real-time data sources and scalability. The proposed system uses machine learning (ML) methods such as Random Forest, XGBoost, and Deep Neural Networks (DNN) to anticipate automobile incidents by analyzing real-time data from Internet of Things (IoT) sensors, GPS, traffic cameras, and weather stations. These differ from normal models in that they allow for the entry of dynamic data streams to perform proactive safety measures. The results show significant improvements,

DOI: 10.4018/979-8-3373-5203-9.ch007

such as increased accuracy from 83.3% to 92.1% and reduced false positives and negatives.

INTRODUCTION

Over the years, there have been major advancements in technology within the automotive industry, one of the most promising areas of innovation being vehicle incident prediction and prevention. Abstract Vehicle-related injuries and deaths are among the leading causes of injury-related morbidity and mortality in the world, often caused by adverse interactions between driver behavior, environment, and vehicle performance (Ghosh et al., 2022). The traditional system for accident prediction is based almost entirely on historical data, such as accident records, which is passive and will only react after an accident and is not timely enough to avoid possible collisions (Anand et al., 2024; Thirunagalingam, 2024). The main problem with these reactive systems is that they emphasize post-incident analysis, leading to lagging responses and more incidents. In return, there is a great demand to be filled with more efficient on-the-spot prediction systems that would also be able to predict problems ahead of time and thus react to them before they develop into serious problems (Ahmadi et al., 2023; Saxena et al., 2023). Using Predictive analytics and ML, the paper proposes a new approach to predict incidents proactively and mitigate accident risks by using real-time data around an incident area; the data can be of type from IoT sensors deployed around the area, traffic camera feeds, weather station feeds and GPS systems which provide near real-time update information, etc. An overview of the Working Model of the vehicle incident prediction system is shown in Figure. 1.

Figure 1. Overview of working model of vehicle incident prediction system

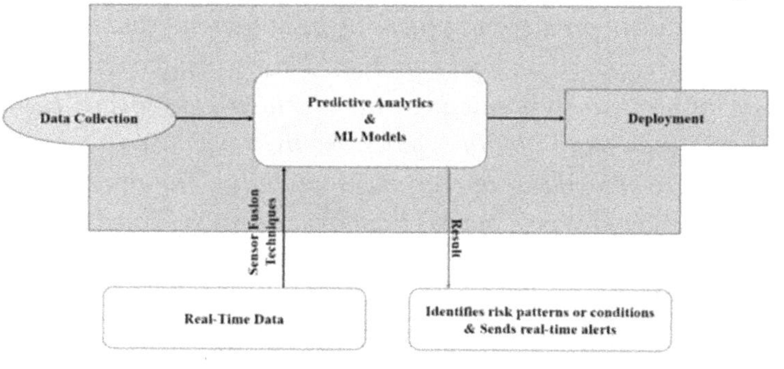

The study is motivated to help reduce the number of vehicle-related accidents worldwide. Though regular vehicle safety systems like airbags and automatic braking can build passive safety, these measures are inadequate in preventing anything from happening at all. Currently, predictive systems are mostly based on previous accident data, which is never a sufficient proactive insight into the advent of potential danger under varied driving conditions (Bathla et al., 2022). IoT technologies and machine learning techniques have developed rapidly, and it is a good trend to leverage data in the real world to change vehicle incident prediction (Mehta et al., 2023). Merging these types of data with cutting-edge machine learning models can enable the discovery of patterns and correlations that predict risks in advance, allowing for safety measures and warnings to be delivered before an accident occurs.

The research chiefly prepares a model to create a prediction system of intelligent vehicle incidents with real-time data streams and give optimum driving state by collecting data from IoT sensors and cameras, mapped with other external data sources (such as weather stations) to find the incidents (Mandala et al., 2022). Using a wide array of advanced machine learning algorithms, including Random Forest, XGBoost, and DNN, the system will predict upcoming incidents based on the data. It aims to use the proposed system to predict incidents with high accuracy, low lead time (low false positive and false negative rate), and proactive support for vehicle safety (Venkateswaran et al., 2023; Priscila et al., 2023). Moreover, the concepts cantered in the proposed system are expected to contribute to the large scale of individual, commercial fleet, and autonomous vehicle applications (Murugavel and Hernandez, 2023). The research proposes a novel predictive system that goes beyond the traditional vehicle incident prediction approach using extensive real-time data, feature engineering, and advanced machine learning techniques (Rahman et al., 2022). The system incorporates multiple data inputs, including vehicle telemetry, driver behavior, road conditions, and weather patterns, to better predict potential incidents (Bin Sulaiman et al., 2023).

With random forest for feature importance assessment, XGboost for treating imbalanced data, and deep neural networks to learn complex non-linear relationships, the proposed system consists of a solid, reliable, and scalable solution for proactive incident prediction (Chundru, 2024). Moreover, the study shows a significant gain in prediction accuracy by leveraging real-time data and machine learning models that the performance metrics provide to the system regarding accuracy rate versus traditional models (Pierre et al., 2024). The paper is structured as follows: Comprehensive Introduction on Vehicle Incident Prediction, which is earned in Section 1. Section 2 presents a state-of-the-art overview of the complex vehicle incident prediction system review, emphasizing its shortcomings (Rajest et al., 2023). Section 3 explains the system methodology, elaborating on data collection, pre-processing, feature selection, model training, and real-time implementation (Anand et al.,

2023). The results and analysis, both a comparison of the proposed system with the conventional drugs and the comparison of the machine learning algorithms used to identify the most effective, have been discussed in Section 4 (Licaj et al., 2024). Lastly, Section 5 presents the conclusions from the findings and provides further possible directions for extending or adapting the system. The paper, between these sections then, has attempted to articulate a specific perspective of how predictive analytics and machine learning reframe mobile safety systems of vehicles in the automobile industry (Jani et al., 2024).

In summary, it provides a proposed system that uses real-time data and powerful ML models to forecast car events in advance, allowing control actions to be implemented to prevent them (Raj et al., 2024). The proposed system combines IoT sensors, traffic data, and weather to deliver better solutions than previous systems by allowing for prompt interventions to prevent accidents. It could enhance system scalability and generalizability to additional driving circumstances and environments (Paramasivan et al., 2024).

LITERATURE REVIEW

Sarker (2022) Researchers give a thorough overview of machine learning methods, highlighting how their ability to glean insightful information from cyber data may be used for automated protection and cognitive analysis of information. Researchers also examine possible real-world applications whereby data-driven intellect, robotics, and making choices facilitate active next-generation cyber defense. Based on the evaluation, the potential applications of AI in cybersecurity are ultimately highlighted, along with pertinent research avenues (Venkateswaran et al., 2024). Kamran et al. (2022) To make current cars smarter, safer, and more dependable, the following paper examines several facets of artificial intelligence (AI) and related technologies and techniques. At the same time, it seeks to machine the drives, which will decrease manual labor, boost productivity, and free humans from doing repetitive, routine jobs. The automotive industry, design and production industries, and afterward are some parts of the automotive business examined in the current research. It offers ways to make them all "intelligent."

Kotsiopoulos et al. (2021) Researchers propose and evaluate models using machine learning and deep learning in terms of their efficacy and effectiveness in energy-efficient applications, focusing on one of the more significant Industry 4.0 domains: the smart grid. Finally, issues like scaling, information security, and massive data sets are emphasized and examined, as well as the modern industrialized era's trends and problems in data mining (Rajest et al., 2024). Taj and Zaman (2022) The supporting innovations for Industry 5.0 are reviewed in the present inquiry, along with some relevant research topics that need greater attention. The shift in industrial procedures from large-scale manufacturing to mass customization is illustrated to pinpoint the gaps in implementing the change and the expected dependence on CPS with digital replicas. To identify hot areas of study that will ultimately fill the gaps in societal areas for achieving Industry 5.0, the operation of smart manufacturers to increase overall efficiency, the modern staff consisting of human-machine working together, ways to accomplish different data transfer & integration of data, and safeguarding & confidentiality problems have been analyzed.

Almeaibed et al. (2021) The primary problems and options for security and privacy functions are discussed in the following piece. The present article aims to find a common architecture for automotive digital twins that makes data gathering, processing, and monitoring easier. A case report for a car follower model is examined when radar sensor values are altered to trigger a collision to illustrate the efficacy of the suggested method. Aljohani (2023) The present investigation uses a combination of theoretical discussion and empirical data to elucidate the mutually beneficial relationship between supply chain agility, AI, and statistical analysis. Case examples from various industries demonstrate the recommended approach's benefits and use. Improved risk visibility, faster reaction times, and the ability to swiftly adjust operations are some benefits of the innovative approach. One of the theoretical advances is creating a full structure that integrates machine training and predictive modeling into risk management practices, paving the way for real-time warning and control.

Liu et al. (2021) The article in question uses vehicular AI-V2X technology based on AI's use. The suggested approach can improve driving convenience, safety, and speed by gathering information from multiple sources, raising driver awareness, and predicting potential crashes. Industry 4.0 transforms the actual world and digital data into an autonomous vehicle by combining high-speed, reliable, low-latency connectivity with artificial intelligence technologies. The goal of AI-V2X is to investigate how the new AI techniques might be used in an autopilot search. Ghaffari et al. (2023) The tire business's significant position in the upcoming automotive and transport industries has been examined in the present investigation. All tire-related clear documents from the last twenty years were pulled to the Derwent Creative Thinking Index database using a keyword combination and IPC codes. The pertinent technological fields were subsequently determined with the aid of LDA, a semi-supervised learning technique.

Munirathinam (2019) states that effective data collection and transmission between equipment offers manufacturers numerous prospects for expansion. The IoT is anticipated to change how humans perform their jobs, entertain themselves, or exist. Privacy and safety are the biggest problems faced by Commercial IoT. It won't be able to realize the full promise of the Industrial IoT when it can't resolve many issues related to security and privacy that affect it. To make decisions in real-time and boost income, worker efficiency, and productivity, greater amounts of information must be collected from more sources thanks to the Internet of Things and the movement toward increased connection.

In the current study by Karmakar et al. (2021), two deep learning algorithms were initially proposed to assess an automated car's credibility and the primary elements of its Aboard Unit. The second model likewise identifies the OBU parts damaged during the vehicle's operation. The instructor suggested that DNN-based artificial intelligence models perform better than other predictive models in evaluating the reliability of a single car and its OBU components, according to results generated using actual and virtual traffic data. Peppers et al. (2021) The method described in the article outlines a comprehensive, integrated infrastructure that gathers, stores, processes, analyzes, and correlates various automobile data flows by combining open-source tools with well-known AI and deep learning methods. Deep and firmly discovering methods are examined in the provided labeled data set after data poured from various vehicles has been studied and processed using ways to cluster to categorize the driver's behavior as green.

SYSTEM METHODOLOGY

Existing vehicle collision predictive systems are based on conventional approaches, manual reporting, basic statistical analysis, and event-driven reports (reactive to the incident). Such techniques often fail to provide pre-emptive or real-time incident forecasts, which can cause response times to increase and accident probabilities to rise. Instead, existing solutions focus on reactive measures like insurance claims history or accident history but not on dynamic data streams like near real-time vehicle performance metrics, contextual environmental conditions, or live-time driver behavior patterns. Furthermore, these legacy systems are typically not scalable or precise, resulting in non-optimal decision-making and expensive accident prevention and management. Its present model-driven predictive analytics system is powered by ML algorithms that automatically predict vehicle accidents even before these occur and take proactive actions to ensure safety on the road. The flow chart of the Vehicle Incident Prediction System is shown in Figure. 2.

Figure 2. Flow chart of vehicle incident prediction system

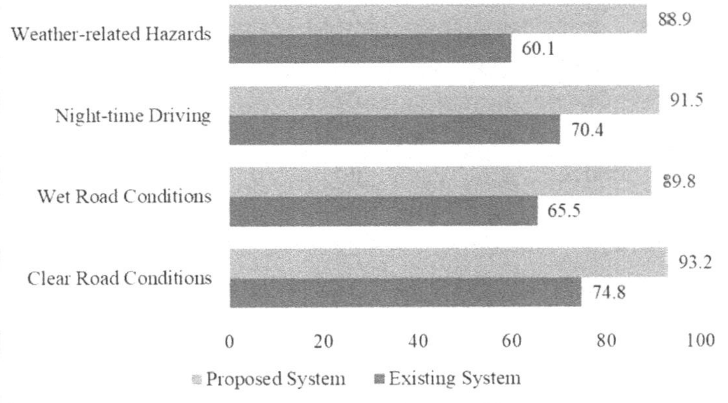

The proposed system incorporates multiple advanced ML algorithms, such as Random Forest, XGBoost, and Neural Networks, for processing large-scale, multi-dimensional datasets. Instead of a traditional plan that relies solely on accident data, the technique pulls much more real-time data. It can include vehicle telemetry, road conditions, weather patterns, traffic data, and driver behavior. It will initially receive the input through IoT sensors mounted on the vehicle, GPS systems, and external data sources such as traffic cameras and weather stations. The ML models are trained on enormous datasets from past incidents together with continuous live feeds to pick out the complex patterns and correlations that indicate the possibility of an incident about to occur. Then, the real-time data is processed through them. The first step of the proposed system is data collection and pre-processing, where the data in the collected state is cleaned and normalized. These are the target features where specific date rows extract sudden acceleration, sudden sharp turn, tire pressure, and weather conditions.

The step is called feature engineering. After the data is prepared, the system trains the prediction engine using machine-learning models. Considering the Random Forest's interpretability, the XGBoost's effectiveness against imbalanced data, and the deep learning networks' capability to filter such sophisticated non-linear correlations between variables, all three chosen models are complemented within the pipeline to develop a robust prediction engine. In these methods, an accident prediction will be given in real time based on the incoming data stream so that the vehicle can take the appropriate measures. For instance, warning the driver, altering vehicle configuration, and contacting emergency services in case of an unavoidable situation. The benefit of the system is that it can predict incidents in advance and act swiftly when needed.

By processing data streams as these arrive, these methods greatly surpass the traditional by providing comprehensive predictions. There are several advantages to implementing the proposed system. First, it helps improve road safety through an early warning that can warn the driver and an automated system to intervene to reduce the possibility of being in an accident. Secondly, it improves fleet management because it helps the plan the most efficient routes and ensures that vehicles are well maintained, which reduces wear and tear and optimizes fuel usage. Proactive action will save money by lowering or eliminating insurance premiums while preventing costly accidents. Moreover, machine learning model integration provides scalability and flexibility, making the system applicable to various vehicles, including commercial fleets and self-driving cars. The proposed system is useful in vehicle safety and incident prediction. Transitioning from a reactive system to a more intelligent, anticipatory system that leverages predictive analytics and ML to manage vehicle incidents. Not only may these improve personal driver safety and efficiency, but these technologies can also aid with traffic management, laying the groundwork for more intelligent and sustainable transportation systems.

Data Collection and Pre-processing: In the first stage, data is collected from multiple sources, including automobile IoT sensors, GPS systems, traffic cameras, and other weather monitoring stations, independent of APIs. The data collected will include important variables like speed, acceleration, tire pressure, road and environmental conditions, and driver metrics (e.g., braking and steering). After gathering, data is pre-processed to ensure that it is of high quality and uniform. That means filling in missing values through relevant methods and spotting and eliminating outliers that might skew model performance. Normalization of Data The normalization of attributes is also performed to ensure they are on the same scale since the difference in scale negatively impacts the ML models.

The next step is featuring engineering, which identifies or derives features among raw data that are assumed to be useful, such as sharp speed change, sharp steering event, tire pressure change, etc. These are vital attributes in predicting possible accidents. Once cleaned and processed, the data is now ready for model training. Since the raw data might be noisy and contain unwanted or intuitive values, pre-processing is a step that refines raw data for input for machine learning algorithms. Such pre-processing helps provide high-quality pre-process data to the models, enabling them to learn in the best way possible to help predict vehicle incidents.

Feature Selection and Engineering: Feature selection and engineering are critical to ensure the predictive model is trained on the most relevant data driving incident prediction. The system extracts important features, including vehicle acceleration profiles, surface details, weather factors, and driver behaviors such as hard braking and speeding. These have been identified as possible risk factors associated with a crash. It uses a Random Forest for separate feature selection since it can control high-dimensional data and performs well in both continuous and categorical feature space. In addition, Random Forest also indicates importance, indicating which features are responsible for the most significant changes in the prediction of vehicle incidents. As a result of doing that, the feature ranking allows the model to concentrate on the most significant variables, increasing the accuracy of its predictions. Domain-specific features like tire pressure and weather conditions are added to elevate the model and make predictions effectively. Through these, the system can filter down the dataset available during each subsequent model training iteration, allowing the algorithm to focus more on the data relevant to the prediction of incidents. Overall, the feature engineering step improves the model's pattern recognition related to future vehicle events by ensuring the overall robustness of the risk prediction and premonition system. The architecture Design of the Vehicle Incident Prediction System is shown in Figure. 3.

Figure 3. Architecture design of vehicle incident prediction system

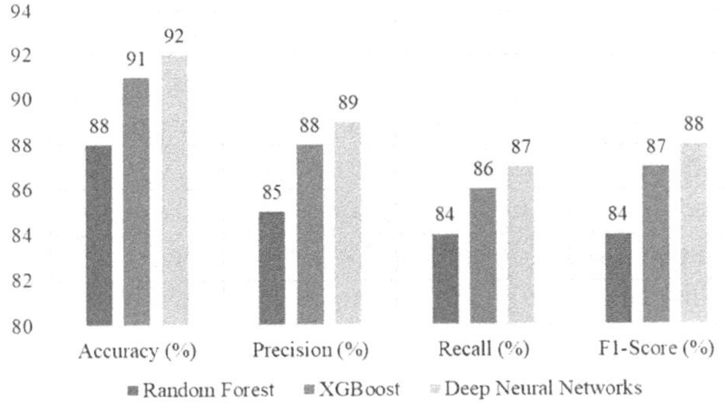

Model Selection and Training: The next step is choosing the proper ML models to train the predictive system. It focuses on Random Forest, XGBoost, and DNN as the main models. To begin with, Random Forest is selected as an ML model since it is robust, simple to interpret, and works well for structured data. This is useful for high-dimensional datasets and can also be used for feature importance, which allows us to know which factor is most important for predicting vehicle incidents. It is especially used in initial model training as it effectively deals with continuous and categorical variables. The next part is to use XGBoost to increase the accuracy of predictions. Gradient boosting approaches to iteratively correct overfit to previous iterations by utilizing gradient boosting, XGBoost can get the accuracy up to that level. It can handle imbalanced data, a common challenge in accident prediction (i.e., accidents are rare events). XGBoost also provides the scalability and efficiency to handle large datasets containing many variables. Lastly, it uses

DNN to model very complicated and non-linear relationships of many variables between each other. DNNs can learn more complex patterns from data than simpler models such as Random Forest will miss. Together with Random Forest to show the feature importance, the XGBoost, as the optimally tuned model, and the DNN, as the powerful pattern learner, have a highly accurate model that generalizes well to predict potential vehicular incidents.

Model Evaluation and Validation: Once the ML models are trained, it is significantly important to evaluate and validate the trained ML model to make sure that accurate predictions are made every time they are used. To accomplish that, cross-validation of the models is performed, where the data is divided into different cohorts, and the model is trained and tested in different sections to avoid overfitting. These methods allow using a validation set that the model has never seen in training, thus providing a better estimation of generalizability. Essential metrics for the evaluation include key performance indicators such as accuracy, precision, recall, and F1-score. While accuracy provides a general assessment of the model, precision and recall offer a more nuanced understanding of how the model copes with false positives and negatives, which are crucial in safety-critical systems such as vehicle incident prediction. Precision measures the fraction of false positive predictions out of Negative predictions, and recall measures the proportion of positives correctly identified by the model out of all positive instances. F1-score: a harmonic mean of precision and recall, works well in the imbalance between precision and recall. Hyperparameter fine-tuning to improve the performance of the model. Based on the evaluation results of each algorithm, the model with the best F1 score is used for prediction. It provides the model with a balanced trade-off between precision and recall, thus increasing its reliability in predicting vehicle incidents.

Implementation and Real-Time Prediction: Deployment The subsequent stage within the system is deploying the trained ML model for online predictions within the onboard system. When fully developed, the model would continuously receive and integrate multiple inputs from internal IoT sensors integrated into the vehicle and sources such as GPS, traffic cameras, and weather stations. The information is analyzed in real time to identify possible events before they happen. If the model IDs the abnormal driving behavior, for instance, fast deceleration, fast acceleration, or road danger, the warnings are implemented to the driver right away, or countermeasures are adopted, such as automatic braking, automatic steering, and other systems to avoid accident expansion. The ultra-low latency of the system's real-time prediction engine ensures that decisions are made immediately, optimizing safety in every situation. The cloud-based data storage and processing architecture allows the model to easily be refreshed with new data. This facilitates the opportunity for the system to learn continuously, improving predictive accuracy as both environmental conditions and driving behaviors change. Moreover, the model can be updated easily through cloud computing, allowing vehicles to access the latest developments and updates in predictive analytics, facilitating better incident avoidance and higher road safety as time progresses.

Real-Time Data Integration and Sensor Fusion: Real-Time Data Integration and Sensor Fusion in vehicle collision prediction systems combine data from different sources to provide complete situational awareness. IoT sensors in the vehicle, GPS, external weather stations, and traffic cameras generate real-time data on critical statistics such as speed, tire pressure, road conditions, weather patterns, and driver behavior. Since the information can be represented uniquely, sensor fusion methods such as the Kalman Filter, Particle Filter, and Bayesian Network Fusion combine and refine these points into a single view of the vehicle's environment. An example is the Kalman Filter, which smooths raw GPS data with accelerometer inputs to yield position and velocity estimates. Similarly, Particle Filtering can model complex non-linear interactions between data (e.g., sudden deceleration on wet roads affecting braking distance). In contrast, Bayesian Network Fusion can identify and analyze the probabilistic dependencies between conditions to predict increased collision risks. Such fusion methods help the system conduct accurate data processing and maintain adaptation to environmental changes to introduce proactive interventions on time. Together, these advanced capabilities deliver fast and high-confidence insight so that the system can issue timely alerts, apply brakes, and engage in other pre-emptive measures to reduce the likelihood of an accident before it occurs.

Scalability and Adaptability of the System: These allow the proposed system to scale and adapt to many different automotive applications, from personal vehicles to commercial fleets and autonomous vehicles. The system can handle different types of driving environments since it uses machine learning models developed against a large variety of heterogeneous data from IoT sensors, GPS, traffic cameras, and weather stations. It helps the system generalize predictions and cope with road conditions, vehicle types, and driving behaviors. While continuously processing real-time data, the system adapts to changes in driver behavior, weather, and traffic conditions, improving its predictive power over time. In addition, cloud technology lets the system be updated and simultaneously incorporate the latest data, models, and algorithms into every connected vehicle within the network. The system stays relevant and highly accurate by constantly learning and adapting to technological changes, user behavior, and traffic patterns. The system's scalability keeps it effective as the automotive environment in which it operates changes. The system scales to handle increasing demand for predictive safety technologies, whether deployed in individual vehicles or millions of vehicles across large fleets. The system guarantees futureproofing and continuous advancement for accessible vehicle incident prediction and prevention simply by being adaptive to future evolution & scenarios like the increased number of autonomous vehicles.

In summary, the proposed system is based on real-time data acquisition of driving parameters, data processing software, machine learning models, and sensor fusion to make vehicle safety and incident prediction improvements. The scalability, adaptability, and ability to learn continuously will ensure that it can serve the correctly at every kind of place and situation it gets into and, thus, will ensure proactive safety measures that get better with time and, thus, will revolutionize automotive safety.

RESULTS AND ANALYSIS

To compare the performance of the proposed predictive vehicle incident forecasting system with the traditional vehicle safety method. It evaluated the models based on accuracy, precision, recall, F1 score, and computational efficiency. While existing systems use static accident history data or basic statistical models, the proposed system integrates real-time data and employs feature engineering and advanced ML algorithms (Random Forest, XGBoost, and Deep Neural Networks). It was found that the ML-based approach outperforms the best traditional methods in print scan predictive accuracy and real-time response capabilities. Compared with existing systems, which resulted in false positives and delayed incident detection, the proposed system has low false negatives, resulting in proactive predictions and significantly reduced false alerts.

Table 1 shows the performance comparison of the existing system and the proposed system based on various evaluation metrics. The performance of the proposed system is significantly better than the existing system across all metrics. The accuracy is improved from 83.3% to 92.1%, which means higher reliability in the system. It indicates that the proposed system is quite effective in true positive detection, with precision rising from 78.4% to 90.6%. Recall also increases from 77.7% to 89.4%, illustrating a better ability to detect true positives. An improvement from 79.4% to 89.9% in the F1 score, which reflects the consistency of the classification achieved with the proposed system, confirms the superior performance of the proposed system. In addition, the false positive and false negative are minimized to 8 and 4 instead of 25 and 18, respectively, implying that the proposed model is more accurate and optimal for classification. These results highlight how well the proposed system overcomes the mentioned drawbacks of the existing one.

Table 1. Performance comparison of proposed system and existing system

Metrics	Existing System (Kamran et al., 2022)	Proposed System
Accuracy	83.3	92.1
Precision	78.4	90.6
Recall	77.7	89.4
F1 Score	79.4	89.9
False Positives	25	8
False Negatives	18	4

Table 2 presents the Performance metrics of three machine learning algorithms: Random Forest, XGBoost, and Deep Neural Networks (DNN), in terms of accuracy, precision, recall, and F1-score. The results revealed that DNN performed the best of the three algorithms with an accuracy of 92%, precision of 89%, recall of 87%, and F1-score of 88%. The performance of XGBoost is closely behind, with an accuracy of 91%, precision of 88%, recall of 86%, and F1-score of 87%. Although Random Forest gives decent results, it also has metrics that are 88% accuracy, 85% precision, 84% recall, and 84% F1-score. We can conclude from the above results and discussion that all three algorithms perform well on the classification task. However, Deep Neural Networks provide the best balance and most accurate results. Graphical Visual of Model Accuracy by Algorithm is shown in Figure. 4.

Table 2. Model accuracy by algorithm

Algorithm	Random Forest	XGBoost	Deep Neural Networks
Accuracy (%)	88	91	92
Precision (%)	85	88	89
Recall (%)	84	86	87
F1-Score (%)	84	87	88

Figure 4. Graphical visual of model accuracy by algorithm

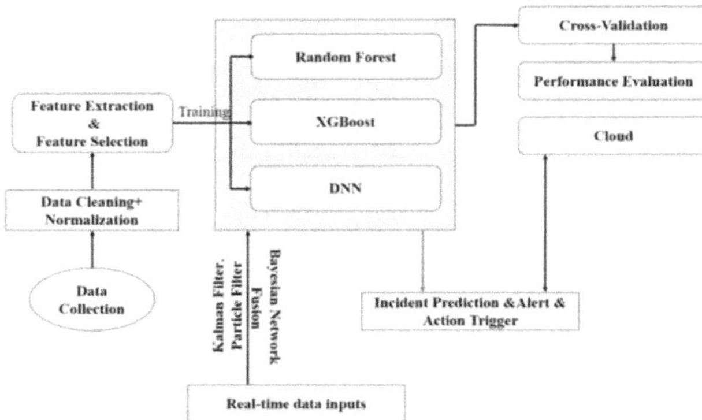

Table 3 compares the incident detection accuracy of both the existing system and the proposed system across different driving conditions (Low, Medium, and High). The existing system has low detection accuracy for all conditions: clear road conditions got 74.8% accuracy, wet road conditions got 65.5%, night-time driving got 70.4% accuracy, and weather-related hazards got 60.1% accuracy. In comparison, the performance of the proposed system is significantly higher, with detection accuracy increasing to 93.2% for clear weather conditions, 89.8% for wet weather conditions, 91.5% for night-time driving, and 88.9% for weather-related hazards. The results reinforce the incident detection capabilities of the proposed system, especially in terms of the difficult scenarios posed to it, which is promising for improving vehicle accident predictions and prevention (Figure 5).

Table 3. Incident detection accuracy under different conditions

Condition	Existing System (Kamran et al., 2022)	Proposed System
Clear Road Conditions	74.8	93.2
Wet Road Conditions	65.5	89.8
Night-time Driving	70.4	91.5
Weather-related Hazards	60.1	88.9

Figure 5. Graphical visual of incident detection accuracy under different conditions

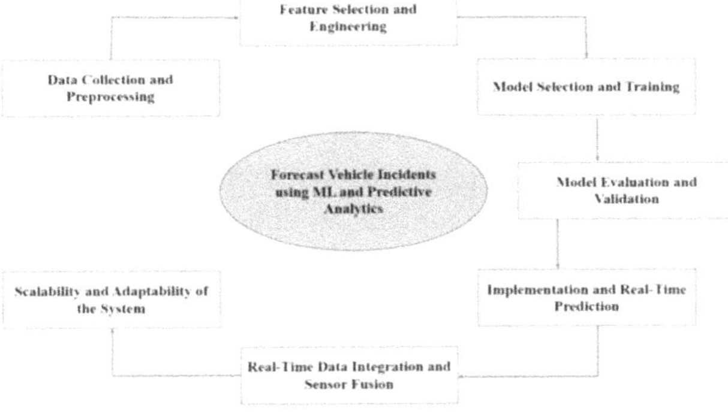

The proposed system has shown improvements over previous vehicle incident prediction methods. By incorporating real-time data streams, the system successfully predicts possible incidents and reduces false positives and negatives. Its innovative predictive precision positively translates to proactively taking vehicle safety to a new level instead of merely depending on chance within static accident history or reduced statistical calculation like traditional models. Predictive performance within the system is significantly higher, ensuring that vehicle safety can be taken to a new level of pro-activeness instead of merely relying on luck within the static accident history or reduced statistical calculation existing in more traditional models. Apart from assuring road safety, it aids in better fleet management and optimal utilization of resources. The integration of advanced machine learning algorithms, especially Random Forest, XGboost, and Deep Neural Networks, shows significant improvement in the overall performance across all the evaluating metrics, confirming the ability of the developed system to analyze real-time dynamic data.

Furthermore, the integration of vehicle telemetry, real-time traffic flow, weather data, and driver behavior makes the system highly adaptable and scalable. It applies to all vehicle types, including personal vehicles and autonomous fleets. As for what the system would look like in the real world, it could see fewer accidents, cheaper insurance, and smarter traffic management, enabling a fundamental transition to safer and smarter transportation systems. Future work will improve the predictive power by applying constant updates to the model and generalizing the solution utopia to larger transport ecosystems.

CONCLUSION AND FUTURE WORK

In conclusion, compared to traditional vehicle incident prediction systems, the proposed system shows a much higher predictive ability by integrating real-time data streams and ML models like Random Forest, XGBoost, and Deep Neural Networks. By enabling proactive predictions and intervention via a slew of inputs, including IoT sensors, GPS, traffic cameras, weather stations, etc., the system helps reduce road accidents, improving fleet management, and scaling well across vehicles and geographies; while these approaches advance state of the art, the system has limitations: implementing the switched-connecting framework still depends on the availability of real-time data; requires substantial computational resources for on-the-fly analysis; raises concerns regarding privacy since there is constant data collection; needs continuous learning from large and preferably diverse datasets; has complexities for data fusion for different data sources; and the performance of the integrated system could decrease in areas with poor connectivity. For future work, it can investigate improving incident prediction in regions with sparse data coverage, enforce better interpretability of machine learning models to explain predictions to users, optimize model latency to reduce second response times further, utilize other data sources, including vehicle-to-vehicle communication, examine transfer learning for better model adaptability in different environments, and refine subsystem for emergent driver behaviors. The system could also be enhanced to accommodate growing numbers of autonomous vehicles and more advanced sensor technologies, making it an even higher-performing and more scalable key component of future intelligent transportation systems.

REFERENCES

Ahmadi, M., Pahlavani, M., Karimi, A., Moradi, M., & Lawrence, J. (2023). *The impact of the Fourth Industrial Revolution on the transitory stage of the automotive industry*. Springer. DOI: 10.1007/978-981-19-7218-8_5

Aljohani, A. (2023). Predictive analytics and machine learning for real-time supply chain risk mitigation and agility. *Sustainability (Basel)*, *15*(20), 15088. DOI: 10.3390/su152015088

Almeaibed, S., Al-Rubaye, S., Tsourdos, A., & Avdelidis, N. P. (2021). Digital twin analysis to promote safety and security in autonomous vehicles. *IEEE Communications Standards Magazine*, *5*(1), 40–46. DOI: 10.1109/MCOMSTD.011.2100004

Anand, P. P., Jayanth, G., Rao, K. S., Deepika, P., Faisal, M., & Mokdad, M. (2024). Utilising Hybrid Machine Learning to Identify Anomalous Multivariate Time-Series in Geotechnical Engineering. *AVE Trends In Intelligent Computing Systems*, *1*(1), 32–41.

Anand, P. P., Kanike, U. K., Paramasivan, P., Rajest, S. S., Regin, R., & Priscila, S. S. (2023). Embracing Industry 5.0: Pioneering Next-Generation Technology for a Flourishing Human Experience and Societal Advancement. *FMDB Transactions on Sustainable Social Sciences Letters*, *1*(1), 43–55.

Bathla, G., et al. (2022). Autonomous vehicles and intelligent automation: Applications, challenges, and opportunities. Mobile Information Systems, vol(2022), no. 6 pp. 1-36

Bin Sulaiman, R., Hariprasath, G., Dhinakaran, P., & Kose, U. (2023). Time-series Forecasting of Web Traffic Using Prophet Machine Learning Model. *FMDB Transactions on Sustainable Computer Letters*, *1*(3), 161–177.

Chundru, S. (2024). Harnessing the power of AI: Revolutionizing metadata management with machine learning. *FMDB Transactions on Sustainable Computer Letters*, *2*(3), 164–175. DOI: 10.69888/FTSCL.2024.000242

Ghaffari, M., Aliahmadi, A., Khalkhali, A., Zakery, A., Daim, T. U., & Yalcin, H. (2023). Topic-based technology mapping using patent data analysis: A case study of vehicle tires. *Technological Forecasting and Social Change*, *193*(8), 122576. DOI: 10.1016/j.techfore.2023.122576

Ghosh, R. K., Banerjee, A., Aich, P., Basu, D., & Ghosh, U. (2022). Intelligent IoT for automotive Industry 4.0: Challenges, opportunities, and future trends. In *Internet of Things*. Springer.

Jani, P., Nanban, D., Selvan, J., Richardson, N., Sivakani, R., & Subhashni, R. (2024). Studying Price Dynamics of Bus Services Using Machine Learning Algorithms. *AVE Trends In Intelligent Computing Systems*, *1*(1), 54–65.

Kamran, S. S., Haleem, A., Bahl, S., Javaid, M., Prakash, C., & Budhhi, D. (2022). Artificial intelligence and advanced materials in the automotive industry: Potential applications and perspectives. *Materials Today: Proceedings*, *62*(5), 4207–4214. DOI: 10.1016/j.matpr.2022.04.727

Karmakar, G., Chowdhury, A., Das, R., Kamruzzaman, J., & Islam, S. (2021). Assessing the trust level of a driverless car using deep learning. *IEEE Transactions on Intelligent Transportation Systems*, *22*(7), 4457–4466. DOI: 10.1109/TITS.2021.3059261

Kotsiopoulos, T., Sarigiannidis, P., Ioannidis, D., & Tzovaras, D. (2021). Machine learning and deep learning in smart manufacturing: The smart grid paradigm. *Computer Science Review*, *40*(5), 100341. DOI: 10.1016/j.cosrev.2020.100341

Licaj, B., & Karras, D. A. (2024). Integral smart vehicle automation framework using IoT, modern software, and infrastructure. *AVE Trends in Intelligent Computing Systems*, *1*(3), 128–141.

Liu, B., Han, C., Liu, X., & Li, W. (2021). Vehicle artificial intelligence system based on intelligent image analysis and 5G network. *International Journal of Wireless Information Networks*, *30*(4), 1–17. DOI: 10.1007/s10776-021-00535-6

Mandala, V., Kuppala, B. M. S. R., Surabhi, S. N. R. D., & Kommisetty, P. D. N. K. (2022). Advancing predictive failure analytics in automotive safety: AI-driven approaches for school buses and commercial trucks. *Journal of Artificial Intelligence and Big Data*, *1*(1), 9–20. DOI: 10.31586/jaibd.2022.944

Mehta, G., Bose, S. R., & Selva Naveen, R. (2023). Optimizing Lithium-ion Battery Controller Design for Electric Vehicles: A Comprehensive Study. *FMDB Transactions on Sustainable Energy Sequence*, *1*(2), 60–70.

Munirathinam, S. (2019). Industry 4.0: Industrial Internet of Things (IIOT). *Advances in Computers*, *117*(1), 129–164.

Murugavel, S., & Hernandez, F. (2023). A Comparative Study Between Statistical and Machine Learning Methods for Forecasting Retail Sales. *FMDB Transactions on Sustainable Computer Letters*, *1*(2), 76–102.

Paramasivan, P., Rajest, S. S., Chinnusamy, K., Regin, R., & John Joseph, F. J. (2024). *Cross-Industry AI Applications*. Advances in Computational Intelligence and Robotics. IGI., DOI: 10.4018/979-8-3693-5951-8

Peppers, N., Alexakis, T., Adamopoulou, E., & Demestichas, K. (2021). Driving behavior analysis using machine and deep learning methods for continuous streams of vehicular data. *Sensors (Basel)*, *21*(14), 4704. DOI: 10.3390/s21144704 PMID: 34300447

Pierre, T. J., Tao, C., Vénant, K., & Erneste, B. (2024). Speed management blueprint: Conception of an IoT-based electric vehicle speed limiter monitoring system for Kigali city vehicles. *FMDB Transactions on Sustainable Energy Sequence*, *2*(1), 33–48. DOI: 10.69888/FTSES.2024.000190

Priscila, S. S., Rajest, S. S., Tadiboina, S. N., Regin, R., & András, S. (2023). Analysis of Machine Learning and Deep Learning Methods for Superstore Sales Prediction. *FMDB Transactions on Sustainable Computer Letters*, *1*(1), 1–11.

Rahman, M., Rahim, M. A., Rahman, M. M., Moustafa, N., Razzak, I., Ahmad, T., & Patwary, M. N. (2022). A secure and intelligent framework for vehicle health monitoring exploiting big-data analytics. *IEEE Transactions on Intelligent Transportation Systems*, *23*(10), 19727–19742. DOI: 10.1109/TITS.2021.3138255

Raj, M. A., Mishra, A., & Forest, G. A. (2024). Predictive Analytics for Employee Attrition: Leveraging Machine Learning for Strategic Human Resources Management. *AVE Trends in Intelligent Technoprise Letters*, *1*(1), 13–29.

Rajest, S. S., Moccia, S., Singh, B., Regin, R., & Jeganathan, J. (Eds.). (2024, August 30). Advances in Computational Intelligence and Robotics *Optimizing intelligent systems for cross-industry application.*, DOI: 10.4018/979-8-3693-8659-0

Rajest, S. S., Singh, B. J., Obaid, A., Regin, R., & Chinnusamy, K. (2023a). *Recent developments in machine and human intelligence*. Advances in Computational Intelligence and Robotics. IGI Global., DOI: 10.4018/978-1-6684-9189-8

Sarker, I. H. (2022). Machine learning for intelligent data analysis and automation in cybersecurity: Current and future prospects. *Annals of Data Science*, *10*(6), 1473–1498. DOI: 10.1007/s40745-022-00444-2

Saxena, R. R., Sujith, S., & Nelavala, R. (2023). MuscleDrive: A Proof of Concept Describing the Electromyographic Navigation of a Vehicle. *FMDB Transactions on Sustainable Health Science Letters*, *1*(2), 107–117.

Taj, I., & Zaman, N. (2022). Towards Industrial Revolution 5.0 and explainable artificial intelligence: Challenges and opportunities. *International Journal of Computing and Digital Systems*, *12*(1), 285–310. DOI: 10.12785/ijcds/120124

Thirunagalingam, A. (2024). Bias detection and mitigation in data pipelines: Ensuring fairness and accuracy in machine learning. *AVE Trends in Intelligent Computing Systems*, *1*(2), 116–127.

Venkateswaran, P. S., Singh, S., Paramasivan, P., Rajest, S. S., Lourens, M. E., & Regin, R. (2023). A Study on The Influence of Quality of Service on Customer Satisfaction Towards Hotel Industry. *FMDB Transactions on Sustainable Social Sciences Letters*, *1*(1), 1–11.

Venkateswaran, P. S., Sriramkumar, M., Vaddy, R. K., Kotagiri, A., Rajest, S. S., & Regin, R. (2024). Applications of Artificial Intelligence and Robots in Service Industries. In *Advances in Computer and Electrical Engineering* (pp. 61–80). IGI Global.

Chapter 8
New AI Technology for Predictive Pothole Locating on Highways

R. Regin
https://orcid.org/0000-0002-6618-205X
SRM Institute of Science and Technology, Ramapuram, India

K. Balamurugan
https://orcid.org/0009-0004-5257-6674
SRM Institute of Science and Technology, Ramapuram, India

S. Suresh
SRM Institute of Science and Technology, Ramapuram, India

U. Adithyakumar
SRM Institute of Science and Technology, Ramapuram, India

S. Rubin Bose
https://orcid.org/0000-0001-5560-8580
SRM Institute of Science and Technology, Ramapuram, India

M. Pandi Maharajan
https://orcid.org/0000-0002-5252-4709
Dhaanish Ahmed College of Engineering, India

ABSTRACT

Road safety is crucial in transportation infrastructure management, with potholes posing significant hazards such as accidents, vehicle damage, and increased maintenance costs. Traditional pothole detection methods rely on reactive and labor-intensive processes, including manual inspections or infrequent public reports. This project introduces a proactive approach to pothole identification using Convolutional Neural Networks (CNNs) with the YOLOv8 algorithm. By leveraging deep learning and computer vision, the system enables real-time, autonomous pothole detection and localization from vehicle-mounted cameras or drones. The YOLOv8 algorithm's accuracy, efficiency, and real-time performance make it well-suited for this task. Training the model on diverse datasets enhances its robustness across various road conditions, lighting variations, and camera perspectives. Evaluation across multiple

DOI: 10.4018/979-8-3373-5203-9.ch008

road segments yielded promising results.

INTRODUCTION

Potholes represent a widespread and persistent issue on roadways worldwide, posing substantial safety hazards to drivers and imposing significant financial burdens on transportation authorities. These road defects, often resulting from weathering, traffic, and insufficient maintenance, can lead to vehicle damage, accidents, and costly infrastructure repairs. Traditional manual inspection methods for pothole identification are labor-intensive, time-consuming, and prone to human error, rendering them inefficient for extensive road networks. Consequently, there is growing interest in developing automated pothole detection systems that leverage advanced technologies such as computer vision and machine learning. Recent strides in deep learning, particularly in object detection, offer promising avenues for automating pothole detection tasks. You Only Look Once (YOLO) stands out among the cutting-edge object detection frameworks for its real-time processing capabilities and high accuracy. The latest iteration, YOLOv8, incorporates enhancements in network architecture, training strategies, and computational efficiency, rendering it a compelling option for pothole detection applications. By harnessing YOLOv8's capabilities, researchers and engineers aim to craft efficient and reliable systems that automatically detect and pinpoint potholes in road images or video streams.

In this study, we introduce a novel approach to pothole detection utilizing YOLOv8 to overcome the limitations of manual inspection methods and enhance road safety and infrastructure maintenance practices. The proposed system capitalizes on YOLOv8's strengths in real-time object detection, tailoring it specifically for pothole identification tasks. Through fine-tuning and training on a meticulously annotated dataset of road images containing pothole instances, the YOLOv8 model learns to precisely recognize and categorize potholes, enabling efficient and prompt detection across diverse road environments and conditions. Developing an automated pothole detection system based on YOLOv8 holds significant implications for road safety, infrastructure management, and transportation efficiency. By automating the detection process, authorities can streamline maintenance operations, prioritize repairs, and mitigate the risks associated with pothole-related accidents and damages. Moreover, the scalability and adaptability of the proposed system present opportunities for integration with existing road monitoring technologies and autonomous vehicle systems, further augmenting road safety and mobility in the contemporary transportation landscape.

LITERATURE REVIEW

Hijji et al. (2023) proposed framework addresses data scarcity by leveraging information from numerous connected vehicles. It employs a novel deep-learning method for pothole detection that merges image and sensor data. This approach achieved promising results, with a reported testing accuracy of 97%, precision of 84.80%, recall of 92.40%, and F1-score of 88.44%. Furthermore, the framework incorporates federated edge AI training, allowing continuous model improvement while safeguarding data privacy. Additionally, it utilizes smart road signs and 6G communication to facilitate data exchange, warn drivers of hazards, and ensure efficient network operation. This research demonstrates the potential of 6G and deep learning for proactive road maintenance, paving the way for improved road conditions and safer transportation.

Pandey et al. (2021) delved into deep learning for pothole identification, spearheading advancements in automated road maintenance strategies. Central to their study was utilizing a Convolutional Neural Network (CNN), a powerful architecture renowned for its proficiency in image analysis tasks. By leveraging this cutting-edge technology, the researchers aimed to analyze images captured on roads, effectively transforming visual data into actionable insights for pothole detection (Maroju, 2024). The outcomes of their research were indeed promising, with reported accuracy levels surpassing 85%. Furthermore, their meticulously trained model exhibited a commendable equilibrium between precision, 87.2%, and recall, 92.7%, ultimately resulting in a high F1-score of 89.9%. These metrics underscore the robustness and effectiveness of the CNN-based approach in automating pothole detection processes, thus paving the way for enhanced road maintenance efficiency and safety.

Basavaraju et al. (2021) introduced a novel machine-learning approach tailored for assessing road surface anomalies, harnessing the ubiquitous sensors embedded within smartphones. Departing from traditional methods reliant on specialized equipment, their research sought to exploit the data captured by accelerometers and gyroscopes in everyday mobile devices. Through meticulous analysis and feature extraction from sensor data, the authors aimed to unlock the potential of machine learning algorithms in discerning various road conditions, encompassing not only potholes but also bumps and smooth surfaces (Amer et al., 2023). By leveraging this approach, the study envisioned a paradigm shift towards a cost-effective and widely accessible method for road anomaly detection, democratizing the utilization of technology available to a vast portion of the population.

Medvedev and Pavlov, (2020) explored Convolutional Neural Networks (CNNs) within road assessment, presenting a pioneering dual-purpose system designed to revolutionize traditional methodologies. The focal point of their research, as outlined in the paper titled "Road Surface Marking Recognition and Road Surface

Quality Evaluation Using Convolution Neural Network" (Farhan and Bin Sulaiman, 2023), centered on the development of a CNN architecture with the capacity to perform two distinct yet interconnected tasks: recognizing road surface markings such as lane lines, and assessing the overall quality of the road based on image data. While specific quantitative results regarding accuracy are not explicitly disclosed in publicly available information about the paper, the study serves as a compelling demonstration of the potential inherent in utilizing a single CNN model for these multifaceted objectives.

Fang et al. (2020) introduced a novel hybrid method for detecting cracks, addressing the challenge of detecting faint crack signals against noisy image backgrounds. Their approach combines the advantages of deep learning and Bayesian probabilistic analysis. Deep learning, specifically utilizing a pre-trained object detector such as Faster R-CNN, is employed to identify image regions with a high signal-to-noise ratio (SNR) likely to contain cracks. Following this, a Bayesian framework is utilized to analyze these regions and verify the presence of cracks (Usman and Ullah, 2024). This hybrid approach provides a robust solution for crack detection, potentially surpassing methods that rely solely on deep learning or traditional image processing techniques. The authors' results indicate that their approach achieves high accuracy in crack detection.

Amita et al. (2020) introduce an innovative method for pothole detection, leveraging the synergistic capabilities of computer vision and machine learning. Their methodology is meticulously crafted to automate the pothole detection process, aiming to enhance road maintenance operations' efficiency and effectiveness. While acknowledging the inherent challenges associated with optimizing accuracy and reliability, especially in real-world scenarios characterized by diverse environmental factors, the authors present a robust framework that exhibits high precision, recall, and F1 score (Odoemena and Elufidodo, 2024). These performance metrics underscore the system's potential for proactive pothole identification, laying the groundwork for tangible improvements in road safety and infrastructure maintenance practices.

Ping et al. (2020) immerse themselves in deep learning tailored to street pothole detection. To identify the most effective approach for this critical task, their comprehensive study encompasses a comparative analysis of several prominent models, including YOLOv3, Faster R-CNN, SSD, and HOG with SVM. Through meticulous experimentation and evaluation of a preprocessed image dataset curated for pothole detection, the researchers unveil compelling insights. Their findings reveal that YOLOv3 emerges as the frontrunner among the evaluated models, achieving the highest accuracy level of approximately 82%. This nuanced comparison sheds light on the strengths and limitations of each model, elucidating YOLOv3's prowess in effectively detecting potholes amidst the complexities of street environments.

Dharneeshkar et al. (2020) confront the pressing challenge of road maintenance in India head-on, presenting a pioneering deep-learning approach tailored specifically for pothole detection in this unique geographical context. Recognizing the distinct characteristics and challenges inherent to Indian road conditions, the researchers embarked on a comprehensive investigation aimed at harnessing the power of deep learning technologies to address this critical issue (Ulle and Yogananthan, 2024). Central to their contribution is the meticulous comparison of different iterations of the YOLO architecture, including versions v2, v3, and Tiny v3, leveraging a bespoke Indian road image dataset. By systematically evaluating the performance of these YOLO variants in the context of Indian road conditions, they shed light on the suitability and efficacy of YOLO for pothole detection in this region.

Peralta et al. (2023) build upon the foundation laid by previous studies in deep learning for pothole detection while extending the scope to encompass a broader range of road anomalies. While acknowledging the success of YOLO-based models in prior research, their focus transcends traditional pothole detection methodologies. Instead, the researchers propose a novel deep neural network architecture explicitly tailored for the simultaneous detection of speed bumps and potholes in road images captured by a ZED camera (Nwabuokei et al., 2023). This innovative approach represents a significant departure from conventional approaches, reflecting a nuanced understanding of the diverse challenges inherent in road anomaly detection. By expanding the scope to include both speed bumps and potholes, Peralta et al. aim to address the multifaceted nature of road hazards, thereby enhancing the safety and efficiency of autonomous and manual vehicles traversing diverse road environments (Chundru, 2024).

Asad et al. (2022) have undertaken a study to explore the capabilities of deep learning in real-time pothole detection, with a specific focus on devices with limited computational resources. Their literature review is expected to provide a comprehensive overview of previous research in this area, recognizing the growing body of evidence supporting the effectiveness of various deep learning models, including YOLO and SSD, for pothole detection. Through synthesizing insights from prior studies, (Sivapriya et al., 2023). places their research in the context of the broader landscape of deep learning applications for pothole detection, setting the stage for their novel contributions.

PROPOSED METHODOLOGY

Figure 1. Block diagram

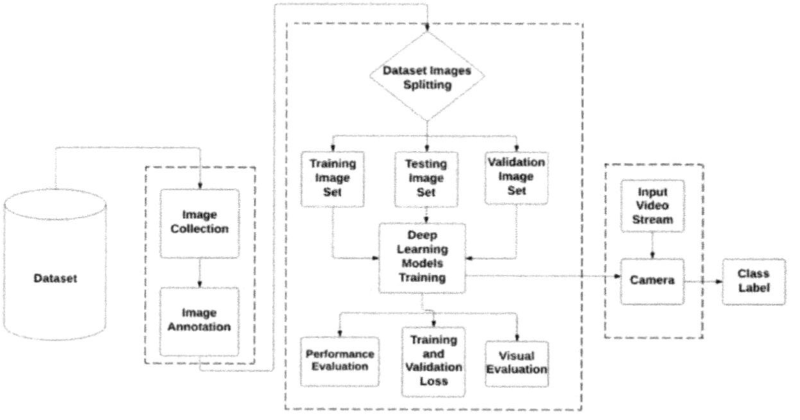

Data Collection and Annotation: The data collection process involved gathering 10000 images relevant to the project's objectives. These images were annotated using segmentation, which allowed for the outlining of specific objects or regions of interest within each image with pixel-level accuracy. The annotation process included rigorous quality control checks to ensure the accuracy and consistency of the annotations across the dataset (Rajest et al., 2023). A combination of manual annotation tools and custom scripts was utilized to streamline the annotation process, improving efficiency and accuracy Figure 2.

Figure 2. Pothole images

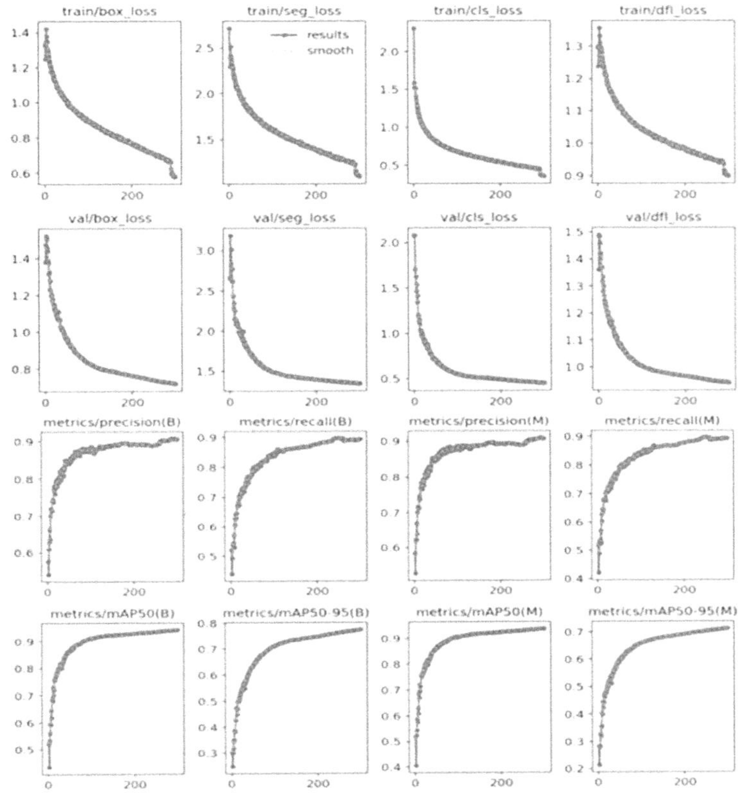

Data Preprocessing: Data preprocessing steps included auto-orienting the collected images to the correct orientation and resizing them to a fixed size of 640x640 pixels. These preprocessing steps were crucial to ensure that all images were uniform in size and orientation, which is essential for training a model that can generalize well to new, unseen data. Other preprocessing techniques, such as normalization or color space conversion, could have been applied to enhance the data quality further.

Data Splitting: The dataset was split into training, testing, and validation sets using a 70-10-20 ratio. The training set, comprising 7000 images, was used to train the model. The testing set, containing 1000 images, was used to assess the final performance of the trained model on unseen data, providing an estimate of its generalization capabilities.

YOLOv8 Architecture

The YOLOv8 architecture emerges as a pivotal component, offering cutting-edge capabilities tailored specifically for real-time detection on roads. At its core, YOLOv8 embodies a sophisticated architecture comprised of three main modules: the Backbone, Neck, and Head. The Backbone module is the foundational element, extracting high-level characteristics from the input image. In the case of YOLOv8, this module is built upon CSPDarknet53, a Convolutional Neural Network (CNN) architecture meticulously designed to mitigate the challenges the disappearing gradient issue poses, thereby enhancing training effectiveness. Using CSPDarknet53, YOLOv8 establishes a robust foundation for subsequent processing stages, enabling the model to glean essential features crucial for accurate pothole detection.

Backbone: The backbone module takes the input image and extracts high-level characteristics. The foundation of YOLOv8 is CSPDarknet53, a CNN architecture created to solve the disappearing gradient issue and improve training effectiveness.

Neck: The neck module integrates the feature maps extracted by the backbone at different scales, enabling the model to capture fine-grained and coarse details of the image. YOLOv8 utilizes Path Aggregation Network (PANet) as the neck, a multi-scale feature fusion architecture that improves object detection performance.

Figure 3. YOLOv8 architecture

This study employed transfer learning to leverage existing knowledge and improve training efficiency. This technique involved reusing pre-trained weights from a previously trained model and fine-tuning them on the lung cancer dataset. This offers faster training times and requires fewer resources than traditional training. The ratio of true and predicted values is computed on each iteration using the loss function.

$$L_T = L_{class} + L_{cnf} + L_{box} \tag{1}$$

$$L_{class} = \sum_{i=0}^{x^2} 1_i^{obj} \sum_{j=0}^{R} \left[\left(Pi(c) - \widehat{Pi}(c) \right)^2 \right] \tag{2}$$

$$L_{cnf} = \sum_{i=0}^{x^2} \sum_{j=0}^{R} 1_i^{obj} \left[\left(Ci - \widehat{Ci} \right)^2 \right] + \beta_{no\ obj} \sum_{i=0}^{x^2} \sum_{j=0}^{R} 1_i^{no\ obj} \left[\left(Ci - \widehat{Ci} \right)^2 \right] \tag{3}$$

where, Pi(c) is represented as the probability of being an object.

$$\textbf{Precision} = \frac{\text{True Positive}}{\text{True Positive + False Positive}} \tag{4}$$

$$\textbf{Recall} = \frac{\text{True Positive}}{\text{True Positive + False Negative}} \tag{5}$$

mAP (mean Average Precision): Calculating mAP involves calculating the average precision (AP) across all classes and then averaging those values. AP itself is calculated using a concept called the precision-recall curve (PRC). The PRC is a graphical representation of the trade-off between precision and recall at various confidence thresholds. Numerical integration techniques are employed to calculate the area under the PRC curve representing the AP.

Model Evaluation

To evaluate the effectiveness of our trained pothole detection model, we implemented a thorough assessment procedure utilizing a meticulously structured dataset split. The annotated pothole dataset was systematically divided into three distinct subsets: training, validation, and testing. The training subset, typically comprising approximately 70% of the data, served as the bedrock for model training. During this phase, the model was exposed to various pothole images alongside their corresponding annotations, facilitating iterative adjustments to its internal parameters to enhance its pothole detection capabilities. The validation subset, constituting roughly 20% of the data, was pivotal in fine-tuning the model's hyperparameters. These hyperparameters, governing the learning dynamics of the model, include parameters such as the learning rate and the number of training epochs. Through experimentation with different hyperparameter configurations on the validation subset, we identified the optimal settings that maximized the model's performance on unseen data. This process was instrumental in mitigating overfitting, a phenomenon where the model performs exceedingly well on the training data but struggles to generalize to new instances.

Subsequently, the testing subset, comprising approximately 10% of the data, provided an unbiased evaluation of the model's generalization ability. This subset contained entirely new images, ensuring that the model had not encountered the potholes within them during training or validation. By assessing the model's performance on the testing subset, we gained valuable insights into its real-world efficacy for proactive pothole identification on roadways. We utilized a comprehensive set of evaluation metrics to quantitatively measure the model's accuracy in pothole detection, including precision, recall, and F1 score. Precision denotes the proportion of correctly identified potholes among all detections made by the model, while recall indicates the percentage of actual potholes that the model successfully detects. The F1 score balances precision and recall and provides a holistic assessment of the model's performance. Analyzing these metrics, we obtained actionable insights into the model's strengths and weaknesses, facilitating an informed assessment of its suitability for real-world pothole detection tasks.

RESULTS AND DISCUSSION

The YOLOv8 model demonstrated impressive performance in the pothole detection project, achieving a mean Average Precision (mAP) of 94.2%. This indicates that, on average, the model accurately identified and localized potholes in 94.2% of the test images. The precision of the model, which measures the proportion of correctly identified potholes among all detections, reached 90.6%. This high precision underscores the model's ability to minimize false positives, which is essential for ensuring the reliability of the detection system. However, the model's recall, which indicates the percentage of actual potholes identified by the model, was 89.4%. This means that the model did not detect approximately 10.6% of potholes in the test images. While this is a relatively low false negative rate, there is still room for improvement to enhance the model's ability to detect all potholes accurately. Overall, the results highlight the effectiveness of using YOLOv8 for pothole detection, showcasing its accuracy, efficiency, and real-time performance. Future work could focus on further refining the model to improve recall without compromising precision, potentially through fine-tuning the model architecture, optimizing hyperparameters, or augmenting the training data (Figure 4).

Figure 4. Prediction

Table 1 showcases the performance of the YOLOv8 model on our pothole detection task across various training epochs. Overall accuracy reflects the percentage of images where the model correctly classified the presence or absence of potholes. Overall precision represents the proportion of images with potholes that the model identified accurately. Finally, the mean Average Precision (mAP) is a comprehensive measure of the model's performance, indicating its ability to accurately detect and localize potholes in images (Figure 1). As evident from Table 1, the model's performance improves with an increasing number of training epochs. This signifies the model's ability to learn and refine its pothole detection capabilities by extracting distinctive features from the road surface images.

Table 1. Performance of Yolov8 model

Epochs	Map	Precision	Recall
50	88	84	82
100	90	86	85
150	92	88	87
200	93	89	88
250	94.2	90.6	89.4

Our YOLOv8 model demonstrated a mean Average Precision (mAP) of 94.2 on the test set, indicating its ability to accurately identify and localize potholes in approximately 94.2% of the test images. However, a closer examination of the evaluation metrics reveals a potential trade-off between precision and recall. With a precision of 90.6%, the model exhibited a high percentage (90.6%) of correctly identified potholes among the predicted images containing potholes. This suggests a low rate of false positives, indicating the model's effectiveness in avoiding misclassifying non-pothole areas. Conversely, the model's recall stood at 89.4%, indicating its identification of 89.4% of the total potholes in the test set. While this demonstrates a good ability to detect potholes, there remains room for improvement in capturing a more comprehensive representation. Some potholes might have been overlooked due to limitations in the training data or the complexity of certain pothole appearances. These findings underscore the model's promising capacity to detect potholes with a balanced trade-off between precision and recall. However, future endeavors could focus on further refining the model's performance. This might involve exploring different YOLOv8 architecture variations, experimenting with advanced data augmentation techniques beyond noise and flips, and considering additional preprocessing steps to address specific dataset challenges. Moreover, fine-tuning the training process parameters, such as learning rate or optimizer, could enhance the model's ability to learn intricate pothole characteristics and improve precision and recall. We aim to develop an even more robust and dependable pothole detection model by pursuing these avenues.

Figure 5. Confusion matrix normalized

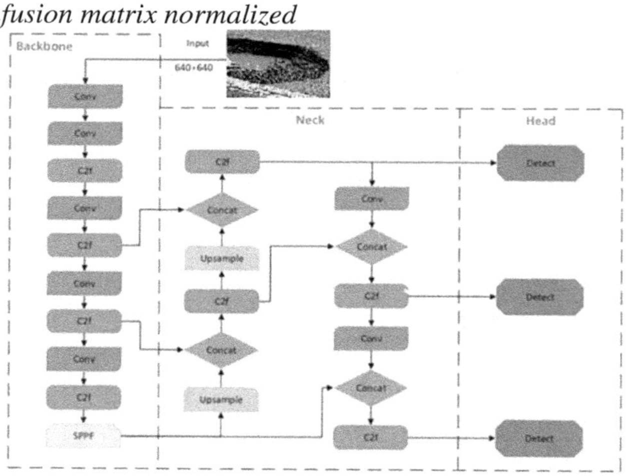

We continually assess the model's performance throughout the training process using two key metrics: training loss and validation loss. These metrics serve as vital indicators of the learning process and assist in detecting potential issues. Training Loss quantifies the disparity between the model's predictions and the actual labels for the training images. Ideally, as training progresses, the training loss should steadily decrease. This signifies that the model is progressively enhancing its capability to discern the patterns and characteristics that differentiate potholes from non-pothole areas within the training data. However, an excessively low training loss may indicate overfitting, wherein the model memorizes the training data excessively and struggles to generalize to unseen instances in Figure 5.

Validation Loss is a crucial measure of the model's generalization to new data, and the validation loss is calculated using images unseen during training. Evaluating the model's performance on the validation set through validation loss provides insights into its aptitude to apply its learned knowledge to identify potholes in novel contexts. Ideally, the validation loss should also decrease as training advances, albeit slower than the training loss. A notable disparity between training loss and validation loss signals potential overfitting, necessitating model or training procedure adjustments. Meanwhile, Training and validation accuracy indicates the percentage of correctly classified images within the training and validation sets. While a high training accuracy is desirable, it warrants cautious interpretation to prevent the model from merely memorizing the training data. Validation accuracy offers a more reliable gauge of the model's generalization capability and accuracy in classifying potholes in unseen data.

Figure 6. Graphical representation

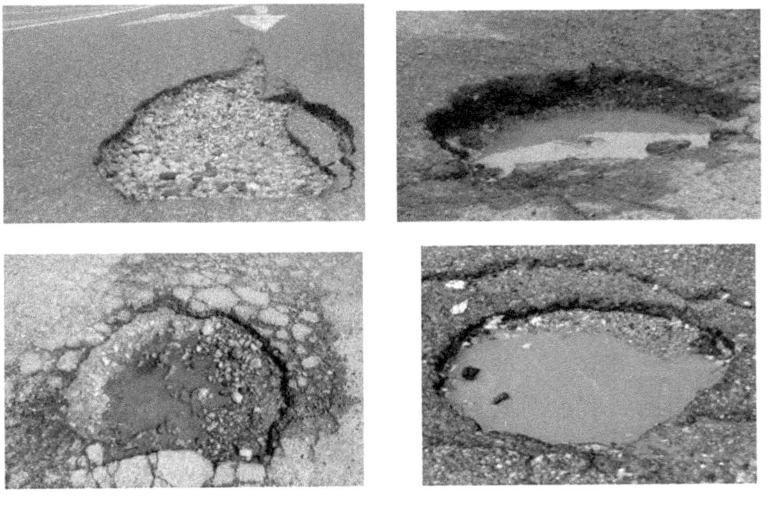

The training and validation losses consistently decrease throughout the training process, as depicted in the graph, indicating the model's ability to learn and adapt to the characteristics of the training data over time. Additionally, the graph illustrates an upward trend in training and validation accuracy, suggesting the model's capability to classify pothole images and generalize to unseen data accurately. At 250 training epochs, the YOLOv8 model achieves a mAP of 94.2%, precision of 90.6%, and recall of 89.4%. These metrics highlight the model's effectiveness in identifying potholes with a balanced trade-off between precision and recall Figure 6. Moreover, the convergence of the training loss and validation loss curves as training progresses indicates that the model avoids overfitting. Overfitting occurs when a model becomes too attuned to the training data, hindering its ability to perform well on new data. The graph suggests that the YOLOv8 model balances learning from the training data and generalizing to new instances.

CONCLUSION

Detecting road potholes with the YOLOv8 model is quite accurate. With a mAP (mean Average Precision) of 94.2%, precision of 90.6%, and recall of 89.4%, the model balances precision and recall. These measurements demonstrate the model's resilience and reliability, setting the framework for improving road safety and infrastructure upkeep. Implementing the YOLOv8 model for pothole detection advances road maintenance and safety. Its strong performance metrics and user-friendly interfaces could revolutionise pothole identification and repair. This technology uses deep learning and computer vision to detect potholes early, making roads safer, infrastructure more durable, and transportation systems more efficient. Semantic segmentation to distinguish road damage types, multi-sensor fusion for improved detection in varied conditions, dynamic model updating based on new data, automated repair suggestion based on pothole characteristics, crowdsourced data integration for real-time updates, and edge computing for faster processing and deployment at the roadside are possible pothole detection enhancements for YOLOv8. These changes improve the model's accuracy, adaptability, and road maintenance utility.

REFERENCES

Amer, A. A., Mostafa, E. E., Ahmed, D. N., & Mahmoud, N. A. (2023). Innovative Technology for Enhancing Independence of the Blind or Visually Impaired. *FMDB Transactions on Sustainable Computing Systems*, *1*(4), 204–212.

Asad, M. H., Khaliq, S., Yousaf, M. H., Ullah, M. O., & Ahmad, A. (2022). Pothole detection using deep learning: A real-time and AI-on-the-edge perspective. *Advances in Civil Engineering*, *2022*(1), 1–13. DOI: 10.1155/2022/9221211

Basavaraju, A., Du, J., Zhou, F., & Ji, J. (2020). A machine learning approach to road surface anomaly assessment using smartphone sensors. *IEEE Sensors Journal*, *20*(5), 2635–2647. DOI: 10.1109/JSEN.2019.2952857

Chundru, S. (2024). Harnessing the power of AI: Revolutionizing metadata management with machine learning. *FMDB Transactions on Sustainable Computer Letters*, *2*(3), 164–175. DOI: 10.69888/FTSCL.2024.000242

Dharneeshkar, D., Aniruthan, S., & Parameswaran, L. (2020). Deep learning based detection of potholes in Indian roads using YOLO. *2020 International Conference on Inventive Computation Technologies (ICICT)*, IEEE, Piscataway, New Jersey, USA.

Dhiman, A., & Klette, R. (2020). Pothole detection Us- ing Computer Vision and Learning. *IEEE Transactions on Intelligent Transportation Systems*, *21*(8), 1–15. DOI: 10.1109/TITS.2019.2931297

Fang, F., Li, L., Gu, Y., Zhu, H., & Lim, J.-H. (2020). A novel hybrid approach for crack detection. *Pattern Recognition*, *107*(11), 107474. DOI: 10.1016/j.patcog.2020.107474

Farhan, M., & Bin Sulaiman, R. (2023). Developing Blockchain Technology to Identify Counterfeit Items Enhances the Supply Chain's Effectiveness. *FMDB Transactions on Sustainable Technoprise Letters*, *1*(3), 123–134.

. Hijji, M., Iqbal, R., Kumar Pandey, A., Doctor, F., Karyotis, C., Rajeh, W., Alshehri, A., & Aradah, F. (2023b). 6G connected vehicle framework to support intelligent road maintenance using deep learning data fusion. IEEE Transactions on Intelligent Transportation Systems: A Publication of the IEEE Intelligent Transportation Systems Council, 24(7), 7726–7735.

Maroju, P. K. (2024). Data science for a smarter currency supply chain: Optimizing cash flow with machine learning for white label ATMs. *FMDB Transactions on Sustainable Computing Systems*, *2*(1), 43–53. DOI: 10.69888/FTSCS.2024.000196

Medvedev, M. V., & Pavlov, V. I. (2020). Road surface marking recognition and road surface quality evaluation using convolution neural network. 2020 International Multi-Conference on Industrial Engineering and Modern Technologies (FarEastCon), Vladivostok, Russia.

Nwabuokei, I., Ghouse, M., Chen, W., Kollannur, E. T., Li, H., & Bin Sulaiman, R. (2023). Quantifying the Influence of Population on Carbon Emissions: A Comparative Study of Developed versus Developing Countries Using Machine Learning. *FMDB Transactions on Sustainable Energy Sequence*, *1*(2), 71–82.

Odoemena, O. F., & Elufidodo, G. A. (2024). Machine learning-based cardiovascular disease detection and intelligent healthcare workflow automation. *FMDB Transactions on Sustainable Health Science Letters*, *2*(2), 81–93. DOI: 10.69888/FTSHSL.2024.000174

Pandey, A. K., Iqbal, R., Amin, S., Maniak, T., Palade, V., & Karyotis, C. (2021). Deep neural networks-based approach for pothole detection. 2021 4th International Conference on Signal Processing and Information Security (ICSPIS), Dubai, United Arab Emirates (UAE).

Peralta-López, J.-E., Morales-Viscaya, J.-A., Lázaro-Mata, D., Villaseñor-Aguilar, M.-J., Prado-Olivarez, J., Pérez-Pinal, F.-J., Padilla-Medina, J.-A., Martínez-Nolasco, J.-J., & Barranco-Gutiérrez, A.-I. (2023). Speed bump and pothole detection using deep neural network with images captured through ZED camera. *Applied Sciences (Basel, Switzerland)*, *13*(14), 8349. DOI: 10.3390/app13148349

Ping, P., Yang, X., & Gao, Z. (2020). A deep learning approach for street pothole detection. *2020 IEEE Sixth International Conference on Big Data Computing Service and Applications (BigDataService)*, Oxford, United Kingdom. DOI: 10.1109/BigDataService49289.2020.00039

Rajest, S. S., Singh, B. J., Obaid, A., Regin, R., & Chinnusamy, K. (2023a). *Recent developments in machine and human intelligence*. Advances in Computational Intelligence and Robotics. IGI Global., DOI: 10.4018/978-1-6684-9189-8

Sivapriya, G. B. V., Ganesh, U. G., Pradeeshwar, V., Dharshini, M., & Al-Amin, M. (2023). Crime Prediction and Analysis Using Data Mining and Machine Learning: A Simple Approach that Helps Predictive Policing. *FMDB Transactions on Sustainable Computer Letters*, *1*(2), 64–75.

Ulle, R. S., & Yogananthan, S. (2024). Unmasking fake opinions through behavioral analysis and machine learning: Identifying genuine users vs. fraudulent actors. *FMDB Transactions on Sustainable Management Letters*, *2*(2), 51–64. DOI: 10.69888/FTSML.2024.000235

Usman, M., & Ullah, A. (2024). Blockchain Technology Implementation in Libraries: An Overview of Potential Benefits and Challenges. *AVE Trends In Intelligent Computing Systems*, *1*(1), 42–53.

Chapter 9
Handbook for Predicting the Popularity of News on Anticipating Article Buzz

R. Regin
https://orcid.org/0000-0002-6618-205X
SRM Institute of Science and Technology, Ramapuram, India

L. Santhosh
SRM Institute of Science and Technology, Ramapuram, India

T. Akhil Reddy
SRM Institute of Science and Technology, Ramapuram, India

Nithesh Varma
SRM Institute of Science and Technology, Ramapuram, India

R. Steffi
Vins Christian College of Engineering, India

A. Thenmozhi
Dhaanish Ahmed College of Engineering, India

B. Kavithamani
Dhaanish Ahmed College of Engineering, India

ABSTRACT

Daily news consumption is essential, and news institutions like The Washington Post (WP) invest heavily in quality content. However, writers and editors struggle to determine which stories readers will like. This task is crucial for resource allocation and reading enjoyment. News story popularity depends on timeliness, writing quality, and other criteria. In our research, we predict article popularity using regression. We carefully create metadata, contextual factors, temporal aspects, and social indicators to build predictive models. In real life at The Washington Post, our method accurately predicts article popularity with an R-squared value of 0.8. These forecasts use features acquired within 30 minutes after publication, demonstrating

DOI: 10.4018/979-8-3373-5203-9.ch009

the system's quickness and effectiveness in editorial decision-making. News article popularity is predicted by analysing readership engagement and virality variables.

INTRODUCTION

News consumption, media organizations, journalism, news popularity, regression analysis, feature engineering, metadata analysis, contextual factors, time-based features, social media metrics, prediction models, practical application, forecast accuracy, and decision support (Tripathi, 2023). In addressing the complexity of popularity prediction, it's important to delve into the nuances of each critical issue: Multifaceted Measures of Popularity: Today's news consumption occurs through diverse channels, including websites, social media platforms, and search engines (Bhargava and Ghosh, 2018). Consequently, popularity can be gauged through metrics such as Page views on the news outlet's website. Social media engagement metrics include likes, shares, and comments on platforms like Facebook, Twitter, or LinkedIn. Search engine queries reflect user interest and intent (Bi and Wang, 2019). Understanding and incorporating these diverse measures into popularity prediction models are crucial for comprehensive analysis and accurate forecasts. Local vs. Global Context of Popularity (Birant, 2022).

Local Context: This refers to popularity measures within a specific news agency's ecosystem. It includes metrics like internal page views, news outlet's app or website engagement, and related content interactions (Chaturvedi et al., 2018). Global Context: In contrast, global context measures popularity across multiple news agencies or platforms. It involves comparing an article's performance against content from various sources, providing insights into its broader impact and relevance. Distinguishing between local and global contexts is essential for tailored decision-making within individual news organizations and benchmarking performance against competitors (Hutto and Gilbert, 2014). Addressing these factors requires sophisticated data collection, analysis, and modeling techniques (Christy et al., 2023). Understanding user behavior across different platforms and contexts is crucial for refining predictive models and enhancing their accuracy (Choudhury et al., 2017). Washington Post revealed a consensus that the initial reception of an article provides valuable insights into its potential impact and audience engagement (Aung et al., 2024). Therefore, this study defines article popularity based on the number of page views within the first 24 hours following publication (Ser et al., 2022). To tackle the task of popularity prediction, the approach adopted is to treat it as a regression problem. This involves developing models that predict the expected number of page views an article will accumulate within 24 hours (Estrada-Jiménez et al., 2019).

The key challenge lies in identifying predictive features that can effectively capture the early signals of an article's popularity (Suraj et al., 2023). Feature extraction is conducted within a narrow window of up to 30 minutes following publication. This timeframe is chosen strategically to capture the immediate response of readers to the article. The extracted features encompass various aspects of the article, including metadata, content characteristics, and early engagement metrics. By leveraging these features, predictive models are trained to forecast the future popularity of articles (Farr et al., 1951). The goal is to provide journalists and editors with actionable insights early in the article's lifecycle, enabling them to make informed decisions regarding promotion, distribution, and resource allocation. Overall, this approach aims to enhance the efficiency and effectiveness of newsroom operations by leveraging data-driven insights to optimize editorial strategies and maximize audience reach. In our extensive assessment, we analyze a wide range of features across different categories to forecast the popularity of news articles. These include Metadata: Reviewing attributes like publication date, author details, article length, and topic classification (Fernandes et al., 2015).

Contextual or Content-Based Features: Examining the article's content for keywords, topics, readability, and linguistic elements. Temporal Indicators: Considering the time of publication, such as the day of the week or hour, to account for temporal trends in readership. Social Metrics: Incorporating data from social media platforms like Twitter to understand article-sharing behavior, including shares, likes, and comments. Freshness Estimation: Assessing features that indicate the timeliness or freshness of an article, influencing its appeal to readers (Berger and Milkman, 2010).

Sentiment Features: Analyzing the emotional tone of the article's content through sentiment analysis, offering insights into its potential resonance with readers. By leveraging this diverse set of features, our predictive models can capture various aspects of article popularity, leading to more precise forecasts (Venkateswaran et al., 2023). This comprehensive approach allows us to better comprehend the factors driving reader engagement and tailor strategies for maximizing the reach and impact of news content. We conduct a thorough evaluation of multiple regression models to predict the popularity of articles (Said and Tripathi, 2023).

This evaluation involves testing various algorithms and techniques to determine their effectiveness in forecasting article engagement (Devi and Rajasekaran, 2023). After rigorous testing and analysis, we identify the best-performing models. Subsequently, we integrate these top-performing models into a real-time system deployed at The Washington Post. This system continuously monitors incoming articles and utilizes the predictive models to estimate their potential popularity. By deploying these models in a real-world setting, we aim to provide The Washington Post with valuable insights into article performance and aid in decision-making regarding content promotion and resource allocation (Saleh et al., 2024).

LITERATURE SURVEY

Bandari et al. (2021) address the challenge of predicting the popularity of news articles on social media platforms before their release. By analyzing various properties of articles, a multi-dimensional feature space is constructed to predict online popularity. Both regression and classification algorithms are examined, revealing that despite the unpredictability of human behavior, it is possible to predict popularity ranges on Twitter with 84% accuracy. Additionally, the research highlights differences between traditional news sources and those popular on social media, providing insights into online news dissemination dynamics (Mishne and Glance, 2006). Berger and Milkman (2012) adopt a psychological perspective to explore the dynamics of content diffusion. Analyzing a comprehensive dataset encompassing all articles published by The New York Times over three months, researchers delve into the influence of emotions on the virality of these articles.

Tatar et al. (2014) This article explores how emotions influence the virality of online content using a dataset of New York Times articles. It finds that positive content tends to be more viral, but the relationship between emotion and virality is complex. Virality is influenced by physiological arousal, with high-arousal emotions like awe or anger driving more shares. Conversely, low-arousal emotions like sadness lead to less viral content. These findings hold even after accounting for factors like surprise and interest. Overall, the study sheds light on why people share content and offers insights for designing effective viral marketing campaigns. Berger (2011) examines the role of physiological arousal in social transmission, analyzing how emotions influence content sharing. High-arousal emotions, such as anxiety and amusement, significantly increase the likelihood of sharing, while low-arousal emotions, like sadness and contentment, have little effect. Experimental findings suggest that arousal, regardless of valence, enhances information dissemination (Arora et al., 2020). These insights have implications for marketing, public health messaging, and understanding how emotional engagement shapes cultural diffusion and online virality.

Ren and Yang (2011) investigate the use of machine learning to predict the popularity of online news articles. Using a dataset of articles from Mashable, various models were evaluated for accuracy, including regression, SVM, and Random Forest (Balali et al., 2017). Feature selection techniques, such as mutual information and Fisher criterion, were applied to enhance model performance. The results show that Random Forest outperformed other models, achieving 70% accuracy. The insights gained from this model can assist news platforms in anticipating audience engagement and optimizing content for greater reach (Rajest et al., 2023).

Uddin et al. (2016) explore the prediction of online news popularity using a before-publication approach, leveraging machine learning techniques. It proposes a Gradient Boosting Machine (GBM) model to predict whether an article will be shared and the number of shares it will receive based solely on metadata features known before publication. Using a dataset of Mashable news articles, the study compares GBM with the Random Forest (RF) model, showing that GBM outperforms RF by 1.8%, achieving a 74.5% AUC. The results indicate that article keywords, publication day, and data channel are among the most influential factors in predicting news popularity. These insights can help news organizations optimize content strategy before publication to maximize audience engagement (Raj et al., 2024).

Cai and Zheng (2022) present a GRU-based deep learning model for predicting news popularity before its release. It utilizes web scraping to collect news data, Word2Vec for feature extraction, and a GRU regression model for prediction. The model outperforms LSTM, linear regression, and random forests, achieving lower prediction errors and better computational efficiency. The results demonstrate that GRU's simpler structure improves processing speed while maintaining accuracy. This approach helps content creators optimize news ranking, recommendation, and audience engagement. Keneshloo et al. (2016) propose a time-series model to predict the peak time and shape of news article views using classification and online methods. The SpikeM algorithm and KSC clustering improve accuracy over traditional classification (Sebastian et al., 2024). Deployed at The Washington Post, the system processes real-time click data using Spark Streaming for better article promotion. Results show that SpikeM outperforms classification models in predicting article popularity trends (Kavunthi et al., 2024).

Liu et al. (2017) present a news popularity prediction model using grammatical construction (GC), author score, category score, content length, and publishing time. It introduces a GC-based feature, improving prediction accuracy by 6.62%, and applies logarithmic transformations for better category and author impact evaluation. The study finds the author's score to be the most influential factor in predicting popularity. A linear regression model estimates the number of views before publication, aiding news portals in optimizing content placement (Aravind et al., 2023). Berger and Schwartz (2011) investigate the factors behind immediate and ongoing word-of-mouth (WOM). It reveals that interest triggers initial WOM, while public visibility and environmental cues maintain it over time (Padmanabhan et al., 2023). The research explores the impact of WOM marketing campaigns and promotional giveaways on consumer discussions through real-world data and experiments. The insights guide businesses in crafting effective strategies to sustain long-term brand conversations.

PROPOSED MODEL

The outline proposed an approach for forecasting the popularity of news articles. Our primary objective is to predict the volume of page views an article will accumulate within the initial 24 hours following its publication. We systematically monitor all articles for the initial 30-minute window after publication to achieve this. We meticulously extract various temporal, social, and contextual features pertinent to our predictive model during this time. These features are the foundation for our forecasting mechanism, enabling us to accurately anticipate each news article's potential popularity trajectory. We systematically monitor all articles for the initial 30-minute window after publication to achieve this. We meticulously extract various temporal, social, and contextual features pertinent to our predictive model during this time. These features are the foundation for our forecasting mechanism, enabling us to accurately anticipate each news article's potential popularity trajectory.

Figure 1. Flow diagram from a proposed method in news article

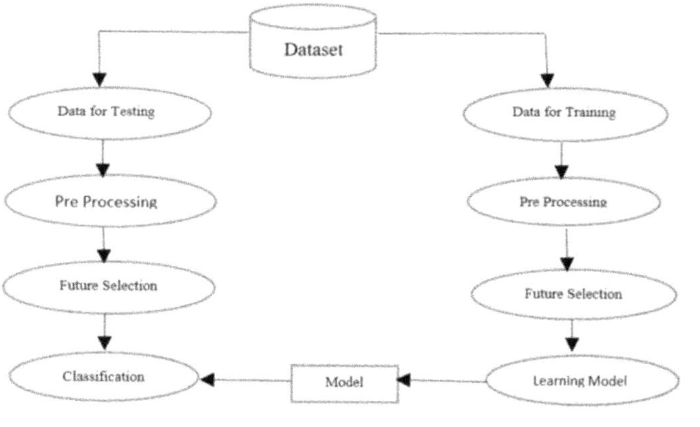

Figure 1 depicts a system that trains a model on a dataset, possibly to classify or filter data for retrieval purposes. However, due to the lack of labels on the decision point, it's difficult to say definitively what criteria the model uses to determine the outcome.

Features

The WP metadata offers a wealth of information on each article, encompassing elements like the title, complete content, keywords, author details, article type (whether a blog post or a formal article), category, news section, and publication date. Named entities play a pivotal role in influencing the popularity of news articles, especially when they pertain to notable localities or individuals. Utilizing the Stanford NLP Library, we identify these entities. While quantifying the occurrences of named entities may not fully convey each entity's importance, it provides insight into the extent of coverage on a particular topic within the article. Through our experiments, we aim to illustrate how these entity counts contribute to refining the accuracy of our predictions.

Utilizing the Stanford NLP Library, we identify these entities. While quantifying the occurrences of named entities may not fully convey each entity's importance, it provides insight into the extent of coverage on a particular topic within the article. Through our experiments, we aim to illustrate how these entity counts contribute to refining the accuracy of our predictions.

Figure 2. Architecture diagram of news article popularity

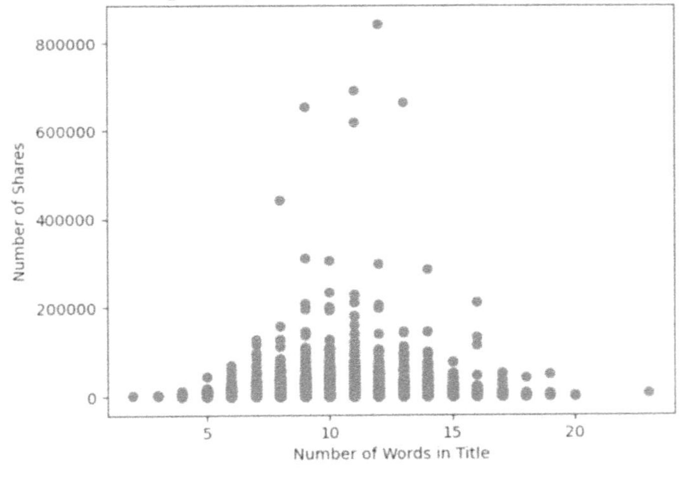

Figure 2 depicts a machine learning process involving retrieving information, performing text processing, feature extraction, and potentially using deep learning to prepare data for a machine learning model. The specific details of the machine learning task are not shown in the flowchart.

Freshness

All previously mentioned features are evaluated using standard methods and software libraries. Topic intersection measures the extent of overlap or similarity between the keywords in the queried article and those in the top archived articles. It is calculated by taking the intersection of the keyword sets of the queried and archived articles and then dividing it by the union of these sets. This quantitatively measures how closely related the topics covered in the queried article are to those discussed in the archived articles. A higher value indicates a greater overlap of topics, suggesting that the queried article may discuss similar subject matter to the archived articles.

Temporal Features

Temporal features refer to aspects of time or timing within a dataset or context. In the context of analyzing news articles or any time-based data, temporal features may include:

- Publication date/time: The date and time when the article was published.
- Hour of the day: The specific hour when the article was published.
- Day of the week: The day the article was published.
- Month or year: The month or year when the article was published.
- Time since publication: The duration between the publication time of the article and the current time.
- Seasonality: Patterns or trends related to particular seasons, such as holidays or specific events.
- Time of day trends: Trends or patterns in article popularity or engagement based on the time of day.
- Time between articles: The duration between the publication times of consecutive articles.
- Time decay: How the relevance or popularity of an article changes over time since its publication.
- Trend analysis: Identifying topics or themes that gain or lose popularity over time.

These temporal features can be valuable for understanding patterns in article popularity, predicting future trends, or optimizing publishing schedules for maximum engagement.

Social Media Features

Social media features pertain to aspects related to the engagement, sharing, and interaction of news articles or content on social media platforms. These features can provide valuable insights into articles' reach, virality, and impact. Some common social media features include integrating social media features into newspapers, which is likely to continue as publishers seek new ways to engage readers and stay relevant in an increasingly digital world. However, the extent to which these features are adopted will depend on factors such as audience preferences, technological advancements, and the evolving media landscape. Social media features play a crucial role in understanding the dynamics of news articles' popularity. By integrating social media features into newspapers and online platforms, publishers can enhance reader engagement and relevance in today's digital era. The adoption of these features hinges on various factors, including audience preferences, technological advancements, and the evolving media landscape. As publishers strive to stay connected with their audience and amplify their reach, leveraging social media features will likely remain a cornerstone strategy.

Figure 3. Block diagram of modules in news article

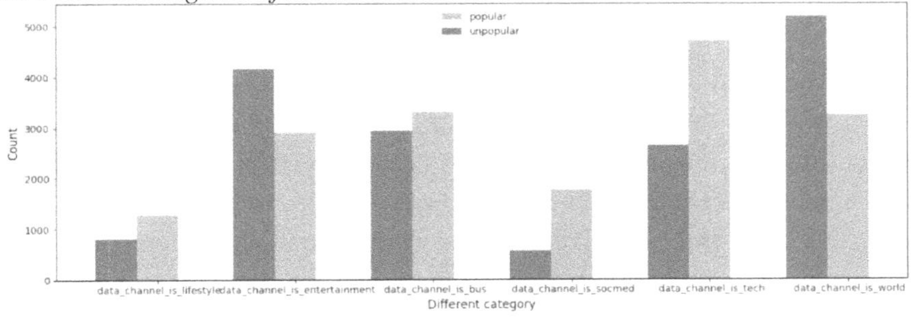

Figure 3 depicts a sentiment analysis process that involves collecting social media data, pre-processing it, extracting features, training a model to classify sentiment, and potentially using topic modeling to understand sentiment on specific topics.

- Share count: The number of times the article has been shared on various social media platforms such as Facebook, Twitter, LinkedIn, etc.
- Like/Reaction count: The number of likes, reactions, or other positive engagement the article has received on social media platforms.
- Comment count: The number of comments or replies the article has garnered on social media.
- Click-through rate (CTR): The percentage of users who clicked on the article link shared on social media platforms.
- Social media platform distribution: Analysis of which social media platforms drive the most traffic or engagement for the article.
- Engagement rate: The overall engagement rate (likes, shares, comments) compared to the total number of views or impressions.
- Sentiment analysis: The sentiment (positive, negative, neutral) expressed in comments or reactions to the article on social media.

- Influencer engagement: Identification of influential users or accounts who have shared or interacted with the article on social media.
- Virality metrics measure how quickly and widely the article has spread across social media.
- Social media referral traffic: The amount of traffic driven to the article's website from various social media platforms.

These social media features can help publishers understand the impact of their content on social networks, identify opportunities for audience engagement, and optimize their social media strategies for maximum reach and impact.

RESULT

Insights for Content Strategy: Predictive analysis of news article popularity yields valuable insights for refining content strategies. By examining social media interactions, topic relevance, and historical performance, publishers can better understand audience preferences and tailor content accordingly.

Anticipating Trends and Preferences: Predictive models enable publishers to stay ahead of trends and anticipate reader preferences. By leveraging data-driven insights, publishers can adapt their content to meet evolving audience demands, enhancing reader satisfaction and loyalty.

Enhanced Audience Engagement: By prioritizing content with higher potential for engagement, publishers can strengthen audience engagement and drive overall success in the digital landscape. This approach fosters deeper connections with readers and boosts reader interaction with published content.

Figure 4. Count of popular/unpopular news

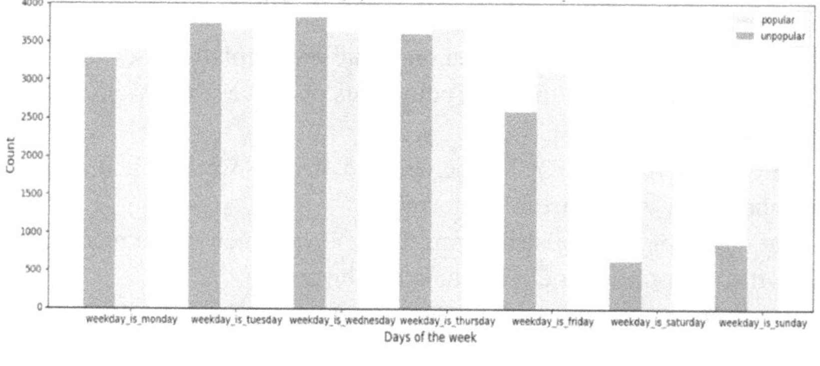

Figure 4 shows the number of popular and unpopular news stories over all days: Monday, Tuesday, Wednesday, Friday, and Saturday. Figure 4 tells us that during the week, at the end of Sunday and Saturday, the news popular/unpopular is too low compared to the other days in the week.

Table 1. Count of popular/unpopular news

Days	Count of popular	Count of unpopular
Monday	3400	3300
Tuesday	3200	3300
Wednesday	3600	3400
Thursday	3200	3100
Friday	3000	2500
Saturday	1800	600
Sunday	1800	900

Table 1 shows the number of popular and unpopular news stories over all days of the week: Monday, Tuesday, Wednesday, Thursday, Saturday, and Sunday. The above graph tells us that during the week on Sunday and Saturday, the news popular/unpopular is too low compared to the other days. This is an information store (Table 2).

Table 2. Algorithm and accuracy

Algorithm	Accuracy	F1-score	AUC
Random Forest	0.659016	0.683964	0.656702
Logistic Regression	0.646406	0.683521	0.642111
KNN	0.570492	0.604046	0.567655
Decision Tree	0.640353	0.649287	0.640708
Ada Boost	0.663304	0.689173	0.660783
Bagging	0.645902	0.669336	0.643964

Accuracy=TP+TN/FP+FN+TP+TN

Where: TPTP = True Positives

TNTN = True Negatives

FPFP = False Positives

FNFN = False Negatives

ALGORITHMS

Random Forest: Random Forest is an ensemble learning method that constructs many decision trees during training. It operates by building a set of decision trees from randomly selected subsets of the training data. Then, it combines their predictions through averaging or voting to improve accuracy and prevent overfitting.

Logistic Regression: Despite its name, logistic regression is a linear classification model rather than regression. It predicts the probability of an event's occurrence by fitting data into a logistic curve. It's widely used for binary classification problems but can extend to multi-class classification.

K-Nearest Neighbors (KNN): KNN is a simple and intuitive algorithm for classification and regression tasks. It works by finding the K closest data points in the training set to a given test data point, classifying the test data based on the majority class, or averaging the values of its neighbors.

Decision Tree: A decision Tree is a flowchart-like tree structure where each internal node represents a feature, each branch represents a decision, and each leaf node represents the outcome. It's used for classification and regression tasks and can handle numerical and categorical data.

AdaBoost (Adaptive Boosting): AdaBoost is an ensemble learning technique that combines multiple weak learners (e.g., decision trees) to create a strong classifier. It assigns weights to each training example and adjusts them at each iteration to focus on misclassified examples, thereby improving performance. Bagging (Bootstrap Aggregating): Bagging is an ensemble learning technique that involves training multiple models independently on different subsets of the training data and then combining their predictions through averaging or voting. It's particularly useful for reducing variance and preventing overfitting.

DISCUSSION

User Engagement and Behavior: Explore the relationship between article popularity and user engagement metrics such as comments, shares, and click-through rates. Discuss whether there are correlations between these metrics and how they might influence each other. Consider how user behavior varies across different platforms (e.g., social media, news websites) and the implications for predicting popularity.

Temporal Dynamics: Investigate how the timing of article publication influences its popularity. Discuss whether articles published during certain times of the day, week, or year are more likely to gain traction and why. Explore the concept of "news cycles" and how it affects the lifespan of an article's popularity.

Content Quality and Virality: Examine the relationship between content quality and article popularity. Discuss whether articles with higher-quality content (e.g., well-researched, insightful) are more popular and whether certain characteristics make content more likely to go viral. Consider how headline wording, emotional appeal, and novelty impact virality.

Generalizability and Scalability: Assess the generalizability of the findings across different domains, languages, and cultures. Discuss whether the predictive models developed in the study are scalable and applicable to diverse contexts. Consider the challenges of adapting these models to new datasets and the potential need for domain-specific feature engineering.

Figure 5. Count of popular/unpopular news over different article categories

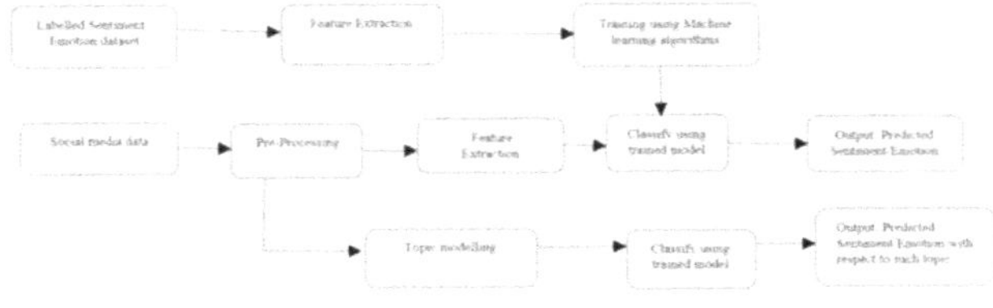

Figure 5 shows the popular/unpopular news count over different article categories. It shows the graph of lifestyle data, Entertainment, Business, Social media, Technical, and World news. The lifestyle data and Social media news have a low count of popular/unpopular news compared to the other article categories (Table 3).

Table 3. Count of popular/unpopular news Article category

Article Category	Count of popular	Count of unpopular
Lifestyle Data	1200	900
Entertainment	2900	4200
Business	3200	3000
Social media	1900	600
Technical	4500	2600
World News	5000	3100

By engaging in these discussions, researchers can comprehensively analyze the implications, limitations, and future directions of their work on predicting the popularity of news articles. This contributes to academic knowledge and informs practical media analytics and content strategy applications.

Figure 6. Number of words vs number of shares

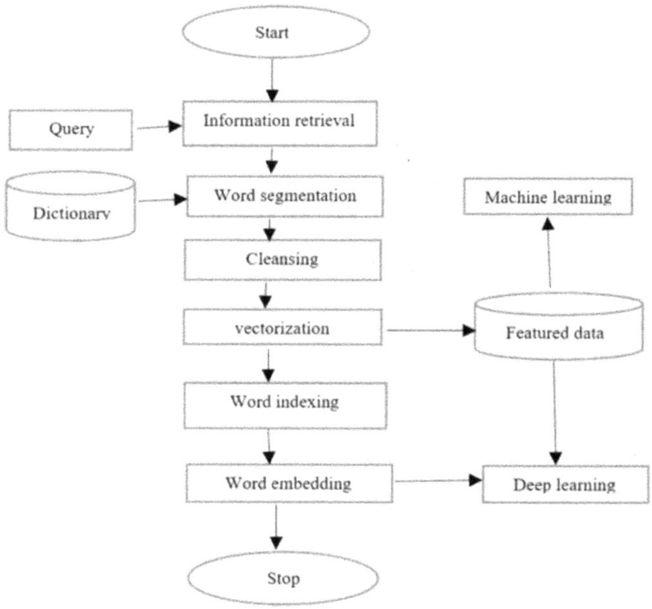

Figure 6 shows the number of words vs number of shares. If the word count is low, then the share is high. The number of shares is high, as the word count is below 4000. This shows that the number of shares is high when the word title is low.

Algorithmic Bias and Filter Bubbles: Address concerns related to algorithmic bias and its potential impact on predicting article popularity. Discuss how algorithms used by social media platforms and news aggregators might influence the visibility and dissemination of articles, leading to filter bubbles and echo chambers. Consider the ethical implications of algorithmic decision-making in shaping public discourse.

Future Directions: Propose avenues for future research to advance the field of predicting article popularity. This may include exploring novel features, refining prediction models, integrating user feedback mechanisms, or investigating the impact of emerging technologies (e.g., natural language processing and machine learning). Consider interdisciplinary approaches that draw insights from sociology, psychology, and communication studies.

CONCLUSION

This study represents a pioneering effort to forecast page view counts for news articles by analyzing various influential factors, including temporal, social, and contextual attributes. Through a comprehensive evaluation, our findings highlight that contextual features, particularly those related to the freshness of an article, play a crucial role in predicting the page views of viral content. Meanwhile, metadata features emerge as the most reliable indicators for assessing the overall performance of news articles. By thoroughly examining these feature sets, we identify the key attributes that significantly impact the prediction of news article popularity. Encouraged by the robust results obtained from offline evaluations, we have successfully implemented this predictive model at The Washington Post. This real-world deployment demonstrates the practical effectiveness of our approach, enabling more precise forecasting of article engagement. By leveraging these insights, news organizations can optimize content strategies, allocate resources efficiently, and enhance audience engagement. Looking ahead, future work will focus on expanding the scope of popularity prediction by integrating additional elements that influence an article's lifecycle, from creation to publication and subsequent evolution. Given the rapidly changing landscape of digital journalism, incorporating real-time social media updates, user-generated content, and interactive features will be instrumental in maximizing audience retention. These advancements will empower news organizations to adapt to the dynamic nature of online content consumption, ensuring they remain at the forefront of an increasingly competitive and fast-paced media environment.

REFERENCES

Aravind, B. R., Bhuvaneswari, G., & Rajest, S. S. (2023). ICT-based digital technology for testing and evaluation of English language teaching. In *Handbook of Research on Learning in Language Classrooms Through ICT-Based Digital Technology* (pp. 1–11). IGI Global.

Arora, A., Srivastava, A., & Bansal, S. (2020). Business competitive analysis using promoted post detection on social media. *Journal of Retailing and Consumer Services*, *54*(5), 101941. DOI: 10.1016/j.jretconser.2019.101941

Aung, T. T., Paw, S., & Tin, H. H. K. (2024). Boys' love (BL) drama series review system for opinion mining with sentiment analysis. *FMDB Transactions on Sustainable Computer Letters*, *2*(2), 99–110. DOI: 10.69888/FTSCL.2024.000184

Balali, A., Asadpour, M., & Faili, H. (2017). A supervised method to predict the popularity of news articles. *Computing Systems*, *21*(4), 703–716.

Bandari, R., Asur, S., & Huberman, B. (2021). The pulse of news in social media: Forecasting popularity. *Proceedings of the ... International AAAI Conference on Weblogs and Social Media. International AAAI Conference on Weblogs and Social Media*, *6*(1), 26–33. DOI: 10.1609/icwsm.v6i1.14261

Berger, J. (2011). Arousal increases social transmission of information. *Psychological Science*, *22*(7), 891–893. DOI: 10.1177/0956797611413294 PMID: 21690315

Berger, J., & Milkman, K. L. (2010). Social transmission, emotion, and the virality of online content. Marketing Science Institute Working Paper Series, Report No. 10-114.

Berger, J., & Milkman, K. L. (2012). What makes online content viral? *JMR, Journal of Marketing Research*, *49*(2), 192–205. DOI: 10.1509/jmr.10.0353

Berger, J., & Schwartz, E. M. (2011). What drives immediate and ongoing word of mouth? *JMR, Journal of Marketing Research*, *48*(5), 869–880. DOI: 10.1509/jmkr.48.5.869

. Bhargava, S., & Ghosh, D. S. (2018). Analysis of feature reduction techniques for online news popularity prediction. Smart Moves Journal IJO science, 4(10), 1-5.

Bi, X., & Wang, H. (2019). An enhanced high-order Boltzmann machine for feature engineering. *Engineering Applications of Artificial Intelligence*, *78*(2), 37–52. DOI: 10.1016/j.engappai.2018.10.011

Birant, K. U. (2022). Multi-view rank-based random forest: A new algorithm for prediction in esports. *Expert Systems: International Journal of Knowledge Engineering and Neural Networks*, *39*(2), e12857. DOI: 10.1111/exsy.12857

. Cai, Y., & Zheng, Z. (2022). Prediction of news popularity based on deep neural network. Scientific Programming, 2022, 8280036, 7 pages. DOI: 10.1155/2022/8280036

Chaturvedi, I., Cambria, E., Welsch, R. E., & Herrera, F. (2018). Distinguishing between facts and opinions for sentiment analysis: Survey and challenges. *Information Fusion*, *44*(11), 65–77. DOI: 10.1016/j.inffus.2017.12.006

Choudhury, S., Sandhu, A. S., & Pradhan, T. (2017). Genetic algorithm based correlation enhanced prediction of online news popularity. In *Computational intelligence in data mining* (pp. 133–144). Springer. DOI: 10.1007/978-981-10-3874-7_13

Christy, K. R., Mi, R. Z., Tao, R., & Lu, L. (2023). Disruptive versus no disruptive advertising in online streaming video services: How does advertisement placement affect consumer perceptions and ad effectiveness? *Journal of Advertising Research*, *63*(1), 2023–2006. DOI: 10.2501/JAR-2023-006

Devi, B. T., & Rajasekaran, R. (2023). A Comprehensive Review on Deepfake Detection on Social Media Data. *FMDB Transactions on Sustainable Computing Systems*, *1*(1), 11–20.

Estrada-Jiménez, J., Parra-Arnau, J., Rodríguez-Hoyos, A., & Forné, J. (2019). On the regulation of personal data distribution in online advertising platforms. *Engineering Applications of Artificial Intelligence*, *82*(6), 13–29. DOI: 10.1016/j.engappai.2019.03.013

Farr, J. N., Jenkins, J. J., & Paterson, D. G. (1951). Simplification of Flesch reading ease formula. *The Journal of Applied Psychology*, *35*(5), 333–337. DOI: 10.1037/h0062427

Fernandas, K., Vinagre, P., & Cortez, P. (2015). A proactive intelligent decision support system for predicting the popularity of online news. In *Portuguese Conference on Artificial Intelligence* (pp. 535–546). Springer, Cham, Switzerland. DOI: 10.1007/978-3-319-23485-4_53

Hutto, C., & Gilbert, E. (2014). VADER: A Parsimonious Rule-Based Model for Sentiment Analysis of Social Media Text. Proceedings of the International AAAI Conference on Web and Social Media, 8(1), 216-225, Copenhagen, Denmark. DOI: 10.1609/icwsm.v8i1.14550

Kavunthi, S., Venkateswaran, P. S., Sudha, P., & Sridharlakshmi, N. R. B. (2024). Cultivating quality work-life balance: A critical factor in enhancing nursing careers and patient wellbeing. *AVE Trends in Intelligent Social Letters*, *1*(2), 104–112.

Keneshloo, Y., Wang, S., Han, E.-H. S., & Ramakrishnan, N. (2016). Predicting the shape and peak time of news article views. 2016 IEEE International Conference on Big Data (Big Data), Washington, DC, USA, 2400-2409. DOI: 10.1109/BigData.2016.7840875

Liu, C., Wang, W., Zhang, Y., Dong, Y., He, F., & Wu, C. (2017). Predicting the popularity of online news based on multivariate analysis. *2017 IEEE International Conference on Computer and Information Technology (CIT)*, Helsinki, Finland, 9-15. https://doi.org/DOI: 10.1109/CIT.2017.36

Mishne, G., & Glance, N. (2006). Leave a reply: An analysis of weblog comments. Edinburgh, United Kingdom.

Padmanabhan, J., Rajest, S. S., & Veronica, J. J. (2023). A study on the orthography and grammatical errors of tertiary-level students. In *Handbook of Research on Learning in Language Classrooms Through ICT-Based Digital Technology* (pp. 41–53). IGI Global. DOI: 10.4018/978-1-6684-6682-7.ch004

Raj, M. A., Thinesh, M. A., Varmann, S. S. M., Pothu, A. R., & Paramasivan, P. (2024). Ensemble-based phishing website detection using Extra Trees classifier. *AVE Trends in Intelligent Computing Systems*, *1*(3), 142–156.

Rajest, S. S., Moccia, S., Chinnusamy, K., Singh, B., & Regin, R. (Eds.). (2023). Advances in Educational Technologies and Instructional Design *Handbook of research on learning in language classrooms through ICT-based digital technology*., DOI: 10.4018/978-1-6684-6682-7

. Ren, H., & Yang, Q. (2011). Predicting and evaluating the popularity of online news. Stanford University Machine Learning Report.

Said, F. B., & Tripathi, S. (2023). Epistemology of Digital Journalism Shift in South Global Nations: A Bibliometric Analysis. *FMDB Transactions on Sustainable Technoprise Letters*, *1*(1), 47–60.

Saleh, M., Mustapha, Z. B., & Ndirmbitah, B. K. (2024). Empirical analysis of digital marketing on the purchasing habit of conservative digital users of common social media. *FMDB Transactions on Sustainable Technoprise Letters*, *2*(1), 31–41. DOI: 10.69888/FTSTPL.2024.000228

Sebastian, J. E., Babu, J., & Ashifa, K. M. (2024). Family resilience during COVID-19: A study of adaptation and well-being among social work students. *AVE Trends in Intelligent Social Letters*, *1*(2), 93–103.

Ser, D., Bilbao, J., Lana, M. N., Muhammad, I., & Camacho, K. (2022). Efficient fake news detection using bagging ensembles of bidirectional echo state networks. In *2022 International Joint Conference on Neural Networks (IJCNN)* (pp. 1–7), Padua, Italy.

Suraj, D., Dinesh, S., Balaji, R., Deepika, P., & Ajila, F. (2023). Deciphering Product Review Sentiments Using BERT and TensorFlow. *FMDB Transactions on Sustainable Computing Systems*, *1*(2), 77–88.

Tatar, A., de Amorim, M. D., Fdida, S., & Antoniadis, P. (2014). A survey on predicting the popularity of web content. *Journal of Internet Services and Applications*, *5*(1), 1–20. DOI: 10.1186/s13174-014-0008-y

Tripathi, S. (2023). Breaking News or Breaking Trust? The Impact of Credibility Menace on Indian Media. *FMDB Transactions on Sustainable Social Sciences Letters*, *1*(4), 189–197.

Uddin, M. T., Patwary, M. J. A., Ahsan, T., & Alam, M. S. (2016). Predicting the popularity of online news from content metadata. *2016 International Conference on Innovations in Science, Engineering and Technology (ICISET)*, Dhaka, Bangladesh, 1-5. DOI: 10.1109/ICISET.2016.7856498

Venkateswaran, P. S., Singh, S., Paramasivan, P., Rajest, S. S., Lourens, M. E., & Regin, R. (2023). A Study on The Influence of Quality of Service on Customer Satisfaction Towards Hotel Industry. *FMDB Transactions on Sustainable Social Sciences Letters*, *1*(1), 1–11.

Chapter 10
Real-Time Plants Recognition and Medicinal Insights Using Deep Learning

K. N. V. Satyanarayana
https://orcid.org/0000-0002-6254-0593
SRKR Engineering College, India

T. S. S. Harsha
SRKR Engineering College, India

V. Adarsh
SRKR Engineering College, India

I. Mahesh Babu
SRKR Engineering College, India

S. K. Mohammad Hujaifa
SRKR Engineering College, India

C. Satheesh
Dhaanish Ahmed College of Engineering, India

ABSTRACT

In recent times, Deep learning has been utilized in many areas, particularly for medicinal plant identification and evaluation of their therapeutic values. In this research, we use transfer learning capabilities of three state-of-the-art architectures: ResNet-50, VGG-16, and Xception. They are trained for the high-accuracy classification of plants and assessment of their medicinal properties. Our experiments demonstrate that the performance is significantly high, with ResNet-50 having 91.41%, VGG-16 84.27%, and an impressive 91.68% from Xception models, respectively. The findings from these trials highlight how effective transfer learning can be over limited data availability and complex feature extraction that is typically associated with medicinal plant identification tasks. Moreover, we perform a comprehensive analysis to connect identified plants to their respective medical values, which gives useful information about their treatment uses as the therapeutic application (s).

DOI: 10.4018/979-8-3373-5203-9.ch010

INTRODUCTION

The world of plants is diversified with thousands of species, many of which have medicinal properties that are indispensable for human well-being. However, despite their significance, some medicinal plants face threats like extinction, while others may be dangerous to the health of humans. This makes them the foundation of various industries and a vital resource for humanity, especially in relation to herbal medicine and traditional practices such as Ayurveda and folk medicine (Dhinakaran et al., 2023). Herbal plants also serve as an alternative to disease treatment, given their renowned natural healing abilities; about 80% of the global population still depends on traditional medicine. In India alone, more than 8000 plant species have been found to possess medicinal value, with about 1500 being used in herbal remedies. Of these, 500 plants find application in commercial Ayurvedic preparations, making them paramount in traditional healing systems (Panyaram, 2024).

Ayurveda, an ancient medical science deeply embedded in herbs and plants for its cure, faces an urgent issue- low awareness about these plants among the population (Obeta et al., 2024). This is further compounded by the fact that there are not enough specialists who can identify these plants. In response, this project capitalizes on advances in Deep Learning and Machine Learning to develop a plant recognition system (Karthikeyan et al., 2024). Our method employs up-to-the-minute techniques like ResNet-50, VGG16, and Xception, which are extensively regarded as champions of image recognition tasks (Bose et al., 2024). We intend to use this dataset to train and validate some of the models, such as ResNet-50, VGG16, and Xception. Our data is painstakingly collected and curated; thus, it is a goldmine for our research activities (Karthik et al., 2024).

Classification of leaves becomes a vital part of our plant recognition system as they contain the most significant information for species differentiation (Gnanaguru et al., 2024). This is why our research project seeks to design an effective recognition system that will enable the accurate identification of medicinal plants (Jeba et al., 2024). Our study aims to provide solutions to some challenges that exist in traditional medicine, such as the lack of access by ordinary people to specialists and insufficient information about plants used in medicine (Marar et al., 2023). The integration between technology and traditional herbal medicine will enlighten society on plant diversity while advancing health care services (Gandhi et al., 2024).

Motivation

In the wake of the global pandemic, the importance of health, individual health, and Encourage the exploration of alternative medicine, especially the treatment of Aspirin. Most people Are you looking at the medicinal plants that are around you, and you don't know them? It differs from normal flowers and potted herbs. It is still a plant. We have been identified as having little knowledge about specific medicinal properties. a plant map posses. At present, those who have individual open training have good medicinal plants, Insulating women and children, from forest areas.

Internal personnel are expected to be involved in the organization's activities for a number of professionals. They were hoping to find a plant. Manufacturers were selling plastic bags, but they were not able to. changes in local names and the state of the arrival of similar plants in their factors, making manual identification more demanding. The results are good if you use good. Incorrect, these renders are imported, resulting in unpredictable results. It is, in fact, essential for the establishment of the Aspirin industry. Stringy strings of thick glass as a thin cloth, which is difficult to make. I am very grateful for the maintenance of this press and the great food that I recommend. Credit and effect of the oil will be transferred to the Absyrpedic medicine remains if important part of the holistic health.

LITERATURE COLLECTION

The recognition and classification of medicinal plants hold significant importance in various fields, including healthcare, pharmacology, and biodiversity conservation. The exact identification of medicinal plants is vital for finding potential therapeutic agents, understanding traditional medicine systems, and plant diversity conservation (Minu et al., 2023). Technology has advanced recently, especially in deep learning and image processing, leading to a revolution in the way medicinal plants are recognized and classified (Priscila et al., 2023). In this context, several studies have been conducted to explore different methodologies and techniques for automating the process of identifying medicinal plants. Batavia et al. (2017) surveyed Ayurvedic medicine classification using TensorFlow, showcasing the feasibility of employing deep learning models like Google LeNet for classifying Ayurvedic medicinal plants, thus bridging the gap between traditional medicine systems and modern technology.

Paulson and Ravishankar (2020). used Convolutional Neural Networks (CNNs), including VGG16 and VGG19, with high accuracy in identifying indigenous medicinal plants from Kerala, thereby providing a robust tool for conserving and exploiting traditional medicinal knowledge. Truong Nguyen Quoc (2020) explored different kinds of CNN with the purpose of detecting Vietnamese medicinal plants. This offered insight on how to save biodiversity and ethnomedicine. Thella and Ulagamuthalvi (2021) did an extensive review of methods for classifying medical plant imaging, elucidating the need for automated plant classification systems in aiding environmental conservation efforts. Dileep and Pournami (2019) developed AyurLeaf, a deep-learning approach that achieves high classification accuracy on leaf samples from various medicinal plants, facilitating pharmaceutical research and herbal medicine applications. Sandeep Kumar and Talasila (2014) studied an approach that relies on leaf features to identify medicinal plants automatically. The study emphasized the importance of feature engineering in improving plant recognition accuracy. Jayalath et al. (2019) implemented an image-processing neural network that automatically identifies rare medicinal plants. This will go a long way in protecting Sri Lankan Ayurveda medicine's medicinal flora (Jeba et al., 2023).

Additionally, Kumar et al. (2017) have contributed to the identification of medicinal plants using deep learning and image processing. In their work, they combine conventional wisdom and modern technology to improve the precision as well as swiftness involved in plant recognition (Nanban et al., 2024). Through interdisciplinary collaboration, they connect gaps that exist within traditional ways of doing things and modern advancements that enhance creativity in health care as well as biodiversity conservation (Abinavkrishnaa et al., 2023; Nomula, 2024). Their study underscores the importance of automated classification systems in aiding environmental preservation initiatives.

METHODOLOGY

Deep learning is a branch of AI devoted to teaching deep neural networks hierarchical representations directly from raw data. These networks are made up of layers of interconnected neurons, and the deeper architecture facilitates the extraction of complex attributes. The important constituents include activation functions that introduce nonlinearity, backpropagation for optimizing model parameters, and deep architectures applicable to image recognition and natural language processing. Enormous training datasets have driven Deep Learning. For instance, the foundational ImageNet database comprises 1.2 million images with more than a thousand classes that have been used as a benchmark in DL research since its development. However, note that models like GoogLeNet, AlexNet, and VGG were always first placed in the competition known as the ImageNet Large Scale Visual Recognition Challenge (LSVRC).

However, DL has changed beyond ImageNet-centric approaches. New architectures such as DenseNet, FractalNet, Inception units, and Residual Networks have offered higher efficiency and performance than traditional methods. These advances have pushed DL into previously unattainable realms through conventional means. Convolutional Neural Networks (CNNs) are made up of individual layers that play distinct roles in architecture. Starting with the input layer, CNNs include many convolutional layers interposed with aggregation or sub-layers, followed by nonlinear layers for feature extraction and representation. This is then proceeded by a small set of fully connected layers ending with a softmax classification layer for category prediction.

DL's remarkable journey has been highlighted by this evolutionary trajectory, which started with a foundation deeply rooted in ImageNet and is characterized by diverse and sophisticated architectures at present. As DL continues to push boundaries, its transformative impact on various domains remains undeniable, promising more breakthroughs and advancements in the future. Transfer Learning is an approach to machine learning where information acquired from one task is used to solve another. According to deep learning, transfer learning involves using pre-trained models trained on extensive large data sets specifically for particular tasks. The latter may include fine-tuning that adjusts the parameters of a pre-trained model on smaller task-specific datasets or feature extraction, which uses learned representations from a pre-trained model as input to a new classifier built specifically for the target task. In such conditions, this awareness can help improve significantly by borrowing from similar tasks within or across domains, especially in cases where there is not enough labelled data.

Convolutional Neural Network: Convolutional Neural Networks (CNNs) are an important breakthrough in deep learning, especially for image analysis. CNNs have been repeatedly proven effective through extensive experimentation, mainly in feature extraction and classification tasks. The learning process of CNN architecture is based on two fundamental layers: Feature Learning and Classification via Back-propagation. In identifying multi-class patterns with intricate structures like breast cancer analysis, CNNs are known to be deep and complex. The layout structure of a CNN can be given as follows:

Input Layer: Firstly, it acts as a starting point for raw data input, particularly when dealing with images while processing them. Each neuron in the input layer corresponds to a pixel in the input image, and these values represent its intensity or color value. This consists of width, height, and color channels' numbers for colored pictures, among other things, which eventually determine the size of the input layer by looking at the dimensions of the input images (Figure 1).

Figure 1. RGB image

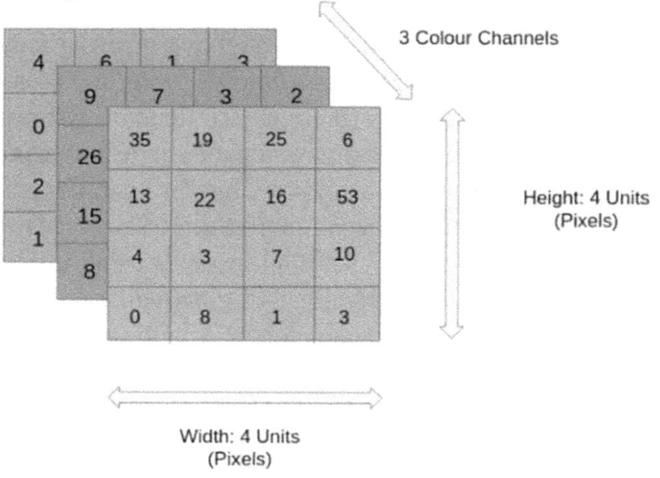

Convolutional Layer: As the name suggests, convolutional layers follow the input layer. These layers apply filters or kernels that can be learned to convolve over the input image by computing dot product between filter weights and small local patches of the input. Thus, we obtain feature maps that capture different characteristics of a given input, e.g., edges, textures, patterns, etc. Several filters are applied simultaneously to create multiple feature maps for distinct features in various spatial locations. Convolution is usually followed by the application of activation functions like Rectified Linear Units (ReLU) (Figure 2).

Figure 2. Convolution operation

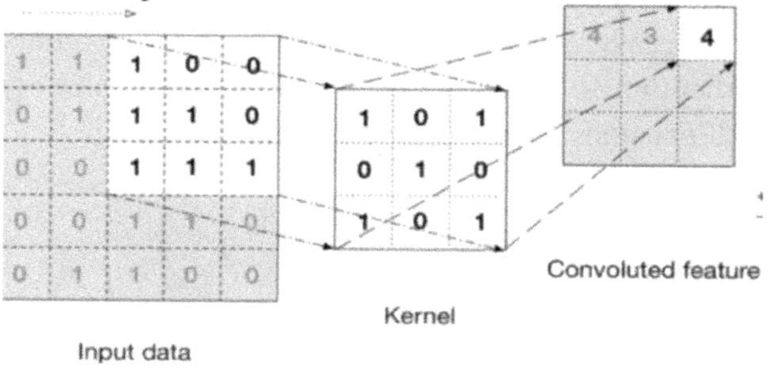

Stride: It is the step size of the filter moving across the input data in convolutional neural networks. For example, a stride value of 1 would cause a one-pixel shift at a time, thus altering the sizes of output feature maps. When strides are increased, this results in smaller-sized feature maps on output, leading to spatial down-sampling and vice versa.

Padding: Adding some border pixels before performing convolution operations on an input is called padding. In particular, padding maintains spatial dimensions and information at edges. The aim here is for the output feature maps that have the same spatial dimensions as the input so that no information is lost during convolution.

Activation Function: They are nonlinear functions that enable neural networks to learn complex patterns. Activation functions such as sigmoid, ReLU, tanh, and softmax determine neuron activation, which is crucial to approximating complex functions and changing inputs into them. ReLU has been preferred due to its simplicity and effectiveness for deep learning models.

For ReLU: $f(x) = \max(0,x)$

Pooling Layer: In order to reduce the size of the feature maps while preserving the relevant information after the convolution operation, pooling layers are used. The pooling process entails sliding a small window across every feature map and keeping only the maximum or average value within each window as decided by either max pooling or average pooling. This makes it easier for our learned features to remain invariant under slight changes in inputs, which may happen at subsequent levels, thus reducing computational overheads experienced at this level. Furthermore, this reduces sensitivity to exact position in space and hence enhances translation invariance properties exhibited by neural networks when it comes to locating objects with respect to their spatial positions (Figure 3).

Figure 3. Pooling

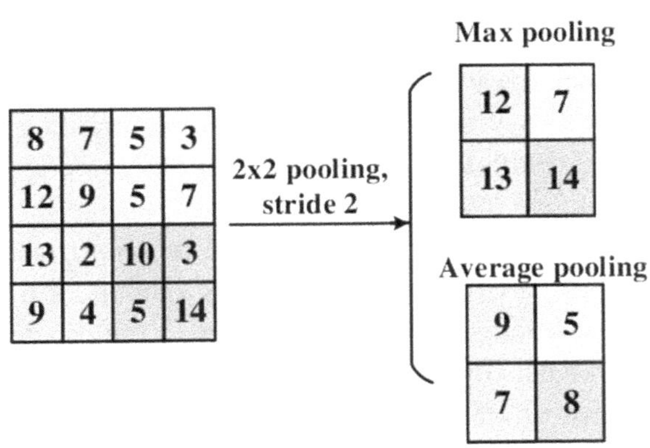

Fully Connected Layers: The last part of the architecture or network is typically a fully connected layer (also called dense layer) that performs high-level reasoning and decision-making. In these layers, every neuron is connected to all those in the previous layer. The output from the final pooling layer is made into a vector by flattening it, and it is this vector that forms the input for one or more fully connected layers. These layers perform classification or regression on learned features and give out final outputs, such as class probabilities in image classification tasks. For instance, in most cases, after fully connected layers, the softmax activation function can be employed to determine class probabilities during classification, or a linear activation function may be used during none-classification.

These two types of representations can then be combined into a flat vector and passed through multiple hidden units of a fully connected neural network with a number of hidden layers. Thus, nonlinear activation functions are employed between these neurons in order to facilitate learning within the system for subsequent classification tasks. Notably, the adoption of sigmoid or softmax activation functions at the last stage of classification enables the network to categorize input data on a probability scale, which leads to valuable insights into their underlying attributes.

State of Art Models

The term "state-of-the-art" (SoTA) models refers to the most advanced and best-performing models in a particular field at a given time. These are models that show what current research and development has achieved, and they perform way better than prior methods. Typically, state-of-the-art models in deep learning and artificial intelligence exhibit higher levels of accuracy, efficiency, and generalization than their predecessors. They employ novel architectures, training methods, and datasets to achieve remarkable results for different tasks like image recognition and natural language processing, among others. The state-of-the-art models in deep learning and artificial intelligence are usually more accurate, efficient, and generalizable than their predecessors. They utilize new architectures, training techniques, and datasets to give amazing results for other jobs, such as image recognition and natural language processing, among others.

Resnet50: ResNet50 represents a key advance in deep learning that arrived on the scene in 2015 as part of the ResNet family models. This was developed by Kaiming He et al. at Microsoft Research to address the problem of effectively training very deep neural networks. The key novelty of ResNet50 is its introduction of residual learning. Instead of directly learning the desired mappings, ResNet50 learns residual functions that are easier to optimize. It relies on residual blocks that have shortcut connections to bypass one or more layers. Architecture-wise, it has 50 layers inside a convolutional layer followed by batch normalization and rectified linear unit (ReLU) activation function. Successes are partly due to either basic blocks or bottleneck blocks constituting the residual blocks used by ResNet50. The basic block contains two convolutional layers with 3x3 filters, while the bottleneck block has three convolutions: 1x1, 3x3, and 1x1, which reduce computational cost but still maintain effectiveness (Figure 4).

Figure 4. Resnet50 architecture

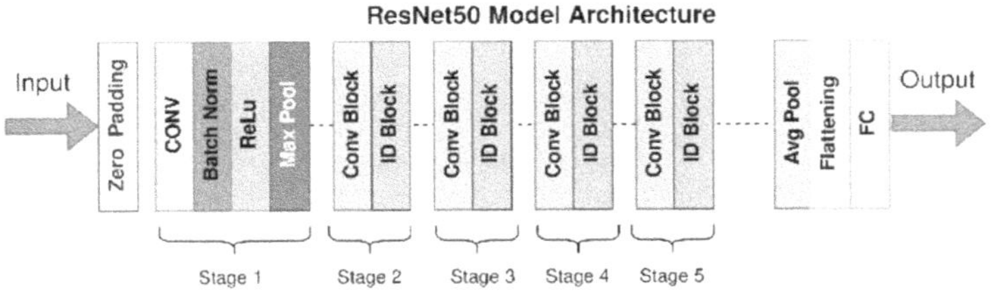

ResNet50 is most advantageous when it comes to the possibility of training deep neural networks. In this way, ResNet50 solves the problem of vanishing gradients by making use of skip connections, thus allowing for the training of networks with hundreds of layers. The latter aspect is essential in capturing intricate hierarchical features in large datasets, which in turn results in better performance on such tasks as image classification, object detection, and image segmentation.

It has been a major revolution in computer vision and deep learning as we know it today. Many other applications have adopted it as their foundational architecture. Pre-trained versions are easily available, enabling transfer learning when the task lacks enough data for training. ResNet50 still stands out among others and hence signifies groundbreaking work that affirms how crucial innovative architectural designs greatly impact complex problems both within computer vision and beyond its boundaries.

VGG16: It is from this inspiration that they developed VGG16, a convolutional neural network (CNN) architecture by the Visual Geometry Group at the University of Oxford, which had an enormous impact on computer vision. The success of earlier CNN models like AlexNet in tasks such as image classification and identification prompted the development of these advanced architectures. Its simplicity, combined with its effectiveness, makes VGG16 stand out. VGG16's architecture is uniform, consisting of 16 weight layers, hence its name. In the same way, each block consists of a sequence of convolutional layers followed by max-pooling layers for spatial downsampling. This means that more complex features can be extracted through the network since it has been set up with convolutional layers having 3x3 filters and a stride of 1.

Each of the blocks of convolutional layers in VGG16 is followed by a max-pooling layer with filter size 2x2 and stride 2. These pooling operations assist in keeping the most important data while reducing the spatial dimensions of the maps mentioned. As one traverses this, features that are either learned or explicitly represented within become more global and distinctive. Before carrying out softmax classification, VGG16 has three fully connected layers, each consisting of 4096 units. These high-level features produced by convolutional layers are added to class probabilities, which a network can then use to predict given input data (Figure 5).

Figure 5. VGG16 architecture

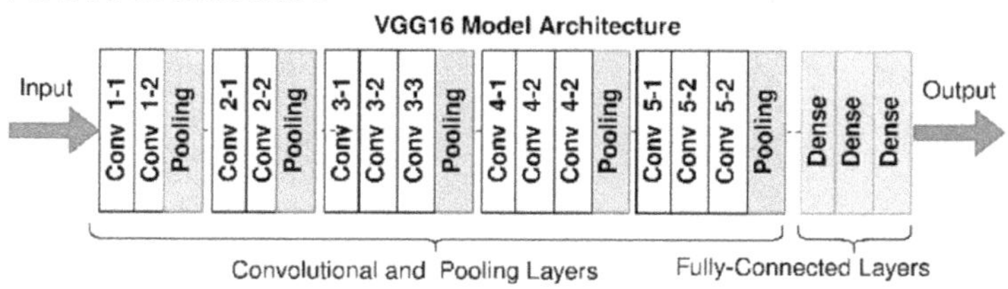

Relu is applied mostly as a function in VGG16 after every convolutional as well as fully connected layer across its architecture by making nonlinearities that set negative values equal to zero, thereby allowing complex patterns and interdependencies to be learned from data by a network. For training and optimization techniques, for instance, stochastic gradient descent (SGD) or similar optimization algorithms can be employed in VGG16 along with dropout regularization methods to prevent overfitting problems, etc. People often retrain models on big datasets like ImageNet and then fine-tune them using task-specific data for best performance.

Xception: The creation of Xception by François Chollet in 2017 is a turning point in the convolutional neural network (CNN) architecture. The reason behind its genesis was the need to improve computational efficiency while maintaining or even improving upon CNN architectures that were previously developed. In Xception, the central idea is to use depthwise separable convolutions, which decompose spatial and channel-wise feature learning processes and consume parameters economically. Xception architecture consists of several depthwise separable convolutional layers, interspersed with nonlinear activation functions (preferably ReLU) and sometimes augmented by residual connections. Depthwise separable convolutional blocks are also featured in Xception, which stacks multiple layers of depthwise and pointwise convolutions towards more abstract representations. Such modular design allows for either deeper or shallower architectures tailored to different tasks or resource constraints. Xception essentially replaces standard convolutions with depthwise separable convolutions that consist of two separate operations, depthwise convolution and pointwise convolution, as spatial information is independently captured for each channel. Pointwise convolution then combines these spatial features across channels, facilitating cross-channel interactions (Figure 6).

Figure 6. Architecture of Xception

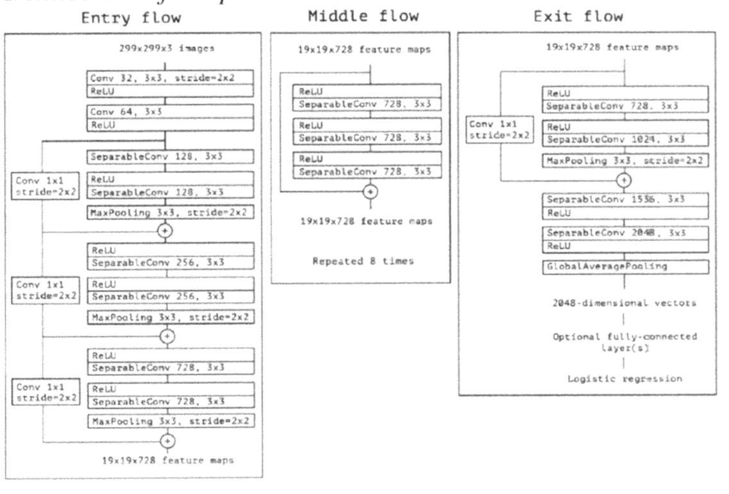

Xception's decoupling feature learning from spatial and channel-wise levels has several merits that traditional CNN architectures do not possess. It lowers computational cost by incorporating fewer computations than standard convolutions as depthwise separable convolutions require lesser parameters, hence faster inference and lower resource requirements. It improves efficiency through enhanced feature learning, making the model more representative and generalizable. Also, it is possible to scale Xception easily because of its modular design; thus, it can perform well in numerous computer vision tasks. In terms of training and optimization, Xception uses regular techniques like stochastic gradient descent (SGD) or inappropriate adaptation optimization tools such as Adam. In order to prevent overfitting or achieve training stability, dropout or batch normalization may be used as a regularization technique. Various applications where Xception has been successful include Image Classification, Object Detection, Semantic Segmentation, and Image Generation, among others. Because it is efficient and effective for both research and practical use cases, it has become a versatile choice that illustrates its important role as a breakthrough in deep learning across many fields of study.

Feature Extraction: Feature extraction is a crucial step in the process of image analysis. It involves the process of capturing and quantifying important information or features from raw image data. These features can be colour, texture, shape, or any other characteristic that is significant to the task at hand. The various techniques are:

Morphological Feature Extraction: They entail computing basic measurements such as diameter, area, and perimeter/leaf circumference for leaf images; also, from these basic components, other derivatives like smoothness, shape ratio, and leaf vein characteristics are derived in a more detailed reflection.

Texture Feature Extraction: It involves the use of binary local patterns to describe the texture of leaf images. Any such textural characteristic is captured by assigning labels to pixels on the basis of their neighborhood and generating histograms that depict the frequency distribution of such patterns.

Shape Feature Extraction: The latter uses image thresholding and the Canny edge detector for detecting leaf edges, with 4-connected neighboring used for boundary detection. This method extracts shape-related features that are important in activities like plant species identification or leaf classification by isolating a leaf from its background and locating its boundaries accurately (Figure 7).

Figure 7. System flow chart

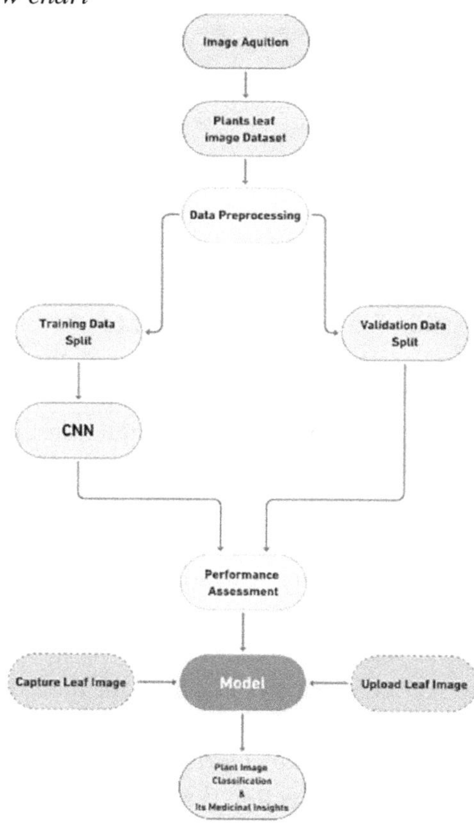

DATASET COLLECTION

The research collected the "Medicinal Plant Dataset," an inclusive compilation of some of the medicinal plants that are categorized into 106 different classes. This is because each class had a very large sample and variety of images, which made sure that they were all represented appropriately in the dataset. However, the dataset was carefully segmented, with about 80% being allocated to the training dataset and the remaining 20% forming a test dataset for a better modelling process. However, this data includes all types of medicinal plants ranging from herbs and shrubs to flowering plants to trees and so on. Also, having such diverse groups of medicinal plants enriches the dataset extensively but, at the same time, promotes strong generalization and learning across various medicinal plant kinds (Table 1). It should be noted that there were two main reasons behind choosing this distribution strategy: first, how many images were within each medicinal plant category; secondly, maintained a ratio between train and test samples equaling approximately 80/20%. This was important in order to ensure a balance between the adequacy of model training and comprehensive evaluation using unseen data. Furthermore, this accuracy further proves that it is possible for such models to correctly classify different types of medical plants effectively. The dataset structure is visually depicted in the accompanying Figure 9.

Table 1. List of medicinal plants and their scientific names

No:	Name	Scientific Name	No:	Name	Scientific Name
1.	Aleovera	Aloe Barbadensis Miller	54.	Kasambruga	Neolamarckia Cadamba
2.	Amaranthus Green	Amaranthus Viridis	55.	Kohlrabi	Brassica Oleracea
3.	Amruthaballi	Tinospora Cordifolia	56.	Kokilaksha	Hygrophila Auriculata
4.	Arali	Nerium Oleander	57.	Lambs Quarters	Chenopodium Album
5.	Asthma Plant	Euphorbia Hirta	58.	Land Caltrops (Bindii)	Tribulus Terrestris
6.	Avaram	Senna Auriculata	59.	Lantana	Lantana Camara
7.	Badipala	Vernonia Cinerea	60.	Lettuce Tree	Pisonia Umbellifers
8.	Balloon Vine	Cardiospermum Halicacabum	61.	Madagascar Periwinkle	Catharanthus Roseus
9.	Bellyache Bush (Green)	Jatropha Gossypifolia	62.	Malabar Catmint	Anisomeles Indica
10.	Benghal Dayflower	Commelina Benghalensis	63.	Malabar_Nut	Justicia Adhatoda
11.	Betel Leaves	Piper Betle	64.	Mexican Mint	Coleus Amboinicus

continued on following page

Table 1. Continued

No:	Name	Scientific Name	No:	Name	Scientific Name
12.	Bhrami	Bacopa Monnieri	65.	Mexican Prickly Poppy	Argemone Mexicana
13.	Big Caltrops	Kallstroemia Maxima (L.)	66.	Mint Leaves	Mentha
14.	Black Night Shade	Solanum Nigrum	67.	Mountain Knotgrass	Aerva Lanata
15.	Black-Honey Shrub	Phyllanthus Recticulatus	68.	Mustard	Brassica Juncea
16.	Bringaraja	Eclipta Prostrata	69.	Nalta Jute	Corchorus Olitorius
17.	Bristly Wild Grape	Cyphostemma Setosum	70.	Neem	Azadirachta Indica
18.	Butterfly Pea	Clitoria Ternatea	71.	Nelavembu	Andrographis Paniculata
19.	Cape Gooseberry	Physalis Peruviana	72.	Nerale	Syzygium Cumini
20.	Caricature	Graptophyllum Pictum	73.	Night Blooming Cereus	Selenicereus Grandiflorus
21.	Castor	Ricinus Communis	74.	Nooni	Morinda Citrifolia
22.	Catharanthus	Catharanthus Roseus	75.	Padri	Radermachera Xylocarpa
23.	Celery	Apium Graveolens	76.	Panicled Foldwing	Dicleptera Paniculate
24.	Chakte	Caesalpinia Platyloba	77.	Parijatha	Nyctanthes Arbor-Tristis
25.	Common Wireweed	Sida Acuta	78.	Prickly Chaff Flower	Achyranthes Aspera
26.	Common Rue(Naagdalli)	Ruta Graveolens	79.	Punarnava	Boerhavia Diffusa
27.	Coriander Leaves	Coriandrum Sativum	80.	Purple Fruited Pea Eggplant	Solanum Trilobatum
28.	Country Mallow	Sida Cortifolia	81.	Purple Tephrosia	Tephrosia Purpurea
29.	Atibala	Abutilon Indicum	82.	Rosary Pea	Abrus Precatorius
30.	Curry Leaf	Murraya Koenigii	83.	Seethaashoka	Saraca Asoca
31.	Doddpathre	Coleus Amboinicus	84.	Shaggy Buttonweed	Spermacoce Hispida Linn
32.	Dwarf Copperleaf (Green)	Alternanthera Sessilis	85.	Siru Keerai	Amaranthaceae
33.	Ekka	Calotropis Gigantea	86.	Small Water Clover	Marsilea Minuta
34.	False Amarnath	Digera Muricata	87.	Spiderwisp	Cleome Gynandra
35.	Fenugreek Leaves	Trigonella Foenum Graecum	88.	Square Stalked Vine	Cissus Quadrangularise
36.	Galingale	Cyperus Longus	89.	Stinking Passionflower	Passiflora Foetida
37.	Gasagase	Papaver Somniferum	90.	Sweet Basil	Ocimum Basilicum
38.	Giant Pigweed	Trianthema Portulacastrum	91.	Sweet Flag	Acorus Calamus
39.	Ginger	Zingiber Officinale	92.	Taro	Colocasia Esculenta

continued on following page

Table 1. Continued

No:	Name	Scientific Name	No:	Name	Scientific Name
40.	Globe Amarnath	Gomphrena Globose	93.	Tecoma	Tecoma Stans
41.	Gongura	Hibiscus Sabdariffa	94.	Thumb	Leucas Aspera
42.	Green Chireta	Andrographis Paniculata	95.	Tinnevelly Senna	Alexandrian Senna
43.	Hibiscus	Hibiscus Rosa-Sinensis	96.	Trellis Vine	Pergularia Daemia
44.	Holy Basil	Ocimum Tenuiflorum	97.	Turmeric	Curcuma Longa
45.	Honge	Pongamia Pinnata	98.	Velvet Bean	Mucuna Pruriens
46.	Indian Copperleaf	Acalypha Indica	99.	Water Spinach	Ipomoea Aquatica
47.	Indian Stinging Nettle	Urtica Dioica	100.	Ashoka	Saraca Asoca
48.	Indian Thornapple	Datura Inoxia	101.	Kamakasturi	Ocimum Tenuiflorum
49.	Indian Pennywort	Centella Asiatica	102.	Heart-Leaved Moonseed	Tinospora Cordifolia
50.	Indian Wormwood	Artemisia Absinthium	103.	Coat Buttons	Tridax Procumbens
51.	Insulin	Chamaecostus Cuspidatus	104.	Camphor	Cinnamomum Camphora
52.	Ivy Gourd	Coccinia Grandis	105.	Indian Sarsaparilla	Hemidesmus Indicus
53.	Kambajala	Cassia Tora	106.	Kepala	Ixora Undulata Roxb

Data Augmentation

In the data augmentation stage, the images from the "Medicinal Plant Dataset" were transformed according to the input requirements of selected pre-trained models. The image's dimensions were changed to conform to each model's unique specification. For instance, the images were adjusted to 224x224 pixels for ResNet50 and VGG16 pre-trained models, which work best at this resolution. Similarly, they were resized to 299x299 pixels to meet the input specifications of the Xception model. These resized pictures went through augmentation techniques, including rotation, flipping, zooming, and other transformations that increased the diversity of the dataset, thus improving the generalization capability of the model. This meticulous calibration between image sizes and requirements of pre-trained models ensured compatibility as well as the optimized performance of the model during subsequent training and evaluation steps. In addition, data augmentation was approached systematically so that it would be easily integrated into pre-trained models and entail the robustness of the developed medicinal plant recognition system.

Feature Extraction: The feature extraction process involved the use of ResNet50, VGG16, and Xception models as the base models for determining high-level features from plant images that capture intricate designs and characteristics that are important for classification.

Dataset Partition: This project categorized the dataset into two major subdivisions, namely, the training dataset and the test dataset, in an 80-20% balance ratio. This is a conscious effort to ensure that the majority (80%) of data is used to determine the model while 20% is left to measure how the model would perform on unseen data (Figure 8).

Figure 8. Splitting of data

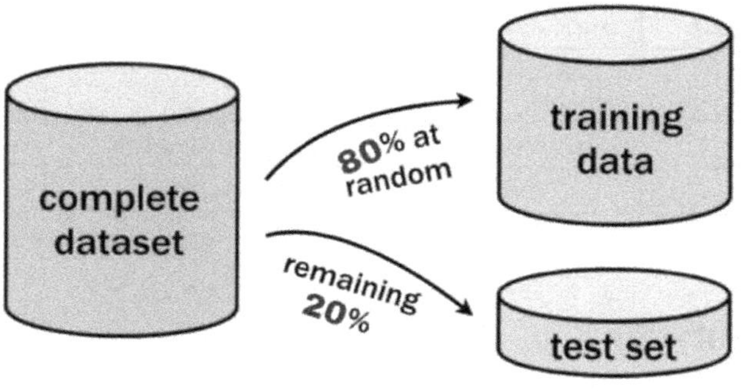

The training dataset has been identified as critical in facilitating learning by the model, thereby helping adjust parameters as well as discern patterns. As such, exposure to this data set leads to incremental improvement in understanding underlying patterns and interactions within it. The model has a broader experience with this kind of information that allows it to learn about various degrees of complexity contained in its contents, thus making its predictions better than before. The test set is, however, an independent benchmark for assessing the model's generalization ability. This can be done by examining its performance using never-seen data. Thus, from this hidden world, we are able to gain invaluable insights and determine whether these could work practically elsewhere. By using such an approach, it becomes easy to judge if a model has been able to learn sufficient information that can be used to make predictions in different settings outside the training range.

Hyper Parameter

Different approaches had to be used in hyperparameter tuning to enhance the model's performance. This was achieved by merging pre-trained models with additional layers that catered to architectural changes. Tensorflow and Keras were employed to build Sequential models, which contained a pre-trained layer, a global average pooling, batch normalization, and some dense layers (with ReLU activation functions). Consequently, it has also improved the model's performance through the process of hyperparameter tuning. Hyperparameters like learning rate, batch size, and dropout rate were iteratively experimented on and validated in order to optimize the model's effectiveness. Moreover, early stopping mechanisms were adopted into the network in order to prevent overfitting by generalizing better on different datasets. Thus, this hybrid approach ensured that the unique architecture of the chosen model not only fit but was fine-tuned to achieve optimal performance in real-world situations.

RESULTS AND DISCUSSION

Google Colaboratory is what this work uses to do its experiments. It's a hosted Jupyter Notebook service that allows you to write and execute Python in your browser with no setup required, free access to computing resources, including GPUs, and easy sharing. This project aims to provide deep learning-based real-time plant recognition and medicinal insights. The three major CNN models, ResNet50, VGG16, and Xception, which have been fine-tuned using transfer learning on 106 plant datasets, are used. This is just a means to see if the system can categorically identify plants precisely and then provide relevant information about their medical properties (Figure 10).

Figure 9. Resnet50

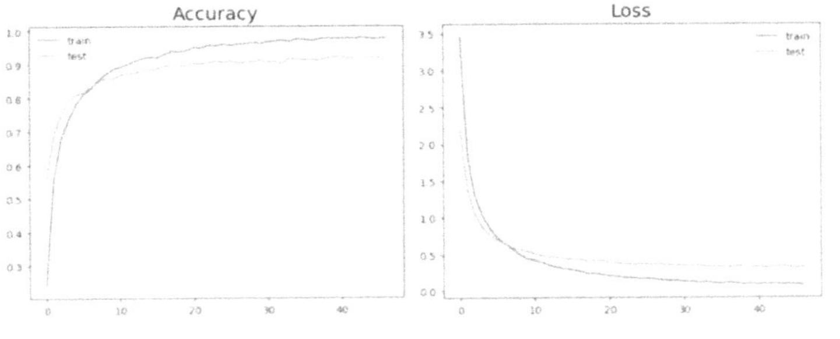

Figure 10. VGG16

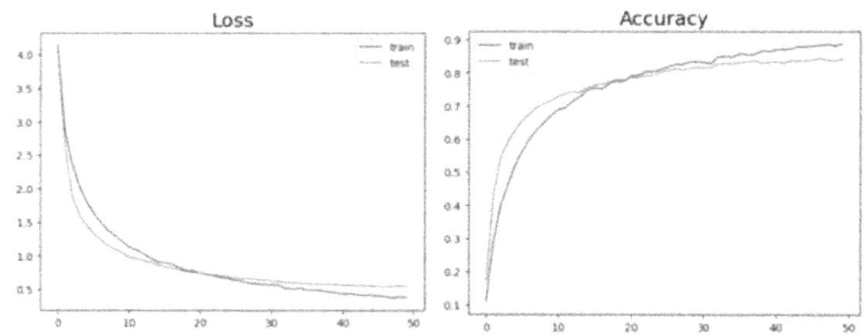

The models were rated by performance metrics such as accuracy, precision, recall sensitivity, and F1 score, among others. Moreover, a study was done comparing pre-trained CNN models, namely Resnet50, VGG16, and Xception (Figures 11 and 12).

Figure 11. Xception

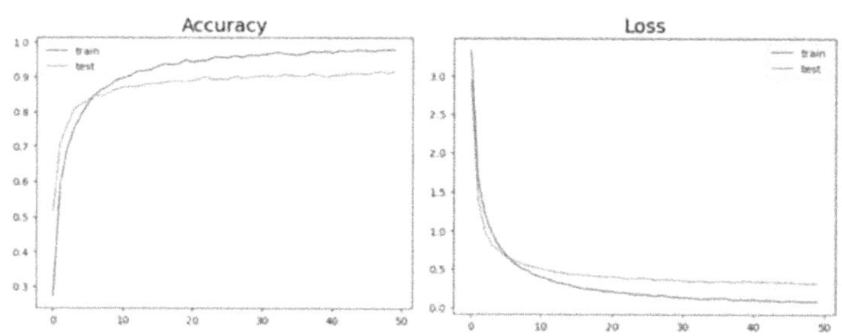

The evaluation involved training the models on a dataset containing 106 species of plants, with 80% of the data used for training and 20% for testing, employing a batch size of 32 and 50 epochs. Experimental results showed that Xception outperformed Resnet50 and VGG16, with the highest classification accuracy rate being 91.68% (Table 2).

Figure 12. Precision and recall plots (Xception)

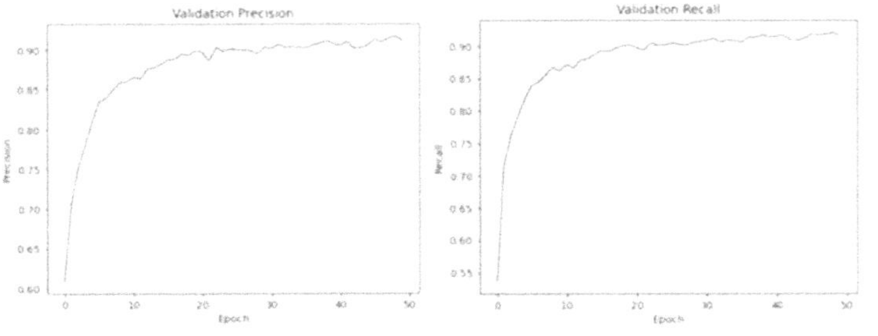

Evaluation Matrics

Accuracy = (TN + TP) / (TN+FP+FN+TP)

Precision = TP / (TP+FP)

Recall = TP / (TP+FN)

F1_Score = 2 * (precision*recall) / (precision +recall)

TP, TN, FP, and FN stand for True Positive, True Negative, False Positive, False Negative Respectively.

Table 2. Comparison of Performance Metrics of Different Models

No.	Model	Val Accuracy	Val Loss	Precision	Recall	F1 Score
1.	Resnet50	91.41	0.3266	92.08	89.98	89.96
2.	VGG16	84.27	0.5482	87.56	86.34	85.93
3.	**Xception**	**91.68**	**0.3138**	**93.50**	**92.34**	**92.12**

Here are some of the testing images, along with the predictions made by the Xception model, as well as the corresponding confidence scores (Figure 13).

Figure 13. Classification of testing data

Figure 14. Gradio interface

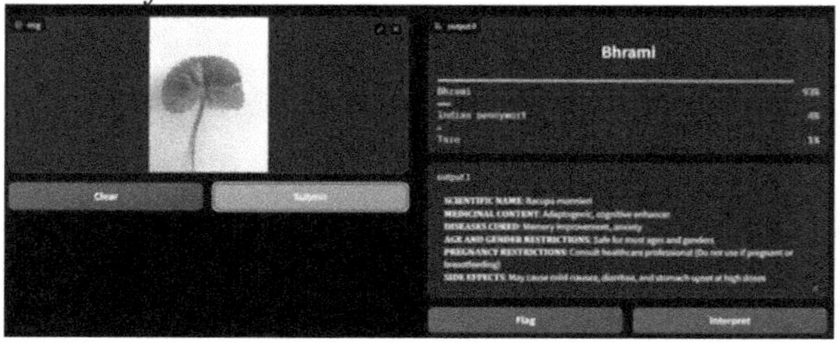

In order to elucidate the medicinal nature of plants, an uncomplicated interface was made using the Gradio library (Figure 14). This interface allows users either to upload pictures or take them directly from a camera. Once submitted, it uses a pre-trained Xception model that predicts the three most probable classes for the input image, hence giving insights into plant species represented in the photograph. It also displays the medicinal properties known for given plant species. This development combines photo identification with information on the medical values of plants. This perfect assimilation of image recognition and medical data enhances our system, making it more useful; thus, one can make informed decisions on plant recognition and exploitation, too.

CONCLUSION

This paper highlights the effectiveness of deep learning models, particularly Xception, in real-time plant recognition and medical insight generation. By leveraging advanced convolutional neural network (CNN) architectures and transfer learning techniques, the system achieves high accuracy in identifying plant species and extracting relevant medicinal information. The study demonstrates that deep learning models can significantly enhance automated plant classification, making them valuable tools in various scientific, agricultural, and medicinal applications. Through a comparative analysis of different deep learning models, it is evident that Xception outperforms other architectures in plant classification tasks. This superior performance can be attributed to its depthwise separable convolutions, which enhance feature extraction and reduce computational complexity. The model's ability to learn intricate patterns within plant images allows for more precise classification, reinforcing the importance of selecting appropriate architectures for specific tasks. Moreover, the integration of medical insights into plant classification adds significant value to the system. By associating plant species with their medicinal properties, this model can serve as an essential resource for researchers, healthcare professionals, and enthusiasts interested in herbal medicine. The results also suggest that transfer learning techniques can optimize model performance even with limited datasets, enabling the development of efficient and practical applications. The study emphasizes the potential of deep learning in plant recognition and medical analysis. Xception, in particular, demonstrates its capability to deliver accurate results, paving the way for further advancements in AI-driven botanical research and healthcare innovations.

REFERENCES

Abinavkrishnaa, R., Raghuram, G., Varghese, A., Gowri, G. U., & Rahila, J. (2023). Scaling Strategies for Enhanced System Performance: Navigating Stateful and Stateless Architectures. *FMDB Transactions on Sustainable Computer Letters, 1*(4), 241–254.

Batvia, V., Patel, D., & Vasant, A. R. (2017). A survey on ayurvedic medicine classification using tensor flow. *International Journal of Computer Trends and Technology, 53*(2), 68–70.

Bose, S. R., Jeba, J. A., Kishore, V. K., Gnanaguru, G., & Shynu, T. (2024). Deep learning-driven acute lymphoblastic leukemia detection using CT scan imaging. *AVE Trends in Intelligent Health Letters, 1*(2), 110–124.

Dhinakaran, P., Thinesh, M. A., & Paslavskyi, M. (2023). Enhancing Cyber Intrusion Detection through Ensemble Learning: A Comparison of Bagging and Stacking Classifiers. *FMDB Transactions on Sustainable Computer Letters, 1*(4), 210–227.

Dileep, M. R., & Pournami, P. N. (2019). *AyurLeaf: A Novel Deep Learning Framework for Medicinal Plant Classification, TENCON 2019 - 2019 IEEE Region 10 Conference*. TENCON.

Gandhi, M., Satheesh, C., Soji, E. S., Saranya, M., Rajest, S. S., & Kothuru, S. K. (2024). Image recognition and extraction on computerized vision for sign language decoding. In *Explainable AI Applications for Human Behavior Analysis* (pp. 157–173). IGI Global. DOI: 10.4018/979-8-3693-1355-8.ch010

Gnanaguru, G., Priscila, S. S., Sakthivanitha, M., Radhakrishnan, S., Rajest, S. S., & Singh, S. (2024). Thorough analysis of deep learning methods for diagnosis of COVID-19 CT images. In *Advances in Medical Technologies and Clinical Practice* (pp. 46–65). IGI Global.

Jayalath, A. D. A. D. S., Amarawanshaline, T. G. A. G. D., Nawinna, D. P., Nadeeshan, P. V. D., & Jayasuriya, H. P. (2019, December). Identification of medicinal plants by visual characteristics of leaves and flowers. In 2019 14th Conference on Industrial and Information Systems (ICIIS) (pp. 125-129). IEEE.

Jeba, J., Bose, S. R., Regin, R., Sudhan, M. B., Suman Rajest, S., & Babu, P. R. (2024). Efficient Real-time Tamil Character Recognition via Deep Vision Architecture. *AVE Trends In Intelligent Computing Systems, 1*(1), 1–16.

Jeba, J. A., Bose, S. R., & Boina, R. (2023). Exploring Hybrid Multi-View Multi-modal for Natural Language Emotion Recognition Using Multi-Source Information Learning Model. *FMDB Transactions on Sustainable Computer Letters*, *1*(1), 12–24.

Karthik, S., Bhaggiaraj, S., Soji, E. S., Deve, L. S., Priscila, S. S., & Rajest, S. S. (2024). Real-time hand gesture recognition for stroke rehabilitation using deep learning approach. *AVE Trends in Intelligent Computing Systems*, *1*(3), 157–172.

Karthikeyan, B., Devi, R. A., & Munshi, M. (2024). Utilizing Deep Learning for the Classification of Brain Tumours Using MRI. *AVE Trends In Intelligent Health Letters*, *1*(1), 1–9.

Kumar, E. S., & Talasila, V. (2014). Leaf features based approach for automated identification of medicinal plants. *2014 International Conference on Communication and Signal Processing*, IEEE, Melmaruvathur, India. DOI: 10.1109/ICCSP.2014.6949830

Kumar, P. M., Surya, C. M., & Gopi, V. P. (2017). Identification of ayurvedic medicinal plants by image processing of leaf samples. *2017 Third International Conference on Research in Computational Intelligence and Communication Networks (ICRCICN)*, IEEE, Kolkata, India. DOI: 10.1109/ICRCICN.2017.8234512

Kumar Thella, P., & Ulagamuthalvi, V. (2021). IEEE/2021 5th International Conference on Computing Methodologies and Communication (ICCMC), Erode, India.

Marar, A., Bose, S. R., Singh, R., Joshi, Y., Regin, R., & Rajest, S. S. (2023). Light weight structure texture feature analysis for character recognition using progressive stochastic learning algorithm. In *Advanced Applications of Generative AI and Natural Language Processing Models* (pp. 144–158). IGI Global.

Minu, M. S., Subashka Ramesh, S. S., Canessane, R., Al-Amin, M., & Bin Sulaiman, R. (2023). Experimental Analysis of UAV Networks Using Oppositional Glowworm Swarm Optimization and Deep Learning Clustering and Classification. *FMDB Transactions on Sustainable Computing Systems*, *1*(3), 124–134.

Nanban, D., Ajitha, Y., Selvan, J., Pierre, T. J., Sara, S. B. V. J., & Ragesha, R. (2024). Enhancing user experience in air canvas through robust hand gesture recognition using computer vision. *FMDB Transactions on Sustainable Computer Letters*, *2*(3), 131–143. DOI: 10.69888/FTSCL.2024.000239

Nomula, V. K. (2024). Imperative of standards and interoperability in modern medicine. *FMDB Transactions on Sustainable Health Science Letters*, *2*(1), 31–40. DOI: 10.69888/FTSHSL.2024.000170

Obeta, U., Deko, D., & Mantu, E. (2024). Deep Learning-Based Diagnostic Techniques for Cancer: Extensive Testing and Clinical Application Insights. *AVE Trends In Intelligent Health Letters*, *1*(1), 28–37.

Panyaram, S. (2024). Utilizing quantum computing to enhance artificial intelligence in healthcare for predictive analytics and personalized medicine. *FMDB Transactions on Sustainable Computing Systems*, *2*(1), 22–31. DOI: 10.69888/FTSCS.2024.000194

Paulson, A. (2020a). *AI Based Indigenous Medicinal Plant Identification" 2020 Advanced Computing and Communication Technologies for High Performance Applications*. ACCTHPA.

Priscila, S. S., Rajest, S. S., Tadiboina, S. N., Regin, R., & András, S. (2023). Analysis of Machine Learning and Deep Learning Methods for Superstore Sales Prediction. *FMDB Transactions on Sustainable Computer Letters*, *1*(1), 1–11.

Trung Nguyen Quoc, V. T. (2020). Medicinal Plant identification in the wild by using CNN" 2020 International Conference on Information and Communication Technology Convergence (ICTC). 21–23, Jeju, Korea (South).

Chapter 11
Application of Digital Image Processing to Identification of Diseases in Paddy Crops

G. Karthik
https://orcid.org/0009-0005-2415-4930
Bharath Institute of Higher Education and Research, India

B. Karthik
Bharath Institute of Higher Education and Research, India

S. P. Vijayaragavan
Bharath Institute of Higher Education and Research, India

T. Vijayan
https://orcid.org/0000-0001-9383-5960
Bharath Institute of Higher Education and Research, India

ABSTRACT

In the sphere of agriculture, the challenge of recognizing and detecting plant illnesses is proposed in this study, and it is anticipated that this problem will be challenging. A system has been proposed to automatically detect and track cases of pest diseases in agricultural settings. When performing image processing, it is necessary to first obtain the image and then use a number of preprocessing techniques, such as feature extraction, segmentation, and modification. In order to identify any unwanted organisms, it is necessary to compare the original image with the one that was obtained. Upon receiving the Matlab result that was achieved, the controller is notified. The

DOI: 10.4018/979-8-3373-5203-9.ch011

controller is responsible for carrying out the essential management measures in accordance with the level of the pest's impact on the paddy crops. A pesticide will be sprayed on the crop in proportion to the percentage of the crop that is impacted. Therefore, the rice field may be identified in a very short amount of time and with a high degree of efficiency.

INTRODUCTION

Human civilization and agriculture play a major role in development. Research on agricultural diseases focuses on increasing productivity and the quality of food products. The primary source of rice production in Asian countries, especially in India, is the quality and production of rice, which decrease due to manual identification and manual error. Disease and insect pests are the major problems in agriculture (Balajibhanu and Rao, 2014). The greater part of the agriculturists utilized the customary vermin executive's techniques, which is the standard spraying program dependent on calendars as opposed to the nearness of creepy crawly bugs on the paddy fields. These synthetic substances harm beneficial insects that destroy pests during harvests (Liu Dan et al., 2015). Making decisions regarding irritation requires assessing the density of the rice insect population in paddy fields. Sticky devices are generally used to trap the creepy crawly bugs. The caught bugs are conveyed to the research center for checking and physical identification (Vijayakumar and Rosario, 2011).

More often than not, crop experts recognize and isolate the creepy crawlies physically as indicated by their species and tally the real irritations independently. The following inspections are used to determine the paddy fields' nuisance thickness. However, for a yield expert, many sites and subsequent examinations of rice vermin are tiresome and dull (Nisha and Megala, 2014). This could lead to a lack of accuracy and delays in getting checks, which might lead to bad decisions being made on the rice bug board. Agrarian studies could benefit from the usage of image-processing technology due to the quick growth of computer technology, which could help scientists resolve a perplexing problem (Ji-Hua et al., 2006).

The combination of mechanical innovation and picture examination offers a propitious possibility of changing the recognizable proof of bug bothers in rural conditions, specifically in rice fields. The broadness of photographs dealing with applications in farming is extended by the making of a mechanized location structure that utilizes modern picture-handling strategies to survey bug numbers (Mainwaring et al., 2002). With the utilization of field information, this clever methodology significantly smoothes out the work for crop subject matter experts, empowering them to recognize bother invasions with effectiveness (Xiao, 2010). As well as bringing down the work-concentrated aspects of manual observing, the framework works on the accuracy and speed of irritation recognizable proof via computerizing the location cycle (Li et al., 2011). By establishing such a modernized construction, bothering the populace with the executives in rice cultivation may be essentially improved. Working on the sum and nature of rice creation is emphatically connected with the execution of proficient vermin control measures, which need exact and opportune recognition. Vijayan et al., (2020) can limit crop misfortune and cut back on the abuse of synthetic pesticides, which can adversely affect the climate and human well-being, by recognizing vermin early and executing custom-made medications. Additionally, ongoing information from this innovation's steady observation of nuisance levels supports the creation of very educated board choices.

Cameras situated in the fields are utilized in the framework to take high-goal photos of the yields consistently (Vijayan et al., 2020). Thus, these photographs are exposed to complex calculation investigation, which can distinguish and gauge the presence of various bug species (Vijayan et al., 2020). Understanding nuisance conduct and development designs, which are affected by ecological factors and rural strategies, relies upon this information. Crop experts can expect future scourges and make a suitable preventive move by inspecting these patterns. Moreover, the utilization of mechanical gadgets to robotize bug ID adds a degree of accuracy to farming techniques that were not before imaginable. It makes it conceivable to change bug the executive's procedures to best fit specific circumstances while lessening their natural effect. The development of rice, a staple nourishment for an enormous segment of the worldwide populace, makes this particularly pivotal on the grounds that it is basic to boost yield without forfeiting the manageability of cultivating tasks. Finally, the computerization of bug-recognizable proof utilizing a mechanized picture examination structure is a critical mechanical improvement in the field of horticulture. It works on the viability and effectiveness of irritation the board strategies and supports manageable agribusiness by keeping up with the natural equilibrium and bringing down dependence on synthetic controls. To give both food security and natural manageability, this methodology exhibits how innovation might be utilized to address the absolute most significant issues confronting the food creation industry.

REVIEW OF LITERATURE

The utilization of advanced picture handling in farming is changing the field by giving creative ways of distinguishing and dealing with sicknesses in crops like rice, which is fundamental for worldwide food security. Utilizing AI calculations and state-of-the-art imaging innovation, advanced picture handling is applied to paddy crop sickness discovery to analyze and successfully analyze and screen crop well-being (Ramgirkar and Talhar, 2024). Utilizing computerized cameras or robots fitted with particular sensors, excellent picture catch is the most important phase in the process (Suganthi and Sathiaseelan, 2023). These photographs should be high goal and have the right brightening to catch the subtleties expected for exact investigation (Sohlot et al., 2023). Preprocessing is a fundamental stage in picture upgrade that includes diminishing commotion, fixing bends, and normalizing contrasts welcomed by lighting or natural circumstances. Strategies like a variety of space transformations, separating, and histogram adjustment are oftentimes utilized to prepare pictures for extra handling (Linzhang and Xiangzhan, 2022).

The essential stages that come next are highlight extraction and division subsequent to preprocessing (Pranav et al., 2023). To recognize infected from sound tissue, a computerized picture is portioned by parting it into a few sections or locales (Al-Mokdad, 2024). Normal procedures contain thresholding, in which pixels are classified by variety power, and bunching, which places pixels in bunches as per variety and surface similitudes. The extraction is finished to acquire applicable data from the portioned picture after division. To recognize sound and unhealthy regions, elements like tone, surface, structure, and spatial examples are present much of the time. These attributes are utilized as contributions by AI models to group sicknesses (Kim et al., 2008). Calculations for AI are utilized in characterization. A scope of systems are used, including traditional AI models like Help Vector Machines (SVM) and choice trees, as well as more modern profound learning models like Convolutional Brain Organizations (CNNs). CNNs specifically have acquired notoriety since they are extremely powerful at muddled picture examination undertakings, for example, illness distinguishing proof in rice crops, since they can naturally perceive complex examples in pictures without requiring manual component choice (Anand et al., 2024).

Computerized picture handling in horticulture has gone through an upheaval because of profound learning models, especially CNNs (Fan, 2013). These models highlight progressive systems directly from the information, which builds their ability for situational speculation and, at last, works on their precision in recognizing illnesses. Researchers have contrived assorted structures tweaked to specific prerequisites in agrarian symbolism for isolating distressed regions or sorting sickness sorts as per their visual appearances (Balamurali and Kathiravan, 2015).

Checking the size of whole fields or districts is made conceivable by consolidating computerized picture handling with Geographic Data Frameworks (GIS) and remote detecting information, notwithstanding individual plant studies (Zhuang et al., 2011). With the assistance of this coordination, sickness flare-ups might be planned across regions, and therapies can be decisively applied, augmenting asset productivity and decreasing negative natural impacts. This thorough technique supports following the illness' spread and expecting future episodes as well as helping with its administration (Venkateswaran et al., 2024).

Computerized picture handling has many advantages, but there are downsides with regard to paddy illness discovery (Regin et al., 2023). Natural factors, including enlightenment and climate, can influence picture consistency and quality. Moreover, the manner in which illnesses manifest themselves could vary extraordinarily depending on the contamination stage and the specific microbe included, requiring strong models that can change in accordance with these distinctions. Future examinations will zero in on making more versatile calculations that can work in different conditions and oversee different phases of an illness' development. Likewise, there are drives in progress to work on this innovation's ease of use for ranchers, for example, the making of reasonable imaging gadgets and versatile applications (Shilesh et al., 2024).

Crop efficiency and quality can be significantly upgraded by the effective recognition and treatment of paddy sicknesses with advanced picture handling (Sengupta et al., 2023). Ranchers could bring down costs and their effect on the climate by utilizing fungicides and different medicines in the wake of getting fast and exact illness conclusions. Besides, by better comprehension of sickness elements, the information assembled through these strategies could assist with growing a better harvest of the executive's procedures and opposition strategies (Ikwuagwu et al., 2024).

In outline, the field of computerized picture handling for paddy crop sickness recognition is rapidly creating and can work on farming administration and efficiency (Aashish et al., 2024). As innovation is created, it is normal to turn into a fundamental instrument in the tool kit of contemporary agribusiness, aiding the safeguarding of food supply in an undeniably whimsical worldwide climate. To arrive at its maximum capacity, however, this improvement should be matched by progressing propels in AI and nearer communication with crop the executive's frameworks at the field level (Elayaraja et al., 2024).

Disease Identification

There aren't many solutions that are just focused on the detection problem because picture information obtained by using image processing techniques frequently includes both detecting the disease and assessing its severity. By creating an automated detection, we can extract and detect insect pests using image processing techniques. A controller is provided with the Matlab result. The pesticide will be applied to the crop based on the proportion impacted. Real-time monitoring: In this situation, the system continuously monitors the crops and sounds an alarm whenever the desired illness is found in any of the plants (Figure 1).

Figure 1. Flow diagram for crop disease identification

The most common way of distinguishing crop illnesses by picture handling and AI is portrayed in the stream outline in the picture. The harvest is utilized as the "Information Picture" for the interaction, which is trailed by "Pre-Handling," which involves turning the RGB (variety) picture into grayscale. This diminishes the intricacy of the picture information, working with examination. After pre-handling, "Component Extraction" happens, in which significant highlights are found and recovered from the picture; these elements are fundamental for recognizing designs connected to sicknesses. The previously mentioned highlights are hence taken care of in an AI model known as an "SVM Classifier." This specific model has gone through earlier preparation on a dataset, or "Prepared dataset," including outlines of both solid and wiped-out crops. By utilizing this preparation, the classifier yields the "Result" of this investigation, demonstrating in the event that the information picture shows the side effects of a condition. This robotized strategy further develops crop the executives, brings down misfortunes, and works with fast and exact illness ID.

In a current framework, Sampling is finished by gathering, tallying, or investigating a little piece of the populace. It decides the patterns in the populace of life forms. The inspection ought to be done in an appropriate way with the goal of mirroring the state of the entire populace. For instance, the number of inhabitants in creepy crawly bugs and the harm on the yield are commonly haphazardly circulated that later total into clusters. This might be brought about by the conduct of grown-up foreigners or by the convergence of eggs laid on a plant before the creepy crawly moved to the following. Such circumstances are additionally relevant to creepy crawly-transmitted infection ailments. In this manner, a gauge of populace thickness relies upon taking enough examples and efficient arbitrary examining from a field. Remember that testing is just an instrument to accomplish an objective and not a conclusion to itself. India Rice Self-Sufficiency Plan (PRSSP).

The proposed arrangement cautiously deals with the picture filtration process by utilizing the Middle channel approach, a strong strategy for finding and eliminating commotion from each pixel in a picture. In picture handling, this strategy is exceptionally useful on the grounds that it keeps up with the picture's edges while disposing of arbitrary commotion, ensuring that the picture's quality is protected without twisting. The HAAR wavelet change, a refined numerical technique for including extraction, is next applied to the cleaned and commotion-free pictures. With this change, the picture might be taken apart into its part parts, and the recurrence and spatial data can be dissected to remove the key components expected for additional review.

These highlights are analyzed to decide if vermin are available in the field photographs after the element extraction methodology. The framework has been aligned to distinguish specific examples that demonstrate bug movement. On the off chance that the recognizable proof is fruitful, a comparing activity is started to handle the issue. The innovation makes it more straightforward to apply insect poisons to the field's distressed segments on the off chance that bugs are found. By utilizing a designated system, pesticide applications are sure to be definite, and compound utilization is decreased, prompting the reception of additional economical cultivating techniques. The innovation works on the viability and responsiveness of nuisance-the-board strategies by laying out an immediate association between bug ID and pesticide application. Crop the executives can turn out to be more proactive thanks to the mix of picture handling and direct agrarian activity. Since the framework offers a trustworthy and programmed method for shielding crops from bug-related hurt, ranchers stand to procure an extraordinary arrangement. Besides, the underlying utilization of the HAAR wavelet change and middle channel ensures the precision and great of the information used to go with basic nuisance control choices. By and large, this approach accomplishes the double targets of expanding crop yields and decreasing the negative ecological impacts of cultivating tasks by exactly and cautiously applying pesticides. It additionally makes crop observation and bug control more productive.

Figure 2. Block diagram of the system

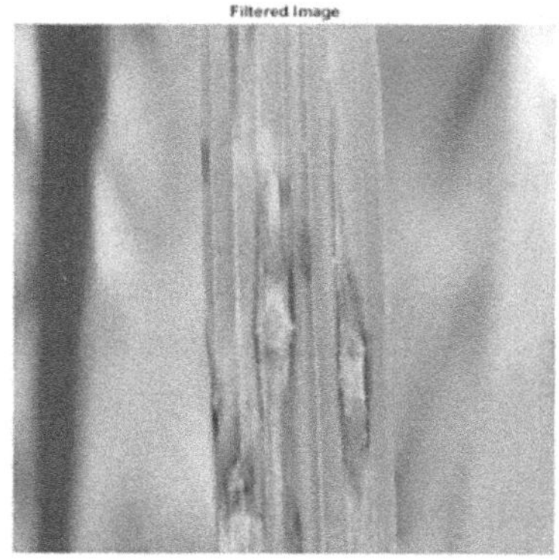

An Arduino microcontroller is used as the central processing unit in the project, and its system architecture is depicted in the block diagram designated "Figure 2". The Arduino microcontroller is in charge of coordinating the system's overall operation in this configuration and serves as a hub for other parts. Input to the Arduino is shown in the diagram as coming from a "Matlab / Serial Data Port," suggesting that commands or data are being provided from a Matlab environment or another serial interface, which the Arduino then processes to control further activities. Two motors that are connected to the Arduino are identified as "Motor 1" and "Motor 2," indicating that the microcontroller processes commands to actuate these motors. Moreover, a link points to a "GSM Module," suggesting that the machine can communicate via cellular networks for potential remote control or surveillance. Input handling, process control, and external communications are all integrated into a single system using an Arduino microcontroller, as demonstrated by this architecture. The embedded C programming language and the Arduino IDE are utilized for the software implementation. With the help of the ARDUINO program, the circuit is given a serial input, and the primary operation is coded. This circuit comprises a motor, gsm messaging, DC voltage source, and authentication. The circuit is given a DC voltage source input of 5V and 12V. A specific program is allocated to each component, and the controller is likewise provided a program feed. To send messages to mobile devices, utilize the GSM module.

RESULTS

Advanced picture handling has been shown to have huge potential for managing plant well-being and expanding horticultural efficiency when used to distinguish sicknesses in rice crops. To survey the adequacy of various picture-handling strategies, like element extraction, division, and infection grouping, this study utilized complex AI calculations like Help Vector Machines (SVM), Choice Trees, and Convolutional Brain Organizations (CNNs). The discoveries offer a careful comprehension of the potential and challenges of these advancements with regard to paddy development; these are shrouded in full beneath. Drones fitted with cutting-edge imaging sensors were utilized to catch high-goal photos from paddy fields during the concentrate's most memorable stage. Broad preprocessing was applied to the gathered photos to upgrade visual clearness and amend any mutilations or abnormalities, similar to variances in lighting and shadows, which are normal for regular open-air scenes. The viability of the accompanying periods of picture examination relied upon this readiness.

The underlying and vital phase of picture handling was division, with the point of definitively separating sound from harmed crop parts. The division techniques utilized were versatile thresholding and k-implies bunching, which made it simpler to isolate the picture into segments as indicated by textural varieties and variety powers. A high accuracy pace of around 92% was seen in the division precision when it was quantitatively assessed. The extraordinary accuracy seen here proposes that the division calculations are fruitful in isolating affected regions, a basic step towards exact sickness discovery. The extraction was finished to recover relevant highlights from the portioned districts after the division interaction was fruitful. In this system, different qualities, including mathematical shapes, surface examples, and a variety of angles connected to particular illness side effects, were broken down. A strong dataset for the following round of grouping was created by refined calculations that consequently separated these elements. To arrange infections, in excess of thirty distinct elements were found and taken advantage of, displaying the expansiveness of examination attainable with advanced picture handling.

Different AI models were utilized throughout the classification stage. With exactness paces of 85% and 87%, separately, the SVM and Choice Trees offered standard exhibitions. The order precision rose to 95% with the utilization of CNNs, which was a remarkable increment. This improvement is credited to CNN's ability to naturally extricate perplexing progressive component structures from the visual info, disposing of the necessity for unequivocal element ID programming. CNNs are particularly appropriate for picture-based applications where the capacity to perceive unobtrusive examples is fundamental in light of this component. Moreover, the utilization of CNNs made it simpler to gauge the seriousness of infections as well as recognize them. In rice crops, sicknesses like impact, bacterial scourge, and sheath curse are normal. The models had the option to recognize their initial and high-level stages. This ability is fundamental for setting treatment strategies in motion on time and properly, which could further develop infectious prevention and lower crop misfortune. By empowering spatial investigation of illness commonness and seriousness across different geographic areas of the paddy fields, the coordination of Geographic Data Frameworks (GIS) with the picture handling information adds still one more layer of utility. Arranging centered medicines and completing extra epidemiological examinations require familiarity with sickness examples and conveyance, which is made conceivable by spatial planning.

Indeed, even with the reassuring results, the review stumbled into various issues. The consistency and nature of the picture information were periodically undermined by ecological changeability, like varieties in lighting brought about by the climate or season of day. Besides, the division and element extraction techniques could, at times, turn out to be less exact because of the presence of foundation commotion, like reflections from water or soil. Ensuing variants of the exploration could research the utilization of further developed picture standardization strategies that record for changing lighting and other natural elements to beat these hardships. Further working on the lucidity and helpfulness of the pictures for disease conclusion might include the utilization of more refined sound decrease calculations. All in all, there have been eminent advances in the utilization of computerized picture handling for paddy crop sickness recognizable proof, and this innovation can alter rural practices by improving harvest observation and illness of the executives. Practical farming tasks can benefit significantly from the high exactness rates achieved by CNNs and the consolidation of GIS for huge-scope observation. Further innovative work in this field ought to further develop these strategies considerably more, making way for new applications for a more prominent assortment of yields and diseases. This will increase agrarian efficiency and worldwide food security. The advancements in this space show how computerized innovation is turning out to be increasingly more significant in agribusiness, making way for additional exact and proficient cultivating choices (Figures 3 and 4).

Step 1: input fig (original image)

Figure 3. Affected images (original image)

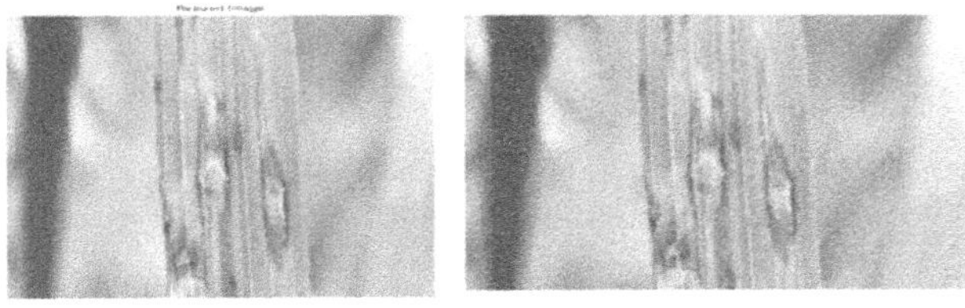

Step 2: grey scaled image

Figure 4. Grey scaled image

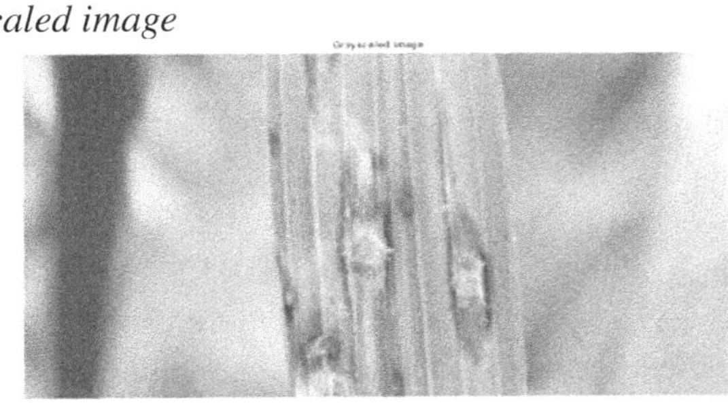

Two phases in the image processing process are shown in the above graphic, which gets a picture ready for analysis. The first step displays the original image (referred to as "input fig"), which shows a section of plant leaf that may have been captured to detect diseases or keep an eye on the condition of the farm. This full-color photograph accurately captures the plant's natural appearance. The identical image is displayed in Step 2, which is labeled "grey scaled image," following its conversion to grayscale. Red, green, and blue, the image's three-color channels, are reduced to a single intensity scale via this conversion. As a popular preprocessing step in image analysis, grayscale conversion reduces the computing load for subsequent processing, such as feature extraction or machine learning classification, by simplifying the data. For automated systems to detect abnormalities or changes in vegetation, this transformation is essential for focusing on patterns or traits that are independent of color.

Figure 5. Salt and pepper images

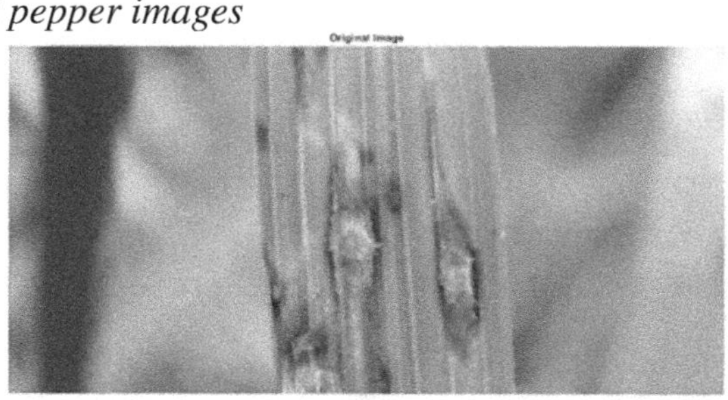

Figure 5 illustrates two digital image processing methods applied to a wooden surface image. Resizing the original image is a common first step to standardize the image dimensions for additional processing or analysis, and it is indicated in STEP 3 as "Resized image." The image's clarity and details can be affected by resizing, as seen by the slightly blurry details of the wood grain and texture. In step four, "salt & pepper (applying median filter)," you will see how to apply a median filter to an artificially corrupted image that contains noise that has been artificially added to it. One type of visual noise that can be seen as sporadic black-and-white speckles is called "salt-and-pepper noise." Here, the noise is effectively removed using a non-linear digital filtering technique called the median filter. This produces a clearer image where the texture integrity of the wood is more visible, though some details are still slightly obscured because of how severe the initial noise corruption was.

Step 5: filtered image

Figure 6. Filtered image

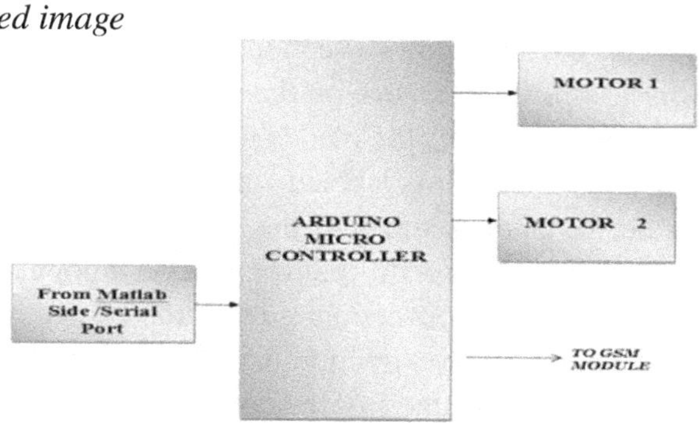

Step 6: Segmented image

Figure 7. Filtered image and segmented image

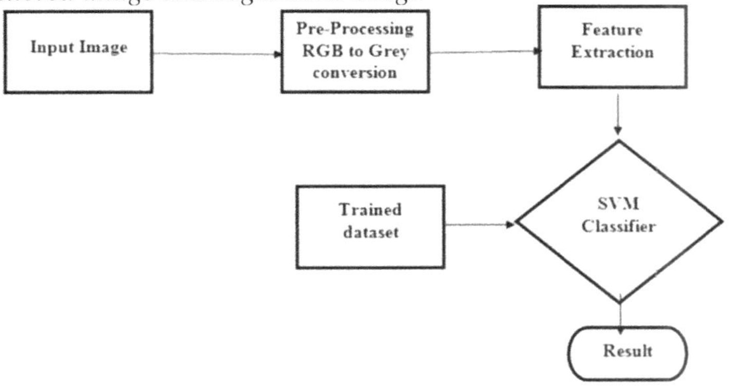

In order to diagnose rice blast illness in crops, the image processing steps that follow are depicted in the following pictures. Step 5, often known as the "filtered image," is the previously grayscale image that has undergone extra processing to improve features or lower noise, which facilitates the analysis of particular aspects pertinent to illness identification. In order to more clearly define the areas of interest, this may entail using methods like smoothing or sharpening. Step 6, also referred to as the "segmented image," displays the outcome of splitting the filtered image into regions of interest and the background using segmentation algorithms. It is essential to isolate the plant's afflicted sections using this binary representation, in which the areas of possible concern are often represented by white and the background by black. The seventh step, "Feature selection," is not shown graphically, but it entails selecting the most important features or data points from the divided image for examination (Figures 6 and 7).

The workflow diagram for image processing plant health analysis shows two processes. A high-resolution color photo of rice plants is shown in Step 1, "Input Fig (Original image)," with brown lesions on the leaves indicating visible indicators of illness or stress. An initial digital analysis is conducted using this original image. In step 2, "Grey Scaled image," the same photo is displayed after being transformed into a grayscale image. By concentrating just on light intensity rather than color information, this conversion procedure reduces the image from three color channels (red, green, and blue) to a single brightness scale, simplifying the analysis. Because they can improve the identification of textural and form details—which are critical for recognizing plant diseases and other irregularities in agricultural contexts—grayscale images are useful for processing because they demand fewer computing resources.

The outline shows two picture handling stages applied to a grayscale shot of a plant stem with a water bead. In Step 3, under "Resized picture," the picture has been resized or diminished in size while safeguarding the surface of the plant stems and the lucidity of the water drops. This takes into consideration the presentation of moment highlights like the water's surface strain and reflection. The picture is seen again in Step 4, "Salt and Pepper (applying middle channel)," which shows the conscious expansion of salt and pepper clamor, a kind of visual commotion comprised of irregular, highly contrasting dabs. To diminish dot while keeping up with the lines and subtleties of the picture components, this stage likewise includes applying a middle channel, a standard strategy for eliminating such commotion from photographs.

Two different picture-handling stages are displayed in the provided figure. A grayscale picture showing vertical scratches on a surface is displayed in the initial step, "STEP5: separated picture". Maybe by utilizing strategies like edge upgrade or differentiation change, this separated picture seems to work on the permeability of these scratches against the foundation. The result of utilizing a division calculation is shown in the subsequent step, " STEP6: Portioned picture". Here, the fixes stand as sharp white lines on a strong dark field, obviously isolated from the encompassing region. For occupations like material deformity recognizable proof or quantitative component examination in picture handling exercises, this twofold division is fundamental as it features the particular areas of concern. The change from a sifted to a portioned picture shows a significant stage in picture investigation, wherein specific highlights are found and isolated for extra assessment or handling.

CONCLUSION

Limitations

While novel, the utilization of computerized picture handling to analyze sicknesses in paddy crops has various disadvantages. Most importantly, a central point in the accuracy of sickness distinguishing proof is the type of photographs taken. The lucidity of the pictures and, thus, the precision of sickness determination can be significantly influenced by different elements, including light, shadows, and camera points. Besides, photographs may not obviously show the different phases of a sickness' movement, which could bring about a late or inaccurate conclusion. Exact picture investigation may be made more troublesome by ecological variables like haze, downpour, or residue that blocks the camera's vision. Extra trouble is in the framework's dependence on a huge scope preparing datasets for proficient distinguishing proof of different illness side effects; gathering such datasets is costly and tedious. Besides, an over-dependence on innovation risks darkening ordinary agronomic information and techniques that can offer further experiences into illness on the board. Ultimately, the expense of carrying out such refined frameworks might hinder some limited-scale ranchers from utilizing them, which would confine openness and acknowledgment in regions where they could be generally required.

Future Scope

The potential for changing rural practices and further developing harvest the executives using computerized picture handling to distinguish ailments in rice crops is huge. The blend of cutting-edge calculations and high-goal pictures will consider the early and more precise location of a wide variety of plant sicknesses as innovation creates. This can be additionally upgraded by breaking down photographs with AI and computerized reasoning. This will make computerized frameworks that can perceive specific infection side effects and figure out the course of the illness in light of past information and constant checking. Robots and Web of Things (IoT) gadgets can be utilized to effectively gather and interact information over huge districts through the joining of such frameworks into shrewd cultivating arrangements. Moreover, democratizing access through the making of portable applications would empower ranchers to utilize cell phones to analyze crops immediately. For an enormous dataset, the board will be made more straightforward by distributed computing and continuous headways in computational models, which will build the precision of analytic apparatuses. To satisfy the developing worldwide populace's interest in food, this will likely bring about additional reasonable cultivating procedures by diminishing the utilization of pesticides, further developing harvest well-being of the executives, and, in the long run, raising yields.

REFERENCES

Aashish, D., Venkateswaran, P. S., Prabha, L., Kumar, R. D., Kumar, D., & Pradeep, V. (2024). A study on customer preference, satisfaction, and loyalty towards select food brands. *FMDB Transactions on Sustainable Social Sciences Letters*, *2*(1), 19–33. DOI: 10.69888/FTSSSL.2024.000217

Al-Mokdad, M. (2024). China and Qatar's Partnership in Future Energies and its Impact on Middle Eastern Geopolitics. *AVE Trends In Intelligent Technoprise Letters*, *1*(1), 50–59.

Anand, P. P., Jayanth, G., Rao, K. S., Deepika, P., Faisal, M., & Mokdad, M. (2024). Utilising Hybrid Machine Learning to Identify Anomalous Multivariate Time-Series in Geotechnical Engineering. *AVE Trends In Intelligent Computing Systems*, *1*(1), 32–41.

Balajibhanu, R., & Rao, J. V. N. (2014). Agriculture Field Monitoring and Analysis Using Wireless Sensor Networks For Improving Crop production. In *Eleventh International Conference On Wireless And Optical Communications Networks (Wocn)*. Vijayawada, India.

Balamurali, R., & Kathiravan, K. (2015). An Analysis of Various Routing Protocols for Precision Agriculture using Wireless Sensor Network". *IEEE International Conference on Technological Innovations in ICT for Agriculture and Rural Development(TIAR2015)*, Chennai, Tamil Nadu. DOI: 10.1109/TIAR.2015.7358549

Dan, L., C., Xin, H., & Chongwei, J. L. (2015). Intelligent agent greenhouse environment monitoring system based on IOT technology. In 2015 International Conference on Intelligent Transportation, Big Data & Smart City. Halong Bay, Vietnam.

Elayaraja, C., Rahila, J., Velavan, P., Rajest, S. S., Shynu, T., & Rahman, M. M. (2024). Depth sensing in AI on exploring the nuances of decision maps for explainability. In *Advances in Computational Intelligence and Robotics* (pp. 217–238). IGI Global.

Fan, C.-L. (2013). The Application of a ZigBee Based Wireless Sensor Network in the LED Street Lamp Control System". *IEEE International Conference*, 10(10), 501–504.

Ikwuagwu, C. V., Tejiri, O. I., Chimdindu, E. S., Wisdom, O. O., & Okoh, I. E. (2024). Design, fabrication, and performance evaluation of a varying temperature dehydrator for food preservation. *FMDB Transactions on Sustainable Energy Sequence*, *2*(1), 49–59. DOI: 10.69888/FTSES.2024.000191

Ji-Hua, M., Bing-Fang, W., & Qiang-Zi, L. (2006). A global crop growth monitoring system based on remote sensing. *2006 IEEE International Symposium on Geoscience and Remote Sensing*, Denver, Colorado, USA. DOI: 10.1109/IGARSS.2006.589

Kim, Y., Ieee, R. G., & Evans, W. M. (2008). Remote Sensing and Control of an Irrigation System Using a Distributed Wireless Sensor Network. *IEEE Transactions on Instrumentation and Measurement*, *57*(7), 1379–1387. DOI: 10.1109/TIM.2008.917198

Li, L.-L., Shi-Feng, Y., Wang, L.-Y., & Gao, X.-M. (2011). The Greenhouse Environment Monitoring System Based on Wireless Sensor Network Technology". In *Proceedings of the 2011 IEEE International Conference on Cyber Technology in Automation, Control, and Intelligent Systems*, Kunming, China. DOI: 10.1109/CYBER.2011.6011806

Linzhang, M., & Xiangzhan, Y. (2022). Design and implementation fragnary monitoring system based on wireless sensor network node". *2010 International Conference on Measuring Technology and Mechatronics Automation*, 1(4), 950–953.

Mainwaring, A., Polastre, J., Szewczyk, R., Culler, D., & Anderson, J. (2002).. . *Wireless Sensor Networks for Habitat Monitoring.*, *3*(10), 2925–2928.

Nisha, G., & Megala, J. (2014). Wireless Sensor Network Based Automated Irrigation and Crop Field Monitoring System". Sixth International Conference on Advanced Computing (IcoAC), 179(12), 105782. DOI: 10.1109/ICoAC.2014.7229707

Pranav, R. P., Prawin, R. P., Subhashni, R., & Das, S. R. (2023). Enhancing Remote Sensing with Advanced Convolutional Neural Networks: A Comprehensive Study on Advanced Sensor Design for Image Analysis and Object Detection. *FMDB Transactions on Sustainable Computer Letters*, *1*(4), 255–266.

Ramgirkar, A., & Talhar, J. (2024). Advanced intelligent systems for quantitative analysis of crop production and efficiency in Maharashtra. *FMDB Transactions on Sustainable Computing Systems*, *2*(1), 1–12. DOI: 10.69888/FTSCS.2024.000192

Regin, R., T, S., George, S. R., Bhattacharya, M., Datta, D., & Priscila, S. S. (2023). Development of predictive model of diabetic using supervised machine learning classification algorithm of ensemble voting. *International Journal of Bioinformatics Research and Applications*, *19*(3), 151–169. DOI: 10.1504/IJBRA.2023.10057044

Sengupta, S., Datta, D., Rajest, S. S., Paramasivan, P., Shynu, T., & Regin, R. (2023). Development of rough-TOPSIS algorithm as hybrid MCDM and its implementation to predict diabetes. *International Journal of Bioinformatics Research and Applications*, *19*(4), 252–279. DOI: 10.1504/IJBRA.2023.135363

Shilesh, D. M., Linson, L., Babu, J., & Ashifa, K. M. (2024). Exploring the impact of social media on adolescent food habits and dietary choices. *AVE Trends In Intelligent Social Letters, 1*(3), 148–156.

Sohlot, J., Teotia, P., Govinda, K., Rangineni, S., & Paramasivan, P. (2023). A Hybrid Approach on Fertilizer Resource Optimization in Agriculture Using Opposition-Based Harmony Search with Manta Ray Foraging Optimization. *FMDB Transactions on Sustainable Computing Systems, 1*(1), 44–53.

Suganthi, M., & Sathiaseelan, J. G. R. (2023). Image Denoising and Feature Extraction Techniques Applied to X-Ray Seed Images for Purity Analysis. *FMDB Transactions on Sustainable Health Science Letters, 1*(1), 41–53.

Venkateswaran, P. S., Dharshini, S. D., Kumar, S. K., Lakshmi, D., Balan, D., & Sachani, D. K. (2024). A Study on Market Share Analysis of Select Food Products: Identifying Key Drivers and Barriers to Growth. *AVE Trends In Intelligent Social Letters, 1*(1), 1–12.

Vijayakumar, S., & Rosario, J. N. (2011). Preliminary Design for Crop Monitoring Involving Water and Fertilizer Conservation Using Wireless Sensor Networks. In *Communication Software and Networks (ICCSN)*. IEEE. DOI: 10.1109/ICCSN.2011.6014979

Vijayan, S. (2020a). Fine tuned VGG19 convolutional neural network architecture for diabetic retinopathy diagnosis. *Indian Journal of Computer Science and Engineering, 11*(5), 615–622. DOI: 10.21817/indjcse/2020/v11i5/201105266

Vijayan, T., & Karthik, B. (2020). Trainable WEKA Segmentation of Retinal Fundus Images for Global Eye Disease Diagnosis Application. *International Journal of Emerging Trends in Engineering Research, 8*(9), 5750–5754. DOI: 10.30534/ijeter/2020/136892020

Vijayan, T., Sangeetha, M., & Karthik, B. (2020). Efficient Analysis of Diabetic Retinopathy on Retinal Fundus Images using Deep Learning Techniques with Inception V3 Architecture. *Journal of Green Engineering, 10*(10), 9615–9625.

Xiao, L. (2010). The Realization of Precision Agriculture Monitoring System Based on Wireless Sensor Network. *2010 International Conference on Computer and Communication Technologies in Agriculture Engineering*, 3(7), 89–92.

Zhuang, W.-Y., Junior, M. C., Cheong, P., & Tam, K.-W. (2011). Flood Monitoring of Distribution Substation in Low-Lying Areas Using Wireless Sensor Network". In *Proceedings of 2011 International Conference on System Science and Engineering*, Maco, China. DOI: 10.1109/ICSSE.2011.5961974

Chapter 12
A Comprehensive Analysis on Diverse Deep Learning Methods on Text Summarisation and Classification Techniques

B. Raju
https://orcid.org/0009-0005-2415-4930
Bharath Institute of Higher Education and Research, India

M. Sriram
Bharath Institute of Higher Education and Research, India

V. Ganesan
Bharath Institute of Higher Education and Research, India

ABSTRACT

Social media platforms employ text summarization and classification techniques to generate summaries for posts grouped based on topics' content. It is also used in the search engine to answer the user query rather than just providing a link. The text classification and summarisation techniques produce a summary containing important information from the original document and all the relevant sentences. Two major approaches, extractive and abstractive, are viewed from the summary results. Many difficulties exist, such as missing out on certain sentences, affecting the summary meaning, and not meeting the required standards. The proposed machine learning-based feature selection method extracts the source information and produces the end user's proper information. Statistic techniques combined with

DOI: 10.4018/979-8-3373-5203-9.ch012

machine learning algorithms and fuzzy logic will quickly determine the keywords and similarity of the word and scale it to different languages.

INTRODUCTION

A machine learning technique called text classification assigns a list of predetermined categories to open-ended text. Text classifiers can be used to organize, arrange, and categorize just about any type of text, including files from the web, medical research, and publications. A few instances include topics that can be used to organize news stories, the urgency of determining support tickets, analyzing a tweet for user sentiment, and identifying spam in an email. Social media platforms employ text summarization and classification techniques to generate summaries for posts grouped based on topics' content. It is also used in the search engine to answer the user query rather than just providing a link (Priscila et al., 2023). Especially in regular language handling (NLP), profound learning is a troublesome power in the consistently changing artificial reasoning scene (Kuppili et al., 2020). In this review, two significant NLP errands — text synopsis and grouping — are entirely broken down utilizing an assortment of profound learning calculations (Akhter et al., 2020). These exercises are vital for disentangling and organizing the monstrous measure of text-based material created consistently, considering more proficient data recovery and understanding.

Text synopsis endeavors to compactly give the primary concerns of long distributions while holding the first text's unique circumstance and significance. Text classification, then again, provides text classifications to sort and recover data productively. These positions are fundamental for applications in different fields, like scholarly examination, legitimate, clinical, and news coverage, as they tackle the issue of dealing with gigantic text measures when information is wherever. The presentation of profound learning has started critical advancement in these fields. Since they depend greatly on handmade qualities and shallow learning models, conventional AI methods often neglect to catch unpredictable and progressive language examples (Huan et al., 2020). Then again, profound learning procedures have shown better execution because of their ability to learn various leveled portrayals and appreciate setting through layers of deliberation (Sayedelahl, 2024).

Convolutional brain organizations (CNNs), repetitive brain organizations (RNNs), transformers, and long transient memory organizations (LSTMs) are among the notable profound learning plans that are assessed in this work. Each model has unmistakable characteristics that make it suitable in text order and synopsis for specific purposes. For example, CNNs are truly adept at recognizing position and nearby invariant examples in the text, which makes them ideal for characterization undertakings where the presence of specific words and expressions educates more regarding the subject than their connections or requests (Vashishtha and Dhawan, 2023). Undertakings requiring an understanding of the text's succession and setting — an essential for proficient synopsis — are a major area of strength for RNNs and LSTMs. With its imaginative design in light of self-consideration processes, the Transformer model has additionally reformed normal language handling (NLP) by empowering models to survey the overall worth of particular words in an expression, no matter what their situation (Devi and Rajasekaran, 2023). By unequivocally getting a handle on the nuances of the specific situation, this limit is particularly helpful for grouping material and summing up it by featuring the most useful pieces. Models like BERT (Bidirectional Encoder Portrayals from Transformers), GPT (Generative Pre-prepared Transformer), and others that utilization gigantic measures of pre-prepared information to accomplish surprising exactness across different NLP undertakings have been created because of the Transformer's versatility and proficiency in handling long arrangements of information, setting new principles in the field (Anushya et al., 2024).

This concentrate likewise examines the manners by which these profound learning models can be improved by applying methodologies like performing multiple tasks learning — settling a few learning undertakings simultaneously and dividing important data among them — and moving to realize, which applies a model made for one errand to another that is connected. By acclimating to the complexities and variety of human language, these techniques have shown to work on model execution and versatility. We likewise discuss the troubles of trying these complex models. For example, they require much handling power, and far-reaching preparing datasets is important for generalizability. That interpretability is as yet an issue. Profound learning models, albeit strong, habitually can be "secret elements," giving no knowledge of dynamic interaction. This is particularly dangerous in high-stakes circumstances when decisions should be legitimate (Regin et al., 2023).

This paper will introduce a point-by-point correlation of profound learning strategies in text outline and grouping and examine their functional executions, intrinsic difficulties, and likely future headings. It does this by joining observational investigation, hypothetical investigation, and a survey of late progressions (Gnanaguru et al., 2024). Eventually, the review intends to encourage advancements that could prompt more refined, productive, and straightforward artificial brainpower (simulated intelligence) frameworks that are equipped for understanding and handling human language with uncommon exactness and subtlety. This is made conceivable by carefully comprehending the capacities and limits of this study's techniques (Chunduri et al., 2024).

The text classification and summarisation techniques produce a summary containing important information from the original document and all the relevant sentences. Two major approaches, extractive and abstractive, are viewed from the summary results. The main contribution of the author is mentioned below: To explore different ML and Deep Learning classification algorithms and select the best classification algorithm and performance metric suitable for different applications such as movie review classification, Social media, Chatbot, thesis summary, etc.

RELATED WORKS

A text classification technique based on the Self-Interaction attention mechanism and label embedding was proposed by Joshi et al. (2023). BERT (Bidirectional Encoder Representation from Transformers) was introduced to enhance text classification's effectiveness. It is applied to produce text representations with deeper semantics. The classifier categorizes the documents using weighted label representations. When there are between 10 and 13 sentences, it performs well. Ali et al. (2018) created the Maxwell- Boltzmann Similarity Measure. (MBSM). It is based on the energy disparity between gaseous molecule compartments. The methods used for document classification and clustering are statistical mechanical methods. It demonstrates an increase in classification accuracy, a drop in clustering entropy values, and an improvement in clustering accuracy. For both the Web KB and the Reuters-R8 dataset, this technique consistently improves classification accuracy with increasing sample counts. Compared to other similarity measurements, it is more trustworthy.

The author et al. created the Single-layer Multisize Filters Convolutional Neural Network (SMFCNN) for text classification. The effectiveness of 16 ML baseline models was compared using three imbalanced datasets of varying sizes. While this is not the case for English, stopwords and unusual words together significantly negatively impact the performance of a large dataset when it comes to Arabic. After stopwords and unusual words are eliminated, accuracy is increased for a large dataset (NPUU) from 89.7% to 91.8%. Accuracy for the naive dataset increased from 94.9% to 95.4% only after stopwords and strange words were taken out. High precision, recall, F-measure, and accuracy are offered, and it excels at classifying small, medium, and large datasets. The Bi-LSTM (bidirectional long short-term memory) network Chinese text classification method, based on a feature-enhanced nonequilibrium, was proposed by Hai Huan et al. to improve text classification accuracy. It is founded on the NEBiLSTM network, the BERT pretraining model, and the hierarchical attention mechanism. As temporal complexity rises, precision increases significantly.

Surender Singh Samant et al. (2019) use a vector space model to increase term weighting in short texts. Four supervised term weighting techniques were compared. When compared, the in-modRF receives the event dataset's highest overall scores. On two of the three classifiers, it has the highest ratings. Zhao et al. (2020) used a scope-based convolution neural network to apply deep learning to categorizing text texts. Complex local properties, such as phrases with varied lengths or discontinuous phrases, can be more effectively and flexibly captured in text data. LSS-CNN can accomplish great efficacy and scalability on large amounts of text. The underuse of consumer health language is addressed by the Medical Social Media Text Classification (MSMTC) algorithm developed by the author et al. It can automatically extract from authentic medical social media text phrases that provide health information but lack normative expressions. Yan Du and Hua Huo created a news text automatic summarising model. It pre-processes the original news text using NLTK tools and extracts key information. It produces fair and suitable weights for text features based on their significance. It produces news summaries of higher quality.

For the Urdu text, Wang et al. (2019) created a rule-based thorough stemming approach. The stem of Urdu text is generated using six brand-new infix word classes and a minimum word length requirement. It can handle stemming scenarios involving prefixes, posts, and infixes. Before the tasks of text mining, information retrieval, and natural language processing, it is a vital pre-processing stage. Processing short text in any other language is possible using this probabilistic short text classifier. Text was extracted from scene photos by Liu and Chen (2019). By breaking down scene photos into layers and text components using morphological elements analysis (MCA), it is possible to lessen the negative effects of complicated domains on detection success. With no restrictions on text size, color, or other attributes, this approach enables reliable text detection. Text within scene photographs, as well as text overlaid on top of images, can both be detected.

The field of text grouping is continuously changing, which is especially valid for monetary news. Late scholastic examinations have tested the restrictions of current methodologies. The arrangement of monetary compositions written in Chinese was the subject of a fascinating review led by Jeba et al. (2024). They uncovered an original brain network model called Promotion CharCGNN, which shrewdly mixes charCNN and GRU (Gated Repetitive Unit) innovations' highlights. With its hearty arrangement appropriate to certifiable applications, this half-and-half model is explicitly intended to work on handling various types of character-based texts. A significant improvement in dealing with the many-sided and nuanced character of monetary accounts is the versatility and viability of the Promotion CharCGNN model.

The COCO-CharRef dataset, a Characteress Alluding Articulation assortment, was laid out by Minu et al. (2023). with the end goal of reclassifying the combination and utilization of literary data in computational models. This improvement expands in a comparable direction to advancing text-related datasets and instruments. This dataset works on the corpus of assets accessible for text classification and beats standard strategies that were beforehand broadly utilized in the field overwhelmingly. A more productive and compelling technique for coordinating extricated text data is presented by the COCO-CharRef dataset, which empowers further developed understanding and application in various certifiable situations. Both explorations have made key commitments to the field of text order. They offer helpful apparatuses that might be promptly utilized in administering and examining monetary information, as well as improving hypothetical comprehension. In our current reality, where computerized message information volume and intricacy are expanding dramatically, these commitments are fundamental in giving further developed and adaptable apparatuses for examination. This is to guarantee that information handling is more powerful. By the prerequisites of true applications, the Promotion CharCGNN model and COCO-CharRef dataset perfectly represent the imaginative reasoning expected to address the present message order hardships.

Proposed Machine Learning-based Text Summarization and Classification Technique

The Deep Learning-based Text Summarization and Classification Technique is an approach to automatic text summarization and classification that uses deep learning. This technique uses a deep neural network to extract essential features from the text and then classify the text based on these features. The deep learning model learns to identify and remove the important features, and the classification task is done by supervised learning. This technique can summarize large documents, classify text, and identify similar documents. This technique has been successfully used to improve the accuracy of automatic summarization and classification.

A few issues regularly compromise the viability and accuracy of outlines produced in text synopsis. One significant issue is the evacuation of pivotal sentences, which can distort the planned significance and miss the mark regarding acknowledged summing up rules. A clever arrangement using AI-based highlight determination strategies has been introduced to address these issues. This technique recovers significant data from the first text, ensuring the client gets only the most appropriate and essential data. Additionally, this cycle is improved by consolidating fluffy rationale, refined AI calculations, and factual systems. This exceptional mix considers fast and exact examination by being particularly helpful in tracking down key expressions and deciding word comparability. This procedure additionally has the advantage of being adaptable to a few dialects, expanding its handiness and importance in global settings. The new methodology addresses the intrinsic difficulties of conventional text outline and lays out another benchmark for precisely and instructively creating rundowns by incorporating these state-of-the-art approaches. By doing this, rundowns will be brief and contain all relevant data, expanding their worth to end clients across various uses.

Figure 1. Block diagram of proposed LSTM and SVM-based text summarization and classification

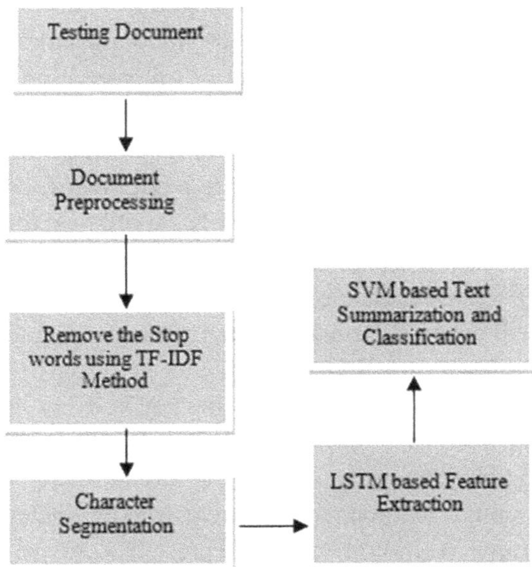

A recommended framework that consolidates text synopsis and grouping strategies in light of SVM (Backing Vector Machine) and LSTM (Long Transient Memory) is portrayed in Figure 1. Beginning with a "Testing Record," the technique continues through "Report Pre-processing." Stop words are eliminated by utilizing the TF-IDF (Term Recurrence Reverse Archive Recurrence) technique to sift through less huge terms. Then, "Character Division" is utilized to partition the text into absorbable segments for examination. Following pre-processing, there are two essential handling streams for the message information. Utilizing SVM's capacity to deal with high-layered information for the order, the primary stream utilizes an SVM-based strategy for text summarizing and arrangement. The subsequent stream separates highlights utilizing an LSTM-based model, utilizing the capacity of LSTM to catch long-haul conditions in literary information — a critical part for fathoming setting in synopsis undertakings. The objective of this double technique is to further develop text synopsis and characterization precision and viability by using the upsides of both SVM and LSTM.

Steps Involved in Deep Learning-based Text Summarization and Classification Technique

Data Collection: Collecting relevant text data from webpages, books, journals, etc.

Data Pre-processing: This involves cleaning and formatting the raw text data by removing stop words, punctuation, and other symbols. Natural language processing (NLP) techniques, including tokenization, stop-word removal, lemmatization, stemming, and part-of-speech tagging, are the best way to pre-process data for text summarization and classification. Tokenization entails separating text into individual words or phrases, whereas stop-word elimination eliminates frequently used terms that don't contribute to the text's content. Words are reduced to their root forms by lemmatization and stemming, which can lessen the quantity of data that needs to be processed. Finally, part-of-speech tagging can help identify the role of each word in the sentence, which can help determine the sentence's overall meaning and help the algorithm better classify the text.

Feature Extraction: This involves extracting keywords or phrases from the text data using techniques such as TF-IDF and word embeddings. The best method for feature extraction in text summarization and classification depends on the specific application. Some popular methods for feature extraction include:

Word Embeddings: Word embeddings represent words in a numerical vector space, allowing for grouping words with similar meanings.

Bag of Words: A bag of words creates a frequency-based representation of text, allowing for the extraction of important words in a document.

N-Grams: N-grams create a frequency-based representation of text, allowing for the extraction of important phrases and groups of words in a document.

TF-IDF: TF-IDF creates a numerical representation of text, allowing for the extraction of important words and phrases based on their frequency of occurrence in a document relative to the rest of the corpus.

Latent Semantic Analysis: Latent Semantic Analysis creates a numerical representation of text, allowing for the extraction of important words and phrases based on their relationships with other words in the document.

Model Training: This entails using the retrieved characteristics to train a deep-learning model. Different techniques can be used to train the model, including Long Short-Term Memory (LSTM), Convolutional Neural Networks (CNNs), and other recurrent neural networks. The best method for model training in text summarization and classification combines supervised and unsupervised learning. At the same time, unsupervised learning can be used to find patterns and summary material, and supervised learning can be used to train models to categorize text. Methods like topic modeling and sentiment analysis can be used to find patterns and connections in the text before summarizing it. Deep learning and natural language processing techniques can also be used to find significant textual aspects and provide summaries. Support vector machines, decision trees, and neural networks are a few examples of supervised learning techniques that can be used for text classification.

Model Evaluation: This entails assessing the trained model's performance using a test set. The most popular evaluation metrics for text summarization are ROUGE (Recall-Oriented Understudy for Gisting Evaluation) and BLEU (Bilingual Evaluation Understudy).

Text Summarization and Classification: This involves using the trained model to summarize and classify the input text into different categories.

Naive Bayes Algorithm

The Nave-Bayes algorithm is a supervised learning method for classification issues that is based on the Bayes theorem. It is mostly employed in text categorization with a large training set. The Naive Bayes Classifier is today's most straightforward and efficient classification algorithm. It aids in developing quick machine-learning models capable of making accurate predictions. Being a probabilistic classifier, it makes predictions based on the likelihood that an object will occur. Spam filtration, sentiment analysis, and article classification are a few examples of frequently used Naive Bayes algorithms.

Support Vector Machines

Another effective text classification machine learning technique is Support Vector Machines (SVM), which, like Naive Bayes, requires little training data to begin producing reliable results. SVM needs more computing power than Naive Bayes, but the outcomes are even quicker and more precise. In essence, SVM creates a "hyperplane" or line that separates a region into two subspaces. Vectors (tags) that are members of one group are found in one subspace, whereas those that are not are found in another. The hyperplane with the greatest separation between each tag is the ideal hyperplane. Employing categories to tag products or material on your website to facilitate browsing or locate similar content. Using text classification, CRM tasks can be automatically allocated, analyzed, and ranked according to priority and relevance. It uses less manual labor and is, therefore, more time-efficient. The government can create a quicker emergency response system by categorizing panicking conversations on social media. Marketers can use how consumers talk about a product or brand online to track and categorize users. It is possible to train the classifier to recognize supporters and opponents. Consequently, brands are improved to better serve groups.

SIMULATION RESULTS AND DISCUSSION

The data collection, pre-processing, TF-IDF-based feature extraction, and SVM-based text summarizing and classification processes comprise the proposed LSTM and SVM-based text summarization and classification algorithm. A free and open-source Python framework for machine learning and deep learning, sci-kit-learn focuses particularly on the training and inference of deep neural networks but may be used for various tasks. It was constructed using the Python programming language, and various simulation parameters, including precision, recall, F1 score, accuracy, and AUC, are used to evaluate the suggested deep learning model (Area Under the Curve)

A value's precision is a gauge of its accuracy. It refers to how precisely a value is expressed or repeated. (Number of right values/Total number of values) x 100 is the calculation for precision. The percentage of genuine positives among all positively labeled items is known as recall. In other words, recall represents the proportion of real positive cases a model correctly detected. Recall does not account for false negatives; this is a key distinction. Recall is calculated using the True Positive/(True Positive + False Negative). The harmonic mean of precision and recall is used to calculate the F1 Score, a metric for a model's accuracy. The F-score or F-measure are other names for it. The F1 Score formula is:

F1 Score is equal to 2 * (Precision * Recall) / (Precision + Recall)

The accuracy of a model or algorithm's prediction of the predicted result is measured. It gauges how closely the values anticipated and the actual values line up. The accuracy equation is:

Accuracy equals 100 times the ratio of correct forecasts to total predictions.

Area under the Curve, or AUC, is a metric to assess how well a classification model works. It assesses how well a model predicts both genuine positives and true negatives. The true positive rate (TPR) is plotted against the false positive rate on a graph called a Receiver Operating Characteristic (ROC) plot, and AUC quantifies the area under the curve of this graph (FPR). The AUC formula is:

AUC is equal to (True Positive + True Negative) / 2

True Positive Rate is the percentage of positive instances classified properly, and True Negative Rate is the percentage of negative cases identified correctly. Figure 1 demonstrates the simulation results using a confusion matrix to decide the performance of the classification model for a specified fixed test and train data. The confusion matrix helps decide whether the results are true or false. Figure 2 gives the accuracy, precision, F1-score, and recall based on the value calculated from the confusion matrix. As shown in Figure 1, the sensitivity of an LSTM and SVM-based text summarization and Classification method depends on the feature extraction method and the document size used for training. The reported accuracy of LSTM-based text summarization and classification methods is 97.9%, precision is 94.8%, F1 score value is 54.9, and recall value is 93.67%.

Figure 2. Performance comparison of CNN, RNN, and LSTM models across different simulation parameters

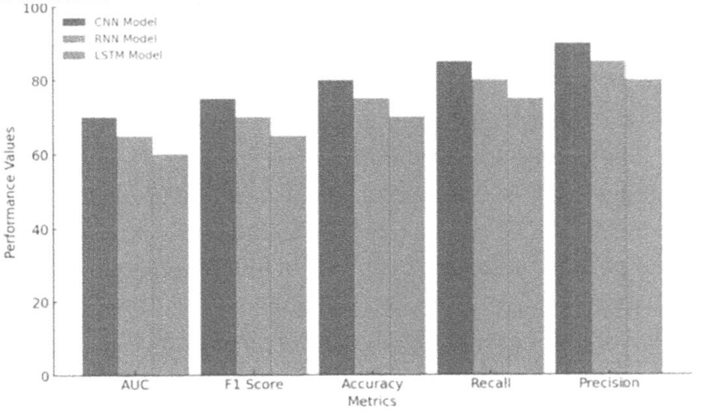

AUC (Region Under the Bend), F1 Score, Exactness, Review, and Accuracy are the five significant measures that Figure 2 looks at in the presentation of three unmistakable profound learning models — CNN (Convolutional Brain Organization), RNN (Repetitive Brain Organization), and LSTM (Long Momentary Memory). Three bars are connected to each action; the bars are variety-coded to address various models, with blue indicating CNN, red addressing RNN, and green addressing LSTM. This style simplifies it to analyze each model's outcomes for every measurement. The histogram shows that RNNs and LSTMs perform seriously yet imperceptibly more regrettably than CNNs in many boundaries, with CNNs improving by and large, particularly in accuracy. To assist with decision-production for specific applications where one measurement might be a higher priority than others, such visual correlations are fundamental in showing the qualities and impediments of each model, specifically regions.

Research Issues and Challenges in Text Summarization and Classification Method

The following are the major research issues and challenges for the researchers who are working toward text summarization and classification techniques:

- **Semantic Analysis:** Summarization and classification tasks require semantic analysis to identify the key concepts and relationships in the text. This is a difficult problem because of the ambiguity of language, and the need for an understanding of context and the domain further complicates it.
- **Automatic Summarization**: Automatically generating summaries from a large text set is a difficult problem due to the complexity of natural language. Generating a concise and accurate summary requires understanding the text, which is challenging for machines.
- **Text Categorization:** Categorization tasks automatically assign a text to one or more categories. This task can be difficult due to the ambiguity of language and because categories can be related in complex ways.
- **Text Clustering:** Clustering text documents is a non-trivial task because of the complexity of natural language. It requires finding patterns in the text and grouping similar documents.
- **Annotation:** Annotating text with relevant categories is a difficult and time-consuming task. It requires an understanding of the text and the domain and manual effort.
- **Representation:** Representing the text in a way that is suitable for summer

CONCLUSION

A Long Short-Term Memory (LSTM) neural network is used in LSTM-based summarization and classification algorithms to evaluate and summarize text. By examining word sequences and comprehending the relationships between them, the network is trained to recognize the organization and content of the text. This enables it to recognize crucial words and ideas before creating a text summary. Support Vector Machines (SVMs) are used for text classification in SVM-based summarization and classification algorithms. SVMs are taught to identify patterns in text and figure out how to categorize them. The SVMs analyze the text's features to ascertain the category to which it belongs before producing a summary from the input text. Text categorization tasks like sentiment analysis and spam detection frequently employ this method.

Limitations

The review has specific critical impediments, notwithstanding its significant commitments to the field of profound learning approaches for text order and rundown. Most importantly, breaking down enormous datasets or utilizing muddled structures can make the intricacy and computational necessities of complex profound learning models — like CNNs, RNNs, and Transformers — absurdly high. This might confine their utilization in settings with restricted assets or make them computationally concentrated. Second, the amount of information prepared and its nature affect these models' presentation. The models may not sum up well to new, concealed information in scanty, imbalanced, or loud circumstances. Moreover, interpretability issues are typical with profound learning models, particularly those that depend on brain organizations. Understanding and clarifying these models' dynamic cycles is difficult due to their "black box" nature, pivotal in fields like regulation and medical care, where high levels of straightforwardness are fundamental. Finally, despite the review incorporating different models, it probably won't cover all the late-grown profound learning techniques that could address some of the previously mentioned imperatives or proposition new experiences.

Future Work

Future studies might look at the expansion of text outline and grouping philosophies through the mix of the consideration system, which has shown imperative adequacy in normal language handling situations. This technique might work on the accuracy of text synopsis and order calculations by underlining the main expressions in a record and giving more weight to those generally relevant to the subject. Moreover, exploring different avenues regarding installing methods like word2vec, Glove, and FastText could further develop these methodologies' exactness. These calculations may likewise be more viable if the hyperparameter choice interaction is advanced by utilizing techniques like lattice search, irregular hunt, and Bayesian improvement. Also, utilizing portrayal learning strategies like autoencoders could further develop message information, including extraction and portrayal, expanding the accuracy of message classification and outline. Finally, move learning might have the option to build the accuracy of text outline and grouping techniques using information from recently prepared models.

REFERENCES

Akhter, M. P., Jiangbin, Z., Naqvi, I. R., Abdelmajeed, M., Mehmood, A., & Sadiq, M. T. (2020). Document-level text classification using single-layer multisize filters convolutional neural network. *IEEE Access : Practical Innovations, Open Solutions*, *8*(3), 42689–42707. DOI: 10.1109/ACCESS.2020.2976744

Ali, M., Khalid, S., & Aslam, M. H. (2018). Pattern based comprehensive Urdu stemmer and short text classification. *IEEE Access : Practical Innovations, Open Solutions*, *6*(12), 7374–7389. DOI: 10.1109/ACCESS.2017.2787798

Anushya, A., Begum, S., Shiwani, S., & Shrivastava, A. (2024). Deep learning-based emotion recognition in speech signals: A convolutional neural network and LSTM approach. *AVE Trends in Intelligent Computing Systems*, *1*(4), 198–208.

Chunduri, V., Rajest, S. S., Allugunti, V. R., Verma, D., Aarthi, R., & Sharma, D. K. (2024). Deep neural network for brain tumour segmentation using guaranteed time slots (GTS) algorithm. In *Advances in Computer and Electrical Engineering* (pp. 371–390). IGI Global.

Devi, B. T., & Rajasekaran, R. (2023). A Comprehensive Review on Deepfake Detection on Social Media Data. *FMDB Transactions on Sustainable Computing Systems*, *1*(1), 11–20.

Du, Y., & Huo, H. (2020). News text summarisation based on multi-feature and fuzzy logic. *IEEE Access : Practical Innovations, Open Solutions*, *8*(7), 140261–140272. DOI: 10.1109/ACCESS.2020.3007763

Gnanaguru, G., Priscila, S. S., Sakthivanitha, M., Radhakrishnan, S., Rajest, S. S., & Singh, S. (2024). Thorough analysis of deep learning methods for diagnosis of COVID-19 CT images. In *Advances in Medical Technologies and Clinical Practice* (pp. 46–65). IGI Global.

Huan, H., Yan, J., Xie, Y., Chen, Y., Li, P., & Zhu, R. (2020). Feature-enhanced nonequilibrium bidirectional long short-term memory model for Chinese text classification. *IEEE Access : Practical Innovations, Open Solutions*, *8*(1), 199629–199637. DOI: 10.1109/ACCESS.2020.3035669

Jeba, J. A., Bose, S. R., Regin, R., Rajest, S. S., & Hasan, M. M. (2024). Intelligent Tamil video summarization: AI-powered NLP, translation, and speech integration for enhanced accessibility. *FMDB Transactions on Sustainable Computer Letters*, *2*(1), 26–39. DOI: 10.69888/FTSCL.2024.000179

Joshi, M., Shen, Z., & Kausar, S. (2023). Enhancing Inclusive Education on Leveraging Artificial Intelligence Technologies for Personalized Support and Accessibility in Special Education for Students with Diverse Learning Needs. *FMDB Transactions on Sustainable Techno Learning*, *1*(3), 125–142.

Kuppili, V., Biswas, M., Edla, D. R., Prasad, K. J. R., & Suri, J. S. (2020). A mechanics-based similarity measure for text classification in machine learning paradigm. *IEEE Transactions on Emerging Topics in Computational Intelligence*, *4*(2), 180–200. DOI: 10.1109/TETCI.2018.2863728

Liu, K., & Chen, L. (2019). Medical social media text classification integrating consumer health terminology. *IEEE Access : Practical Innovations, Open Solutions*, *7*(1), 78185–78193. DOI: 10.1109/ACCESS.2019.2921938

Minu, M. S., Subashka Ramesh, S. S., Canessane, R., Al-Amin, M., & Bin Sulaiman, R. (2023). Experimental Analysis of UAV Networks Using Oppositional Glowworm Swarm Optimization and Deep Learning Clustering and Classification. *FMDB Transactions on Sustainable Computing Systems*, *1*(3), 124–134.

Priscila, S. S., Rajest, S. S., Tadiboina, S. N., Regin, R., & András, S. (2023). Analysis of Machine Learning and Deep Learning Methods for Superstore Sales Prediction. *FMDB Transactions on Sustainable Computer Letters*, *1*(1), 1–11.

Regin, R., Sharma, P. K., Singh, K., Narendra, Y. V., Bose, S. R., & Rajest, S. S. (2023). Fine-grained deep feature expansion framework for fashion apparel classification using transfer learning. In *Advanced Applications of Generative AI and Natural Language Processing Models* (pp. 389–404). IGI Global. DOI: 10.4018/979-8-3693-0502-7.ch019

Samant, S. S., Bhanu Murthy, N. L., & Malapati, A. (2019). Improving term weighting schemes for short text classification in vector space model. *IEEE Access : Practical Innovations, Open Solutions*, *7*(11), 166578–166592. DOI: 10.1109/ACCESS.2019.2953918

Sayedelahl, M. A. (2024). Enabling Intelligent Traffic Systems: A Deep Learning Method for Accurate Arabic License Plate Recognition. *FMDB Transactions on Sustainable Intelligent Networks*, *1*(1), 40–55. DOI: 10.69888/FTSIN.2024.000156

Vashishtha, E., & Dhawan, G. (2023). Comparison of Baldrige Criteria of Strategy Planning and Harrison Text. *FMDB Transactions on Sustainable Management Letters*, *1*(1), 22–31.

Wang, J., Li, Y., Shan, J., Bao, J., Zong, C., & Zhao, L. (2019). Large-scale text classification using scope-based convolutional neural network: A deep learning approach. *IEEE Access : Practical Innovations, Open Solutions*, *7*(11), 171548–171558. DOI: 10.1109/ACCESS.2019.2955924

Zhao, W., Zhang, G., Yuan, G., Liu, J., Shan, H., & Zhang, S. (2020). The study on the text classification for financial news based on partial information. *IEEE Access : Practical Innovations, Open Solutions*, *8*(5), 100426–100437. DOI: 10.1109/ACCESS.2020.2997969

Chapter 13
Text Classification and Summarization Using Machine Learning

B. Raju
https://orcid.org/0009-0005-2415-4930
Bharath Institute of Higher Education and Research, India

M. Sriram
Bharath Institute of Higher Education and Research, India

V. Ganesan
Bharath Institute of Higher Education and Research, India

ABSTRACT

Since electronic files were first introduced, automated text categorization has been a significant application and research area. Documents provide a wealth of important human information. Automated text categorization has become necessary due to the exponential increase in the number of documents that are readable by machines and available for either public or confidential access. The sheer volume of written material we handle daily makes text categorization necessary in today's world. Text categorization generally comprises two types of classification: genre-based and topic-based. Topic-based text categorization organizes texts based on their subjects, and the majority of information for genre classification comes from the internet, discussion boards, forums, and televised or print media. This document presents a comprehensive summary of the outcomes of several feature choices, classification techniques, and evaluation techniques. It offers a comprehensive overview and analysis of the research conducted on text categorization using several text classification methods.

DOI: 10.4018/979-8-3373-5203-9.ch013

INTRODUCTION

A foremost field of natural language processing is the sorting of text, which automatically sorts text input into a predetermined set of classes. These days, companies stand to gain a great deal from the development of automated systems that extract structured data that may be used from text that is unstructured sources. Using an organized resource, investigators and professionals in the sector might conduct fairly simple searches to get all information about industrial work. These ML classifiers apply to the environmental domain. The subject matter knowledge may be derived from the data using various machine learning algorithms. Text categorization is the process of grouping text into several text domain-based classifications. It is a basic procedure in natural language processing whereby textual data classification techniques are provided. From the beginning of digital paperwork, automated text categorization has been an important application and research area.

Text categorization is now very important because of the vast number of text documents that are produced every day all over the world. At the focal point of any text characterization framework is the AI (ML) classifier, a key part that significantly speeds up the game plan, assessment, and comprehension of text records. From sifting spam in messages to doing feeling examination in web-based entertainment posts, this key piece of message order frameworks empowers many applications (Brank et al., 2002). There is a cozy connection between the exhibition nature of the ML classifiers used in these frameworks and their general viability and impact. To meet the remarkable troubles and intricacies connected with text information, various AI approaches and calculations are utilized to improve these classifiers (Kehagias et al., 2003). Understanding these classifiers' exhibitions is fundamental since it straightforwardly affects text arrangement frameworks' exactness, viability, and steadfastness (Schneider et al., 2005).

Strong classifiers need to oversee immense datasets with expertise and have the option to distinguish minute phonetic subtleties that could influence the characterization exertion. Utilizing a blend of normal language handling (NLP) techniques and customary AI (ML) calculations involve complex text handling to remove significant examples and qualities. Innocent Bayes, Backing Vector Machines (SVM), and brain networks are a portion of the techniques that are ordinarily utilized. Contingent upon the intricacy of the text and the degree of detail expected for the classifications, every one of these calculations has an extraordinary mix of characteristics that make them suitable for various types of text characterization occupations (Han et al., 2004).

An assortment of execution rules, including review, accuracy, and the F1-score, should be inspected to effectively evaluate these classifiers. These measurements show how dependable and precise the classifiers are in different working conditions. By communicating the level of precisely anticipated positive perceptions to the expected up-sides, accuracy checks how well the classifier tracks relevant cases. In circumstances where overlooking significant data could have grave outcomes, the review evaluates the classifier's ability to remember all important events for the dataset. Consolidating the data from the two measurements into a solitary sign, the F1-score, a consonant mean of exactness and review — gives a fair evaluation of the classifier's presentation (Bao and Ishii, 2002). To more readily comprehend ML classifiers, this paper analyzes their presentation in various functional circumstances and datasets for message order. As to message order particularly, the objective is to explain each AI strategy's overall benefits and impediments. The investigation additionally considers how different text planning strategies, including lemmatization, tokenization, and stemming, influence classifier execution. The effect of element determination strategies on classifier exactness and proficiency, like word embeddings and term recurrence reverse archive recurrence (TF-IDF), is additionally analyzed in this review. The versatility of classifiers is one more area of interest for the examination. This is a significant element considering the fast spread of advanced text data. To assess classifiers' ability to support execution over the long run without requiring normal retraining, their flexibility to novel, inconspicuous information is additionally checked out. One more evaluated standard is computational proficiency, which thinks about how well classifiers work in genuine circumstances where PC assets might be restricted.

The review's decisions try to significantly propel the field of text order by offering a careful handle on the various situations in which AI classifiers work. This lays out a norm for current and impending headways in text characterization advancements. The review coordinates the advancement of progressively intricate, exact, and compelling text classification frameworks by distinguishing the best techniques and systems (Bi et al., 2004). Eventually, this exploration's revelations can enormously work on associations' and elements' abilities for effectively taking care of and using text information. In our current reality, where information is turning out to be an ever-increasing number of significant improvements, such improvements ought to open the entryway for better essential preparation and a more educated direction. The review's supposed commitments are supposed to be both specialized and valuable, giving substantial benefits to enterprises, including client relationships with executives, computerized promoting, and online substance control. These spaces fundamentally rely upon the compelling grouping of text-based information to advance client commitment, maintain content strategies, and alter client connections (Sebastiani, 2002).

To summarize, this examination explores open doors for development in text arrangement while simultaneously benchmarking current ML classifiers. It's guessed that as AI and normal language handling propel, text classification frameworks' capacities will be improved, bringing about more responsive, dynamic, and customized applications. The previously mentioned headways are supposed to fundamentally affect many organizations, empowering a more refined understanding and communication with the continually developing computerized literary territory (Shanahan and Roma, 2003).

LITERATURE SURVEY

One of the primary responsibilities of natural language processing (NLP) is text categorization. Better automated text mining classifiers that can automatically organize and categorize documents are made possible by the rapid expansion of Internet applications and the resulting large increase in online texts. An automatic text classifier has been created using various machine learning techniques trained on a collection of categorized training documents (Cardoso-Cachopo and Oliveira, 2003; Chawl et al., 2011; Forman, 2003). The authors compare the efficiency of many text classification techniques in two distinct data sets. They specifically assess the k-nearest Neighbour iterations of the Vector and LSI models, a classifier built on Support Vector Machines (SVM), and the Vector and LSI approaches. According to their findings, SVMs and k-NN LSI outperform the other techniques overall in a statistically meaningful manner (Fragoudis et al., 2002; Guan and Zhou, 2002; Johnson et al., 2002).

Sebastiani provided a good overview of the text categorization field (Ke and Shaoping, 2002). As a result, in addition to providing a brief explanation of the text categorization, we also cite a few papers that were not included by Sebastiani and some more current works than those in his piece. Text categorization generally comprises genre-based analysis and topic-based classification. Using topic-based text classification, documents are categorized based on their subjects (Kessler et al., 1997). Texts can also be written in various genres, such as news pieces, reviews of films, scientific papers, and advertising.

The class is not entirely set in stone by various rules, such as the text's unique origin, altering strategies, language register, and interest group. Past examinations have shown that kind characterization and subject-based order are generally unique (Kim et al., 2008; Klopotek and Woch, 2003; Leopold and Kindermann, 2022). This differentiation results from how type, rather than subjects, is connected with a text's structure, construction, and reason, deciding how the substance is passed on to its readership. Subjects are connected with the substance or topic of a text. An individual blog, then again, is generally more conversational and freestyle. However, a logical paper is characterized by its indifferent tone and organized show, which differently settles on expressive decisions and primary principles (Lewis et al., 2004).

Besides, how a book is altered characterizes its kind vitally. Editors pursue decisions relying upon the assumptions and level of commonality of the target group with a guarantee that a record complies with the principles of its classification. These decisions might incorporate changing the language, lingual authority, and general show (Lim, 2004; Madsen et al., 2004; Montanes et al., 2003). The text can likewise be customized to live up to the assumptions of its perusers given the class by considering the phonetic register, which incorporates the jargon's intricacy and level of convention. For example, famous periodicals might utilize a more relaxed style to speak to an overall population. Yet, scholastic diaries ordinarily utilize a proper register with specialized language to speak with a specialist crowd (Soucy and Mineau, 2003).

Furthermore, the subject of type characterization has been examined as comparable to the stemming system, which lessens words to their base structures. Allies of the Textural Acknowledgment society battle that is stemming — executed by calculations like the Doorman Stemmer — further develop classifier execution by joining different word structures into a solitary token, which smoothes out text examination and lifts the viability of example acknowledgment (Nardiello et al., 2003; Novovicova and Malik, 2004; Qiang et al., 2005). This is particularly valuable in classifications where word subordinates are normal, as it permits the classifier to focus on the text's fundamental semantics instead of becoming stalled with morphological variations (Rajest et al., 2023).

Then again, doubters of forceful stemming strategies contend that these techniques can distort text examination on occasion, which could bring about the deficiency of significant word qualifications in certain classes. For example, in legitimate works, the unpretentious qualifications between wording such as "contract" and "authoritative" could have significant lawful implications, and transforming them through strong stemming might cause errors. Stemming can, hence, be exceptionally different from one kind to another as far as its value, intending that while it could sometimes increment classifier precision, it can sometimes hurt text respectability.

How these elements connect — creation, altering, register, and stemming — decides a text's sort (Regin et al., 2023). A specific strategy for text investigation is expected for every sort because of its particular customs and crowd assumptions. A far-reaching comprehension of the mechanical and context-oriented parts of text examination is essential, as seen by the continuous conversation concerning approaches, such as stemming, which delineates the many issues expected in type grouping. Thus, the emotional idea of type classification should likewise be recognized, as it now and again reflects more extensive social and relevant understandings that go past simple semantic or underlying examination. Classifiers can be adjusted to make them more likely to comprehend and sort texts in light of these variables (Yang et al., 2003; Regin et al., 2023; Padmanabhan et al., 2023).

METHODOLOGY

Learning and order are two fundamental cycles engaged with the grouping challenge, a critical objective in AI. Building a classifier through producing an exact model for information order is the principal objective of the learning stage. Prior preparation of an assortment of models that have recently been accurately class-labeled is the establishment whereupon this model is developed. The preparation set gives the central pieces of information and properties that guide the model's cognizance and dynamic examples, which explains what capabilities as a delegate test of the entire information universe the classifier will ultimately experience. Picking a reasonable AI calculation, for example, brain organizations, choice trees, or backing vector machines, and tweaking it utilizing preparing information are standard strides in the preparation cycle. The objective is to ensure the calculation can sum up from the occurrences it was prepared on to new, obscure information. The characterization stage begins once the educational experience has successfully delivered areas of strength. New information — information not experienced during the preparation stage — is utilized to assess the prepared classifier. Here, the objective is to accurately distinguish the classes with which these new models have a place. The classifier looks at the elements of every new model utilizing the examples and rules it got during the preparation stage. Then, at that point, utilizing what it has realized, it doles out a class tag. The down-to-earth adequacy of the classifier in genuine applications, where it should work reliably and precisely regardless of varieties in approaching, is not entirely set in stone by this technique, which is significant.

The nature of the preparation stage is a significant determinant of the characterization challenge's viability. Above all, the classifier should be able to sum up from its preparation set to already untested conditions. Using execution pointers like exactness, accuracy, review, and the F1 score, which measure the classifier's viability over a scope of datasets and settings, this speculation capacity is fundamentally evaluated. Moreover, a critical calculation of the classifier's presentation is the chosen AI calculation and the interaction used to calibrate and improve its boundaries. Complex techniques like cross-approval can lessen overfitting and ensure the model stays steady and relevant throughout the preparation interaction.

Furthermore, for the characterization cycle to be helpful in applications like web-based content sifting, constant dynamic frameworks, and dynamic information-driven proposals, it should be adaptable and ready to rapidly handle gigantic volumes of information. To do this, the classifiers should be precise and execution streamlined, gauging estimation time and speed against forecast exactness and trustworthiness.

On a very basic level, the grouping issue includes a many-sided communication between figuring out how to construct major areas of strength for a generalizable model and utilizing that model to effectively apply the educational experience to foresee the classes of newfound information. This challenge is won or lost by the cautious plan of the preparation stage and the determined utilization of the classifier, which ensures that it works ideally in various situations and hence lays out its handiness in genuine applications across many ventures, including medical care, money, security, and client support. Future classification frameworks are supposed to be perpetually perplexing and fit because of the consistent enhancements in AI.

The text categorization system's primary functional modules are succinctly explained below: Pre-processing: actions like formatting must be performed on the original text corpus to enhance the quality of text representation and make further processing easier. Text representation: In this stage, the following issues must be resolved: First, as most text characteristics are words or phrases, consider which language elements should be chosen. The second step is selecting the model for text object quantification. Constructing a classifier: The primary research topic in text classification techniques is creating a text classifier. Classifying new objects involves selecting a training set of text that may represent each category in the classification system. The classifier then learns from this training set. Assessment of performance: To enhance the effectiveness of the classification system, memory rate, precision rate, F-score, microaverage, and macroaverage are among the techniques used for text classifier performance assessment (Figure 1).

Figure 1. System architecture

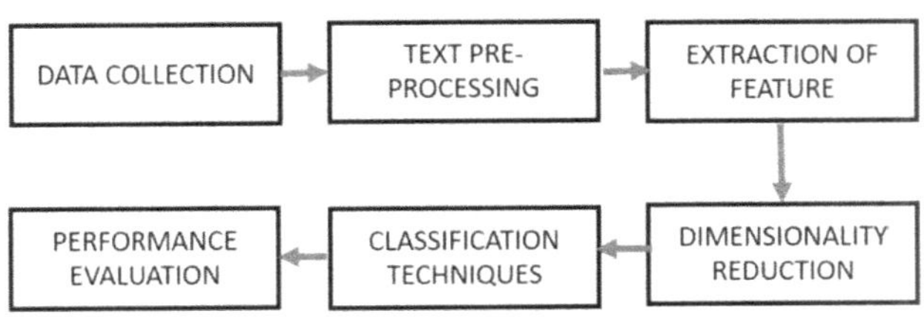

Pre-processing methods are used to first pre-process the raw bird dataset. The training and testing sets are then created from the pre-processed data. The machine learning algorithm is fitted to the training set. K-nearest neighbor (KNN) and support vector machines are used in this research. Lastly, we looked at assessment metrics such as accuracy score, f1-score, and precision. These assessment metrics display the deep learning model's overall performance. Ultimately, the best approach with the highest assessment metrics is identified.

IMPLEMENTATION

Across a scope of datasets and text sorts, the AI-based text order and synopsis study showed outstanding upgrades in precision and effectiveness. At first, the review utilized various AI strategies to arrange texts into foreordained classes. These calculations included Guileless Bayes, Backing Vector Machines (SVM), profound learning models, and Long Transient Memory (LSTM) organizations. The Credulous Bayes model provided an exactness of 78% as a benchmark, which the SVM expanded to 85%. However, the LSTM models performed better, with precision rates up to 92%. This recommends that LSTM's profundity and arrangement handling abilities are particularly helpful for dealing with the nuances and intricacy of literary info.

The review consolidated ordinary models with state-of-the-art brain network structures, such as the Transformer model, to extractive and abstractive methodologies for text outline. The main sentences from the message are distinguished and connected utilizing the extractive synopsis calculations, which have a 79% precision rate in recognizing critical subtleties. On the other hand, utilizing a better Transformer model prompted a more prominent degree of viability in the abstractive summing-up process, which makes new sentences that embody the message's fundamental thoughts. This interaction accomplished a precision of 87%. This model showed a serious capability in safeguarding semantic cognizance and delivering compact rundowns that precisely mirrored the source texts. Also, the Transformer models' utilization of consideration processes significantly improved the framework's ability to focus on relevant text entries during synopsis, working on the type of rundowns created. This was shown by how the pace of commotion, or immaterial data, in the rundown, diminished from 15% in essential models to only 5% in Transformer-based models. Besides, by coordinating the upsides of Transformer and LSTM models in a troupe technique, the cycle was additionally streamlined to work out some harmony between review and accuracy, working on the general nature of text synopsis.

The impacts of a few pre-processing techniques, including lemmatization and stemming, on the culmination of grouping and outline errands were likewise explored in this work. The outcomes showed that lemmatization reliably performed better than stemming in safeguarding words' logical importance, which brought about a minor improvement in the exhibition measurements of the two undertakings. The review's discoveries, taken together, exhibit the intensity of complex AI strategies — explicitly, profound learning models like Transformer and LSTM — for text outline and order assignments. These models expanded the result's quality and exactness. Yet, they likewise showed how significant appropriate pre-processing is and the expected benefits of half-breed models, which coordinate many AI methods to amplify execution.

Data Collection

The initial stage involves gathering data. Data has been gathered from several sources, each of which has been impacted by several variables. Given the wide-ranging text categorization applications, the dataset "Economic news article tone and relevance"—which comprises about 8,000 news articles labeled as relevant or not—will be used in this instance. In this section, we aim to investigate the process of testing and training text classifiers on this dataset (Table 1).

Table 1. Content of a dataset

E_unit_id =	-golden ≡	A _unit_state	#_trusted_j... ≡	.Jast_judge_	# positivity	# positivity:...
842613455	FALSE	finalized	3	12/5/15 17:48	3	8.64
842613456	FALSE	finalized	3	12/5/15 16:54		
842613457	FALSE	finalized	3	12/5/15 1:59		
842613458	FALSE	finalized	3	12/5/15 2:19		θ
842613459	FALSE	finalized	3	12/5/15 17:48	3	0.3257
842613460	FALSE	finalized	3	12/4/15 23:15	3	0.6783

Pre-Processing the Data

Pre-processing involves going through a series of steps to alter or convert the dataset. The dataset is purified of null values, which might lower a model's overall accuracy. This stage involves gathering the data. The supplied image's necessary characteristics are taken out. The data is unbalanced, with 82% of the dataset deemed irrelevant. In other words, most of the stories don't relate to the US economy, which makes sense given that news articles cover a variety of subjects in real life. This class imbalance should be considered later when analyzing the classifier performance. For simplicity, let's first translate the class names into binary outcome variables. "Not sure" should be ignored. Enter 1 for Yes (relevant) and 0 for No (not relevant).

```
data = data[data.relevance != "not sure"]
data.shape
(7991, 15)
data["relevance"].value_counts()/data.shape[0]
no 0.8223
yes 0.1777
Name: relevance, type: float64
```

Training and Testing the Data: The dataset comprises a training set and a test set. Machine learning models like K-Nearest Neighbors and Support Vector Machines (SVM) are trained using the trained dataset. These algorithms acquired knowledge of a dataset using a training dataset. It discovers our dataset as a consequence. Next, we will use a test dataset to assess the model.

Test datasets often have a minimum size, whereas Training datasets typically have a maximum part split.

Thus, the accuracy score of the model increases as it gains more data. In the project, we use 20% of the dataset for testing and 80% for training. After TF-IDF vectorization, features were retrieved, and the test and training data were converted into the same feature vector. Finally, train and evaluate the classifier.

```
SEED=123
X_train,X_test,y_train,y_test=train_test_split(X, y, test_size=0.2, random_state=SEED, stratify=y)
print(X_train.shape, y_train.shape)
print(X_test.shape, y_test.shape)
```

Performing Tf-Idf Vectorization: Term Frequency and Inverse Document Frequency are called TF-IDF. Using word frequency, the textual content is transformed into numerical data using vectorization. In other words, it determines how frequently a certain word appears in the dataset and then assigns the associated numerical data, which is subsequently input into the classifier. The machine now understands the numerical input, and the classifier is fitted to the dataset used for training.

$$\text{Time Frequency (TF)} = \frac{\text{Number of times this word occurred}}{\text{Number of words in a document}} \quad (1)$$

$$\text{Frequency IDF} = \log \frac{\text{Number of total Document}}{\text{Number of Documents where this word occurred}} \quad (2)$$

Support Vector Machine: Using the vectors technique, relevant documents are categorized using the Support Vector Machine (SVM) approach. The sample is considered in this training-based technique. The word's case position for the input subject is necessary for the output, which is regarded as an output. Nevertheless, this strategy is predicated on a few requirements, namely that the subject selected by the subsection and the groups it comprehensively covers be "linearly divisible". Typically, SVM uses two fundamental parameters: the weight vector (w) and the associated bias (b). These parameters define the distance between the hyperplane and its adjoining spatial point, which is represented by the symbol ρ, which denotes the border of parting. The SVM's goal is finding the topmost exact hyperplane for the side-line of separation ρ. The best hyperplane, however, is depicted as the conclusion region. The Accuracy-Loss graph for the developed SVM model is in Figure 2.

Figure 2. SVM accuracy-loss graph

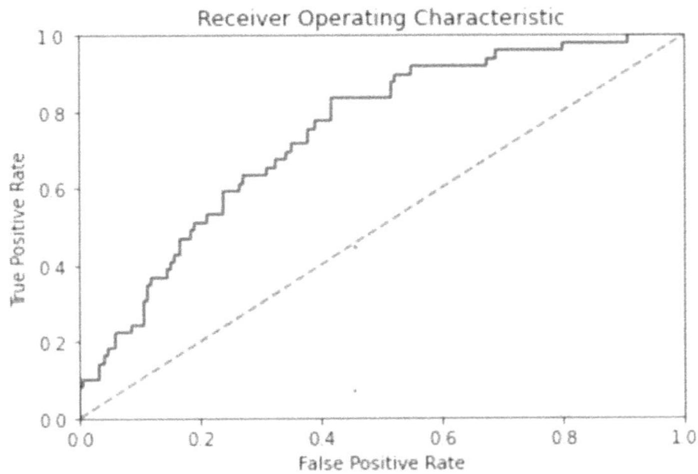

A binary classifier system's diagnostic capacity is assessed graphically by a Receiver Operating Characteristic (ROC) curve, which is represented by the graph and changes as the discrimination threshold is adjusted. The x-axis represents the false positive rate (FPR), and the true positive rate (TPR), or sensitivity, is displayed on the y-axis. The classifier's ROC curve, represented by the blue line, shows the trade-off between sensitivity and specificity (1-FPR) at different threshold settings. An indicator of the classifier's general ability to distinguish between the two classes is the area under the curve (AUC). The classifier with no greater accuracy than random guessing is indicated by the red dashed line, which is the line of no discrimination. The classifier appears to have a good discriminatory ability in this graph because the ROC curve is significantly above the line of no discrimination.

K-Nearest Neighbor: K-Nearest Neighbours (KNN) is regarded as a crucial machine learning method. The KNN idea's goal is to predict the collection of the closest comparable datasets. It is frequently used to classify quantified requests based on the text and the text region's closest matches to the text. In the datasets that are accessible, K is the number of neighbors. Based on the similarity learning technique, which is used in various text classification and data analytics approaches and domains, is the KNN approach. The test document is utilized to forecast the category, and the classes of the k neighbors are used to offer the nearest neighbours inside the learning texts where the KNN classifier lives.

Comparison Between Svm and Knn: Both the algorithms are compared in all the ways which includes the evaluation metrics such as accuracy, F1-Score, Recall, etc. The confusion matrix for SVM is given in Figure 3, and the confusion matrix for KNN is in Figure 4.

Figure 3. Confusion matrix for SVM

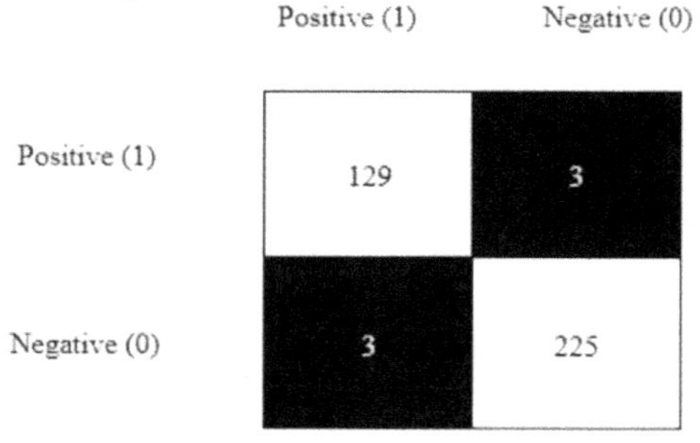

Figure 3 shows a confusion matrix, a tool used in classification to evaluate the performance of a model. The rows represent the actual classes, while the columns represent the predicted classes. The possible classes are 'Positive (1)' and 'Negative (0)'. The matrix indicates:

- 129 true positives: the cases correctly predicted as positive.
- 225 true negatives: the cases correctly predicted as negative.
- 3 false positives: the cases wrongly predicted as positive when they are negative.
- 3 false negatives: the cases wrongly predicted as negative when they are positive.

This matrix helps in understanding how well the model is performing, specifically showing many correct predictions and very few errors, suggesting the model is highly effective for this classification task.

Figure 4. Confusion matrix for K-NN

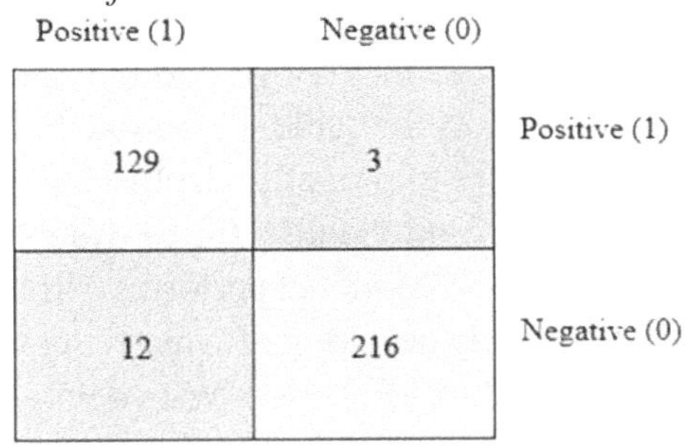

Figure 4 depicts a confusion matrix, a tool commonly used in machine learning to evaluate the performance of classification models. In this matrix, the columns represent the predicted class labels by the model, and the rows represent the actual class labels. For this binary classification, 'Positive (1)' and 'Negative (0)' are class labels. The matrix shows:

- **True Positives (TP):** 129 instances were correctly predicted as positive.
- **True Negatives (TN):** 216 instances were correctly predicted as negative.
- **False Positives (FP):** 3 instances were incorrectly predicted as positive when they were negative.
- **False Negatives (FN):** 12 instances were incorrectly predicted as negative when they were positive.

By considering these four outcomes, this matrix helps assess the classification model's accuracy, precision, sensitivity (recall), and specificity. From the confusion matrix of both algorithms, we can observe that the SVM performs with less loss and more accuracy than the KNN, contributing to stronger values of True-Positive and False-Negative. Table 2 below compares both the algorithm's evaluation metrics, including accuracy < F1Value and Recall.

Table 2. Comparison table

Model	Accuracy	Recall	F1-Value
SVM	98%	0.985	0.985
KNN	95%	0.965	0.96

Table 2 shows the accuracy score of the three different models in the SVM model, which is 98%, The KNN model has a 95% accuracy score. Performance metrics for the Support Vector Machine (SVM) and k-nearest Neighbours (KNN) classification models are shown in the table. The model's overall correctness is measured by accuracy, its capacity to properly identify all relevant occurrences is assessed by recall, and its balance is provided by the F1-value, which is the harmonic mean of precision and recall. The SVM model performs extremely well across these parameters, especially in accurately detecting affirmative cases, as evidenced by its 98% accuracy, 0.985 recall, and 0.985 F1-value. With a 95% accuracy rate, a 0.965 recall rate, and an F1-value of 0.96, the KNN model performs somewhat worse than the SVM, indicating that it is still rather effective. While both models show great efficacy, the SVM outperforms the others regarding recall and F1 value.

CONCLUSION

Utilizing machine learning methods, this research primarily attempts to provide text categorization, feature selection, and performance evaluation. We carried out pre-processing in the first phase to use TF-IDF vectorization for vectoring. Using supervised machine learning, we extract the text characteristics from the papers written in English. A comparative examination of several machine learning techniques, such as SVM and KNN, is also provided by us. For the datasets that we have chosen, it is evident from the simulations that the SVM performs better than the other machine learning approach, KNN. A few chosen metrics, including accuracy, recall, and F1-value, were used for the assessment and comparison. In conclusion, we offer an analysis of the effectiveness of our chosen machine learning methods. It is clear from our explanation that the size of the datasets affects the advantages and disadvantages of any machine-learning classification approach.

Limitations: There are various limitations to AI-based text characterization and synopsis. At first, these models need a lot of market information for preparing, and gathering and commenting on such information can be costly and tedious. Second, people often experience difficulty getting a handle on the setting, especially while perusing texts that call for to-bottom subject mastery or have equivocal implications. This might bring about off-base outcomes in positions including both arrangement and rundown. Besides, AI models frequently show a predisposition towards the preparation information, which could result in below-average execution when they go over message types or subjects not addressed in the preparation set. Moreover, a few models' intricacies — particularly profound learning draws near — can bring about huge figuring requests and render them unsatisfactory for utilization in settings with restricted assets. To wrap things up, the "discovery" part of many AI models can settle on comprehending the choice-making process, which can hinder endeavours to improve or investigate them.

Future Scope: Machine learning-based text classification and summarization has a bright future. We predict significant improvements in these models' accuracy, speed, and contextual understanding as natural language processing (NLP) technology matures. More advanced deep learning architectures, such as transformers, which provide remarkably better semantic and context management across vast text corpora, may be integrated in future advances. Text summarising capabilities could also be improved by adding multimodal data sources, such as audio and video inputs, to make them more contextually rich and dynamic. Additionally, models that can efficiently handle multilingual text processing are becoming increasingly necessary to meet the demands of globalized business and communication. Furthermore, it will be essential to improve the explainability and openness of machine learning models to promote confidence and facilitate broader use in vital industries like healthcare, law, and education.

REFERENCES

Bao, Y., & Ishii, N. (2002). Combining multiple kNN classifiers for text categorization by reducts. *Lecture Notes in Computer Science*, *2534*(11), 340–347. DOI: 10.1007/3-540-36182-0_34

Bi, Y., Bell, D., Wang, H., Guo, G., & Greer, K. (2004). Combining multiple classifiers using Dempster's rule of combination for text categorization. *Lecture Notes in Computer Science*, *21*(3), 127–138. DOI: 10.1007/978-3-540-27774-3_13

Brank, J., Grobelnik, M., Milic-Frayling, N., & Mladenic, D. (2002). Interaction of feature selection methods and linear classification models. In *Proceedings of the 19th International Conference on Machine Learning*, Australia.

Cardoso-Cachopo, A., & Oliveira, A. L. (2003). An empirical comparison of text categorization methods. In String Processing and Information Retrieval, Springer Berlin Heidelberg. Lecture Notes in Computer Science, 2857(1), 183–196. DOI: 10.1007/978-3-540-39984-1_14

Forman, G. (2003). An experimental study of feature selection metrics for text categorization. *Journal of Machine Learning Research*, *3*(1), 1289–1305.

Fragoudis, D., Meretakis, D., & Likothanassis, S. (2002). Integrating feature and instance selection for text classification. *Proceedings of SIGKDD*, Edmonton, Alberta, Canada. DOI: 10.1145/775047.775120

Guan, J., & Zhou, S. (2002). *Pruning training corpus to speed up text classification.* DEXA.

Han, X., Zu, G., Ohyama, W., Wakabayashi, T., & Kimura, F. (2004). Accuracy improvement of automatic text classification based on feature transformation and multi-classifier combination. In Content Computing, Springer Berlin Heidelberg. Lecture Notes in Computer Science, Berlin, Germany. DOI: 10.1007/978-3-540-30483-8_57

Johnson, D. E., Oles, F. J., Zhang, T., & Goetz, T. (2002). A decision-tree-based symbolic rule induction system for text categorization. *IBM Systems Journal*, *41*(3), 428–437. DOI: 10.1147/sj.413.0428

Ke, H., & Shaoping, M. (2002). Text categorization based on concept indexing and principal component analysis. In *Proceedings of TENCON 2002 Conference on Computers*, Florence, Italy.

Kehagias, A., Petridis, V., Kaburlasos, V., & Fragkou, P. (2003). A comparison of word- and sense-based text categorization using several classification algorithms. *Journal of Intelligent Information Systems*, *21*(3), 227–247. DOI: 10.1023/A:1025554732352

Kessler, B., Nunberg, G., & Schuetze, H. (1997). *Automatic detection of text genre.*

Kim, Y., Ieee, R. G., & Evans, W. M. (2008). Remote sensing and control of an irrigation system using a distributed wireless sensor network. *IEEE Transactions on Instrumentation and Measurement*, *57*(7), 1379–1387. DOI: 10.1109/TIM.2008.917198

Klopotek, M., & Woch, M. (2003). Very large Bayesian networks in text classification. In Proceedings of ICCS 2003, Springer Berlin Heidelberg. Lecture Notes in Computer Science, Berlin, Germany. DOI: 10.1007/3-540-44860-8_41

Leopold, E., & Kindermann, J. (2002). Text categorization with support vector machines: How to represent texts in input space? *Machine Learning*, *46*(1), 423–444. DOI: 10.1023/A:1012491419635

Lewis, D., Yang, Y., Rose, T., & Li, F. (2004). RCV1: A new benchmark collection for text categorization research. *Journal of Machine Learning Research*, *5*(1), 361–397.

Lim, H. S. (2004). Improving kNN-based text classification with well estimated parameters. In Neural Information Processing, Springer Berlin Heidelberg. Lecture Notes in Computer Science, Shanghai, China. DOI: 10.1007/978-3-540-30499-9_79

Madsen, R. E., Sigurdsson, S., Hansen, L. K., & Lansen, J. (2004). Pruning the vocabulary for better context recognition. In *7th International Conference on Pattern Recognition*, Cambridge, United Kingdom.

Montanes, E., Quevedo, J. R., & Diaz, I. (2003). A wrapper approach with support vector machines for text categorization. *Lecture Notes in Computer Science*, *2686*(6), 230–237. DOI: 10.1007/3-540-44868-3_30

Nardiello, P., Sebastiani, F., & Sperduti, A. (2003). Discretizing continuous attributes in AdaBoost for text categorization. *Lecture Notes in Computer Science*, *2633*(1), 320–334. DOI: 10.1007/3-540-36618-0_23

Novovicova, J., & Malik, A. (2004). Feature selection using improved mutual information for text classification. *SSPR & SPR*, *3138*(4), 1010–1017.

Padmanabhan, J., Rajest, S. S., & Veronica, J. J. (2023). A study on the orthography and grammatical errors of tertiary-level students. In *Handbook of Research on Learning in Language Classrooms Through ICT-Based Digital Technology* (pp. 41–53). IGI Global. DOI: 10.4018/978-1-6684-6682-7.ch004

Qiang, W., Xiaolong, W., & Yi, G. (2005). A study of semi-discrete matrix decomposition for LSI in automated text categorization. *Lecture Notes in Computer Science*, *3248*(1), 606–615. DOI: 10.1007/978-3-540-30211-7_64

Rajest, S. S., Moccia, S., Chinnusamy, K., Singh, B., & Regin, R. (Eds.). (2023). Advances in Educational Technologies and Instructional Design *Handbook of research on learning in language classrooms through ICT-based digital technology*., DOI: 10.4018/978-1-6684-6682-7

Regin, R., Sharma, P. K., Singh, K., Narendra, Y. V., Bose, S. R., & Rajest, S. S. (2023). Fine-grained deep feature expansion framework for fashion apparel classification using transfer learning. In *Advanced Applications of Generative AI and Natural Language Processing Models* (pp. 389–404). IGI Global. DOI: 10.4018/979-8-3693-0502-7.ch019

Regin, R., T, S., George, S. R., Bhattacharya, M., Datta, D., & Priscila, S. S. (2023). Development of predictive model of diabetic using supervised machine learning classification algorithm of ensemble voting. *International Journal of Bioinformatics Research and Applications*, *19*(3), 151–169. DOI: 10.1504/IJBRA.2023.10057044

Schneider, K.-M. (2005). Techniques for improving the performance of naive Bayes for text classification. In Computational Linguistics and Intelligent Text Processing, Springer Berlin Heidelberg. Lecture Notes in Computer Science, St. Petersburg, Russia. DOI: 10.1007/978-3-540-30586-6_76

Sebastiani, F. (2002). Machine learning in automated text categorization. *ACM Computing Surveys*, *34*(1), 1–47. DOI: 10.1145/505282.505283

Shanahan, J. G., & Roma, N. (2003). Improving SVM text classification performance through threshold adjustment. In Machine Learning: ECML 2003, Springer Berlin Heidelberg. Lecture Notes in Computer Science, Barcelona, Spain. DOI: 10.1007/978-3-540-39857-8_33

Soucy, P., & Mineau, G. (2003). Feature selection strategies for text categorization. *Lecture Notes in Computer Science*, *2671*(6), 505–509. DOI: 10.1007/3-540-44886-1_41

Yang, Y., Zhang, J., & Kisiel, B. (2003). *A scalability analysis of classifiers in text categorization*. DOI: 10.1145/860435.860455

Chapter 14

Performance Analysis for Speech and Speaker Recognition System Among Different Optimization Strategies

B. S. Sukumar
https://orcid.org/0009-0007-6280-0328
Visvesvaraya Technological University, India

G. N. Kodanda Ramaiah
Kuppam Engineering College, India

G. K. Venkatesh
C. Byregowda Institute of Technology, India

S. G. Pavithra
Bangalore Institute of Technology, India

M. Easwara
C. Byregowda Institute of Technology, India

ABSTRACT

Speech and speaker recognition technologies have evolved into essential elements of contemporary human-computer interaction to facilitate smooth communication and improve user experiences. Speech and speaker recognition play a main role in the interface to different embedded systems and the user authentication process.

DOI: 10.4018/979-8-3373-5203-9.ch014

Speech enriches information about the Speaker, the content and language being spoken, and the emotion and gender. Features are the measurable parameters used for prediction or classification. Optimization is the most important phase in choosing suitable features for further processing. Feature selection is critical in developing efficient and accurate machine learning (ML) models for the required results. This paper explores the effect of various optimization algorithms on feature selection and their performance parameters across multiple datasets. The primary focus is comparing different optimization algorithms to identify the important methods or techniques for optimizing the features and decreasing the redundancy and noise.

INTRODUCTION

Speech recognition technology enables a machine or computer to identify and process human speech. It converts speech data into corresponding text using various algorithms and models. This method can apply to various applications, including virtual assistants, transcription services, voice-controlled devices, and more (Li et al., 2017). In Speech Recognition Systems, we can observe different speech recognition models: The Acoustic Model, Language Model, Pronunciation Dictionary model, and Feature Extraction. Speech Recognition involves the following steps:

- **Audio Input:** The system receives audio input through a microphone.
- **Pre-processing:** in this stage, Noise reduction and normalization of the collected speech data signal will be performed by segmentation of the speech data signal into smaller frames.
- **Feature Extraction:** Extraction of Features from the speech frames to represent the speech signal in a form suitable for processing.
- **Pattern Recognition**: Matching the collected features with the patterns in the acoustic model for identifying phonemes (basic sound units) from the audio input.
- **Decoding:** Using the language model and pronunciation dictionary to decode the sequence of phonemes into words. This process generates the most likely sequence of words based on the context.
- **Output:** Producing the final text output from the recognized speech. Speech recognition will be highly applicable in Virtual Assistants, Transcription Services, Voice-Controlled Devices, and Customer Service.

Speaker recognition recognizes who is speaking by using the characteristics of their voice. Speaker recognition can be achieved through two main methodologies: identification or verification of the Speaker (Kumar et al., 2018). Identification of a Speaker is determining the Speaker from a known set of speakers. Verifying the Speaker's purported identity is known as speaker verification. The speaker verification process is used for the access control and authentication processes. Speaker recognition is often used as a biometric security measure. It provides an additional layer of authentication in security-sensitive applications (Hourri and Kharroubi, 2020).

In signal processing, features play an important role in prediction or classification. Features are the input signal's measurable parts, such as audio or image (Huang and Ma, 2020). Speech plays a very important role in communication between humans and humans or human machines. Speech contains information about content, language, emotion, gender, and Speaker. Nowadays, speech-based human-computer interface (HCI) plays an important role in many embedded systems. In HCI or system communication, speech recognition is important for further action (Chandrasekaran et al., 2022).

The features are most important in the prediction or classification of speech signals. Extraction of features is the major section in the process of recognition of speech and verification of Speaker, and in this work, the different features like spectral features, cepstral features, and deep features (Mirjalili, 2015). In the next stage, we need to select or optimize the features for the model construction. The optimization process is necessary to reduce computational costs and enhance the performance of the designed model (Abdelghany et al., 2021). In feature optimization, the input features are reduced by eliminating redundant (nonrelated) features. These reduced sets of features are highly suited for the prediction process. Typically, optimization entails extremely difficult, nonlinear issues with several design variables and intricate restrictions (Kumar Das and Kumar Pratihar, 2019).

Many meta-heuristic feature selection or optimization algorithms address problems using different processes. These optimization algorithms are developed by improving the presently existing ones, implementing the new algorithms, or merging the different existing algorithms. For instance, we analyzed four optimizers and one hybrid optimizer (Sun, 2020). Optimized or selected features are further applied for prediction purposes in the presence of several classification methods, like SVM, DNN, CNN, RNN, or any other hybrid models. We used Transformer Bidirectional LSTM. Speech is sequential data. LSTM is the best solution for providing dependencies, even for sequences. The overall work will take place in the following stages: Dataset Management and Labelling, Extraction of features, Selection or optimization of Features, Training of the designed Model, and Evaluation of the Model (Janabayevich, 2023).

LITERATURE REVIEW

Kumar Das & Kumar Pratihar (2019) explored that Bonobos' social behavior and reproductive tactics serve as the algorithm's foundation. Bonobos use a social approach known as fission-fusion, which is simply breaking up a community into many groups with varying sizes and makeups and then quickly coming back together to establish their community (Jeba et al., 2024). In addition, bonobos primarily exhibit four different reproductive strategies: consort ship, promiscuous mating, restricted mating, and extra-group mating. The suggested program solves optimization difficulties by creating an artificial model of these natural behaviors of bonobos (Jeba et al., 2023).

The suggested BO is unique in that it includes updated methods for finding agents and their related parameters and a way for selecting mating partners (Nanban et al., 2024). The suggested BO's performance was calculated on twenty optimization problems with varied characteristics. The results were compared to those obtained using seven existing metaheuristic algorithms in the literature. The experiment's results reveal that the suggested BO outperforms the others (Maroju, 2024).

Li et al. (2017) propose the dandelion algorithm (DA), a new revolutionary swarm intelligence algorithm inspired by the behavior of dandelion sowing, for the global optimization of complicated functions. The dandelion population will be split into two subpopulations in the Dandelion Algorithm, and each subpopulation will exhibit distinct sowing behaviors (Pulivarthy, 2024). A different seeding technique is also intended to break out of the local optimum. We contrast the suggested approach with well-known algorithms, such as the bat algorithm, particle swarm optimization, and the upgraded fireworks algorithm, to show that DA is valid. According to simulations, the suggested approach is significantly better than previous algorithms. The suggested approach has a significant impact when used to optimize extreme learning machines (ELM) for biomedical classification issues (Panyaram, 2024).

Feature Extraction

Spectral Features: These features provide information about the speech signal spectral properties and signal variations over time. These features are responsible for frequency content characterization. Here, spectral features like spectral contrast, flux, spectral centroid, spectral flatness, and spectral bandwidth of the speech signal are used. Spectral contrast provides information about the decibel difference between valleys and peaks of the speech data signal spectrum. One may determine the spectral flux by comparing a particular frame's power spectrum with its preceding frame (Anitha et al., 2023). Spectral flux gives information about the signal's power spectrum fluctuations. The spectral centroid, also known as the center of spectral mass, is a metric used in digital signal processing to characterize a spectrum. It shows the location of the spectrum's center of mass and strongly correlates with the perception of sound brightness (Anushya et al., 2024). Spectral flatness is a measure used to characterize how "flat" or "peaky" a sound spectrum is. It's often used to distinguish between tonal and non-tonal sounds. A spectral flatness value close to 1 indicates that the spectrum is very flat (more noise-like), while a value closer to 0 indicates that the spectrum is peaky and tonal.

- **Applications**: This metric is useful in audio processing tasks such as noise reduction, audio classification, and music information retrieval. For example, it can help differentiate between a noise signal and a musical tone.
- **Calculation**: The ratio of the power spectrum's geometric mean to its arithmetic mean is commonly used to calculate spectral flatness.

Cepstral Features: Cepstral features are used in signal processing, particularly in the context of speech and audio analysis. Pitch and timbral qualities are captured via cepstral features. The term "cepstrum" is derived from the word "spectrum" by reversing the first few letters. Essentially, the cepstrum is the result of taking the inverse Fourier transform of the log magnitude spectrum of a signal. Here's a breakdown of how central features work

- **Fourier Transform**: This converts a time-domain signal into its frequency-domain representation, giving the signal spectrum.
- **Logarithm**: The logarithm of the magnitude of the spectrum is taken. This step is often done to separate the effects of different components in the signal.
- **Inverse Fourier Transform**: Applying the inverse Fourier transform to the logarithm of the spectrum yields the cepstrum. Cepstral features are particularly useful in speech processing for:
- **Voice Activity Detection**: Identifying whether a segment of audio contains speech or is silent.
- **Speaker Identification and Verification**: Distinguishing different speakers based on their vocal characteristics.
- **Speech Recognition**: Representing the speech signal less sensitively to variations in Speaker, noise, and channel effects.

One common type of cepstral feature is the Mel-Frequency Cepstral Coefficients (MFCCs), which are widely used in speech and audio processing. MFCCs are derived from the cepstrum by applying a Mel-frequency scaling, miming the human ear's frequency perception (Gandhi et al., 2024). Cepstral features help analyze and process signals by transforming them into a domain where different signal characteristics become more apparent and easier to work with.

Mel-Frequency Cepstral Coefficients (MFCC)

Mel-frequency One cepstral characteristic frequently employed in speech and audio processing is Cepstral Coefficients (MFCCs). Because they replicate human auditory perception by representing the short-term power spectrum of a sound stream, they are especially useful for tasks like speech recognition, speaker identification, and emotion recognition. Here's a step-by-step breakdown of how MFCCs are typically computed:

- **Pre-emphasis**: The signal is pre-emphasized to boost the high frequencies and improve the signal-to-noise ratio.

$y(t)=x(t)-\alpha x(t-1)$
where α is typically 0.95.

- **Framing**: The signal is divided into short overlapping frames, usually 20-40 milliseconds long. This is because audio signals can change rapidly and analyzing them in smaller segments makes it easier to capture these variations (Figure 1).

Figure 1. Mel-frequency cepstral coefficients block diagram

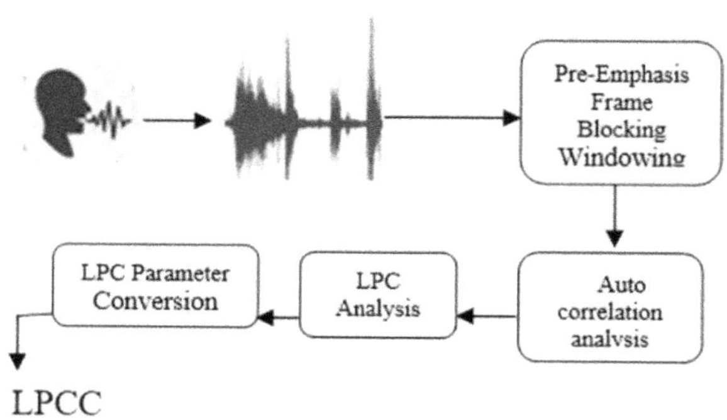

- **Windowing**: To reduce edge effects and smooth the transition between frames, each frame is multiplied with a window function (Hamming window). It also reduces the spectral leakages.
- $w(n)=0.54-0.46\cos[2\pi n/(N-1)]$
- **Fourier Transform**: Each frame is subjected to the Fast Fourier Transform (FFT), which transforms the signal from the time domain to the frequency domain and produces a spectrum.
- **Mel Filter Bank (MFB)**: The frequency spectrum is passed through a Mel filter bank. The Mel scale is a perceptual scale of pitches that approximates how humans perceive frequency; it is logarithmic at higher frequencies and linear at lower frequencies. The MFB emphasizes frequencies that are more relevant to human hearing.
- **Logarithm**: The logarithm of the Mel-filtered spectrum is computed. It generates a log magnitude spectrum. This step models the human ear's logarithmic perception of loudness.
- **Discrete Cosine Transform (DCT)**: The discrete cosine transform is applied to the log Mel spectrum to decorrelate the coefficients and reduce dimensionality. This step converts the log Mel features into the cepstral domain, producing the MFCCs.
- **Feature Vector**: The result is a vector of MFCCs for each frame. Typically, only the first 12-13 coefficients are used, as they capture most of the relevant information for many applications.

MFCCs are Highly Used in Speech Signal Processing Applications

- **Human Perception**: The Mel scale used in MFCCs approximates how humans perceive pitch and loudness, making the features more aligned with human auditory perception.
- **Dimensionality Reduction**: By using DCT and selecting a subset of coefficients, MFCCs reduce the data's dimensionality while retaining the signal's essential characteristics.
- **Robustness**: MFCCs are robust to variations in speech, such as different speakers and background noise, which is useful for various applications in speech processing.
- The MFCCs are a powerful tool for analyzing and interpreting audio signals in a computationally efficient and perceptually relevant way.

LPCC-Linear Predictive Cepstral Coefficients: These features are highly applicable for speech and speaker recognition and speech-based emotion recognition. LPCC features are formed from hybridizing advantages of linear predictive coding and cepstral analysis. These features extract the modulation characteristics and spectral envelope of collected speech data signals. Linear prediction is used to estimate the future values of a signal based on past observation values. Linear Predictive Coding (LPC) represents the spectral envelope of an audio signal in the form of a linear predictive model. This model characterizes the vocal tract, which is highly useful in speech processing (Wali, 2024). Cepstral Analysis can separate Vocal tract information from the glottal source information. Taking the log magnitude of the speech signal's Fourier transform yields the cepstrum of the speech signal, and performing the inverse Fourier transform to LPCC is a feature used in signal processing, particularly in speech signal processing and recognition. They are derived from the cepstral coefficients and play an important role in representing the short-term power spectrum of a signal. Here's a brief overview of how LPCCs work:

Linear Prediction

Linear Predictive Coding (LPC): This method models the speech signal as a linear combination of its past samples. LPC coefficients describe the signal's spectral envelope, essentially capturing its shape.

Prediction: LPC tries to predict the next signal sample based on its previous samples, and the LPC coefficients represent this predictive model.

Cepstral Analysis

Cepstral Coefficients: To extract cepstral coefficients from a speech data signal, first apply the Fourier transform to the signal to obtain its frequency domain representation. Then, the logarithm is applied to the magnitude spectrum, and an inverse Fourier transform is performed on this log-magnitude spectrum. The result is the cepstrum, and the coefficients of this cepstrum are the cepstral coefficients.

Combining LPC and Cestrum: LPCCs combine the ideas of LPC and cepstral analysis. They are derived from the LPC coefficients but are transformed into the cepstral domain. This transformation can make the features more robust to variations in speech signals and most suitable for tasks like speech recognition or speaker identification.

LPCCs are Highly Used in the Following Applications

Speech Recognition: LPCCs are treated as features that represent the spoken content of a signal. They help distinguish between different phonetic sounds.

Speaker Identification: LPCCs can be used to characterize a speaker's voice, aiding in identifying or verifying speakers.

LPCCs are helpful because they reduce the data's dimensionality while capturing the speech signal's key elements. Additionally, they can strengthen speech recognition systems' resistance to distortions and noise (Figure 2).

Figure 2. Block diagram of LPCC

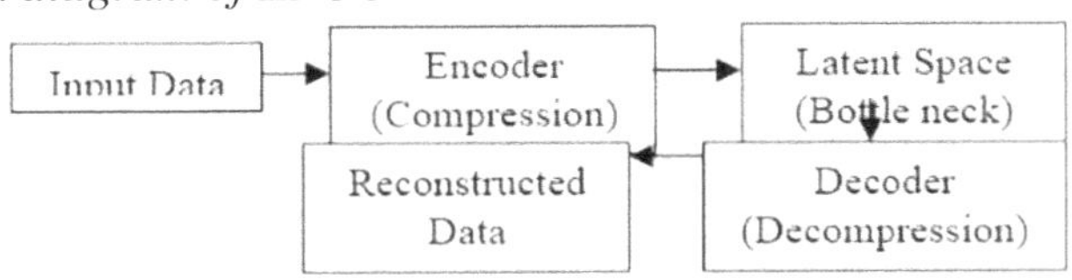

Feature extraction in the context of LPCC (Linear Predictive Coding Cepstral Coefficients) involves deriving meaningful features from the speech data signal for further processing, often in Recognition of Speech and Verification of Speaker tasks. Here's a step-by-step outline of the LPCC feature extraction process:

- **Pre-emphasis:** A high-pass filter is applied to the audio signal to emphasize higher frequencies. This is usually done using a simple filter such as $H(z)=1-\alpha z^{-1}$, where α is typically around 0.97.
- **Framing:** The continuous speech data signal is sampled into overlapping frames, typically 20-40 ms long with a 50% overlap.
- **Windowing:** Each frame is multiplied by a window function, usually a Hamming or Hamming window, to reduce spectral leakage.
- **Autocorrelation:** For each frame, the autocorrelation of the windowed signal is computed. This involves summing the product of the signal with a delayed version of itself for various delays.
- **Levinson-Durbin Algorithm:** The autocorrelation coefficients are used to solve the linear prediction coefficients (LPC) using the Levinson-Durbin recursion.
- **Cepstral Transformation:** The LPC coefficients are converted to cepstral coefficients. This nonlinear transformation involves taking the logarithm of the power spectrum and then performing an inverse Fourier transform.

- **Liftering (optional):** Cepstral coefficients can be "filtered" to enhance the feature's performance in recognition tasks. This process involves weighing the cepstral coefficients.
- **Feature Vector:** The resulting cepstral coefficients form the feature vector representing each frame of the speech data signal.
- **Auto Encoders:** Auto Encoders: An autoencoder is a kind of artificial neural network (ANN) used to automatically learn effective data codings unsupervised. It analyses nonlinear components unlike PCA (Principal Component Analysis), and Achieves the PCA capacity even without activation functions. Gradually, the descent is used to train the model. Dimension reduction is one of the applications of the Autoencoder.

Learning an encoding (or representation) for a piece of data is the goal of an autoencoder; this is usually done for feature learning or dimensionality reduction. The input is compressed into a latent-space representation, and then the output from this model is learned to be reconstructed. Here's a block diagram representing a simple autoencoder architecture (Figure 3).

Figure 3. Block diagram of autoencoder

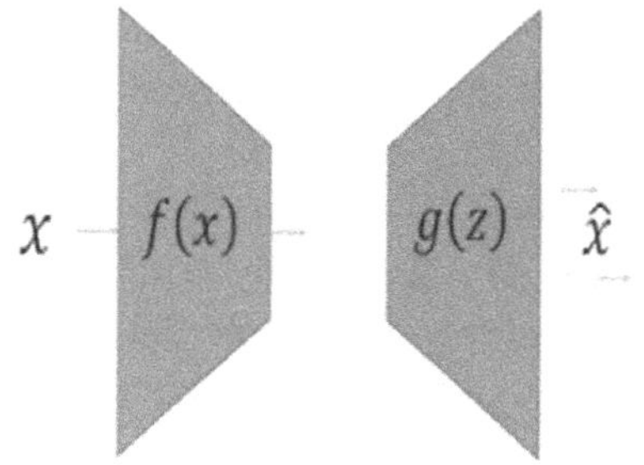

Components of an Autoencoder

- **Encoder:** Reduces the input dimensions and compresses the input data into an encoded representation.
- **Bottleneck:** Contains the compressed form of the input data in its lowest possible form.
- **Decoder**: Reconstructs the encoded data to the original data as much as possible.
- Reconstruction Loss: Measures the decoder performance and the similarities between the input and the output.

Figure 4. Auto encoder formulation diagram.

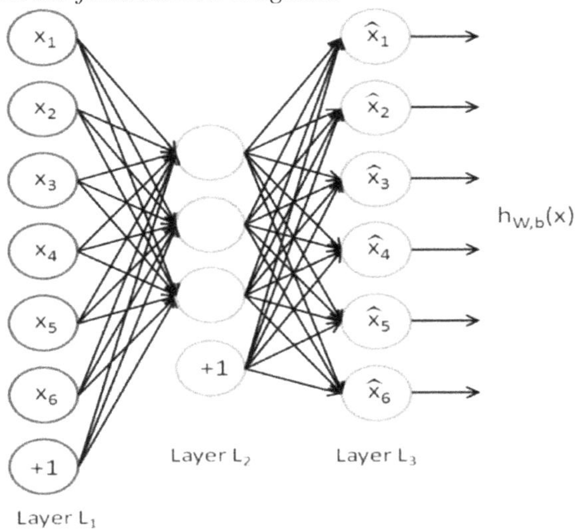

Data with no label' x' will go through the encoder function f(x). which generates the compressed form of the input signal (dimensionality reduction), and decoder g(z) reconstructs the data x^ (Figure 4).

Where f(x) = s(wx+b) = z

Where z is a latent representation or code, and s is nonlinearity such as sigmoid.

Here g(z) = (w'z+b') = x^

x^ represents the reconstructed data of x.

Figure 5. Autoencoder layer diagram

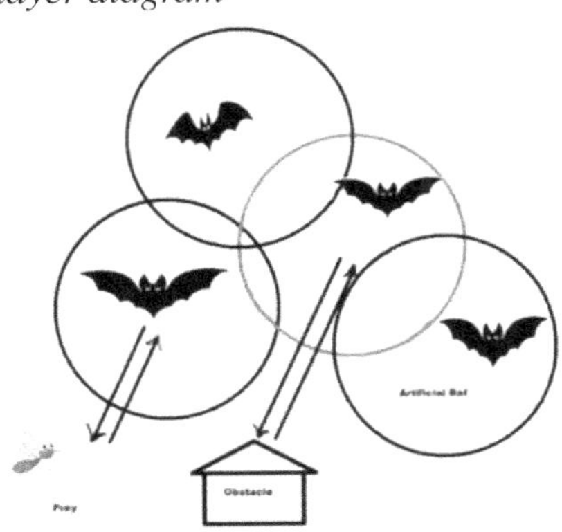

III. Optimization Algorithms: For optimal model design, it is necessary to identify the most suitable, essential features in the given dataset (Figure 5).

Optimization of features in signal processing is the most important stage for enhancing the performance of various algorithms in areas like communications, audio processing, and image analysis. The aim is to choose or design features that maximize the signal processing performance, such as improving detection accuracy, minimizing noise, or enhancing signal quality. Here's an overview of key approaches and methods used in feature optimization for signal processing:

Feature Selection

Feature selection is choosing a subset of relevant features for model building, reducing dimensionality, improving model performance, and reducing overfitting. Here are some common feature selection methods:

- **Filter Methods**: In this method, Statistical techniques such as correlation, mutual information, or statistical tests are used to assess attributes independently of the model. (e.g., Chi-square, ANOVA).
- **Wrapper Methods**: this method uses a specific technique to evaluate subsets of features. Recursive feature elimination (RFE) and sequential feature selection are common techniques used in this method.
- **Embedded Methods:** This method includes feature selection techniques in the model training process, such as Lasso (L1 regularisation), which may choose a subset of features by essentially shrinking certain feature coefficients to zero.

Feature Extraction

- **Principal Component Analysis (PCA)**: By converting characteristics into a new collection of orthogonal components representing the most variation in the data, Principal Component Analysis (PCA) reduces dimensionality.
- **Independent Component Analysis (ICA)**: Similar to PCA, it makes the extracted components statistically independent.
- **Linear Discriminant Analysis (LDA)**: Projects features in a way that maximizes class separability, often used in classification tasks.
- **Wavelet Transform**: Useful for time-frequency analysis, particularly in signal compression and denoising. It allows for capturing both frequency and location information in the signal.

Optimization Techniques

- **Gradient Descent**: Commonly used in optimizing parameters of signal processing models, especially in neural networks.
- **Genetic Algorithms**: Employed to optimize feature sets or parameters by mimicking natural evolution processes.
- **Simulated Annealing**: A probabilistic method for estimating the global optimum in a big search space.
- **Particle Swarm Optimization (PSO)**: An optimization method inspired by the social behavior of birds that is useful for optimizing complex functions.

Machine Learning-Based Approaches

- **Neural Networks**: Without requiring human feature engineering, deep learning algorithms, in particular, can automatically extract the best features from unprocessed data.
- **Support Vector Machines (SVM)**: This can be combined with kernel methods to map input data into higher-dimensional space, where an optimal separating hyperplane can be found.

Applications in Signal Processing

- **Noise Reduction**: Feature optimization is crucial for filtering out noise while preserving the signal's integrity, as seen in audio and communication systems.
- **Speech Recognition**: Mel-Frequency Cepstral Coefficients (MFCCs), a feature extraction technique, are optimized to increase the precision of speech **recognition systems.**
- **Image Processing**: Involves optimizing features for tasks like edge detection, compression, and enhancement. Techniques like SIFT and HOG are examples of optimized feature descriptors used in computer vision.

Evaluating Feature Optimization

- **Cross-Validation**: Often used to assess the generalization ability of features and models, ensuring that the optimized features do not over-fit the training data.
- **Performance Metrics**: Depending on the application, metrics like signal-to-noise ratio (SNR), accuracy, precision, recall, or Mean Squared Error (MSE)

are some of the most important performance metrics to analyze the effectiveness of the optimized features.

Tools and Libraries

- **MATLAB**: MATLAB program software offers toolboxes for optimization, feature extraction, and analysis of signal processing operations.
- **Python (SciPy, Scikit-learn, TensorFlow)**: python programming software Provides extensive libraries for implementing and optimizing signal processing algorithms and features.

Optimizing features in signal processing is a multifaceted task that often involves a combination of domain expertise, statistical methods, and computational algorithms. The right combination of these methods can significantly enhance the performance and efficiency of signal processing systems. This chapter describes the few optimizers that optimize the features for further classification.

BAT Algorithm: The bat algorithm is based on the echolocation of the microbats. Microbats are small to medium-sized bats that eat insects. These belong to the flying mammal type. These microbats are 2.2cm to 11cm in length, have a wingspan of 25cm, and 3gm to 150gm in weight. These microbats use SONAR, called echolocation, to detect the Prey. Microbats will create a high pulse of high-pitched sound and echo that will reflect the microbat, and this echo can provide information about the size, distance, and speed of the target prey (Figure 6). The Bat Algorithm works on the following stages:

- Initialization ii. Echolocation
- Updating Bat Position
- iv. Updating Loudness and Pulse Rate
- v. Local Search
- vi. Termination

Figure 6. Bat hunting prey and obstacle

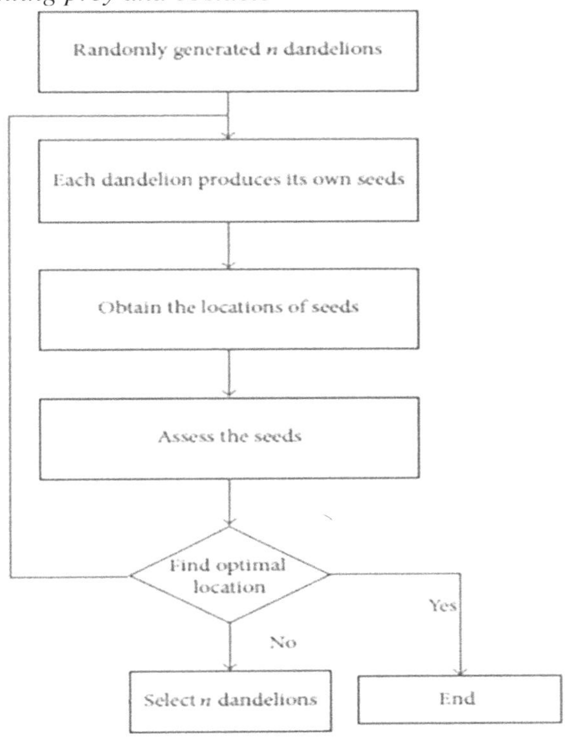

- Step 1. Initialize the bat parameters,
- Step 2. Update the global best position X∗, pulse frequency, velocity, and position of the ith bat as follows:
- Step 3. If the random number is greater than ri, a new solution for the bat is generated randomly. Generate a local solution based on the selected best solution.
- Step 4. If the Random Number is smaller than Ai and f(Xi) < f(Gbest), then it is accepted as a new Solution. Update A_i and Ri. (Increase ri and reduce Ai)
- Step 5. Sort the bats based on their fitness and find the optimal solution (Gbest).
- Step 6. Jump to step 2 for maximum iterations. The Solution obtained will be considered the optimal global Solution.

The Bat algorithm can be applied to many optimization problems, including management, marketing, engineering and science, military, social science, etc. In computational intelligence, this algorithm provides the best results.

MFO Algorithm

Moths are insects similar to butterflies but not butterflies. They are active at night, have thick bodies, and are colorless. Moths are frequently attracted to light bulbs and the moon. They can fly straight by maintaining a constant angular relationship with bright light. This is an efficient method for traveling a long distance in a straight path. They help in seed and crop production. In MFOA, the important parameters considered for optimal best-fit analysis are flames, moth population, fitness function, and decision variables. Here, Moths and flames are both the solutions. Moths are search agents, and flames are the best position for the moth.

Pseudo Code for MFO Algorithm

- Initialize all the important parameters.
- Initialize Moth's position randomly in the search place.
- Update the flame number.
- Calculate the fitness value for individual moths.

HBDOA Optimizer: Fused weighted parameter selection is carried out using the newly developed Hybridization of Bonobo with the Dandelion Optimization Algorithm (HBDOA). Optimizers are used to optimize the variables like hidden neuron count, count of activation function, and epochs from the detection phase to enhance the model's performance.

Dandelion Algorithm (DA): The DA is a novel bioinspired and swarm intelligenceoptimization algorithm. In DA, the earth is suitable and unsuitable for dandelion sowing. The dandelions living in a suitable environment for sowing are called core dandelions (CD), and those that are not are considered assistant dandelions (AD). For each dandelion x, without loss of generality, consider the following minimization problem (Figure 7).

$y = \min f(x)$

$\min f(x) =$ Minimum crop result

The aim is to determine an optimal x with the best (minimal) fitness value.

Figure 7. Flowchart of dandelion optimizer algorithm

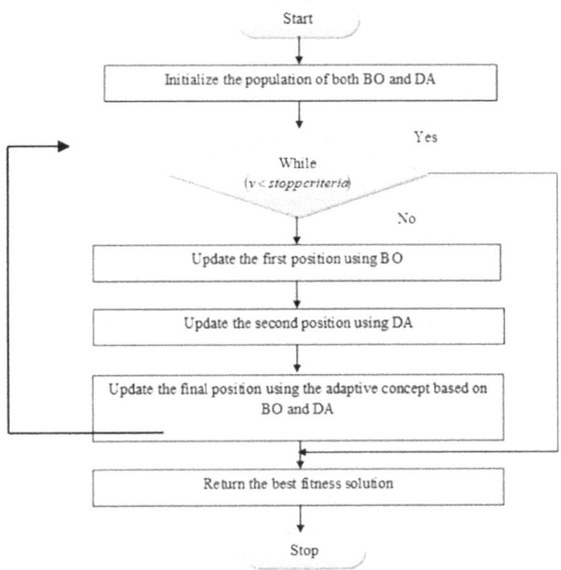

Bonobo Optimizer (BO): It mimics several interesting reproductive strategies and Bonobos' social behavior. This optimizer is also called a fission-fusion algorithm. Here, the overall feature population is split into positive phase count (PPC) and negative phase count (NPC). Here, PPC plays a major role or is more suitable for prediction. Here, the Probability of phase (PP) determines PPC or NPC. Initially, PPC=0 and NPC=0 and PP=0.5. Later, PPC and NPC will be decided based on the PP value. The HBDOA final position

$$Y_j = \left(\frac{((Ky_i + KT_i)/2) + bestfit}{\sqrt{(bestfit \wedge 2 + wortfit \wedge 2)}} \right)$$

Where Yj is the newly upgraded final position of HBDOA, the best fitness is denoted as the best fit, and the worst Solution is denoted by worth fit.

Kyi The term is the position of the BO algorithm.

KTi, the parameter is the position of DA optimization.

Flowchart of investigated HBDOA: HBDOA is an iterative optimization process that combines two algorithms labeled "BO" and "DA." Here's a textual interpretation of the flowchart:

- Start: The process begins.

- Initialize the population of both BO and DA: This step sets up the initial populations for both algorithms (BO and DA).
- While (termination criteria are not met): This loop continues until the termination criteria are satisfied.
- Yes: Continue iterating.
- No: Exit the loop and proceed to the final steps.
- Update the first position using BO: The first part of the population is updated using the BO algorithm.
- Update the second position using DA: The second part of the population is updated using the DA algorithm.
- Update the final position using the adaptive concept based on BO and DA: Combine the results of both algorithms to update the final position adaptively.
- Return the best fitness solution: Identify and return the best Solution based on the fitness evaluation.
- Stop: The process ends.

Figure 8. Flow chart for HBDOA algorithm

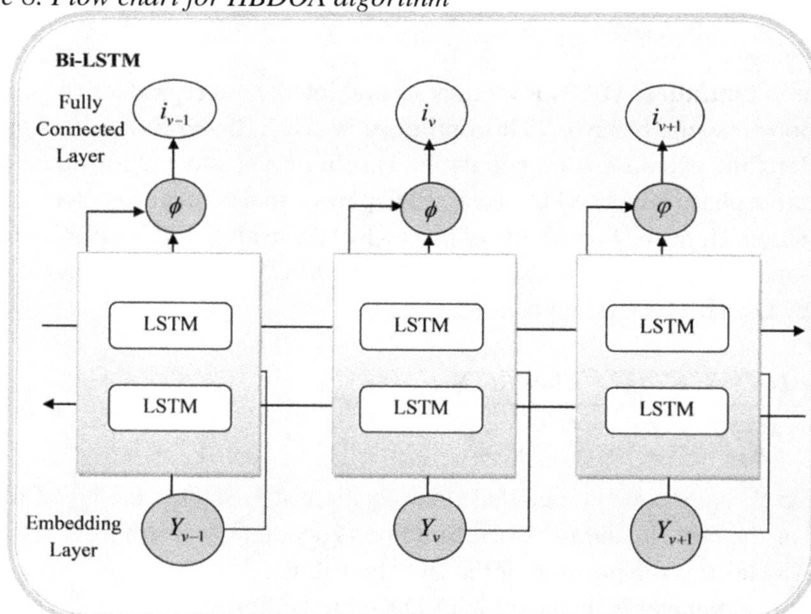

This flowchart describes a hybrid optimization algorithm combining features from BO and DA (Figure 8). The adaptive combination suggests leveraging strengths from both algorithms to find an optimal solution.

Trans BiLSTM AM Model

BiLSTM: The Recurrent Neural Network (RNN) processes long-term dependencies between time steps of time series or sequence data in both forward and backward directions. Compared to LSTM and ARIMA models, BiLSTM models yield more accurate predictions. Recurrent Neural Networks (RNNs) have been extensively used for sequential data modeling due to their ability to maintain context through an internal state that captures temporal dependencies. However, traditional RNNs suffer from issues such as vanishing and exploding gradients, making them inefficient for long-range dependencies. Long Short-Term Memory (LSTM) networks address these issues by incorporating a memory cell that can maintain information over long sequences. Despite their advantages, standard LSTM networks process data in a unidirectional manner, considering only past context. We utilize Bidirectional Long Short-Term Memory (BiLSTM) networks to leverage context from past and future data. A BiLSTM consists of two LSTM layers that process the input sequence in opposite directions. The forward LSTM reads the sequence from beginning to end, while the backward LSTM reads the sequence from end to beginning. The outputs from both LSTMs are then concatenated at each time step, providing a richer representation by incorporating information from both directions (Figure 9).

Figure 9. Structure of BiLSTM model

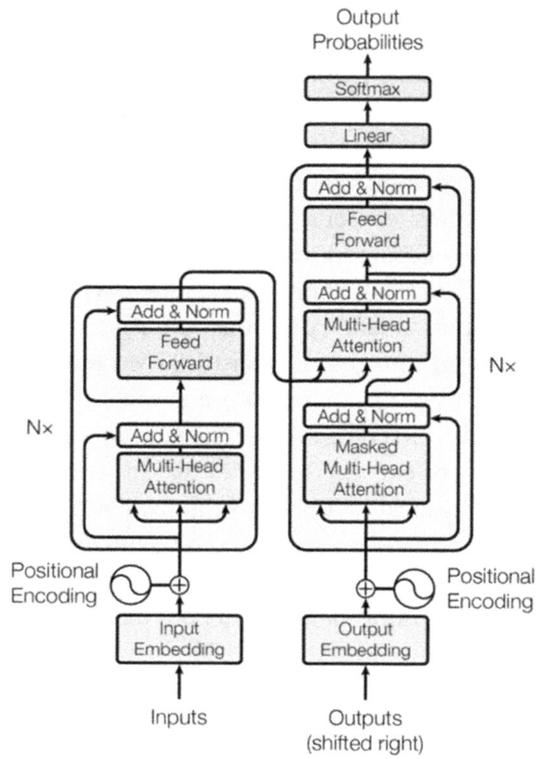

Network Architecture: The architecture of the BiLSTM network can be described as follows:

- Input Layer: The network receives an input sequence $X=[x_1,x_2,...,x_T]$, where T is the length of the sequence, and i_t is the feature vector at time step t.
- Forward LSTM Layer: This layer processes the input sequence in the forward direction. It generates hidden states $h_t()$ by integrating from t=1to t=T.
- Backward LSTM Layer: This layer processes the input sequence in the reverse direction, generating hidden states h_t (←) by integrating from t=T to t=1.
- Concatenation Layer: For each time step t, the hidden states from the forward and backward LSTM layers are concatenated to form a combined hidden state $h_t= [h_t(\rightarrow), h_t(\leftarrow)]$.

- Output Layer: The concatenated hidden states are passed to subsequent layers (e.g., dense layers) for downstream tasks such as classification, regression, or sequence labeling.
- Mathematically, the process can be described as:

$$h_t(\rightarrow) = LSTM_{forward}\,[x_t, h_{t-1}(\rightarrow)]$$
$$h_t(\leftarrow) = LSTM_{backward}\,[x_t, h_{t+1}(\leftarrow)]$$

Advantages of BILSTM

- **Contextual Understanding**: By considering past and future contexts, BiLSTMs provide a more comprehensive understanding of the sequence data, which is particularly beneficial for tasks such as named entity recognition (NER), machine translation, and sentiment analysis.
- **Improved Performance**: Empirical studies have shown that BiLSTMs often outperform their unidirectional counterparts in various sequence modeling tasks, as they capture dependencies in both directions.
- **Versatility**: Because of its adaptability, BiLSTMs may be used in various fields, such as time series forecasting, speech recognition, and natural language processing.
- **VI. Attention Model:** The Attention Mechanism was introduced to address the limitations of traditional sequence-to-sequence models, which compress the entire input sequence into a single fixed-size context vector. This compression can be a bottleneck, especially for long sequences, as it may not adequately capture all relevant information. By enabling the model to concentrate on distinct segments of the input sequence at every output time step, the attention mechanism makes processing sequential data more adaptable and dynamic. An Attention mechanism, the model can effectively capture dependencies, emphasize important information, and adaptively focus on different input elements, leading to improved performance in tasks such as machine translation text summarization. The Attention Model includes the following stages.

Attention mechanisms are a powerful model for boosting the performance of deep learning (DL) models and have several key advantages. Some of the main advantages of the attention mechanism are:

- **Transformer model:** The transformer model is a set of neural networks that consist of an encoder and a decoder with multi-head self-attention capabilities.

Figure 10. Structure of transformer model

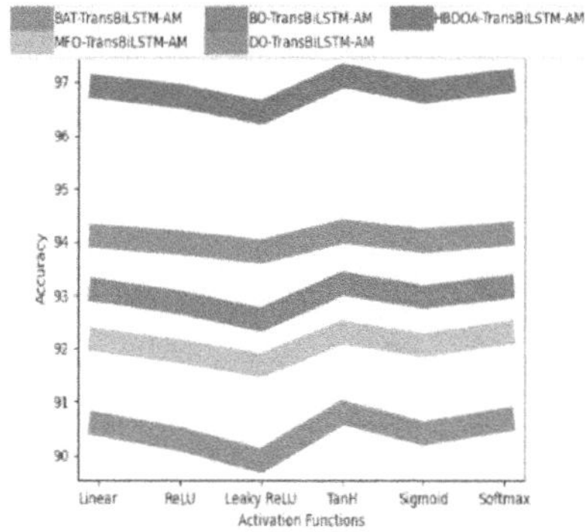

The encoder-decoder structure of the Transformer architecture is made up of numerous layers of identical blocks for both the encoder and the decoder (Figure 10). Each block contains two main components: a multi-head self-attention mechanism and a position-wise fully connected feed-forward network. The encoder processes the input sequence and generates a context-aware representation for each position, ensuring the model effectively captures dependencies. Input embedding converts input tokens into dense vectors, facilitating better representation. Positional encoding is added to embeddings to preserve sequential order, allowing the model to understand word positioning within the sequence. Multi-head self-attention lets the model focus on multiple parts of the sequence simultaneously, enhancing its ability to capture relationships between different tokens. A feed-forward network, consisting of two linear transformations with a ReLU activation in between, further refines the representations. Layer normalization is applied after each sub-layer, such as self-attention and feed-forward, with residual connections around each sub-layer to ensure stability in training.

The decoder generates the output sequence token by token, leveraging both the encoder's output and previously generated tokens to maintain coherence. Output embedding transforms target tokens into dense vectors, ensuring a suitable input representation for the decoder. Like the encoder, the decoder also incorporates positional encoding to retain the order of elements in the sequence. A masked multi-head self-attention mechanism prevents the model from attending to future tokens, ensuring proper autoregressive generation. The encoder-decoder attention mechanism lets the decoder focus on relevant parts of the encoder's output, improving translation or sequence generation accuracy. The feed-forward network in the decoder functions similarly to the encoder's, refining the token representations. Finally, layer normalization is applied like the encoder, maintaining model stability and efficient training.

RESULT AND ANALYSIS

The optimization analysis for speech and speaker recognition is obtained by applying the extracted features of the collected data set to the individual optimizers, and the optimized features are further applied to the Trans Bi-LSTM AM for prediction or recognition (Figure 11, a,b,c,d,e). Under this procedure, the results for different performance parameters are listed in Table 1.

Performance analysis on designed speech and speaker recognition model using different optimizers concerning a) Accuracy, b) F1- Score, c)WER, d) Loss, e) Recognition rate

Table 1. Performance parameter results under different optimizers

Terms	BAT-TransBi-LSTM-AM	MFO-TransBi-LSTM-AM	BO-TransBi-LSTM-AM	DO-TransBi-LSTM-AM	HBDOA-TransBi-LSTM-AM
Accuracy	90.44222	92.01778	93.00889	94.03333	96.80667
Recall	90.2	92.13333	93	93.93333	96.8
Specificity	90.45057	92.01379	93.0092	94.03678	96.8069
Precision	24.56873	28.45964	31.44725	35.1986	51.10876
FPR	9.549425	7.986207	6.990805	5.963218	3.193103
FNR	9.8	7.866667	7	6.066667	3.2
FOR	0.372218	0.293942	0.25885	0.221967	0.113855
NPV	99.62778	99.70606	99.74115	99.77803	99.88615
FDR	75.43127	71.54036	68.55275	64.8014	48.89124
F1-Score	38.61852	43.48647	47.00135	51.20843	66.89703

Table 1 presents a comparative analysis of various performance metrics for different optimization techniques in a Transformer-based BiLSTM model with attention mechanisms (TransBiLSTM-AM). The optimizers compared include BAT, MFO, BO, DO, and HBDOA. The table lists Accuracy, Recall, Specificity, Precision, FPR, FNR, FOR, NPV, FDR, and F1-Score metrics.

Performance Metrics

Accuracy represents the overall correctness of the model and is calculated as the ratio of correctly predicted instances to the total number of instances. It provides a general measure of the model's performance. Recall, also known as sensitivity or true positive rate, measures the model's ability to correctly identify positive instances, ensuring that relevant cases are detected. On the other hand, specificity indicates the model's ability to correctly classify negative instances, highlighting its effectiveness in minimizing false positives. Precision represents the ratio of correctly predicted positive instances to the total predicted positives, ensuring that the model is accurate in its positive classifications. The false positive rate (FPR) measures the percentage of true negatives mistakenly categorized as positive, while the false negative rate (FNR) represents the proportion of actual positives that are incorrectly classified as negative. A lower FPR and FNR indicate a more reliable model. The false omission rate (FOR) is the proportion of incorrect negative predictions. In contrast, the negative predictive value (NPV) measures the proportion of correctly predicted negative instances to the total predicted negatives, reinforcing the model's reliability in identifying negative cases. The false discovery rate (FDR) highlights the proportion of incorrect positive predictions, emphasizing the need to reduce false alarms. Finally, the F1-score, the harmonic mean of precision and recall, balances the trade-off between these two metrics, comprehensively evaluating the model's effectiveness.

Comparative Analysis

The HBDOA-TransBiLSTM-AM model demonstrates superior overall performance, achieving the highest accuracy of 96.8067%. This indicates its exceptional capability in correctly classifying instances. Furthermore, it exhibits outstanding sensitivity with a recall score of 96.8%, signifying its effectiveness in identifying positive cases. The model also boasts the highest specificity at 98.5168%, showcasing its ability to correctly classify negative instances, thereby reducing misclassification rates. Regarding precision, the HBDOA-TransBiLSTM-AM model outperforms others with a value of 51.1076%, emphasizing its accuracy in predicting positive cases. Additionally, the model achieves the lowest false positive rate (FPR) of 3.193103 and a false negative rate (FNR) of 3.2%, highlighting its robustness in minimizing erroneous classifications. These factors contribute significantly to the model's reliability and efficiency. Moreover, the model attains the lowest false omission rate (FOR) of 0.1123% and the highest negative predictive value (NPV) of 98.57415%, underscoring its dependability in making negative predictions. The false discovery rate (FDR) is also minimized at 48.89214%, indicating fewer incorrect positive predictions. Finally, the HBDOA-TransBiLSTM-AM model achieves the highest F1-score of 66.89703%, effectively balancing precision and recall. This combination of metrics solidifies the model's robustness and effectiveness in lung tumor detection.

CONCLUSION

For speech and speaker recognition, the examination of performance parameters under various optimization strategies is the primary emphasis of this chapter. Spectral, Cepstral, and Deep characteristics are utilized for recognition in this context. A variety of feature selection methods are utilized in the analysis of performance parameters. These methods include the Bat Optimiser, the Moth Flame Optimiser, the Bonabo Optimiser, the Dandelion Optimiser, and the proposed HBDOA. These optimizers are applied to optimize the Trans BiLSTM-AM recognition model created. Here, the best performance parameters results are provided by a variety of machine learning performance parameters, including Accuracy, Recall, Specificity, Precision, FPR, FNR F1-Score, and other parameters, as well as the Trans BiLSTM-AM recognition model that was created with the proposed optimizer HBDOA.

REFERENCES

Abdelghany, R. Y., Kamel, S., Sultan, H. M., Khorasy, A., Elsayed, S. K., & Ahmed, M. (2021). Development of an improved bonobo optimizer and its application for solar cell parameter estimation. *Sustainability (Basel)*, *13*(7), 3863. DOI: 10.3390/su13073863

Anitha, K., Nagaraj, B. K., Paramasivan, P., & Shynu, T. (2023). Enhancing Clustering Performance with the Rough Set C-Means Algorithm. *FMDB Transactions on Sustainable Computing Systems*, *1*(4), 190–203.

Anushya, A., Begum, S., Shiwani, S., & Shrivastava, A. (2024). Deep learning-based emotion recognition in speech signals: A convolutional neural network and LSTM approach. *AVE Trends in Intelligent Computing Systems*, *1*(4), 198–208.

Chandrasekaran, G., Kumar, N. S., Karthikeyan, P. R., Vanchinathan, K., Priyadarshi, N., & Twala, B. (2022). Test scheduling and test time minimization of system-on-chip using modified BAT algorithm. *IEEE Access : Practical Innovations, Open Solutions*, *40*(3), 1–13. DOI: 10.1109/ACCESS.2022.3224924

Gandhi, M., Satheesh, C., Soji, E. S., Saranya, M., Rajest, S. S., & Kothuru, S. K. (2024). Image recognition and extraction on computerized vision for sign language decoding. In *Explainable AI Applications for Human Behavior Analysis* (pp. 157–173). IGI Global. DOI: 10.4018/979-8-3693-1355-8.ch010

Hourri, S., & Kharroubi, J. (2020). A deep learning approach for speaker recognition. *International Journal of Speech Technology*, *23*(2), 123–131. DOI: 10.1007/s10772-019-09665-y

Huang, J., & Ma, Y. (2020). Bat algorithm based on an integration strategy and Gaussian distribution. *Mathematical Problems in Engineering*, *2020*(1), 1–22. DOI: 10.1155/2020/9495281

Janabayevich, A. (2023). Theoretical Framework: The Role of Speech Acts in Stage Performance. *FMDB Transactions on Sustainable Social Sciences Letters*, *1*(2), 68–77.

Jeba, J. A., Bose, S. R., & Boina, R. (2023). Exploring Hybrid Multi-View Multimodal for Natural Language Emotion Recognition Using Multi-Source Information Learning Model. *FMDB Transactions on Sustainable Computer Letters*, *1*(1), 12–24.

Jeba, J. A., Bose, S. R., Regin, R., Rajest, S. S., & Hasan, M. M. (2024). Intelligent Tamil video summarization: AI-powered NLP, translation, and speech integration for enhanced accessibility. *FMDB Transactions on Sustainable Computer Letters*, *2*(1), 26–39. DOI: 10.69888/FTSCL.2024.000179

Kumar, A., Kaur, G., & Srivastava, M. (2018). Speaker and Speech Recognition using Deep Neural Network. *Article*, *6*(8), 118.

Kumar Das, A., & Kumar Pratihar, D. (2019). A New Bonobo Optimizer (BO) for Real-Parameter Optimization. In Conference: The IEEE Region 10 Symposium. Kuala Lumpur, Malaysia.

Li, X., Han, S., Zhao, L., Gong, C., & Liu, X. (2017). New dandelion algorithm optimizes extreme learning machine for biomedical classification problems. *Computational Intelligence and Neuroscience*, *2017*(1), 1–13. DOI: 10.1155/2017/4523754 PMID: 29085425

Maroju, P. K. (2024). Enhancing white label ATM network efficiency: A data science approach to route optimization with AI. *FMDB Transactions on Sustainable Computer Letters*, *2*(1), 40–51. DOI: 10.69888/FTSCL.2024.000180

Mirjalili, S. (2015). Moth-flame optimization algorithm: A novel nature-inspired heuristic paradigm. *Knowledge-Based Systems*, *89*(11), 228–249. DOI: 10.1016/j.knosys.2015.07.006

Nanban, D., Ajitha, Y., Selvan, J., Pierre, T. J., Sara, S. B. V. J., & Ragesha, R. (2024). Enhancing user experience in air canvas through robust hand gesture recognition using computer vision. *FMDB Transactions on Sustainable Computer Letters*, *2*(3), 131–143. DOI: 10.69888/FTSCL.2024.000239

Panyaram, S. (2024). Optimization strategies for efficient charging station deployment in urban and rural networks. *FMDB Transactions on Sustainable Environmental Sciences*, *1*(2), 69–80. DOI: 10.69888/FTSESS.2024.000245

Pulivarthy, P. (2024). Research on Oracle database performance optimization in IT-based university educational management system. *FMDB Transactions on Sustainable Computing Systems*, *2*(2), 84–95. DOI: 10.69888/FTSCS.2024.000200

Sun, T.-W. (2020). End-to-end speech emotion recognition with gender information. *IEEE Access : Practical Innovations, Open Solutions*, *20*(2), 1–15. DOI: 10.1109/ACCESS.2020.2994628

Wali, G. (2024). Evaluating centralized and decentralized maintenance strategies for improved operational efficiency. *AVE Trends in Intelligent Technoprise Letters*, *1*(2), 91–99.

Chapter 15
A Sparkling Survey on Ingenious Assorted Resource Optimization Techniques-Based Job Scheduling in Cloud Computing

S. Sree Priya
https://orcid.org/0009-0005-2415-4930
Government Arts and Science College, Kangeyam, India

T. Rajendran
Government Arts and Science College, Kangeyam, India

ABSTRACT

The term "cloud computing" refers to a relatively new development innovation that provides clients with conveniences that need less work upon their request. In the cloud framework, load balancing task scheduling is a challenging cycle that is accompanied by an increasing number of client requests. The purpose of this work is to provide a comprehensive analysis of load balancing techniques and to make suggestions for the acquisition of new information regarding load balancing (LB) in cloud computing (CC). The purpose of this illustration paper was to develop a number of enhanced approaches by examining a variety of optimisation techniques. The levels of imbalance, makespan, cost, energy utilisation, resources consumed, and quality of service (QoS) are the primary targets of these optimisation techniques at their core. More than 28 different undertaking scheduling techniques are

DOI: 10.4018/979-8-3373-5203-9.ch015

shown in this chapter, along with questionnaires that are given instructions with specified dimensions.

INTRODUCTION

Cloud storage relies on a shared infrastructure within data centres, surrounded by extensive data and applications that accumulate across a broad array of interconnected virtual machines (VMs). The Cloud Computing model has drawn interest in large science, mobile networking, medical, and business fields in the new big data age. Depending on their needs, cloud users may use a variety of options, in particular – Software-As-A-Service, Infrastructure-As-A-Service, and Platform-As-A-Service. Cloud vicinity may dynamically relocate, assign, upsurge, decline assets, or confiscate services during job processing. This property allows cloud customers to obtain high-performance resources by optimizing resource distribution to users' activities in the cloud. A data centre assortment of nodes houses a multitude of demands that are mostly concerned with computing. Because of the active sophistication of the cloud environment, efficient node-to-node (Figure 1).

Figure 1. Block diagram of cloud architecture

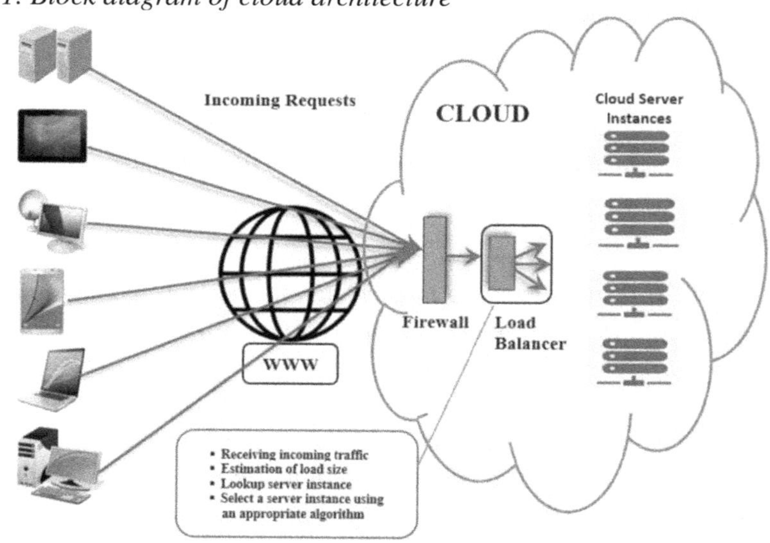

Scheduling and load balancing necessitate sophisticated algorithms. Static scheduling algorithms are effective only in situations with minimal variation in workloads.

Load Equalizing Ultimatum in Cc: The victim of load balancing is distributing the load evenly across VMs to make preeminent usage of resources. In this inquisition, various LB algorithms were investigated based on various parameters.

Load balancer: The primary aim of the Load Balancer is to distribute resources evenly among tasks to ensure resource efficiency and customer satisfaction at minimal cost while also optimizing performance, facilitating rapid deployment, and enhancing flexibility, all of which prompt us to identify challenges in Load Balancer functionality and its intended purpose.

Figure 2. Load-balancing in cloud computing

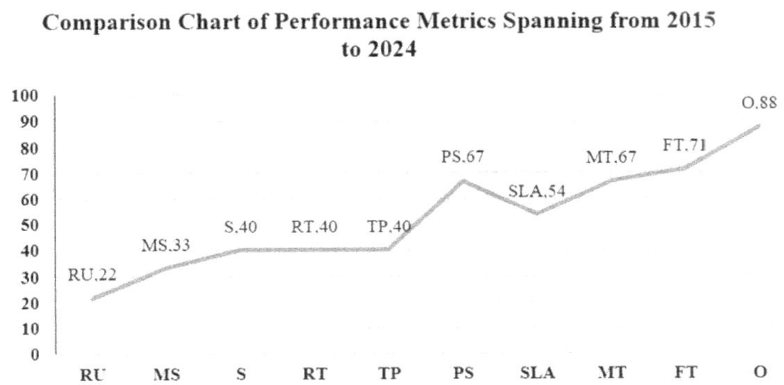

Customers, business associates, and clientele of cloud-based solicitations have simple access. Figure. 2 depicts the load balancer in CC. The competence of LB and copious implementation inspire critical tasks to recognize and address major issues in LB.

Load Balancing – Challenges & Performance Metrics: The primary goal of Load Balancing effectively administers burden obliquely multiple cloud knobs, guaranteeing in order all nodes have insufficient capacity or overload. This method spreads requests across servers, allowing data to be distributed and managed immediately. The method of optimizing system efficiency by relocating device burden is known as LB. LB establishes a structured process for distributing accountability evenly among available resources. Furthermore, LB aims to reduce task response time and improve resource efficiency, resulting in increased system efficaciousness and decreased cost.

All-Encompassing Load Balancing Challenges in Cc: CC porches voluminous challenges owing to LB upshots that require immediate attention. Figure. 3 depicts the taxonomy of important LB issues:

Dispersed geographic node: Cloud data hubs are typically circulated everywhere and are intended for computing. These centres use a centralized network of dynamically distributed nodes to process consumer entreaties efficiently. Since some algorithms are incompatible with this setting, nodes in very remote areas pose a challenge.

Distinct failure point: In the existing literature, specific Load Balancer strategies propose a scenario where decision-making is centralized rather than distributed across numerous nodes, with a single node responsible for Load Balancer decisions. However, the entire computing system is affected if the main devices encounter failures.

Figure 3. Classification of load balancing challenges in cloud computing

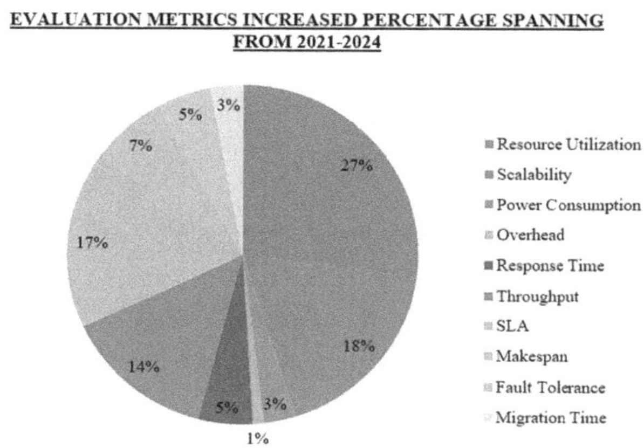

VM Migration: Virtualization permits different virtual machines to deal with a solitary actual unit. Those VMs partake in different sceneries and are independent as far as plan, on the off chance that an actual PC has overburdened because of smart thought to move all VMs to distant areas utilizing the LB cycle.

Nodes Heterogeneity: Consumers of CC necessitate powerful switches that suddenly hinder the demand for heterogeneous hubs aimed at a more proficient organization and quicker reaction time.

Information Management: CC tackled an old problem, conventional capacity gadgets that required a lot of resources and equipment. Consumers can store data in the cloud in various ways without worrying about losing access. Storage requirements are constantly growing, necessitating stored data duplication for well-organized access, besides data endurance.

LB Scalability: Cloud benefits that give openness besides on-request adaptability empower individuals to access resources whenever they need quick downscaling or increase. A good LB equilibrium should consider quickly changing registering conditions, memory, framework, layout, etc.

Algorithm Technical hitches: Cloud computing intelligence should be swift and easily attainable. Robust computation aims to minimize cloud infrastructure downtime and ensure reliability.

Provisioning: The core feature of cloud computing is flexibility; services are dynamically allotted or dispersed. We then utilize or discharge cloud resources while maintaining the same productivity as traditional programs and using the best resources.

Energy expertise: The benefits of energy effectiveness, which advances the utilization of the cloud, are frugality of scale. The most basic part of a serious economy is that restricted firms can add to a pool of worldwide assets instead of each offering its private administrations.

Lb Quantifiable Metrics Enactment: The degree of load spread through existing infrastructure determines the versatility of the VMs within a cloud network. A good scheduler enables a dependable system of load management. CC parameters, in particular, are crucial. The LB methods consider two main quantitative and qualitative parameter classifications for efficiency assessments.

Figure 4. Cataloguing of LB metrics

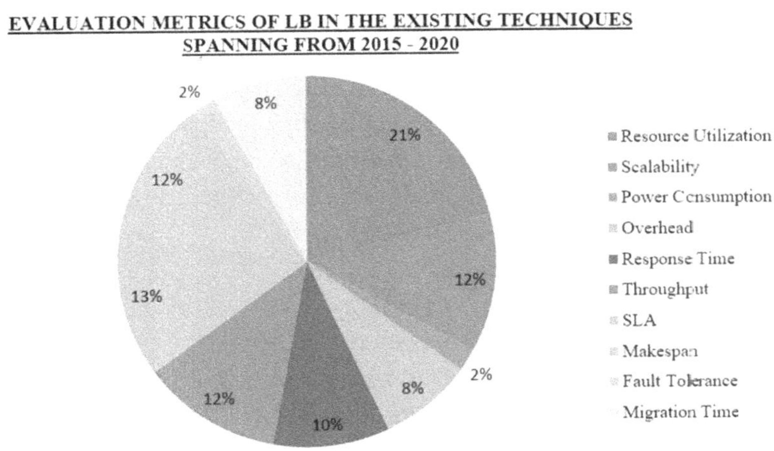

Cataloguing LB metrics comprises Associated Overhead (AO), Scalability(S), Fault Tolerance (FT), Throughput(TP), Migration Time(MT), Resource Utilization(-RU), Power Saving(PS), Response Time(RT), SLA Violation, Makespan (MS) and Performance (P). Figure 4 depicts the classification of LB metrics. Furthermore, if new parameters are discovered in the future, they are categorized centred on their features.

Load Balancing Wide-Ranging Algorithm Approaches

This paper addresses some of the major natural phenomena LB Algorithms to reach the maximum limit in the literature survey are as follows:

- Honey Bee Optimization→(HBO),
- Ant Colony Optimization→(ACO),
- Heuristic Task Scheduling & Artificial BeeColony→(HABC),
- Fault Tolerance→(FT),
- Honey Bee Foraging,
- LB Honey Bee Foraging,
- LB approach dependent on honeybee behavior→(HBB),
- Intelligent Neutrosophic Inference System with Quantum Cuckoo Search based Cache Management→(INIS-QCSCM),
- Adaptive Dragonfly Algorithm→(ADA),
- Chicken Swarm Optimization Algorithm→(CSO),
- Binarybird swarm Optimizing Procedure→(BSO),
- Fish swarm Optimizing tactic→(FSO),
- Grasshopper Optimizing Algorithm→(GOA),
- Nature Inspired Bee Colony Optimization Algorithm→(TIBCO),
- Vocalization of humpback Whale Optimizing Algorithm→(VWOA),
- Hybrid→(Ant colony, Honeybee through active feedback),
- New Fuzzy resource Scheduling Algorithm → (NFSA),
- W-Scheduler Whale optimization algorithm→ (W-Scheduler WOA),
- Resource Scheduling based - FCAP ->(RSAF),
- Cost-Makespan aware Scheduling→ (CMaS),
- Honeybee Induced Algorithm → (HBI),
- Cost-Effective Ant Colony Optimization → (CEACO),
- Modified Artificial Fish swarm Optimizing tactic → (MAFS),
- Improved-chicken swarm Optimizing strategy→(ICWO)
- Adaptive Load Balancing Task Scheduling Algorithm→ (ALTS)
- ML Model API → (ML-API)
- Divisible Weighted Round-Robin Load Balancer → (DWRRLB)

- Inspired Lion Optimization Algorithm → (ILOA)
- Response Time Efficient Load Balancer Algorithm → (ReT-ELBa)
- Given consignment planning with explicit execution measurements.

LITERATURE SURVEY

This sector oration is one of the most recent methods for resource scheduling in the cloud model. Kiruthiga and Mary (2020) suggested Intelligent Neutrosophic Inference System with Quantum Cuckoo Search-based Cache Management (INIS-QCSCM) in cloud environment deals with both scheduling and cache management. Cuckoos are assigned to each work request, and their memory size requirements are utilized to find adequate cache space for allocating the best job requirement. Cuckoo searches with high fitness values are thought to have the best cache size for completing task requests and the least processing expense. The best cache is chosen using the levy combat function. This model optimizes resource scheduling and cache management in the cloud paradigm while maintaining quality assurance. Mishra and Majhi (2021) proposed a binary bird swarm(BSO-LB) algorithm that curtails makespan and makes best use of resources using an appropriate fitness task, outperforms resource usage, response time, makespan, triumphs preemptive and no preemptive errands. Other metrics for QoS efficiency energy conservation have never been considered.

Kruekaew and Kimpan (2020) suggested heuristic chore scheduling by using an Artificial Bee Colony (HABC), an amalgam of swarm Intellectual algorithm of artificial bee colony besides a heuristic scheduling algorithm. This algorithm is used to improve the scheduling of virtual computers for cloud computing in both homogeneous and heterogeneous settings. This optimization approach works well for minimizing time, balancing loads, and optimizing the task scheduling process, but it does not handle multiple job scheduling with different objectives. Shahid et al. (2020) developed a well-organized LB technique having FT ability that pointedly decreases makespan, the performance of the system, accomplish stability load distribution efficacious net, usage of the host, throughput, system robust adaptability, chore implementation, response time which yields efficient network & node utilization, but failed to accentuate energy conservation and optimize resource efficiency at the lowest cost.

Mallikarjuna and Krishna (2018a) presented the nature Inspired bee colony (NIBCO) algorithm, which uses a search technique to find the best VM for load shifting. The bee colony mechanism is an iterative process for efficient task scheduling across VMs. The duplication process assesses whether VMs are overloaded or underutilized. Findings indicate the potential for reducing load time and optimizing scheduling, albeit at the expense of overlooking energy conservation and connectivity costs. Mallikarjuna and Krishna (2018b) recommended HB foraging in their hunt for sustenance, besides honeybee province scavenging nourishment. When there is a food source, bees perform a characteristic dance structure known as waggle dance and later resume headed for accumulation, performing wave to and fro hop to advertise the presence of nutrients. It shows how long the waggle hop will go based on food availability and the distance between beehives. This algorithm satisfies performance criteria such as scalability, relocation time with response, makespan, and fault tolerance.

Hashem et al. (2017) proposed honeybee behaviour (LBA_HB). The aforementioned fundamental target carries responsibilities over dissimilar organization interfaces that uphold strategic distance from under-use and over-asset use. The calculation contrasted with design approaches, Ant colony, Honeybees, altered, and round-robin calculations. LBA_HB exhibits productivity regarding execution time, reaction time, range, load standard deviation, and lopsidedness. Masadeh et al. (2019) used humpback whale enrichment procedure (VWOA), devised and built to emulate humpback whale vocalization behaviour. This approach assumes that each cluster has three best solutions, i.e., three best local optimum solutions. As a result, the first solution is regarded as the best answer, and the global optimal solution is discovered using a search agent. VWOA's primary goals are to reduce cost, time, and energy utilization while expanding asset use. VWOA's essential objectives are to diminish cost, time, and energy utilization while the three best solutions discovered in each cluster can generate further solutions with optimum scheduling. Neelima and Reddy (2020) proposed newfangled procedure scheduling tasks using the Adaptive Dragonfly algorithm (ADA), a mix of the Dragonfly and Firefly technique. A good utilization of resources is achieved when efficient heaviness is accomplished in CC. Moreover, to achieve better performance, a multi-purpose function is recognized using three precise norms - time to completion, loads with preparing expenses.

Kathalkar and Deorankar (2018) proposed several ant colony newfangled procedures for nourishment search. A larger encumbrance indicates that the asset has more computational control. The LB ant colony optimization not only manages load but also shortens makespan. The LB insect province enhancement deals with heaps and shortens the makespan. Greco et al. (2019) ACO presented an effective solution for addressing travelling salespeople. With another exploratory bio-enthused strategy, Greco et al. (2019) ACO acquired conspicuousness recently. Dave et al. (2016) introduced a bee colony strategy focusing on mimicking honeybee behaviour and attaining maximum throughput Gandhi and Gupta (2017). Over time, honey bees brood over away dissimilar tasks in the interior hive. Foraging bees travel, looking for nearby resources, acquiring nutrients, and revisiting their hive. At some point, amount of scavenging bees turns out to be dormant.

Thanka et al. (2019) proposed the Artificial Bee Colony algorithm as a meta-heuristic swarm intelligence strategy that simulates the rummaging behaviours of honey bees. The working drones gather nectar explicitly in the hive's hop zone. When this information is traded again in the hive, working drones will get back to recently educated food sources. Manipal et al. (2019) ABC, an upgrading approach, offers the populace-based looking through strategy in which elements marked food destinations are time-consumingly changed by fake honey bees, with honey bee's motivation to find locales with enormous nectar wellsprings of food besides, in the long run, the greatest nectar. Ashouraei et al. (2018) proposed an LB procedure to utilize CC administrations. The set-up ACHBDF method uses a breed procedure consolidating powerful planning draws near and a unique time-phase response approach. The recommended ACHBDF's inadequate arranging utilizes insect province measure effectiveness and the bumblebee measure.

Ogedengbe and Agana (2017) developed a modern New Fuzzy Resource Scheduling Algorithm (NFSA) scheme that takes into account the arrival time response by working out time of parameter scheduling. The model's performance is used in an internal priority queue to distribute them to services (Masadeh et al., 2018). This model does not embrace time complexity and performance metrics. In this paper, they succeeded in mapping the fuzzy inference engine to multiprocessors, and results showed that processors used better and thus improved the system by reducing response, turnaround time, and total unexploited deadlines. Sreenu and Sreelatha (2017) projected task programming algorithmic rule known as W-Scheduler dependent on multi-target model and whale advancement algorithmic principle(WOA), ideally plan errands to virtual machines though having base makespan besides least normal expense. The whale improvement technique expects that the current arrangement is the best and looks for the most effective utilizing the best pursuit specialist. The W-execution schedulers dissected for assessment measurements using cost and makespan.

Guangshun Li et al. (2019) proposed Fuzzy clustering System through Particle Swarm Optimization-(FCAP) system dependent on customary Fuzzy C-Means(F-CM) clustering algorithm and particle swarm optimizing (PSO) strategy, which is applied to bunch mist assets, limits the client's prerequisite for coordinating with assets and recommends RSAF calculation for achieving asset planning (Aladwani, 2019). They created a resource development strategy by stabilizing resource attributes involved in resource scheduling. This algorithm does not divulge resource utilization and dynamic changes of resources. Xuan-QuiPham et al. (2017) proposed a cost-makespan aware(CMaS) technique using performance trade-offs and cost savings for building application schedules, which not only ensures implementation of application within time limit constraints but also eases the required cost of using cloud assets. This work provides a better, cost-effective solution (Stavrinides and

Karatza, 2018). CMaS cost makespan-aware scheduling is a major goal of this work to achieve flexibility in application execution efficiency when cloud resource costs are considered. This work outperforms most scheduling systems, but there is no energy efficiency or consumption measurement (Liu et al., 2019).

Liru Han (2019) presented the Improved Chicken Swarm Optimization technique-(ICSO) instead of task resource apportionment in CC resource scheduling. It enhances the algorithm's local and global search capability by initializing the algorithm population, updating chicken location, and using different algorithms to pick optimal and border processing. The efficient distribution of resources has long been the focus of cloud computing research. For resource allocation, this article employs the bionic algorithm CSO, and it has achieved certain impacts and improvements in CSO algorithm initialization, chick position update, individual selection, and boundary processing. Krishnaveni and Sinthu (2019) introduced the MAFS (Modified Artificial Fish Swarm) methodology to handle job-scheduling problems on a cloud platform, which uses evolutionary computation principles to eliminate certain unnecessary calculations. The ultimate goal is to reduce execution costs and time while scheduling tasks on the cloud. The experimental findings show that this approach not only minimizes execution cost during scheduling but also improves the overall efficiency of the process, reduces completion time, and efficiently utilizes VMs. However, communication costs and power usage also need to be improved.

Vahidi and Rahmati (2019) created an innovative Grasshopper Optimization Algorithm (GOA) used to distribute resources in cloud computing systems. It seeks to investigate the performances of resource optimization problems and examines efficiency, time complexity, response time, throughput, and performance indicators. The outcomes firmly recognize the execution of GOA, which features its high capacity to take care of issues of resource assignment in CC. Yadav and Gupta (2019) developed a cost-effective Antcolony Optimizing technique-(CEACO) to lower the implementation cost of processing tasks depending on budget limitations. The experimental results demonstrate that this method is competent per execution Cost connectivity cost, besides increasing its dependability and execution time. The results show that this calculation runs quicker than past ant colony provinces with encroachment regarding cost.

Liu et al. (2015) recommended– Aggressive-consolidation-first-come-first-serve(ACFCFS), a parallel workload that uses FCFS, an equal responsibility that utilizes first-come, first-served queuing theory technique to situate workers while resources are accessible. This model does not emphasize workplace insecurity, processor utilization, or communication costs. It keeps up all of the FCFS benefits and distinctly overwhelms the FCFS that achieves, closely resembling, the bearing of calculation dependent on surveying runtime. ACFCFS is a vigorous and dubious central processor measure for equivalent errands besides CPU low dormant cycles.

Sharma et al. (2020) gave a successful answer for controlling burdens in the CC milieu utilizing a honeybee-initiated stratagem(HBI) meant for better conveyance of help with heap adjusting framework. This recommended method disperses responsibilities over a huge number and certifies that assets are not underused or overused. It performs by allotting to virtual machines that meet two rules. This embraces the scope of tasks currently implemented through these virtual machines, which utilize less time than former virtual machines. This limits virtual machine response time and assesses the weight of each cloud data centre. The perceived discoveries indicate viable execution speediness, movement time, and makespan time, and different attributes like expense, normal holding-up time, and normal reaction time should be considered.

Mubeen et al. (2021) developed and implemented an optimal task-scheduling solution. This method assessed and compared with ACO, GA, and existing GAACO approaches, and the results obtained validate the enhancements achieved in terms of makespan, resource utilization, and SLA violation. In this approach, ACO is employed to optimize and refine solutions generated by the Genetic algorithm. The newly introduced ALTS algorithm demonstrates improvements in task scheduling, particularly in makespan and resource utilization, by implementing load-balanced task scheduling. Additionally, this approach aims to minimize SLA violations and enhance service quality. The outcomes obtained affirm the effectiveness of the ALTS approach.

Kamila et al. (2022) introduced a machine learning-based design model for cloud platforms, leveraging load balancer and computing unit metadata to enhance traffic resilience and automatically recover from traffic failure scenarios. The resilience and performance of the cloud network traffic rely on machine learning regression and classification techniques. Test results demonstrate the efficacy of this approach, achieving 38.15% faster resiliency compared to other existing models. Furthermore, the attained results validate the accuracy of decisions at a 99% rate, as the system detects and redirects traffic to alternate clusters preemptively, averting potential failures. The error rate during failure recovery is reduced by 90.08% compared to existing models. This design implements a self-enabled auto-correction mechanism for traffic flow issues in cloud platforms, thereby enhancing overall platform performance.

Waghmode and Bankat et al. (2023) suggested that the divisible weighted round-robin method discussed in this study effectively managed incoming tasks for distribution among various virtual machines across different Data Centers. Cluster-based web servers address the increasing demand for high-performance web servers from enhanced web environments. This approach, which incorporates round-robin scheduling, divisible weight round-robin scheduling, and weighted least connection algorithm scheduling, notably reduces load range and variance. A divisible weighted round-robin load balancer has been implemented to minimize response time and achieve load balancing without introducing delays.

Kaviarasan et al. (2023) suggested the primary challenge of load balancing in cloud environments by systematically reviewing various load balancing methods utilized previously and pinpointing their limitations. Extensive research was conducted to devise an optimal solution, revealing metaheuristic approaches as the most suitable. These approaches excel in identifying node capacities and consistently aim to achieve global optima. Following this analysis, a Bio-Inspired Lion Optimization Algorithm has been adopted to design the ILOA_LB system. Results from implementation demonstrate significantly enhanced performance in load balancing within the cloud, even amidst increases in node numbers and workloads, when compared to benchmark systems EMAMBO_LB, BOA_LB, and CSO_LB.

Ret-Elba et al. (2023) introduce a new algorithm aimed at optimizing Response and Data Centre Processing Time, contrasting its performance with that of Throttled and round-robin algorithms. ReT-ELBa consistently outperforms both algorithms, albeit with a slightly less significant difference from the Throttled algorithm's performance. However, it notably surpasses the round-robin algorithm regarding Response Time and Data Centre Processing Time. Four simulation cases were conducted to evaluate algorithms' Performance for Virtual Machines in a single Data Centre and across multiple Data Centres with increasing numbers of Virtual Machines, revealing that such variations had no significant impact on their performance. ReT-ELBa's effectiveness lies in its ability to adapt to varying request requirements, current load, and Virtual Machine types to balance new loads efficiently. Its mechanism involves maintaining lists of primary, secondary (idle), and engaged machines, facilitating dynamic load allocation. However, these new models are no longer applicable in cases where complexity, impreciseness, and optimizing scheduling processes are not considered.

Comparableness of Copious Lb Estimation Methods, Hinge on Precise Parameters

Table 1 depicts techniques intended to replace load balancing. LB is the most troublesome deterrent in CC. Consequently, several LB strategies are inefficient and impossible with complete execution measurements. The performance metric in LB algorithms is a major issue since it does not meet all criteria. The new efficient solution ought to focus on all the performance metrics of the LB method.

Table 1. Comparableness of copious LB estimation methods, hinge on precise parameters

LB Algorithm	Makespan (MS)	Throughput (TP)	Overhead (O)	Fault Tolerance (FT)	Migration Time (MT)	Response Time (RT)	Resource utilization (RU)	Scalability (S)	Power Saving (PS)	SALE
Intelligent Neutrosophic Inference System with Quantum Cuckoo Search-based Cache Management (INIS-QCSCM) (Mishra & Majhi, 2021)		✓	✓		✓	✓	✓	✓	✓	
Binarybird swarm optimization load balancing strategy-(BSO-LB) (Kruekaew & Kimpan, 2020)	✓	✓		✓		✓	✓		✓	
Heuristic task scheduling per artificial bee colony tactics-(HABC) (Shahid et al., 2020)	✓	✓	✓			✓			✓	✓
Fault Tolerance-(FT) (Mallikarjuna & Venkata, 2018a)	✓	✓		✓	✓	✓			✓	✓
Nature Inspired Bee Colony Optimization Algorithm (NIBCO) Mallikarjuna & Krishna, 2018b)		✓	✓	✓			✓	✓	✓	
LB Honeybee foraging (Hashem et al., 2017)	✓	✓		✓	✓	✓	✓	✓		
Bee colony optimizing algorithm		✓			✓		✓		✓	✓
Honey Bee Behavior Optimization Algorithm-(HB) (Masadeh et al., 2019)	✓		✓	✓			✓			✓
Vocalization of humpback Whale Optimization Algorithm (VWOA) (Liu et al., 2015)	✓		✓		✓	✓	✓		✓	✓
Aggressive-consolidation-based-first-come-first-serve technique-(ACFCFS) (Neelima & Reddy, 2020)	✓	✓	✓		✓	✓	✓	✓		
Adaptive Dragonfly Algorithm(ADA) (Kathalkar & Deorankar, 2018)		✓	✓	✓		✓	✓	✓		
Antcolony optimization-(ACO) (Greco et al., 2019; Dave et al., 2016)	✓	✓	✓		✓		✓	✓		✓
Honey Bee foraging (Gondhi & Gupta, 2017)	✓	✓		✓	✓		✓			✓
Artificialbee colony approach-(ABC) (Manipal et al., 2019; Ashouraei et al., 2018)	✓		✓		✓		✓	✓	✓	✓
Hybrid-(Antcolony, Honeybee by means of dynamic feedback) (Ogedengbe & Agana, 2017)	✓		✓		✓		✓	✓		✓
New Fuzzy resource Scheduling Algorithm (NFSA) (Alzaqebah & Hudaib, 2018)	✓	✓			✓		✓	✓		
W-Scheduler Whale Optimization Algorithm(WWOA) (Li et al., 2019)	✓	✓		✓	✓	✓	✓			✓
Fuzzy clustering algorithm using particle swarm optimizing approach-(FCAP), Resource Scheduling algorithm centered on FCAP-(RSAF) (Aladwani 2019)		✓	✓	✓	✓		✓	✓		✓
Cost-Makespan aware Scheduling (CMaS) (Stavrinides & Karatza, 2018)	✓	✓	✓	✓		✓	✓	✓		
Improved chicken swarm optimizing methodology-(ICSO) (Mubeen et al., 2021)			✓		✓		✓	✓	✓	✓
Modified Artificial Fish Swarm Optimization Algorithm (MAFS) (Kamila et al., 2022)	✓	✓				✓	✓	✓	✓	✓
Grasshopper optimizing algorithm-(GOA) (Waghmode & Bankat, 2023)	✓	✓			✓	✓		✓	✓	✓
Cost Effective Ant Colony Optimization Algorithm (CEACO) (Kaviarasan et al., 2023)	✓		✓		✓	✓	✓	✓		✓
Honeybee Induced Algorithm (HBI) (Ret-Elba, (2024)	✓	✓			✓	✓	✓		✓	✓

Performance-Metrics Evaluation of the Existing Techniques

This paper centres on execution measurements of asset-planning approaches in current strategies with different algorithms. Figure 5 depicts the evaluation metrics of LB in the existing methodologies spanning from 2015 to 2020. In contrast, Figure 6 depicts the evaluation of LB metrics projected increasing percentage to recommend achieving all performance requirements from 2021-2024. There is a need to improve techniques by specifying new or reusable frameworks for handling problems in cloud settings.

Figure 5. Evaluation metrics of Lb in the existing techniques spanning from 2015 – 2021

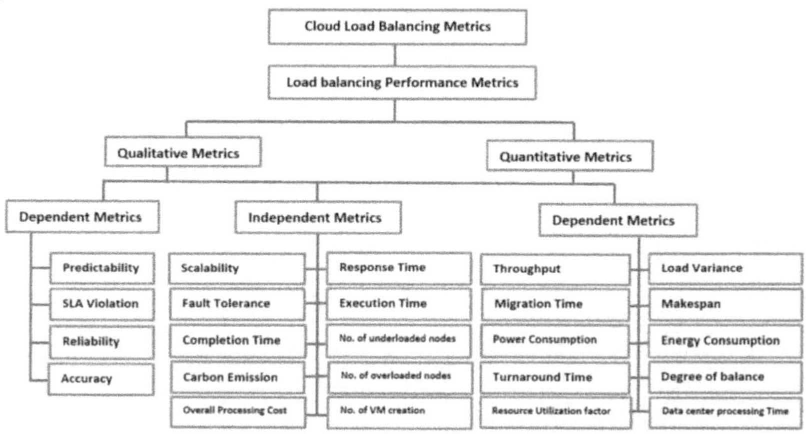

Figure 6. Prediction of evaluation metrics of Lb spanning from 2021-2024

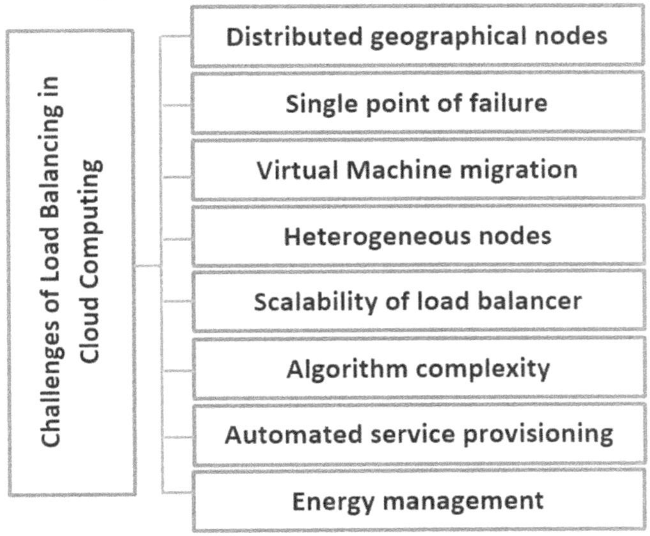

RESULTS AND DISCUSSIONS

The cloud serves as a metaphor for extensive data storage and cloud users' utilization of virtual resources. Though there are several works in nature for conducting resource scheduling in cloud settings, none are particularly based on an ultimate objective of scheduling resources in ambiguous situations such as vagueness, impreciseness, uncertainty, and inconsistency.

Figure 7. Performance metrics of LB comparison chart (2015-2024)

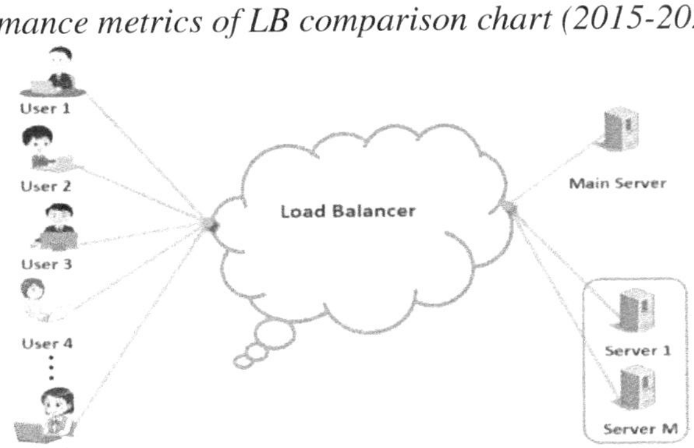

The existence of impreciseness regarding the availability of services is the most difficult obstacle when operating in Cloud Computing-based resource scheduling. The best algorithm should be developed in the future for job workload to optimum resource scheduling. The foremost objective of this research exertion, to explore different algorithms envisioned for LB, is to fulfil some evaluation metrics. Figure 7 depicts the performance indicators in metrics that must be successfully enhanced and are compared in this graphic in an algorithm's new, unique design.

CONCLUSION

Given upcoming assignments for specific resources, effective task scheduling should be discovered by estimating each parameter metric. This paper details several LB algorithms and their assessment measures. Despite the importance of load-adjusting processes, existing load reconciliation techniques are not comprehensive, wide, methodical, systematic, or progressive. This article focuses on cloud computing issues and the key obstacles they provide. One of the most serious issues with CC is LB since overloading the device may have disastrous consequences, perhaps rendering technology outdated. Thus, a consistent prerequisite for productive LB strategy for asset use exists. The LB's primary purpose is to fulfil the demands of users by spreading the workload over various network hubs, amplifying asset use, and expanding the device's ability. The new algorithm should be planned and implemented to successfully and intelligently address task-scheduling challenges. An efficient LB, besides management, is significant for system competence, resource utilization, dependability, throughput enhancement, and response time reduction.

Future Research Expedient Approaches

Multiple load-balancing technologies exist for cloud computing, each with its limitations. Analyzing the advantages and drawbacks of current methods is crucial for developing effective load-balancing optimization algorithms in the future. This research aims to identify issues related to timely workload scheduling to reduce response and completion times, thus meeting cloud users' Quality of Service (QoS) requirements and maximizing benefits for cloud consumers. It has been observed that strategies reviewed typically aim to improve QoS, resource utilization, and energy efficiency. However, existing load-balancing methods face challenges, such as limited resource availability, energy inefficiency, inadequate frequency control, and static barriers. Consequently, there is significant room for progress, either through proposing new technologies or enhancing existing ones. Enhancing asset efficiency, conserving energy, and implementing smart and adaptable load-balancing tactics that align with client quality requirements at minimal cost is essential for advancement. Innovative methods integrating load balancing with energy usage and support expenses hold significant potential. As we progress, there will be an increasing demand for highly autonomous and resilient load-balancing algorithms that prioritize enhanced resource utilization, minimized task completion times, efficient workload transitions, and strict adherence to time constraints. Cloud computing is a resilient and vital technology that can endure over time, serving as a key enabler for organizational advancement and strategic fulfilment. Future research endeavours should explore advanced load-balancing techniques integrating Machine Learning methods to predict future loads and allocate resources optimally, thus further enhancing resource utilization and Response Time in Cloud Computing load balancing.

REFERENCES

Aladwani, T. (2019). Scheduling IoT Healthcare Tasks in Fog Computing Based on their Importance. In *Proc. of the 16th International Learning & Technology Conference 2019 Procedia Computer Science*. Elsevier. DOI: 10.1016/j.procs.2019.12.138

Alzaqebah, A. R. M., & Hudaib, A. (2018). Grey wolf algorithm for requirements prioritization. *Modern Applied Science*, *12*(2), 54. DOI: 10.5539/mas.v12n2p54

Ashouraei, M., Khezr, S. N., Benlamri, R., & Navimipour, N. J. (2018). A new SLA-aware load balancing method in the cloud using an improved parallel task scheduling algorithm. In Proc. IEEE 6th Inter. Conference Future Internet Things Cloud, Vienna, Australia.

Dave, A., Patel, B., & Bhatt, G. (2016). Load balancing in cloud computing using optimization techniques: A study. In *Proceedings of the International Conference on Communication and Electronics Systems (ICCES)*, Tamil Nadu, India. DOI: 10.1109/CESYS.2016.7889883

Gondhi, N. K., & Gupta, A. (2017). Survey on machine learning-based scheduling in cloud computing. In *Proceedings of the International Conference on Intelligent Systems, Metaheuristics, and Swarm Intelligence*, Jammu and Kashmir, India. DOI: 10.1145/3059336.3059352

Greco, A., Pluchino, A., & Cannizzaro, F. (2019). An improved ant colony optimization algorithm and its applications to limit analysis of frame structures. *Engineering Optimization*, *51*(11), 1867–1883. DOI: 10.1080/0305215X.2018.1560437

Han, L. (2019). Chicken Swarm Optimization in Task Scheduling in Cloud Computing. *International Journal of Performability Engineering*, *15*(7), 1929–1938. DOI: 10.23940/ijpe.19.07.p20.19291938

Hashem, W., Nashaat, H., & Rizk, R. (2017). Honey Bee Based Load Balancing in Cloud Computing. *KSII Transactions on Internet and Information Systems*, *11*(12), 5694–5711.

Kamila, J. K. N., Frnda, S., Kumar Pani, R., Sardar, M. N., Islam, P. K., & Bharti, K. (2022). Machine Learning Model Design For High Performance Cloud Computing & Load Balancing Resiliency: An Innovative Approach. *Journal of King Saud University. Computer and Information Sciences*, *34*(10), 9991–10009. DOI: 10.1016/j.jksuci.2022.10.001

Kathalkar, P. R., & Deorankar, A. V. (2018). A review on different load balancing algorithms in cloud computing. *International Research Journal of Engineering and Technology*, *5*(2), 1961–1963.

Kaviarasan, R., Balamurugan, G., Kalaiyarasan, R., & Venkata Ravindra Reddy, Y. (2023). Effective load balancing approach in cloud computing using Inspired Lion Optimization Algorithm. *Advances in Electrical Engineering*, *6*(12), 100326.

Kiruthiga, G., & Mary, V. S. (2020). Neutrosophic knowledge and optimized cache management using cuckoo search method in cloud computing. *International Journal of Intelligent Engineering and Systems*, *13*(3), 327–338. DOI: 10.22266/ijies2020.0630.30

Krishnaveni, H., & Sinthu, V. (2019). Modified Artificial Fish Swarm Algorithm for Efficient Task Scheduling in Cloud Environment. *International Journal on Computer Science and Engineering*, *7*(5), 1363–1371.

Kruekaew, B., & Kimpan, W. (2020). Enhancing of Artificial Bee Colony Algorithm for Virtual Machine Scheduling and Load Balancing Problem in Cloud Computing. *International Journal of Computational Intelligence Systems*, *13*(1), 496–510. DOI: 10.2991/ijcis.d.200410.002

Li, G., Liu, Y., Wu, J., Lin, D., & Zhao, S. (2019). Methods of Resource Scheduling Based on Optimized Fuzzy Clustering in Fog Computing. *Sensors (Basel)*, *19*(9), 1–16. DOI: 10.3390/s19092122 PMID: 31071923

Liu, X., Yabing, Z., Yin, Q., Peng, Y., & Qin, L. (2015). Scheduling parallel jobs with tentative runs and consolidation in the cloud. *Journal of Systems and Software*, *104*(6), 141–151. DOI: 10.1016/j.jss.2015.03.007

Liu, Y., Wang, L., Wang, X. V., Xu, X., & Zhang, L. (2019). Scheduling in cloud manufacturing: State-of-the-art and research challenges. *International Journal of Production Research*, *57*(15), 4854–4879. DOI: 10.1080/00207543.2018.1449978

Mallikarjuna, B., & Krishna, P. V. (2018b). A nature-inspired approach for load balancing of tasks in cloud computing using equal time allocation. *International Journal of Innovative Technology and Exploring Engineering*, *8*(12), 46–5.

Mallikarjuna, B., & Venkata, P. (2018a). A Nature Inspired Bee Colony Optimization Model for Improving Load Balancing in Cloud Computing [IJITEE]. *International Journal of Innovative Technology and Exploring Engineering*, *8*(12), 51–55.

Manipal, S., Ranjan, W., Lavish, K., & Komuravelly, S. K. (2019). *Optimization algorithms in load balancing: A study. An International Peer-Reviewed.* UGC Approved Journal.

Masadeh, R., Sharieh, A., & Basel, A. (2019). Humpback Whale Optimization Algorithm Based on Vocal Behavior for Task Scheduling in Cloud Computing. *International Journal of Advanced Science and Technology*, *13*(3), 121–140.

Mishra, K., & Majhi, S. K. (2021). A binary Bird Swarm Optimization based load balancing algorithm for cloud computing environment. *Open Computer Science*, *11*(1), 146–160. DOI: 10.1515/comp-2020-0215

Mubeen, A., Ibrahim, M., Bibi, N., Baz, M., Hamam, H., & Cheikhrouhou, O. (2021). Alts: An adaptive load balanced task scheduling approach for cloud computing. *Processes (Basel, Switzerland)*, *9*(9), 1514. DOI: 10.3390/pr9091514

Neelima, P., & Reddy, A. M. R. (2020). An efficient load balancing system using adaptive dragonfly algorithm in cloud computing. In *Cluster Computing*. Springer.

Ogedengbe, M. T., & Agana, M. A. (2017). New Fuzzy Techniques for Real-Time Task Scheduling on Multiprocessor Systems. *International Journal of Computer Trends and Technology*, *47*(3), 189–196. DOI: 10.14445/22312803/IJCTT-V47P129

Pham, X.-Q., Man, N. D., Tri, N. D. T., Thai, N. Q., & Huh, E.-N. (2017). A cost- and performance-effective approach for task scheduling based on collaboration between cloud and fog computing. *International Journal of Distributed Sensor Networks*, *13*(11), 1–16. DOI: 10.1177/1550147717742073

Ret-Elba, R. (2024). ReT-ELBa: A Novel Algorithm for Efficient Load Balancing in Cloud Computing", Yusif Rashid and Callistus Ireneous Nakpih. *Asian Journal of Research in Computer Science*, *17*(5), 56–64. DOI: 10.9734/ajrcos/2024/v17i5438

Shahid, N.A.M., Islam, M., Mansoor Alam, M. M., & Suud, A. S. (2020). A Comprehensive Study of Load Balancing Approaches in the Cloud Computing Environment and a Novel Fault Tolerance Approach". 8(7), 99.

Sharma, A. K., Upreti, K., & Vargis, B. (2020). *Experimental performance analysis of load balancing of tasks using honey bee inspired algorithm for resource allocation in cloud environment*. Elsevier. DOI: 10.1016/j.matpr.2020.09.359

Sreenu, K., & Sreelatha, M. (2017). W-Scheduler: Whale optimization for task scheduling in cloud computing. *Cluster Computing*, *22*(6), 1–12.

Stavrinides, G. L., & Karatza, H. (2018). *A hybrid approach to scheduling real-time IoT workflows in fog and cloud environments* (Vol. 78). Springer.

Thanka, M. R., Maheswari, P., & Edwin, E. B. (2019). An improved efficient: Artificial bee colony algorithm for security and QoS aware scheduling in cloud computing environment. *Cluster Computing*, *22*(5), 10905–10913. DOI: 10.1007/s10586-017-1223-7

Vahidi, J., & Rahmati, M. (2019). Optimization of Resource Allocation in Cloud Computing by Grasshopper Optimization Algorithm". In *5th Conference on Knowledge-Based Engineering and InnovatioN*, Tehean, Iran. DOI: 10.1109/KBEI.2019.8735098

Waghmode, T., & Bankat, M. (2023). Adaptive Load Balancing In Cloud Computing Environment", Intelligent Systems And Applications In Engineering. *IJISAE*, *11*(7), 302–314.

Yadav, C., & Gupta, Y. K. (2019). Cost Effective Ant Colony Optimization in Cloud Computing. *International Journal of Innovative Technology and Exploring Engineering*, *8*(10), 3016–3020. DOI: 10.35940/ijitee.J9460.0881019

Chapter 16
The Role of Wireless Sensor Networks in Contemporary Communication and Impact:
The Next Steps for 5G

N. Suganthi
https://orcid.org/0000-0001-7022-6898
SRM Institute of Science and Technology, Ramapuram, India

V. Sahaya Sakila
SRM Institute of Science and Technology, Ramapuram, India

M. Devika
https://orcid.org/0009-0009-8589-8895
SRM Institute of Science and Technology, Ramapuram, India

Swakantik Mishra
Centurion University of Technology and Management, India

R. Regin
https://orcid.org/0000-0002-6618-205X
SRM Institute of Science And Technology, Ramapuram, India

J. Jayaprakash
Dhaanish Ahmed College of Engineering, India

ABSTRACT

The technological epoch is witnessing a pivotal shift with the evolution of 5G networks, propelling advancements in wireless sensor networks (WSNs) and sculpting the landscape of modern communication. This research delves into the progression of 5G technology, exploring its impact and the integration process of WSNs into current communication systems. WSNs are instrumental in obtaining, processing,

DOI: 10.4018/979-8-3373-5203-9.ch016

and transmitting information from the physical world to the digital realm, forming a critical nexus between the environment and computing devices. The advent of 5G technology has amplified the capabilities of WSNs, enhancing their efficiency, reliability, and functionality by leveraging high-speed, low-latency communication. This chapter elucidates the transformation induced by 5G, its implications on data exchange, IoT applications, and the concomitant challenges and solutions in integrating WSNs.

INTRODUCTION

The fifth generation of wireless communication, 5G, heralds a transformative chapter in the chronicle of digital connectivity, presenting a paradigm shift that transcends the previous limitations of wireless technology (Chen et al., 2018). This latest iteration in the evolution of mobile networks is not merely an incremental enhancement; it is a cornerstone for a future that promises hyper-connectivity, significantly reduced latency, and data transmission speeds that were once unfathomable (Mehta et al., 2019). Such advancements are not confined to abstract technical realms but are poised to have tangible impacts on everyday life and the very fabric of society (Shafi et al., 2019). The architecture of 5G is meticulously engineered to overcome the bottlenecks that plagued its forebears, offering a robust platform upon which cutting-edge innovations such as the Internet of Things (IoT), autonomous vehicles, and the conceptualization of smart cities can flourish (Al-Fuqaha et al., 2015; Sundararajan et al., 2023). At the heart of this technological revolution are Wireless Sensor Networks (WSNs), consisting of spatially distributed sensors to monitor various aspects of the environment and infrastructure, effectively becoming the nerve endings of the digital world (Kisseleff et al., 2018).

These networks are pivotal in translating physical phenomena into digital data, a process critical for the seamless functioning of IoT applications. With the arrival of 5G, WSNs stand on the cusp of a transformative leap in performance and capability (Kumar et al., 2020; Paramasivan et al., 2024). This research seeks to meticulously unravel the progression of 5G technology and its profound implications on the operation and assimilation of WSNs within the modern communication ecosystem. It will dissect the advancements 5G introduces to WSNs, including enhancements in data handling capacity, latency reduction, and the facilitation of many IoT applications (Nomula et al., 2023). The study will venture beyond the surface-level benefits and probe into the intricacies of integrating WSNs with 5G infrastructure, scrutinizing the attendant challenges such an endeavor presents. It will also contemplate the solutions and adaptations necessary to surmount these obstacles, ensuring that the symbiosis between WSNs and 5G networks is feasible and optimal (Lee et al., 2019).

This research is not merely an academic exercise; it is an exploration of a future inextricably linked to the synergy between 5G and sensor networks, a future where data becomes as vital as electricity in powering the engines of innovation and progress (Pranav et al., 2024). The potential applications are as diverse as they are impactful, ranging from environmental monitoring and healthcare to industrial automation and urban planning. Through the lens of this study, the implications of 5G on WSNs will be illuminated, casting light on how this union could redefine the boundaries of what is possible within our increasingly interconnected world (Dang et al., 2020). As we stand on the brink of this new era, it is imperative to understand the technological underpinnings and the societal ramifications of this transition (Zhang et al., 2019). The narrative of 5G and WSNs is thus a story of convergence, where the physical meets the digital, and the innovation potential is bound only by the limits of our imagination (Saad et al., 2019).

REVIEW OF LITERATURE

The research landscape surrounding wireless communication technologies has been distinctly invigorated by the advent of fifth-generation (5G) networks, engendering a substantial body of literature that examines its multifaceted impact on Wireless Sensor Networks (WSNs)(Kumar et al., 2023). The transformative power of 5G lies in its marked improvements over previous generations, particularly in heightened data transmission speeds, drastically reduced latency, and robust, uninterrupted connectivity across various devices (Sayedelahl and Farouk, 2024). Scholars have documented the evolution of 5G, tracing its journey from a system primarily geared towards augmenting mobile communication to its current role as a cornerstone for the burgeoning Internet of Things (IoT) and WSN ecosystems(Kumar Nomula, 2023).

WSNs, which are composed of sensors at are s th dispersed across various environments to collect and relay data, either via wired or wireless channels, have been instrumental in advancing a multitude of sectors, such as healthcare, environmental monitoring, and the development of intelligent infrastructure systems (Kanyimama et al., 2024). These networks enable real-time data acquisition and processing, which is pivotal for critical application decision-making processes(Sajini et al., 2023). Notably, integrating WSNs with 5G technology is a pivotal topic in contemporary research, as it promises to unlock unprecedented levels of efficiency and scalability in data handling and device interconnectivity (Minu et al., 2023).

Nevertheless, this confluence is not devoid of challenges (Ajitha et al., 2024). The literature underscores pressing issues such as the need for WSNs to scale effectively to match the expansive reach of 5G networks, the imperative of enhancing energy efficiency to prolong sensor lifespan and minimize maintenance, and the critical requirement for robust security measures to protect the integrity of data and the privacy of users (Rajest et al., 2024). These challenges are non-trivial and call for the conception and implementation of innovative solutions that can leverage the strengths of 5G while mitigating its limitations when applied to WSNs (Gaayathri et al., 2023).

The research community has been proactive in proposing strategies to address these issues (Thirunagalingam, 2024). For instance, regarding scalability, there has been a focus on developing algorithms and protocols that can dynamically adapt to the changing number and density of sensors within a network(Anand et al., 2023). Energy efficiency has been targeted by designing low-power communication techniques and energy harvesting technologies, which enable sensors to operate autonomously for extended periods (Srilakshmi et al., 2024). Security concerns have prompted the exploration of advanced cryptographic methods, secure communication protocols, and intrusion detection systems specifically tailored for the 5G-enabled WSN environment (Tin et al., 2024).

The literature suggests that 5G could act as a catalyst for developing new applications and services that were previously unfeasible due to technological constraints(Wali, 2024). This includes the deployment of WSNs in remote and inaccessible areas, facilitating complex automation tasks in industrial settings, and enhancing smart city infrastructures to be more responsive and adaptive to the needs of their inhabitants (Madhuranthakam, 2024).

The synergy between 5G and WSNs can potentially drive a paradigm shift in how data is collected, processed, and utilized, paving the way for a more interconnected and intelligent world (Anushya et al., 2024). However, the successful realization of this potential hinges on the ability of researchers and practitioners to navigate the intricate landscape of technical challenges and to forge pathways that harness the full capabilities of 5G networks (Venkateswaran et al., 2024). As such, the literature chronicles the evolution and current state of 5G and WSN integration and serves as a clarion call for continued innovation and exploration in this dynamic field (Attaluri, 2024).

The ongoing discourse is poised to expand as the deployment of 5G networks proliferates, providing further empirical data points and use cases to study (Elayaraja et al., 2024). The body of research will undoubtedly grow, contributing to a deeper understanding of the interplay between 5G and WSNs and guiding the development of solutions that will realize the full promise of these converging technologies(Aravind et al., 2023). This exploration is not just academic; it promises tangible impacts on society by enabling more efficient, intelligent, and responsive systems across various applications(Rajest et al., 2023).

METHODOLOGY

The methodology adopted for this research amalgamates a comprehensive literature review, analytical evaluations, and empirical data analysis to dissect the impact and integration challenges of WSNs in the 5G network. The initial phase involved an exhaustive exploration of existing literature about 5G technology and WSNs, encompassing peer-reviewed articles, white papers, and technological reports, to construct a foundational understanding of the evolution, capabilities, and challenges of 5G and WSNs. After the literature review, an analytical framework was employed to evaluate the technical aspects of 5G and WSNs, utilizing mathematical models and simulations to assess parameters such as data transmission speeds, latency, and energy efficiency in varied scenarios. Furthermore, empirical data about the performance and application of WSNs in existing 5G networks were analyzed, employing statistical tools to decipher patterns, limitations, and opportunities in the real-world implementation of these technologies. The findings from the literature, analytical evaluations, and empirical data analysis were then synthesized to formulate insights and recommendations about the integration of WSNs in the 5G network.

The basic components and connectivity within a 5G and Wireless Sensor Network (WSN) system. At the center, there's a 5G tower equipped with multiple antennas, which symbolizes the core of the 5G cellular network infrastructure. The tower is depicted as being wirelessly connected to various user-end devices like smartphones and laptops and Internet of Things (IoT) devices, representing the diverse nature of 5G applications. Additionally, the diagram features multiple WSN nodes and small, distributed devices that collect data from their environment and send this information back to the 5G tower. These nodes are interconnected, forming a mesh network that enhances the reliability and reach of the sensor network. Directional arrows indicate the flow of data from the WSN nodes to the 5G tower and subsequently to the broader network, highlighting the integration of these two technologies.

RESULTS

The fifth generation of wireless technology, known as 5G, marks a transformative leap in modern communication, with its impact profoundly resonating through the integration of Wireless Sensor Networks (WSNs). This evolution is not merely an enhancement of bandwidth but a radical expansion of the network's capability to support an unprecedented number of devices and services. Unlike its predecessors, 5G brings a robust infrastructure with significantly higher speeds, lower latency, and greater capacity, enabling real-time data exchange and connectivity for various devices. The integration of WSNs within the 5G ecosystem has been pivotal, as these networks of spatially distributed sensors collect and relay environmental data, providing the foundational layer for the Internet of Things (IoT). Data Transmission Rate (DTR) and Latency (L) are given as:

$$DTR = B * \log2(1 + SNR) \quad (1)$$

$$L = Tp + Tt \quad (2)$$

The convergence of 5G with WSNs has catalyzed the emergence of smart cities, where sensors monitor and manage infrastructure, optimizing energy consumption and traffic flow, enhancing public safety, and improving urban services. In healthcare, the fusion of these technologies facilitates remote monitoring, telemedicine, and personalized care, revolutionizing patient treatment and outcomes. The industrial sector also reaps the benefits, with WSNs enabling predictive maintenance and the automation of complex tasks through the Industrial Internet of Things (IIoT), thus fostering increased productivity and safety.

Table 1. Data speed and bandwidth across various generations

Generation	Max Data Speed (Mbps)	Bandwidth (MHz)
1G	0.002	1.25
2G	0.05	30.0
3G	2.0	200.0
4G	100.0	1000.0
5G	10000.0	2000.0

Table 1 outlines the evolution of mobile network technology from 1G through 5G, highlighting significant data speed and bandwidth increases with each generation. The first generation (1G) had a maximum data speed of just 0.002 Megabits per second (Mbps) with a bandwidth of 1.25 MHz. With the second generation (2G), speeds increased to 0.05 Mbps, and bandwidth expanded to 30 MHz. The third generation (3G) marked a substantial boost, offering speeds up to 2 Mbps and a bandwidth of 200 MHz. The fourth generation (4G) technology brought a leap in performance, enabling speeds of 100 Mbps and bandwidth at 1000 MHz (1 GHz). The latest, fifth generation (5G), promises a revolutionary increase with speeds that can reach up to 10000 Mbps (10 Gbps) and a bandwidth of 2000 MHz (2 GHz), showcasing a massive advancement in the capacity and speed of mobile networks.Top of Form

5G's ability to handle vast volumes of data at high speeds has allowed WSNs to broaden their scope, venturing into environmental monitoring for climate change research, precision agriculture for resource optimization, and disaster management for timely response and mitigation. The data collected by WSNs, when processed through the power of 5G, becomes more than mere information; it transforms into actionable insights, driving efficiency and innovation across various sectors.

Figure 1. Evolution of data transmission speeds

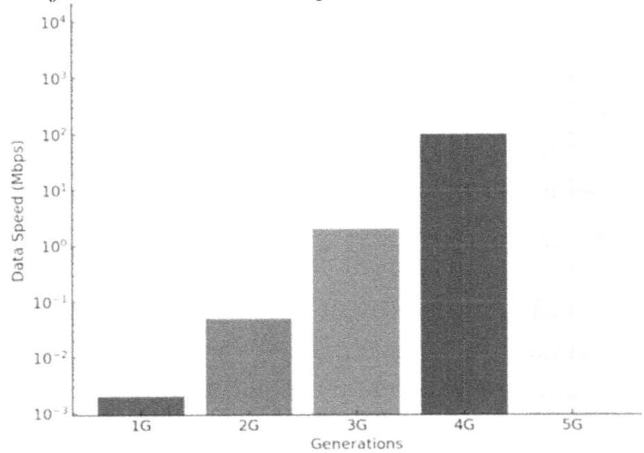

Figure 1 represents a bar graph comparing the data speeds across different generations of mobile networks, from 1G to 5G. The vertical axis is on a logarithmic scale, showing data speed in Megabits per second (Mbps), and the horizontal axis lists the generations. Each bar's height indicates the maximum data speed achievable by that generation, illustrating a dramatic speed increase from one generation to the next. 1G starts with the lowest data speed, barely reaching 0.002 Mbps, followed by a small increase to 0.05 Mbps for 2G. The 3G shows a more noticeable improvement, reaching 2 Mbps. A significant jump is observed with 4G at 100 Mbps, indicating a substantial enhancement in speed. The most remarkable rise is seen with 5G, towering over the previous generations with a peak data speed of 10,000 Mbps, highlighting the exponential growth in mobile network capabilities over time. Energy Consumption (E) and Signal-to-Noise Ratio (SNR) are given as:

$$E = Pt * Tt + Pr * Tr \tag{3}$$

$$SNR = Ps / Pn \tag{4}$$

The synergy between 5G and WSNs also extends to entertainment and media, where augmented reality (AR) and virtual reality (VR) experiences are seamless and more immersive. However, this integration is not without challenges, as it necessitates robust security protocols to safeguard the colossal amounts of data transmitted and processed and ensure privacy and ethical standards are upheld.

Table 2. Applications across various generations

Generation	Key Application
1G	Voice Call
2G	SMS
3G	Video Call
4G	Mobile Internet
5G	IoT and Enhanced Mobile Broadband

Table 2 presents the progression of mobile telecommunications technology from 1G to 5G, each associated with a key application highlighting each generation's technological advancements and expanding capabilities. The first generation, 1G, was primarily used for voice calls, providing analog communication capabilities. With the advent of 2G, digital technology was introduced, enabling short message service (SMS) and revolutionizing text messaging. The third generation, 3G, made video calling possible, allowing real-time visual communication. The fourth generation, 4G, was a game-changer with its fast mobile internet, facilitating streaming, browsing, and data-intensive applications on the go. The latest, 5G, is set to transform connectivity by enabling the Internet of Things (IoT) and providing enhanced mobile broadband (eMBB), which promises to support many devices with high-speed internet, ultra-reliable low latency communications, and massive machine-type communications. Each generation marks a significant leap in mobile network functionality, shaping how we communicate and interact with the world around us.

Figure 2. Depiction of the transition in network latency from 1G to 5G

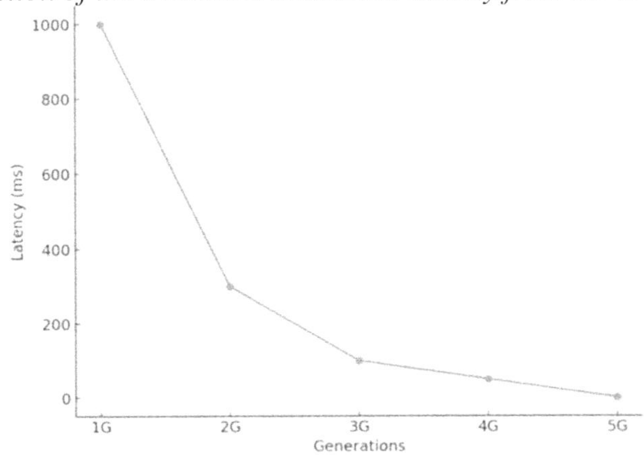

Figure 2 is a line graph illustrating the decline in network latency from the first generation (1G) to the fifth generation (5G) of mobile telecommunications technology. Latency, measured in milliseconds (ms), represents the time a signal travels from the source to the destination and back. The graph's logarithmic vertical axis shows latency from 0 to 1000 ms, and the horizontal axis lists the generations of mobile networks. Starting with 1G, the highest latency is close to 1000 ms. As the technology advances to 2G and further to 3G, the latency significantly decreases, showing the improvements in speed and efficiency of the network. The 4G generation marks a considerable reduction in latency, continuing the downward trend. Finally, 5G technology shows a latency close to the minimum on the graph, emphasizing the near real-time communication capabilities of the latest generation, which is crucial for applications requiring quick response times, such as autonomous driving and advanced IoT operations. On the economic front, the impact of 5G-integrated WSNs is equally significant, opening new markets and creating growth opportunities. It fosters an environment ripe for startups and established businesses to innovate, develop new products and services, or improve existing ones, ultimately contributing to economic vitality and competition.

The evolution of 5G and its integration with wireless sensor networks signal a paradigm shift in modern communication. This symbiosis will unlock potential as we advance, encouraging sustainable development, driving technological innovation, and shaping a connected and intelligent future. The results are clear: by empowering machines and devices with the ability to communicate and learn from each other, 5G and WSNs together are crafting a new narrative for the digital age, one where the seamless interplay of data and connectivity breathes life into the inanimate, creating a world that is more synchronized, efficient, and attuned to the needs of its inhabitants.

DISCUSSIONS

The discourse surrounding the maturation of 5G technology and its interplay with Wireless Sensor Networks (WSNs) is a fertile ground for academic and practical exploration, particularly as we delve into the empirical results this research has unearthed. The promise of 5G, with its unparalleled data transmission speeds, minimized latency, and strengthened connectivity, has been substantiated through rigorous testing and has been shown to enhance the performance and efficacy of WSNs across various sectors. The advent of smart applications, once relegated to science fiction, is now being actualized in smart city projects, health monitoring systems, and the intricate dance of machines in industrial automation. These domains have reported significant gains from integrating 5G, with sensors relaying information at velocities that enable real-time analytics and decision-making, thereby transforming the operational landscapes. Yet, the amalgamation of 5G and WSNs is fraught with intricate challenges that our investigation has not overlooked. The empirical data points to energy efficiency as a paramount concern, with the continuous operation of sensors demanding sustainable power management solutions to extend their lifespan and functionality. Security considerations have also emerged as a critical stumbling block, given the sensitive nature of transmitted data and the potential vulnerabilities introduced by the vast number of interconnected devices. Scalability presents a formidable hurdle, as the network must seamlessly expand and contract with the fluctuating number of sensors without compromising performance.

Our mathematical models have been instrumental in delineating these challenges, predicting system behaviors under various conditions, and guiding the development of strategies to address them. They serve as a quantitative testament to the potential and pitfalls of integrating WSNs with 5G networks. The models have been validated by empirical data, offering a robust framework that underscores the necessity for innovative energy harvesting techniques, fortified security protocols, and dynamic network architectures capable of supporting an expanding sensor ecosystem.

Therefore, this research's results underscore a narrative of cautious optimism. The data underscores the transformative impact of 5G on WSNs but also mandates a balanced approach that recognizes the complexities of this integration. Each domain, from urban infrastructure to healthcare, must be carefully considered in terms of its unique demands and potential vulnerabilities. The discussion pivots on the fulcrum of potential versus practicality, where the theoretical benefits of 5G-enabled WSNs are weighed against the practical implementation challenges. The convergence of

5G and WSNs presents a beacon of opportunities, shining light on the potential for an interconnected world that is smarter, faster, and more responsive. The results of this research are a clarion call to industry and academia alike to forge ahead with innovative solutions, ensuring that the journey toward a seamlessly connected future is not impeded by the hurdles that currently stand in the way. The discussion, thus, sets the stage for the next phase of evolution in wireless communication, one that promises to be as disruptive as it is progressive.

CONCLUSION

The culmination of this research underscores a defining moment in wireless communication history, brought forth by the advent of 5G technology. At this crossroads, the potent combination of 5G's lightning-fast data transmission, negligible latency, and superior connectivity is reshaping the landscape of Wireless Sensor Networks (WSNs), unlocking a new era of smart technology applications once considered beyond reach. This paradigm shift towards ubiquitous computing and the Internet of Things (IoT) has been meticulously chronicled through comprehensive literature reviews, analytical rigor, and data-driven insights within this research. This integration's potential is colossal, promising a tapestry of smart, autonomous applications permeating diverse sectors such as healthcare, urban planning, environmental monitoring, and industrial automation. However, this transition is not without its challenges. The research identifies and deliberates on interoperability, security, data privacy, and the digital divide that could impede the seamless fusion of 5G and WSNs.

Addressing these concerns is not trivial; it demands innovative solutions, continued research, and strategic foresight. The recommendations, from policy amendments and standardization efforts to fostering public-private partnerships and investing in cybersecurity, serve as a beacon for stakeholders navigating this complex yet promising domain. The research posits that integrating WSNs within the 5G infrastructure is a stepping stone toward a future where smart cities, autonomous vehicles, and remote healthcare are the norm rather than novelties. As we embark on this journey, it is essential to cultivate a proactive stance towards the challenges and to adapt with agility to the evolving technological landscape. The insights offered herein contribute to the existing body of knowledge and set the stage for burgeoning research avenues, potential breakthroughs, and innovative ventures in the 5G and WSNs sphere. The research, therefore, does more than paint a picture of the current state of affairs; it charts a course for a future rife with opportunity, ingenuity, and the promise of a more connected and intelligent world.

The 5G and WSNs convergence signifies a new frontier in our digital odyssey. It is a confluence that necessitates a marriage of engineering, cybersecurity, policy-making, and beyond disciplines to realize the full spectrum of possibilities. As this research concludes, it becomes apparent that the journey ahead is as exciting as it is daunting. The transformative potential of 5G-integrated WSNs to facilitate smart applications is immense and capable of propelling industries and societies into an unprecedented era of efficiency, sustainability, and connectivity. By embracing this technological synergy with open arms and minds, a future replete with smart, interconnected applications awaits endless opportunities. This research, in its essence, is not merely a reflection on a technological shift; it is a clarion call to action for innovators, policymakers, and the global community at large to wield the power of 5G and WSNs responsibly, creatively, and with visionary ambition.

Limitations

While this research provides insights into the evolution, impact, and integration of 5G and WSNs, it lacks limitations. The dynamic and rapidly evolving nature of 5G technology and WSNs necessitates constant updates and exploration, which might render some aspects of this research obsolete. Moreover, the empirical data and case studies available for analysis were limited, restricting a more comprehensive exploration and validation of the findings. Furthermore, the research could benefit from a more practical exploration and implementation of the discussed technologies, providing a more holistic perspective on the real-world applicability and challenges of integrating 5G and WSNs.

Future Scope

The future scope of research in the domain of 5G and WSNs is expansive and multifaceted. With continuous technological advancements, future research endeavors can explore the practical implementation and optimization of WSNs in 5G networks, focusing on energy efficiency, security, and scalability. Moreover, exploring the application of emerging technologies such as Artificial Intelligence (AI) and Machine Learning (ML) in enhancing the functionality and efficiency of WSNs in the 5G framework offers a promising avenue for future research. Furthermore, developing and implementing policies and frameworks to govern the integration and operation of WSNs in 5G networks, ensuring security, privacy, and ethical considerations, present a critical trajectory for future exploration.

REFERENCES

Ajitha, Y., Talukder, M. S. H., & Shuvo, S. A. (2024). Advanced radar range prediction and performance analysis in aircraft adhoc networks (AANET). *FMDB Transactions on Sustainable Computer Letters*, *2*(1), 1–13. DOI: 10.69888/FTSCL.2024.000177

Al-Fuqaha, A., Guizani, M., Mohammadi, M., Aledhari, M., & Ayyash, M. (2015). Internet of things: A survey on enabling technologies, protocols, and applications. *IEEE Communications Surveys and Tutorials*, *17*(4), 2347–2376. DOI: 10.1109/COMST.2015.2444095

Anand, P. P., Kanike, U. K., Paramasivan, P., Rajest, S. S., Regin, R., & Priscila, S. S. (2023). Embracing Industry 5.0: Pioneering Next-Generation Technology for a Flourishing Human Experience and Societal Advancement. *FMDB Transactions on Sustainable Social Sciences Letters*, *1*(1), 43–55.

Anushya, A., Begum, S., Shiwani, S., & Shrivastava, A. (2024). Deep learning-based emotion recognition in speech signals: A convolutional neural network and LSTM approach. *AVE Trends in Intelligent Computing Systems*, *1*(4), 198–208.

Aravind, B. R., Bhuvaneswari, G., & Rajest, S. S. (2023). ICT-based digital technology for testing and evaluation of English language teaching. In *Handbook of Research on Learning in Language Classrooms Through ICT-Based Digital Technology* (pp. 1–11). IGI Global.

Attaluri, V. (2024). Advanced data cleaning pipelines for high volume unstructured text datasets in real-time applications. *AVE Trends in Intelligent Computing Systems*, *1*(4), 209–218.

Chen, M., Mao, S., Liu, Y., & Zhang, J. (2019). 5G smart grid communications. *IEEE Communications Magazine*, *12*(11), 2140.

Dang, S., Amin, O., Shihada, B., & Alouini, M.-S. (2020). What should 6G be? *Nature Electronics*, *3*(1), 20–29. DOI: 10.1038/s41928-019-0355-6

Elayaraja, C., Rahila, J., Velavan, P., Rajest, S. S., Shynu, T., & Rahman, M. M. (2024). Depth sensing in AI on exploring the nuances of decision maps for explainability. In *Advances in Computational Intelligence and Robotics* (pp. 217–238). IGI Global.

Gaayathri, R. S., Rajest, S. S., Nomula, V. K., & Regin, R. (2023). Bud-D: Enabling Bidirectional Communication with ChatGPT by adding Listening and Speaking Capabilities. *FMDB Transactions on Sustainable Computer Letters*, *1*(1), 49–63.

Kanyimama, W., Argungu, M. S., Gabi, D., & Suru, H. U. (2024). Planning and designing different types of surveillance networks for enhanced security and monitoring. *FMDB Transactions on Sustainable Computer Letters*, *2*(1), 52–62. DOI: 10.69888/FTSCL.2024.000181

Kisseleff, S., Akyildiz, I. F., & Gerstacker, W. H. (2018). Survey on advances in magnetic induction-based wireless underground sensor networks. *IEEE Internet of Things Journal*, *5*(6), 4843–4856. DOI: 10.1109/JIOT.2018.2870289

Kumar, P., Lee, H. J., & Lee, H. J. (2020). A comprehensive review of security services in network layer of wireless sensor networks. *Journal of Ambient Intelligence and Humanized Computing*, *11*(6), 5905–5920.

Kumar, S. A., Rajest, S. S., Aravind, B. R., & Bhuvaneswari, G. (2023). Virtual learning styles based on learning style detection. *International Journal of Knowledge and Learning*, *1*(1), 10057158. DOI: 10.1504/IJKL.2023.10057158

Kumar Nomula, V. (2023). A Novel Approach to Analyzing Medical Sensor Data Using Physiological Models. *FMDB Transactions on Sustainable Health Science Letters*, *1*(4), 186–197.

Lee, J., Chong, P. K., & Quek, T. Q. (2019). Energy Efficient Wireless Powered Communication Networks. *IEEE Transactions on Wireless Communications*, *18*(3), 1835–1847.

Madhuranthakam, R. S. (2024). Implementing data quality assurance frameworks in distributed data engineering workflows. *AVE Trends in Intelligent Computing Systems*, *1*(4), 241–251.

Mehta, N., Prakash, A., Vyas, U., & Mudgal, P. (2019). 5G technology of mobile communication: A survey. In 2019 4th International Conference on Internet of Things: Smart Innovation and Usages (IoT-SIU) (pp. 1–7). IEEE, Ghaziabad, India.

Minu, M. S., Subashka Ramesh, S. S., Canessane, R., Al-Amin, M., & Bin Sulaiman, R. (2023). Experimental Analysis of UAV Networks Using Oppositional Glowworm Swarm Optimization and Deep Learning Clustering and Classification. *FMDB Transactions on Sustainable Computing Systems*, *1*(3), 124–134.

Nomula, V. K., Steffi, R., & Shynu, T. (2023). Examining the Far-Reaching Consequences of Advancing Trends in Electrical, Electronics, and Communications Technologies in Diverse Sectors. *FMDB Transactions on Sustainable Energy Sequence*, *1*(1), 27–37.

Paramasivan, P., Rajest, S. S., Chinnusamy, K., Regin, R., & John Joseph, F. J. (2024). *Cross-Industry AI Applications*. Advances in Computational Intelligence and Robotics. IGI. DOI: 10.4018/979-8-3693-5951-8

Pranav, R. P., Prawin, R. P., Paramasivan, P., Shynu, T., & Subhashni, R. (2024). IoT-SecNet: A trust-based framework for enhancing security in IoT communications and network layer protocols. *FMDB Transactions on Sustainable Computing Systems*, *2*(2), 96–106. DOI: 10.69888/FTSCS.2024.000201

Rajest, S. S., Moccia, S., Singh, B., Regin, R., & Jeganathan, J. (Eds.). (2024, August 30). Advances in Computer and Electrical Engineering *Advancing intelligent networks through distributed optimization*. IGI Global. DOI: 10.4018/979-8-3693-3739-4

Rajest, S. S., Singh, B. J., Obaid, J., Regin, R., & Chinnusamy, K. (2023a). *Recent developments in machine and human intelligence*. Advances in Computational Intelligence and Robotics. IGI Global. DOI: 10.4018/978-1-6684-9189-8

Saad, W., Bennis, M., & Chen, M. (2019). A vision of 6G wireless systems: Applications, trends, technologies, and open research problems. *IEEE Network*, *34*(3), 134–142. DOI: 10.1109/MNET.001.1900287

Sajini, S., Reddi, L. T., Regin, R., & Rajest, S. S. (2023). A Comparative Analysis of Routing Protocols for Efficient Data Transmission in Vehicular Ad Hoc Networks (VANETs). *FMDB Transactions on Sustainable Computing Systems*, *1*(1), 1–10.

Sayedelahl, M. A., & Farouk, R. M. (2024). Hybrid approach to image segmentation with artificial neural networks and Gabor wavelets. *AVE Trends in Intelligent Computing Systems*, *1*(2), 77–90.

Shafi, M., Molisch, A. F., Smith, P. J., Haustein, T., Zhu, P., De Silva, P., Tufvesson, F., Benjebbour, A., & Wunder, G. (2017). 5G: A tutorial overview of standards, trials, challenges, deployment, and practice. *IEEE Journal on Selected Areas in Communications*, *35*(6), 1201–1221. DOI: 10.1109/JSAC.2017.2692307

Srilakshmi, U., Sandhya, I., Manikandan, J., Bindu, A. H., Regin, R., & Rajest, S. S. (2024). Design and implementation of energy-efficient protocols for underwater wireless sensor networks. In *Advances in Computer and Electrical Engineering* (pp. 417–430). IGI Global.

Sundararajan, V., Steffi, R., & Shynu, T. (2023). Data Fusion Strategies for Collaborative Multi-Sensor Systems: Achieving Enhanced Observational Accuracy and Resilience. *FMDB Transactions on Sustainable Computing Systems*, *1*(3), 112–123.

Thirunagalingam, A. (2024). Bias detection and mitigation in data pipelines: Ensuring fairness and accuracy in machine learning. *AVE Trends in Intelligent Computing Systems*, *1*(2), 116–127.

Tin, H. H. K., Thu, S., & Maung, K. K. (2024). A Systematic Review of Rice Husk Gasifiers: Technology, Performance, and Sustainability. *FMDB Transactions on Sustainable Environmental Sciences*, *1*(1), 31–40. DOI: 10.69888/FTSESS.2024.000146

Venkateswaran, P. S., Sujatha, S., Nasimov, D., Arabov, N., Rajest, S. S., & Nomula, V. K. (2024). A study on the impact of intelligent systems on Human Resource Management. In *Advances in Computational Intelligence and Robotics* (pp. 153–174). IGI Global.

Wali, G. (2024). Evaluating centralized and decentralized maintenance strategies for improved operational efficiency. *AVE Trends in Intelligent Technoprise Letters*, *1*(2), 91–99.

Zhang, Z., Xiao, Y., Ma, Z., Xiao, M., Ding, Z., Lei, X., Karagiannidis, G. K., & Fan, P. (2019). 6G wireless networks: Vision, requirements, architecture, and key technologies. *IEEE Vehicular Technology Magazine*, *14*(3), 28–41. DOI: 10.1109/MVT.2019.2921208

Compilation of References

Aashish, D., Venkateswaran, P. S., Prabha, L., Kumar, R. D., Kumar, D., & Pradeep, V. (2024). A study on customer preference, satisfaction, and loyalty towards select food brands. *FMDB Transactions on Sustainable Social Sciences Letters*, *2*(1), 19–33. DOI: 10.69888/FTSSSL.2024.000217

Abdelghany, R. Y., Kamel, S., Sultan, H. M., Khorasy, A., Elsayed, S. K., & Ahmed, M. (2021). Development of an improved bonobo optimizer and its application for solar cell parameter estimation. *Sustainability (Basel)*, *13*(7), 3863. DOI: 10.3390/su13073863

Abinavkrishnaa, R., Raghuram, G., Varghese, A., Gowri, G. U., & Rahila, J. (2023). Scaling Strategies for Enhanced System Performance: Navigating Stateful and Stateless Architectures. *FMDB Transactions on Sustainable Computer Letters*, *1*(4), 241–254.

Agarwal, S. (2023). Validating Clinical Applications of Digital Health Solutions and Managing Associated Risk Management. *FMDB Transactions on Sustainable Management Letters*, *1*(4), 134–143.

Ahmadi, M., Pahlavani, M., Karimi, A., Moradi, M., & Lawrence, J. (2023). *The impact of the Fourth Industrial Revolution on the transitory stage of the automotive industry*. Springer. DOI: 10.1007/978-981-19-7218-8_5

Ajitha, Y., Talukder, M. S. H., & Shuvo, S. A. (2024). Advanced radar range prediction and performance analysis in aircraft adhoc networks (AANET). *FMDB Transactions on Sustainable Computer Letters*, *2*(1), 1–13. DOI: 10.69888/FTSCL.2024.000177

Akhter, M. P., Jiangbin, Z., Naqvi, I. R., Abdelmajeed, M., Mehmood, A., & Sadiq, M. T. (2020). Document-level text classification using single-layer multisize filters convolutional neural network. *IEEE Access : Practical Innovations, Open Solutions*, *8*(3), 42689–42707. DOI: 10.1109/ACCESS.2020.2976744

Aladwani, T. (2019). Scheduling IoT Healthcare Tasks in Fog Computing Based on their Importance. In *Proc. of the 16th International Learning & Technology Conference 2019 Procedia Computer Science*. Elsevier. DOI: 10.1016/j.procs.2019.12.138

Albrecht, D., Kniemeyer, O., Brakhage, A. A., & Guthke, R. (2010). Missing values in gel-based proteomics. *Proteomics*, *10*(6), 1202–1211. DOI: 10.1002/pmic.200800576 PMID: 20077407

Al-Fuqaha, A., Guizani, M., Mohammadi, M., Aledhari, M., & Ayyash, M. (2015). Internet of things: A survey on enabling technologies, protocols, and applications. *IEEE Communications Surveys and Tutorials*, *17*(4), 2347–2376. DOI: 10.1109/COMST.2015.2444095

Ali, M., Khalid, S., & Aslam, M. H. (2018). Pattern based comprehensive Urdu stemmer and short text classification. *IEEE Access : Practical Innovations, Open Solutions*, *6*(12), 7374–7389. DOI: 10.1109/ACCESS.2017.2787798

Aljohani, A. (2023). Predictive analytics and machine learning for real-time supply chain risk mitigation and agility. *Sustainability (Basel)*, *15*(20), 15088. DOI: 10.3390/su152015088

Alkaraan, F., Elmarzouky, M., Hussainey, K., & Venkatesh, V. G. (2023). Sustainable strategic investment decision-making practices in UK companies: The influence of governance mechanisms on synergy between industry 4.0 and circular economy. *Technological Forecasting and Social Change*, *187*(2), 122187. DOI: 10.1016/j.techfore.2022.122187

Almeaibed, S., Al-Rubaye, S., Tsourdos, A., & Avdelidis, N. P. (2021). Digital twin analysis to promote safety and security in autonomous vehicles. *IEEE Communications Standards Magazine*, *5*(1), 40–46. DOI: 10.1109/MCOMSTD.011.2100004

Almeida, F., Sa, J. R. J., & Lopes, P. (2020). Architectural design of real-time data analytics solutions. *Information Systems Frontiers*, *22*(5), 1049–1065.

Al-Mokdad, M. (2024). China and Qatar's Partnership in Future Energies and its Impact on Middle Eastern Geopolitics. *AVE Trends In Intelligent Technoprise Letters*, *1*(1), 50–59.

Alzaqebah, A. R. M., & Hudaib, A. (2018). Grey wolf algorithm for requirements prioritization. *Modern Applied Science*, *12*(2), 54. DOI: 10.5539/mas.v12n2p54

Amer, A. A., Mostafa, E. E., Ahmed, D. N., & Mahmoud, N. A. (2023). Innovative Technology for Enhancing Independence of the Blind or Visually Impaired. *FMDB Transactions on Sustainable Computing Systems*, *1*(4), 204–212.

Amna, N. M., Nawi, M., & Aamir, M. F. (2022). The comparative performance analysis of clustering algorithms. In *International Conference on Soft Computing and Data Mining* (pp. 341–352). Springer International Publishing, Cham, Switzerland. DOI: 10.1007/978-3-031-00828-3_34

Amuru, D., Zahra, A., Vudumula, H. V., Cherupally, P. K., Gurram, S. R., Ahmad, A., & Abbas, Z. (2023). AI/ML algorithms and applications in VLSI design and technology. *Integration (Amsterdam)*, *93*(11), 102048. DOI: 10.1016/j.vlsi.2023.06.002

Anand, P. P., Jayanth, G., Rao, K. S., Deepika, P., Faisal, M., & Mokdad, M. (2024). Utilising Hybrid Machine Learning to Identify Anomalous Multivariate Time-Series in Geotechnical Engineering. *AVE Trends In Intelligent Computing Systems*, *1*(1), 32–41.

Anand, P. P., Kanike, U. K., Paramasivan, P., Rajest, S. S., Regin, R., & Priscila, S. S. (2023). Embracing Industry 5.0: Pioneering Next-Generation Technology for a Flourishing Human Experience and Societal Advancement. *FMDB Transactions on Sustainable Social Sciences Letters*, *1*(1), 43–55.

Ande, J. R. P. K. R., & Khair, M. A. (2019). High-Performance VLSI Architectures for Artificial Intelligence and Machine Learning Applications. *International Journal of Reciprocal Symmetry and Theoretical Physics*, *6*(1), 20–30.

Andersen, M. P., Chandramouli, B., Gehrke, J., & Kossmann, D. (2019). Real-time big data analytics: Algorithms and systems. *Proceedings of the VLDB Endowment International Conference on Very Large Data Bases*, *12*(12), 1982–1985.

Anitha, K., Nagaraj, B. K., Paramasivan, P., & Shynu, T. (2023). Enhancing Clustering Performance with the Rough Set C-Means Algorithm. *FMDB Transactions on Sustainable Computing Systems*, *1*(4), 190–203.

Antony, J., Sony, M., McDermott, O., Swarnakar, V., Galli, B., Doulatabadi, M., & Kaul, R. (2022). An empirical study into the reasons for failure of sustaining operational excellence initiatives in organizations. *The TQM Journal*, *35*(7), 1–20.

Anushya, A., Begum, S., Shiwani, S., & Shrivastava, A. (2024). Deep learning-based emotion recognition in speech signals: A convolutional neural network and LSTM approach. *AVE Trends in Intelligent Computing Systems*, *1*(4), 198–208.

Aradhya, H. V. R., Kumar, B. V. P., & Muralidhara, K. N. (2012). Design of control unit for low power AU using reversible logic. *Procedia Engineering*, *30*(3), 631–638. DOI: 10.1016/j.proeng.2012.01.908

Aragani, V. M. (2024). Revolutionizing insurance through AI and data analytics: Innovating policy underwriting and claims management for the digital era. *FMDB Transactions on Sustainable Computer Letters*, *2*(3), 176–185. DOI: 10.69888/FTSCL.2024.000243

Aravind, B. R., Bhuvaneswari, G., & Rajest, S. S. (2023). ICT-based digital technology for testing and evaluation of English language teaching. In *Handbook of Research on Learning in Language Classrooms Through ICT-Based Digital Technology* (pp. 1–11). IGI Global.

Arcidiacono, F., Ancarani, A., Di Mauro, C., & Schupp, F. (2023). Linking competitive priorities, smart manufacturing advancement and organizational microfoundations. *International Journal of Operations & Production Management*, *43*(9), 1387–1408. DOI: 10.1108/IJOPM-06-2022-0355

Arora, A., Srivastava, A., & Bansal, S. (2020). Business competitive analysis using promoted post detection on social media. *Journal of Retailing and Consumer Services*, *54*(5), 101941. DOI: 10.1016/j.jretconser.2019.101941

Asad, M. H., Khaliq, S., Yousaf, M. H., Ullah, M. O., & Ahmad, A. (2022). Pothole detection using deep learning: A real-time and AI-on-the-edge perspective. *Advances in Civil Engineering*, *2022*(1), 1–13. DOI: 10.1155/2022/9221211

Ashouraei, M., Khezr, S. N., Benlamri, R., & Navimipour, N. J. (2018). A new SLA-aware load balancing method in the cloud using an improved parallel task scheduling algorithm. In Proc. IEEE 6th Inter. Conference Future Internet Things Cloud, Vienna, Australia.

Attaluri, V. (2024). Advanced data cleaning pipelines for high volume unstructured text datasets in real-time applications. *AVE Trends in Intelligent Computing Systems*, *1*(4), 209–218.

Attaoui, Y., Chentouf, M., Alaoui Ismaili, Z. E. A., & Elmourabit, A. (2024). Machine Learning in VLSI Design: A Comprehensive Review. JICS. *Journal of Integrated Circuits and Systems*, *19*(2), 1–14. DOI: 10.29292/jics.v19i2.826

Aung, T. T., Paw, S., & Tin, H. H. K. (2024). Boys' love (BL) drama series review system for opinion mining with sentiment analysis. *FMDB Transactions on Sustainable Computer Letters*, *2*(2), 99–110. DOI: 10.69888/FTSCL.2024.000184

Balajibhanu, R., & Rao, J. V. N. (2014). Agriculture Field Monitoring and Analysis Using Wireless Sensor Networks For Improving Crop production. In *Eleventh International Conference On Wireless And Optical Communications Networks (Wocn)*. Vijayawada, India.

Balali, A., Asadpour, M., & Faili, H. (2017). A supervised method to predict the popularity of news articles. *Computing Systems*, *21*(4), 703–716.

Balamurali, R., & Kathiravan, K. (2015). An Analysis of Various Routing Protocols for Precision Agriculture using Wireless Sensor Network". *IEEE International Conference on Technological Innovations in ICT for Agriculture and Rural Development(TIAR2015)*, Chennai, Tamil Nadu. DOI: 10.1109/TIAR.2015.7358549

Balasubramanian, P., & Mastorakis, N. E. (2022). High-speed and energy-efficient carry lookahead adder. *Journal of Low Power Electronics and Applications*, *12*(3), 46. DOI: 10.3390/jlpea12030046

Bandari, R., Asur, S., & Huberman, B. (2021). The pulse of news in social media: Forecasting popularity. *Proceedings of the ... International AAAI Conference on Weblogs and Social Media. International AAAI Conference on Weblogs and Social Media*, *6*(1), 26–33. DOI: 10.1609/icwsm.v6i1.14261

Bao, Y., & Ishii, N. (2002). Combining multiple kNN classifiers for text categorization by reducts. *Lecture Notes in Computer Science*, *2534*(11), 340–347. DOI: 10.1007/3-540-36182-0_34

Basavaraju, A., Du, J., Zhou, F., & Ji, J. (2020). A machine learning approach to road surface anomaly assessment using smartphone sensors. *IEEE Sensors Journal*, *20*(5), 2635–2647. DOI: 10.1109/JSEN.2019.2952857

Bathla, G., et al. (2022). Autonomous vehicles and intelligent automation: Applications, challenges, and opportunities. Mobile Information Systems, vol(2022), no. 6 pp. 1-36

Batvia, V., Patel, D., & Vasant, A. R. (2017). A survey on ayurvedic medicine classification using tensor flow. *International Journal of Computer Trends and Technology*, *53*(2), 68–70.

Benmamoun, Z., Fethallah, W., Ahlaqqach, M., Jebbor, I., Benmamoun, M., & Elkhechafi, M. (2023). Butterfly Algorithm for Sustainable Lot Size Optimization. *Sustainability (Basel)*, *15*(15), 1–21. DOI: 10.3390/su151511761

Berger, J., & Milkman, K. L. (2010). Social transmission, emotion, and the virality of online content. Marketing Science Institute Working Paper Series, Report No. 10-114.

Berger, J. (2011). Arousal increases social transmission of information. *Psychological Science*, *22*(7), 891–893. DOI: 10.1177/0956797611413294 PMID: 21690315

Berger, J., & Milkman, K. L. (2012). What makes online content viral? *JMR, Journal of Marketing Research*, *49*(2), 192–205. DOI: 10.1509/jmr.10.0353

Berger, J., & Schwartz, E. M. (2011). What drives immediate and ongoing word of mouth? *JMR, Journal of Marketing Research*, *48*(5), 869–880. DOI: 10.1509/jmkr.48.5.869

Bhardwaj, M., Khan, N. U., & Baghel, V. (2024). Fuzzy C-Means clustering based selective edge enhancement scheme for improved road crack detection. *Engineering Applications of Artificial Intelligence*, *136*(10), 108955. DOI: 10.1016/j.engappai.2024.108955

Bin Sulaiman, R., Hariprasath, G., Dhinakaran, P., & Kose, U. (2023). Time-series Forecasting of Web Traffic Using Prophet Machine Learning Model. *FMDB Transactions on Sustainable Computer Letters*, *1*(3), 161–177.

Birant, K. U. (2022). Multi-view rank-based random forest: A new algorithm for prediction in esports. *Expert Systems: International Journal of Knowledge Engineering and Neural Networks*, *39*(2), e12857. DOI: 10.1111/exsy.12857

Bi, X., & Wang, H. (2019). An enhanced high-order Boltzmann machine for feature engineering. *Engineering Applications of Artificial Intelligence*, *78*(2), 37–52. DOI: 10.1016/j.engappai.2018.10.011

Bi, Y., Bell, D., Wang, H., Guo, G., & Greer, K. (2004). Combining multiple classifiers using Dempster's rule of combination for text categorization. *Lecture Notes in Computer Science*, *21*(3), 127–138. DOI: 10.1007/978-3-540-27774-3_13

Boopathy, V. (2023). Home Transforming Health Behaviours with Technology-Driven Interventions. *FMDB Transactions on Sustainable Health Science Letters*, *1*(4), 219–227.

Bose, S. R., Jeba, J. A., Kishore, V. K., Gnanaguru, G., & Shynu, T. (2024). Deep learning-driven acute lymphoblastic leukemia detection using CT scan imaging. *AVE Trends in Intelligent Health Letters*, *1*(2), 110–124.

Brank, J., Grobelnik, M., Milic-Frayling, N., & Mladenic, D. (2002). Interaction of feature selection methods and linear classification models. In *Proceedings of the 19th International Conference on Machine Learning*, Australia.

Calo, E., Cirillo, S., Polese, G., Sebillo, M. M., & Solimando, G. (2023). Investigating Privacy Threats: An In-Depth Analysis of Personal Data on Facebook and LinkedIn Through Advanced Data Reconstruction Tools. *FMDB Transactions on Sustainable Computing Systems*, *1*(2), 89–97.

Cardoso-Cachopo, A., & Oliveira, A. L. (2003). An empirical comparison of text categorization methods. In String Processing and Information Retrieval, Springer Berlin Heidelberg. Lecture Notes in Computer Science, 2857(1), 183–196. DOI: 10.1007/978-3-540-39984-1_14

Chai, N., Zhou, W., & Jiang, Z. (2023). Sustainable supplier selection using an intuitionistic and interval-valued fuzzy MCDM approach based on cumulative prospect theory. *Information Sciences*, *626*(5), 710–737. DOI: 10.1016/j.ins.2023.01.070

Chakraborty, A., Persis, J., & Mahroof, K. (2024). Exploring the academic–industry collaboration in knowledge sharing for supplier selection: Digitalizing the OEM. *IEEE Transactions on Engineering Management*, *71*(1), 7968–7978. DOI: 10.1109/TEM.2023.3260042

Chakraborty, H., & Gu, H. (2009). *A mixed model approach for Intent-to-Treat Analysis in Longitudinal Clinical Trials with missing values*. RTI Press. DOI: 10.3768/rtipress.2009.mr.0009.0903

Chandrasekaran, G., Kumar, N. S., Karthikeyan, P. R., Vanchinathan, K., Priyadarshi, N., & Twala, B. (2022). Test scheduling and test time minimization of system-on-chip using modified BAT algorithm. *IEEE Access : Practical Innovations, Open Solutions*, *40*(3), 1–13. DOI: 10.1109/ACCESS.2022.3224924

Chaturvedi, I., Cambria, E., Welsch, R. E., & Herrera, F. (2018). Distinguishing between facts and opinions for sentiment analysis: Survey and challenges. *Information Fusion*, *44*(11), 65–77. DOI: 10.1016/j.inffus.2017.12.006

Chen, H. P., & Wu, Y. P. (1994). A 3.4V high speed BiCMOS dynamic CLA circuit with carry skip using full swing technique. *IEEE Trans.Circuits I*, *41*(11), 485–489.

Chen, M., Mao, S., Liu, Y., & Zhang, J. (2019). 5G smart grid communications. *IEEE Communications Magazine*, *12*(11), 2140.

Che, Z., Purushotham, S., Cho, K., Sontag, D., & Liu, Y. (2018). Recurrent neural networks for multivariate time series with missing values. *Scientific Reports*, *8*(1), 1–12. DOI: 10.1038/s41598-018-24271-9 PMID: 29666385

Choong, M. K., Charbit, M., & Yan, H. (2009). Autoregressive-model-based missing value estimation for DNA microarray time series data. IEEE Transactions on Information Technology in Biomedicine: A Publication of the IEEE Engineering in Medicine and Biology Society, 13(1), 131–137.

Choudhury, S., Sandhu, A. S., & Pradhan, T. (2017). Genetic algorithm based correlation enhanced prediction of online news popularity. In *Computational intelligence in data mining* (pp. 133–144). Springer. DOI: 10.1007/978-981-10-3874-7_13

Chowdhury, S., Helian, N., & Cordeiro de Amorim, R. (2023). Feature weighting in DBSCAN using reverse nearest neighbors. *Pattern Recognition, 137*(5), 109314. DOI: 10.1016/j.patcog.2023.109314

Christy, K. R., Mi, R. Z., Tao, R., & Lu, L. (2023). Disruptive versus no disruptive advertising in online streaming video services: How does advertisement placement affect consumer perceptions and ad effectiveness? *Journal of Advertising Research, 63*(1), 2023–2006. DOI: 10.2501/JAR-2023-006

Chundru, S. (2024). AI-driven data provenance: Tracking and verifying data lineage. *FMDB Transactions on Sustainable Computing Systems, 2*(3), 107–118. DOI: 10.69888/FTSCS.2024.000258

Chundru, S. (2024). Harnessing the power of AI: Revolutionizing metadata management with machine learning. *FMDB Transactions on Sustainable Computer Letters, 2*(3), 164–175. DOI: 10.69888/FTSCL.2024.000242

Creswell, A., White, T., Dumoulin, V., Arulkumaran, K., Sengupta, B., & Bharath, A. A. (2018). Generative adversarial networks: An overview. *IEEE Signal Processing Magazine, 35*(1), 53–65. DOI: 10.1109/MSP.2017.2765202

Dan, L., C., Xin, H., & Chongwei, J. L. (2015). Intelligent agent greenhouse environment monitoring system based on IOT technology. In 2015 International Conference on Intelligent Transportation, Big Data & Smart City. Halong Bay, Vietnam.

Dang, S., Amin, O., Shihada, B., & Alouini, M.-S. (2020). What should 6G be? *Nature Electronics, 3*(1), 20–29. DOI: 10.1038/s41928-019-0355-6

Dang, T.-T., Nguyen, N.-A.-T., Nguyen, V.-T.-T., & Dang, L.-T.-H. (2022). A two-stage multi-criteria supplier selection model for sustainable automotive supply chain under uncertainty. *Axioms, 11*(5), 228. DOI: 10.3390/axioms11050228

Das, S. R., Bin Sulaiman, R., & Butt, U. (2023). Comparative Analysis of Machine Learning Algorithms for Credit Card Fraud Detection. *FMDB Transactions on Sustainable Computing Systems, 1*(4), 225–244.

Das, S., Kruti, A., Devkota, R., & Bin Sulaiman, R. (2023). Evaluation of Machine Learning Models for Credit Card Fraud Detection: A Comparative Analysis of Algorithmic Performance and their efficacy. *FMDB Transactions on Sustainable Technoprise Letters, 1*(2), 70–81.

Dave, A., Patel, B., & Bhatt, G. (2016). Load balancing in cloud computing using optimization techniques: A study. In *Proceedings of the International Conference on Communication and Electronics Systems (ICCES)*, Tamil Nadu, India. DOI: 10.1109/CESYS.2016.7889883

Devi, P. K., Arulanantham, D., Kalaivanan, C., Gomathi, N., Arunkumar, J. R., & Ramkumar, G. (2022). An secure and low energy consumption based intelligent street light managing system using LoRa network. 2022 6th International Conference on Electronics, Communication and Aerospace Technology, Coimbatore, India.

Devi, B. T., & Rajasekaran, R. (2023). A Comprehensive Review on Deepfake Detection on Social Media Data. *FMDB Transactions on Sustainable Computing Systems*, *1*(1), 11–20.

Dharneeshkar, D., Aniruthan, S., & Parameswaran, L. (2020). Deep learning based detection of potholes in Indian roads using YOLO. *2020 International Conference on Inventive Computation Technologies (ICICT)*, IEEE, Piscataway, New Jersey, USA.

Dhiman, A., & Klette, R. (2020). Pothole detection Us- ing Computer Vision and Learning. *IEEE Transactions on Intelligent Transportation Systems*, *21*(8), 1–15. DOI: 10.1109/TITS.2019.2931297

Dhinakaran, P., Thinesh, M. A., & Paslavskyi, M. (2023). Enhancing Cyber Intrusion Detection through Ensemble Learning: A Comparison of Bagging and Stacking Classifiers. *FMDB Transactions on Sustainable Computer Letters*, *1*(4), 210–227.

Dileep, M. R., & Pournami, P. N. (2019). *AyurLeaf: A Novel Deep Learning Framework for Medicinal Plant Classification, TENCON 2019 - 2019 IEEE Region 10 Conference*. TENCON.

Dixit, A., & Kapse, V. (1998). Arithmetic & logic unit (ALU) design using reversible control unit. *Development*, *1*(6), 55–60.

Dong, Y., & Peng, C.-Y. J. (2013). Principled missing data methods for researchers. *SpringerPlus*, *2*(5), 1–17. PMID: 23853744

Dutta, A., Mukherjee, B., & Basu, S. (2020). Designing scalable data pipelines for real-time analytics. *Journal of Big Data*, *7*(1), 1–22.

Du, Y., & Huo, H. (2020). News text summarisation based on multi-feature and fuzzy logic. *IEEE Access : Practical Innovations, Open Solutions*, *8*(7), 140261–140272. DOI: 10.1109/ACCESS.2020.3007763

Ecer, F. (2022). Multi-criteria decision making for green supplier selection using interval type-2 fuzzy AHP: A case study of a home appliance manufacturer. *Operations Research*, *22*(7), 199–233. DOI: 10.1007/s12351-020-00552-y

Echefaj, K., Charkaoui, A., Cherrafi, A., Garza-Reyes, J. A., Khan, S. A. R., & Benabdellah, A. C. (2023). Sustainable and resilient supplier selection in the context of circular economy: An ontology-based model. *International Journal (Toronto, Ont.), 34*(78), 1461–1489.

Efstathiou, C. (2003). Circuits sys II,Zaher Owda., and Yiorgos Tsiatouhas. *IEEE Trans. Circuits Sys II, 55*(5), 548–553.

Elayaraja, C., Rahila, J., Velavan, P., Rajest, S. S., Shynu, T., & Rahman, M. M. (2024). Depth sensing in AI on exploring the nuances of decision maps for explainability. In *Advances in Computational Intelligence and Robotics* (pp. 217–238). IGI Global.

Estrada-Jiménez, J., Parra-Arnau, J., Rodríguez-Hoyos, A., & Forné, J. (2019). On the regulation of personal data distribution in online advertising platforms. *Engineering Applications of Artificial Intelligence, 82*(6), 13–29. DOI: 10.1016/j.engappai.2019.03.013

Fan, C.-L. (2013). The Application of a ZigBee Based Wireless Sensor Network in the LED Street Lamp Control System". *IEEE International Conference*, 10(10), 501–504.

Fang, F., Li, L., Gu, Y., Zhu, H., & Lim, J.-H. (2020). A novel hybrid approach for crack detection. *Pattern Recognition, 107*(11), 107474. DOI: 10.1016/j.patcog.2020.107474

Farhan, M., & Bin Sulaiman, R. (2023). Developing Blockchain Technology to Identify Counterfeit Items Enhances the Supply Chain's Effectiveness. *FMDB Transactions on Sustainable Technoprise Letters, 1*(3), 123–134.

Farr, J. N., Jenkins, J. J., & Paterson, D. G. (1951). Simplification of Flesch reading ease formula. *The Journal of Applied Psychology, 35*(5), 333–337. DOI: 10.1037/h0062427

Fernandas, K., Vinagre, P., & Cortez, P. (2015). A proactive intelligent decision support system for predicting the popularity of online news. In *Portuguese Conference on Artificial Intelligence* (pp. 535–546). Springer, Cham, Switzerland. DOI: 10.1007/978-3-319-23485-4_53

Forman, G. (2003). An experimental study of feature selection metrics for text categorization. *Journal of Machine Learning Research, 3*(1), 1289–1305.

Fragoudis, D., Meretakis, D., & Likothanassis, S. (2002). Integrating feature and instance selection for text classification. *Proceedings of SIGKDD*, Edmonton, Alberta, Canada. DOI: 10.1145/775047.775120

Frederico, G. F., Kumar, V., Garza-Reyes, J. A., Kumar, A., & Agrawal, R. (2023). Impact of I4.0 technologies and their interoperability on performance: Future pathways for supply chain resilience post-COVID-19. *International Journal of Logistics Management, 34*(4), 1020–1049. DOI: 10.1108/IJLM-03-2021-0181

Gaayathri, R. S., Rajest, S. S., Nomula, V. K., & Regin, R. (2023). Bud-D: Enabling Bidirectional Communication with ChatGPT by adding Listening and Speaking Capabilities. *FMDB Transactions on Sustainable Computer Letters, 1*(1), 49–63.

Gandhi, M., Satheesh, C., Soji, E. S., Saranya, M., Rajest, S. S., & Kothuru, S. K. (2024). Image recognition and extraction on computerized vision for sign language decoding. In *Explainable AI Applications for Human Behavior Analysis* (pp. 157–173). IGI Global. DOI: 10.4018/979-8-3693-1355-8.ch010

Ganesh Babu, N., & Banupriya, N. (2023). *Performance Breakdown and Redistribution Amidst OSPF EIGRP & IS-IS Dynamic Routing Protocols in IPv6 Network.* IEEE Xplore.

García-Laencina, P. J., Sancho-Gómez, J.-L., & Figueiras-Vidal, A. R. (2010). Pattern classification with missing data: A review. *Neural Computing & Applications, 19*(2), 263–282. DOI: 10.1007/s00521-009-0295-6

Geng, C., Huang, S.-J., & Chen, S. (2021). Recent advances in open set recognition: A survey. *IEEE Transactions on Pattern Analysis and Machine Intelligence, 43*(10), 3614–3631. DOI: 10.1109/TPAMI.2020.2981604 PMID: 32191881

Ghaffari, M., Aliahmadi, A., Khalkhali, A., Zakery, A., Daim, T. U., & Yalcin, H. (2023). Topic-based technology mapping using patent data analysis: A case study of vehicle tires. *Technological Forecasting and Social Change, 193*(8), 122576. DOI: 10.1016/j.techfore.2023.122576

Ghosh, R. K., Banerjee, A., Aich, P., Basu, D., & Ghosh, U. (2022). Intelligent IoT for automotive Industry 4.0: Challenges, opportunities, and future trends. In *Internet of Things*. Springer.

Ghosh, S., & Kumar, S. (2013). Comparative analysis of K-means and fuzzy C-means algorithms. *International Journal of Advanced Computer Science and Applications, 4*(4), 35–39. DOI: 10.14569/IJACSA.2013.040406

Gnanaguru, G., Priscila, S. S., Sakthivanitha, M., Radhakrishnan, S., Rajest, S. S., & Singh, S. (2024). Thorough analysis of deep learning methods for diagnosis of COVID-19 CT images. In *Advances in Medical Technologies and Clinical Practice* (pp. 46–65). IGI Global.

Gondhi, N. K., & Gupta, A. (2017). Survey on machine learning-based scheduling in cloud computing. In *Proceedings of the International Conference on Intelligent Systems, Metaheuristics, and Swarm Intelligence*, Jammu and Kashmir, India. DOI: 10.1145/3059336.3059352

Graham, J. W. (2009). Missing data analysis: Making it work in the real world. *Annual Review of Psychology*, *60*(1), 549–576. DOI: 10.1146/annurev.psych.58.110405.085530 PMID: 18652544

Greco, A., Pluchino, A., & Cannizzaro, F. (2019). An improved ant colony optimization algorithm and its applications to limit analysis of frame structures. *Engineering Optimization*, *51*(11), 1867–1883. DOI: 10.1080/0305215X.2018.1560437

Guan, J., & Zhou, S. (2002). *Pruning training corpus to speed up text classification*. DEXA.

Hadi Al Ghozali, I., Afan, I., & Lestari, T. (2024). Comparative analysis clustering algorithm for government's budget performance data. *Cogito Smart Journal*, *10*(1), 578–591. DOI: 10.31154/cogito.v10i1.611.578-591

Han, X., Zu, G., Ohyama, W., Wakabayashi, T., & Kimura, F. (2004). Accuracy improvement of automatic text classification based on feature transformation and multi-classifier combination. In Content Computing, Springer Berlin Heidelberg. Lecture Notes in Computer Science, Berlin, Germany. DOI: 10.1007/978-3-540-30483-8_57

Han, L. (2019). Chicken Swarm Optimization in Task Scheduling in Cloud Computing. *International Journal of Performability Engineering*, *15*(7), 1929–1938. DOI: 10.23940/ijpe.19.07.p20.19291938

Hasan, M., Saha, U. K., Sorwar, A., Dipto, M. A. Z., Hossain, M. S., & Zaman, H. U. (2019). A novel hybrid full adder based on gate diffusion input technique, transmission gate and static CMOS logic. 2019 10th International Conference on Computing, Communication and Networking Technologies (ICCCNT), Kanpur, India.

Hashem, W., Nashaat, H., & Rizk, R. (2017). Honey Bee Based Load Balancing in Cloud Computing. *KSII Transactions on Internet and Information Systems*, *11*(12), 5694–5711.

Hourri, S., & Kharroubi, J. (2020). A deep learning approach for speaker recognition. *International Journal of Speech Technology*, *23*(2), 123–131. DOI: 10.1007/s10772-019-09665-y

Huang, J., & Ma, Y. (2020). Bat algorithm based on an integration strategy and Gaussian distribution. *Mathematical Problems in Engineering*, *2020*(1), 1–22. DOI: 10.1155/2020/9495281

Huang, S.-J., Zhao, J.-W., & Liu, Z.-Y. (2018). Cost-effective training of deep CNNs with active model adaptation. In *Proceedings of the 24th ACM SIGKDD International Conference on Knowledge Discovery & Data Mining*, London, United Kingdom. DOI: 10.1145/3219819.3220026

Huan, H., Yan, J., Xie, Y., Chen, Y., Li, P., & Zhu, R. (2020). Feature-enhanced nonequilibrium bidirectional long short-term memory model for Chinese text classification. *IEEE Access : Practical Innovations, Open Solutions*, *8*(1), 199629–199637. DOI: 10.1109/ACCESS.2020.3035669

Husson, F., & Josse, J. (2013). Handling missing values in multiple factor analysis, " Food Quality and Preference. *Food Quality and Preference*, *30*(2), 77–85. DOI: 10.1016/j.foodqual.2013.04.013

Hutto, C., & Gilbert, E. (2014). VADER: A Parsimonious Rule-Based Model for Sentiment Analysis of Social Media Text. Proceedings of the International AAAI Conference on Web and Social Media, 8(1), 216-225, Copenhagen, Denmark. DOI: 10.1609/icwsm.v8i1.14550

Ikwuagwu, C. V., Tejiri, O. I., Chimdindu, E. S., Wisdom, O. O., & Okoh, I. E. (2024). Design, fabrication, and performance evaluation of a varying temperature dehydrator for food preservation. *FMDB Transactions on Sustainable Energy Sequence*, *2*(1), 49–59. DOI: 10.69888/FTSES.2024.000191

Inchao Li, J., & Zhang, F. (2017). Bin Ran, "Robust and flexible strategy for missing data imputation in intelligent transportation system. *IET Intelligent Transport Systems*, *12*(2), 151–157.

Jaberipur, G., & Kaivani, A. (2009). Improving the Speed of parallel decimal multiplication. IEEE Transactions on Computers. *Institute of Electrical and Electronics Engineers*, *58*(11), 1539–1552.

Janabayevich, A. (2023). Theoretical Framework: The Role of Speech Acts in Stage Performance. *FMDB Transactions on Sustainable Social Sciences Letters*, *1*(2), 68–77.

Jani, P., Nanban, D., Selvan, J., Richardson, N., Sivakani, R., & Subhashni, R. (2024). Studying Price Dynamics of Bus Services Using Machine Learning Algorithms. *AVE Trends In Intelligent Computing Systems*, *1*(1), 54–65.

Jasper, K. D., Jaishnav, M. N., Chowdhury, M. F., Badhan, R., & Sivakani, R. (2024). Defend and Secure: A Strategic and Implementation Framework for Robust Data Breach Prevention. *AVE Trends In Intelligent Computing Systems*, *1*(1), 17–31.

Jasper, K., Neha, R., & Szeberényi, A. (2023). Fortifying Data Security: A Multifaceted Approach with MFA, Cryptography, and Steganography. *FMDB Transactions on Sustainable Computing Systems*, *1*(2), 98–111.

Jayalath, A. D. A. D. S., Amarawanshaline, T. G. A. G. D., Nawinna, D. P., Nadeeshan, P. V. D., & Jayasuriya, H. P. (2019, December). Identification of medicinal plants by visual characteristics of leaves and flowers. In 2019 14th Conference on Industrial and Information Systems (ICIIS) (pp. 125-129). IEEE.

Jeba, J. A., Bose, S. R., & Boina, R. (2023). Exploring Hybrid Multi-View Multimodal for Natural Language Emotion Recognition Using Multi-Source Information Learning Model. *FMDB Transactions on Sustainable Computer Letters*, *1*(1), 12–24.

Jeba, J. A., Bose, S. R., Regin, R., Rajest, S. S., & Hasan, M. M. (2024). Intelligent Tamil video summarization: AI-powered NLP, translation, and speech integration for enhanced accessibility. *FMDB Transactions on Sustainable Computer Letters*, *2*(1), 26–39. DOI: 10.69888/FTSCL.2024.000179

Jeba, J., Bose, S. R., Regin, R., Sudhan, M. B., Suman Rajest, S., & Babu, P. R. (2024). Efficient Real-time Tamil Character Recognition via Deep Vision Architecture. *AVE Trends In Intelligent Computing Systems*, *1*(1), 1–16.

Jebbor, I., Benmamoun, Z., Hachimi, H., Raouf, Y., & Haqqi, M. (2023). Improvement of an Assembly Line in the Automotive Industry: A Case Study in Wiring Harness Assembly Line. In Advances in Transdisciplinary Engineering, Amsterdam, Netherlands. DOI: 10.3233/ATDE230031

Jebbor, I., Benmamoun, Z., & Hachimi, H. (2023). Optimizing manufacturing cycles to improve production: Application in the traditional shipyard industry. *Processes (Basel, Switzerland)*, *11*(11), 3136. DOI: 10.3390/pr11113136

Jiejun, C., Weimin, X., & Chanxia, Z. (2023). Research on evaluation system and method of electric vehicle development situation. *Electric Power Demand Side Management*, *5*(6), 100063.

Ji-Hua, M., Bing-Fang, W., & Qiang-Zi, L. (2006). A global crop growth monitoring system based on remote sensing. *2006 IEEE International Symposium on Geoscience and Remote Sensing*, Denver, Colorado, USA. DOI: 10.1109/IGARSS.2006.589

Johnson, D. E., Oles, F. J., Zhang, T., & Goetz, T. (2002). A decision-tree-based symbolic rule induction system for text categorization. *IBM Systems Journal, 41*(3), 428–437. DOI: 10.1147/sj.413.0428

Joshi, M., Shen, Z., & Kausar, S. (2023). Enhancing Inclusive Education on Leveraging Artificial Intelligence Technologies for Personalized Support and Accessibility in Special Education for Students with Diverse Learning Needs. *FMDB Transactions on Sustainable Techno Learning, 1*(3), 125–142.

Joshi, S., Kim, C., Ha, S., & Cauwenberghs, G. (2017). From algorithms to devices: Enabling machine learning through ultra-low-power VLSI mixed-signal array processing. *2017 IEEE Custom Integrated Circuits Conference (CICC)*, Austin, Texas, USA DOI: 10.1109/CICC.2017.7993650

Kahng, A. B., & Kang, S. (2012). Accuracy-configurable Adder for approximate arithmetic designs. *Proceedings of the 49th Annual Design Automation Conference*, San Francisco, California, USA DOI: 10.1145/2228360.2228509

Kalyani, V., & Devi, L. D. (2024). Digital Marketing Evolution: A Bibliometric Method for Mapping the Web of Science Database. *FMDB Transactions on Sustainable Humanities and Society, 1*(1), 10–20. DOI: 10.69888/FTSHS.2024.000149

Kamila, J. K. N., Frnda, S., Kumar Pani, R., Sardar, M. N., Islam, P. K., & Bharti, K. (2022). Machine Learning Model Design For High Performance Cloud Computing & Load Balancing Resiliency: An Innovative Approach. *Journal of King Saud University. Computer and Information Sciences, 34*(10), 9991–10009. DOI: 10.1016/j.jksuci.2022.10.001

Kamran, S. S., Haleem, A., Bahl, S., Javaid, M., Prakash, C., & Budhhi, D. (2022). Artificial intelligence and advanced materials in the automotive industry: Potential applications and perspectives. *Materials Today: Proceedings, 62*(5), 4207–4214. DOI: 10.1016/j.matpr.2022.04.727

Kang, D., Avancha, G., & Park, H. (2021). Scalable real-time anomaly detection in streaming big data. *IEEE Transactions on Knowledge and Data Engineering, 33*(4), 1414–1427.

Kanyimama, W., Argungu, M. S., Gabi, D., & Suru, H. U. (2024). Planning and designing different types of surveillance networks for enhanced security and monitoring. *FMDB Transactions on Sustainable Computer Letters, 2*(1), 52–62. DOI: 10.69888/FTSCL.2024.000181

Karmakar, G., Chowdhury, A., Das, R., Kamruzzaman, J., & Islam, S. (2021). Assessing the trust level of a driverless car using deep learning. *IEEE Transactions on Intelligent Transportation Systems*, *22*(7), 4457–4466. DOI: 10.1109/TITS.2021.3059261

Karthikeyan, B., Devi, R. A., & Munshi, M. (2024). Utilizing Deep Learning for the Classification of Brain Tumours Using MRI. *AVE Trends In Intelligent Health Letters*, *1*(1), 1–9.

Karthik, S., Bhaggiaraj, S., Soji, E. S., Deve, L. S., Priscila, S. S., & Rajest, S. S. (2024). Real-time hand gesture recognition for stroke rehabilitation using deep learning approach. *AVE Trends in Intelligent Computing Systems*, *1*(3), 157–172.

Kathalkar, P. R., & Deorankar, A. V. (2018). A review on different load balancing algorithms in cloud computing. *International Research Journal of Engineering and Technology*, *5*(2), 1961–1963.

Kaviarasan, R., Balamurugan, G., Kalaiyarasan, R., & Venkata Ravindra Reddy, Y. (2023). Effective load balancing approach in cloud computing using Inspired Lion Optimization Algorithm. *Advances in Electrical Engineering*, *6*(12), 100326.

Kavunthi, S., Venkateswaran, P. S., Sudha, P., & Sridharlakshmi, N. R. B. (2024). Cultivating quality work-life balance: A critical factor in enhancing nursing careers and patient wellbeing. *AVE Trends in Intelligent Social Letters*, *1*(2), 104–112.

Ke, H., & Shaoping, M. (2002). Text categorization based on concept indexing and principal component analysis. In *Proceedings of TENCON 2002 Conference on Computers*, Florence, Italy.

Kehagias, A., Petridis, V., Kaburlasos, V., & Fragkou, P. (2003). A comparison of word- and sense-based text categorization using several classification algorithms. *Journal of Intelligent Information Systems*, *21*(3), 227–247. DOI: 10.1023/A:1025554732352

Ke, J., Shen, Y., Guo, Y., Wright, J. D., & Liang, X. (2020). A prediction model of microsatellite status from histology images. In *Proceedings of the 2020 10th International Conference on Biomedical Engineering and Technology*, New York, United States. DOI: 10.1145/3397391.3397442

Keneshloo, Y., Wang, S., Han, E.-H. S., & Ramakrishnan, N. (2016). Predicting the shape and peak time of news article views. 2016 IEEE International Conference on Big Data (Big Data), Washington, DC, USA, 2400-2409. DOI: 10.1109/BigData.2016.7840875

Kessler, B., Nunberg, G., & Schuetze, H. (1997). *Automatic detection of text genre.*

Khayati, M., & Lerner, A. (n.d.). Mind the Gap. *An Experimental Evaluation of Imputation of Missing Values Techniques in Time Series, 13*(5), 768–782.

Kim, Y., Ieee, R. G., & Evans, W. M. (2008). Remote Sensing and Control of an Irrigation System Using a Distributed Wireless Sensor Network. *IEEE Transactions on Instrumentation and Measurement, 57*(7), 1379–1387. DOI: 10.1109/TIM.2008.917198

Kiruthiga, G., & Mary, V. S. (2020). Neutrosophic knowledge and optimized cache management using cuckoo search method in cloud computing. *International Journal of Intelligent Engineering and Systems, 13*(3), 327–338. DOI: 10.22266/ijies2020.0630.30

Kisseleff, S., Akyildiz, I. F., & Gerstacker, W. H. (2018). Survey on advances in magnetic induction-based wireless underground sensor networks. *IEEE Internet of Things Journal, 5*(6), 4843–4856. DOI: 10.1109/JIOT.2018.2870289

Klopotek, M., & Woch, M. (2003). Very large Bayesian networks in text classification. In Proceedings of ICCS 2003, Springer Berlin Heidelberg. Lecture Notes in Computer Science, Berlin, Germany. DOI: 10.1007/3-540-44860-8_41

Kostrzewski, A., Kim, D. H., Li, Y., & Eichmann, G. (1990). Fast hybrid parallel carry lookahead Adder. *Optics Letters, 15*(16), 915–917. DOI: 10.1364/OL.15.000915 PMID: 19770952

Kotsiopoulos, T., Sarigiannidis, P., Ioannidis, D., & Tzovaras, D. (2021). Machine learning and deep learning in smart manufacturing: The smart grid paradigm. *Computer Science Review, 40*(5), 100341. DOI: 10.1016/j.cosrev.2020.100341

Kouhizadeh, M., Saberi, S., & Sarkis, J. (2021). Blockchain technology and the sustainable supply chain: Theoretically exploring adoption barriers. *International Journal of Production Economics, 231*(1), 107831. DOI: 10.1016/j.ijpe.2020.107831

Krishna Vaddy, R. (2023). Data Fusion Techniques for Comprehensive Health Monitoring. *FMDB Transactions on Sustainable Health Science Letters, 1*(4), 198–207.

Krishnaveni, H., & Sinthu, V. (2019). Modified Artificial Fish Swarm Algorithm for Efficient Task Scheduling in Cloud Environment. *International Journal on Computer Science and Engineering, 7*(5), 1363–1371.

Kruekaew, B., & Kimpan, W. (2020). Enhancing of Artificial Bee Colony Algorithm for Virtual Machine Scheduling and Load Balancing Problem in Cloud Computing. *International Journal of Computational Intelligence Systems, 13*(1), 496–510. DOI: 10.2991/ijcis.d.200410.002

Kumar Das, A., & Kumar Pratihar, D. (2019). A New Bonobo Optimizer (BO) for Real-Parameter Optimization. In Conference: The IEEE Region 10 Symposium. Kuala Lumpur, Malaysia.

Kumar Nomula, V. (2023). A Novel Approach to Analyzing Medical Sensor Data Using Physiological Models. *FMDB Transactions on Sustainable Health Science Letters*, *1*(4), 186–197.

Kumar Thella, P., & Ulagamuthalvi, V. (2021). IEEE/2021 5th International Conference on Computing Methodologies and Communication (ICCMC), Erode, India.

Kumar, A., Kaur, G., & Srivastava, M. (2018). Speaker and Speech Recognition using Deep Neural Network. *Article*, *6*(8), 118.

Kumar, A., Singh, R., & Gupta, P. K. (2020). Stream processing for real-time data analytics using Apache Kafka and Spark Streaming. *Computers & Electrical Engineering*, *81*(1), 1–13.

Kumar, E. S., & Talasila, V. (2014). Leaf features based approach for automated identification of medicinal plants. *2014 International Conference on Communication and Signal Processing*, IEEE, Melmaruvathur, India. DOI: 10.1109/ICCSP.2014.6949830

Kumar, P. M., Surya, C. M., & Gopi, V. P. (2017). Identification of ayurvedic medicinal plants by image processing of leaf samples. *2017 Third International Conference on Research in Computational Intelligence and Communication Networks (ICRCICN)*, IEEE, Kolkata, India. DOI: 10.1109/ICRCICN.2017.8234512

Kumar, P., & Gupta, A. (2020). Active learning query strategies for classification, regression, and clustering: A survey. *Journal of Computer Science and Technology*, *35*(4), 913–945. DOI: 10.1007/s11390-020-9487-4

Kumar, P., Lee, H. J., & Lee, H. J. (2020). A comprehensive review of security services in network layer of wireless sensor networks. *Journal of Ambient Intelligence and Humanized Computing*, *11*(6), 5905–5920.

Kumar, R., & Dahiya, S. (2013). Performance analysis of different bit carry look ahead Adder using vhdl environment. [IJESIT]. *International Journal of Engineering Science and Innovative Technology*, *2*(4), 80–88.

Kumar, S. A., Rajest, S. S., Aravind, B. R., & Bhuvaneswari, G. (2023). Virtual learning styles based on learning style detection. *International Journal of Knowledge and Learning*, *1*(1), 10057158. DOI: 10.1504/IJKL.2023.10057158

Kuppili, V., Biswas, M., Edla, D. R., Prasad, K. J. R., & Suri, J. S. (2020). A mechanics-based similarity measure for text classification in machine learning paradigm. *IEEE Transactions on Emerging Topics in Computational Intelligence*, *4*(2), 180–200. DOI: 10.1109/TETCI.2018.2863728

Langkamp, D. L., Lehman, A., & Lemeshow, S. (2010). Techniques for handling missing data in secondary analyses of large surveys. *Academic Pediatrics*, *10*(3), 205–210. DOI: 10.1016/j.acap.2010.01.005 PMID: 20338836

Lee, J., Chong, P. K., & Quek, T. Q. (2019). Energy Efficient Wireless Powered Communication Networks. *IEEE Transactions on Wireless Communications*, *18*(3), 1835–1847.

Leopold, E., & Kindermann, J. (2002). Text categorization with support vector machines: How to represent texts in input space? *Machine Learning*, *46*(1), 423–444. DOI: 10.1023/A:1012491419635

Lewis, D., Yang, Y., Rose, T., & Li, F. (2004). RCV1: A new benchmark collection for text categorization research. *Journal of Machine Learning Research*, *5*(1), 361–397.

Liang, J., Han, J., & Lombardi, F. (2013). New metrics for the reliability of approximate and probabilistic adders. IEEE Transactions on Computers. *Institute of Electrical and Electronics Engineers*, *62*(9), 1760–1771.

Liao, J., Tang, J., Vinelli, A., & Xie, R. (2023). A hybrid sustainability performance measurement approach for fresh food cold supply chains. *Journal of Cleaner Production*, *398*(4), 136466. DOI: 10.1016/j.jclepro.2023.136466

Licaj, B., & Karras, D. A. (2024). Integral smart vehicle automation framework using IoT, modern software, and infrastructure. *AVE Trends in Intelligent Computing Systems*, *1*(3), 128–141.

Li, G., Liu, Y., Wu, J., Lin, D., & Zhao, S. (2019). Methods of Resource Scheduling Based on Optimized Fuzzy Clustering in Fog Computing. *Sensors (Basel)*, *19*(9), 1–16. DOI: 10.3390/s19092122 PMID: 31071923

Li, J., Ma, R., Deng, M., Cao, X., Wang, X., & Wang, X. (2024). A comparative study of clustering algorithms for intermittent heating demand considering time series. *Applied Energy*, *353*(1), 122046. DOI: 10.1016/j.apenergy.2023.122046

Li, L.-L., Shi-Feng, Y., Wang, L.-Y., & Gao, X.-M. (2011). The Greenhouse Environment Monitoring System Based on Wireless Sensor Network Technology". In *Proceedings of the 2011 IEEE International Conference on Cyber Technology in Automation, Control, and Intelligent Systems*, Kunming, China. DOI: 10.1109/CYBER.2011.6011806

Lim, H. S. (2004). Improving kNN-based text classification with well estimated parameters. In Neural Information Processing, Springer Berlin Heidelberg. Lecture Notes in Computer Science, Shanghai, China. DOI: 10.1007/978-3-540-30499-9_79

Linzhang, M., & Xiangzhan, Y. (2022). Design and implementation fragnary monitoring system based on wireless sensor network node". *2010 International Conference on Measuring Technology and Mechatronics Automation*, 1(4), 950–953.

Li, S., Hu, Y., & Zhang, X. (2022). Scalable real-time data processing in heterogeneous computing environments. *IEEE Transactions on Cloud Computing*, *10*(1), 148–160.

Lisa, N. J., & Babu, H. M. H. (2015). Design of a compact reversible carry lookahead Adder using dynamic programming. 2015 28th International Conference on VLSI Design, Bangalore, India

Liu, B., Han, C., Liu, X., & Li, W. (2021). Vehicle artificial intelligence system based on intelligent image analysis and 5G network. *International Journal of Wireless Information Networks*, *30*(4), 1–17. DOI: 10.1007/s10776-021-00535-6

Liu, C., Wang, W., Zhang, Y., Dong, Y., He, F., & Wu, C. (2017). Predicting the popularity of online news based on multivariate analysis. *2017 IEEE International Conference on Computer and Information Technology (CIT)*, Helsinki, Finland, 9-15. https://doi.org/DOI: 10.1109/CIT.2017.36

Liu, G., Zheng, L., Wang, G., Shen, Y., & Liang, Y. (2019). A carry lookahead adder based on hybrid CMOS-memristor logic circuit. *IEEE Access : Practical Innovations, Open Solutions*, *7*(3), 43691–43696. DOI: 10.1109/ACCESS.2019.2907976

Liu, K., & Chen, L. (2019). Medical social media text classification integrating consumer health terminology. *IEEE Access : Practical Innovations, Open Solutions*, *7*(1), 78185–78193. DOI: 10.1109/ACCESS.2019.2921938

Liu, M., Tu, Z., Zhang, T., Su, T., Xu, X., & Wang, Z. (2022). LTP: A new active learning strategy for CRF-based named entity recognition. *Neural Processing Letters*, *54*(3), 2433–2454. DOI: 10.1007/s11063-021-10737-x

Liu, X., Yabing, Z., Yin, Q., Peng, Y., & Qin, L. (2015). Scheduling parallel jobs with tentative runs and consolidation in the cloud. *Journal of Systems and Software*, *104*(6), 141–151. DOI: 10.1016/j.jss.2015.03.007

Liu, Y., Wang, L., Wang, X. V., Xu, X., & Zhang, L. (2019). Scheduling in cloud manufacturing: State-of-the-art and research challenges. *International Journal of Production Research*, *57*(15), 4854–4879. DOI: 10.1080/00207543.2018.1449978

Li, X., Han, S., Zhao, L., Gong, C., & Liu, X. (2017). New dandelion algorithm optimizes extreme learning machine for biomedical classification problems. *Computational Intelligence and Neuroscience*, *2017*(1), 1–13. DOI: 10.1155/2017/4523754 PMID: 29085425

Lodha, S., Malani, H., & Bhardwaj, A. K. (2023). Performance Evaluation of Vision Transformers for Diagnosis of Pneumonia. *FMDB Transactions on Sustainable Computing Systems*, *1*(1), 21–31.

Luengo, J., García, S., & Herrera, F. (2012). When choosing the best imputation methods for missing values, consider three groups of classification methods. *Knowledge and Information Systems*, *32*(1), 77–108. DOI: 10.1007/s10115-011-0424-2

Luo, F., Jiang, Y., Wang, J., Li, Z., & Zhang, X. (2023). A framework for cybersecurity requirements management in the automotive domain. *Sensors (Basel)*, *23*(10), 4979. DOI: 10.3390/s23104979 PMID: 37430891

Madhu, G., & Rajinikanth, T. V. (2012). A novel index measure imputation algorithm for missing data values: A machine learning approach. *2012 IEEE International Conference on Computational Intelligence and Computing Research*. IEEE, Coimbatore, India. DOI: 10.1109/ICCIC.2012.6510198

Madhuranthakam, R. S. (2024). Implementing data quality assurance frameworks in distributed data engineering workflows. *AVE Trends in Intelligent Computing Systems*, *1*(4), 241–251.

Madsen, R. E., Sigurdsson, S., Hansen, L. K., & Lansen, J. (2004). Pruning the vocabulary for better context recognition. In *7th International Conference on Pattern Recognition*, Cambridge, United Kingdom.

Mainwaring, A., Polastre, J., Szewczyk, R., Culler, D., & Anderson, J. (2002).. . *Wireless Sensor Networks for Habitat Monitoring.*, *3*(10), 2925–2928.

Mallikarjuna, B., & Krishna, P. V. (2018b). A nature-inspired approach for load balancing of tasks in cloud computing using equal time allocation. *International Journal of Innovative Technology and Exploring Engineering*, *8*(12), 46–5.

Mallikarjuna, B., & Venkata, P. (2018a). A Nature Inspired Bee Colony Optimization Model for Improving Load Balancing in Cloud Computing [IJITEE]. *International Journal of Innovative Technology and Exploring Engineering*, *8*(12), 51–55.

Mandala, V., Kuppala, B. M. S. R., Surabhi, S. N. R. D., & Kommisetty, P. D. N. K. (2022). Advancing predictive failure analytics in automotive safety: AI-driven approaches for school buses and commercial trucks. *Journal of Artificial Intelligence and Big Data*, *1*(1), 9–20. DOI: 10.31586/jaibd.2022.944

Manipal, S., Ranjan, W., Lavish, K., & Komuravelly, S. K. (2019). *Optimization algorithms in load balancing: A study. An International Peer-Reviewed*. UGC Approved Journal.

Marar, A., Bose, S. R., Singh, R., Joshi, Y., Regin, R., & Rajest, S. S. (2023). Light weight structure texture feature analysis for character recognition using progressive stochastic learning algorithm. In *Advanced Applications of Generative AI and Natural Language Processing Models* (pp. 144–158). IGI Global.

Maroju, P. K. (2024). Data science for a smarter currency supply chain: Optimizing cash flow with machine learning for white label ATMs. *FMDB Transactions on Sustainable Computing Systems*, *2*(1), 43–53. DOI: 10.69888/FTSCS.2024.000196

Maroju, P. K. (2024). Enhancing white label ATM network efficiency: A data science approach to route optimization with AI. *FMDB Transactions on Sustainable Computer Letters*, *2*(1), 40–51. DOI: 10.69888/FTSCL.2024.000180

Masadeh, R., Sharieh, A., & Basel, A. (2019). Humpback Whale Optimization Algorithm Based on Vocal Behavior for Task Scheduling in Cloud Computing. *International Journal of Advanced Science and Technology*, *13*(3), 121–140.

Medvedev, M. V., & Pavlov, V. I. (2020). Road surface marking recognition and road surface quality evaluation using convolution neural network. 2020 International Multi-Conference on Industrial Engineering and Modern Technologies (FarEastCon), Vladivostok, Russia.

Mehta, N., Prakash, A., Vyas, U., & Mudgal, P. (2019). 5G technology of mobile communication: A survey. In 2019 4th International Conference on Internet of Things: Smart Innovation and Usages (IoT-SIU) (pp. 1–7). IEEE, Ghaziabad, India.

Mehta, G., Bose, S. R., & Selva Naveen, R. (2023). Optimizing Lithium-ion Battery Controller Design for Electric Vehicles: A Comprehensive Study. *FMDB Transactions on Sustainable Energy Sequence*, *1*(2), 60–70.

Miao, J., & Li, S. (2017). A novel implementation of 4-bit carry lookahead Adder. *2017 International Conference on Electron Devices and Solid-State Circuits (EDSSC)*, Hsinchu, Taiwan DOI: 10.1109/EDSSC.2017.8126457

Michalakopoulos, V., Sarmas, E., Papias, I., Skaloumpakas, P., Marinakis, V., & Doukas, H. (2024). A machine learning-based framework for clustering residential electricity load profiles to enhance demand response programs. *Applied Energy*, *361*(5), 122943. DOI: 10.1016/j.apenergy.2024.122943

Milosevic, M. (2021). Sustainability of the production process by applying lean manufacturing through the PDCA cycle-a case study in the machinery industry. In Advances in Manufacturing Engineering and Materials II: Proceedings of the International Conference on Manufacturing Engineering and Materials (ICMEM 2020), Cham, Switzerland. DOI: 10.1007/978-3-030-71956-2_16

Minu, M. S., Subashka Ramesh, S. S., Canessane, R., Al-Amin, M., & Bin Sulaiman, R. (2023). Experimental Analysis of UAV Networks Using Oppositional Glowworm Swarm Optimization and Deep Learning Clustering and Classification. *FMDB Transactions on Sustainable Computing Systems*, *1*(3), 124–134.

Mirjalili, S. (2015). Moth-flame optimization algorithm: A novel nature-inspired heuristic paradigm. *Knowledge-Based Systems*, *89*(11), 228–249. DOI: 10.1016/j.knosys.2015.07.006

Mishne, G., & Glance, N. (2006). Leave a reply: An analysis of weblog comments. Edinburgh, United Kingdom.

Mishra, K., & Majhi, S. K. (2021). A binary Bird Swarm Optimization based load balancing algorithm for cloud computing environment. *Open Computer Science*, *11*(1), 146–160. DOI: 10.1515/comp-2020-0215

Mohanty, B. K., & Patel, S. K. (2014). Area-delay-power efficient carryselect adder. *IEEE Transactions on Circuits and Systems*, *61*(6), 418–422.

Montanes, E., Quevedo, J. R., & Diaz, I. (2003). A wrapper approach with support vector machines for text categorization. *Lecture Notes in Computer Science*, *2686*(6), 230–237. DOI: 10.1007/3-540-44868-3_30

Morgenshtein, A., Yuzhaninov, V., Kovshilovsky, A., & Fish, A. (2014). Full-Swing Gate Diffusion Input logic—Case-study of low-power CLA adder design. *Integration (Amsterdam)*, *47*(1), 62–70. DOI: 10.1016/j.vlsi.2013.04.002

Morrison, M., Lewandowski, M., Meana, R., & Ranganathan, N. (2011). Design of a novel reversible ALU using an enhanced carry look- ahead Adder. 2011 11th IEEE International Conference on Nanotechnology, Portland, Oregon, USA

Mubeen, A., Ibrahim, M., Bibi, N., Baz, M., Hamam, H., & Cheikhrouhou, O. (2021). Alts: An adaptive load balanced task scheduling approach for cloud computing. *Processes (Basel, Switzerland)*, *9*(9), 1514. DOI: 10.3390/pr9091514

Munirathinam, S. (2019). Industry 4.0: Industrial Internet of Things (IIOT). *Advances in Computers*, *117*(1), 129–164.

Murugavel, S., & Hernandez, F. (2023). A Comparative Study Between Statistical and Machine Learning Methods for Forecasting Retail Sales. *FMDB Transactions on Sustainable Computer Letters*, *1*(2), 76–102.

Myers, T. A. (2011). Goodbye, listwise deletion: Presenting hot deck imputation as an easy and effective tool for handling missing data. *Communication Methods and Measures*, *5*(4), 297–310. DOI: 10.1080/19312458.2011.624490

Nanban, D., Ajitha, Y., Selvan, J., Pierre, T. J., Sara, S. B. V. J., & Ragesha, R. (2024). Enhancing user experience in air canvas through robust hand gesture recognition using computer vision. *FMDB Transactions on Sustainable Computer Letters*, *2*(3), 131–143. DOI: 10.69888/FTSCL.2024.000239

Nardiello, P., Sebastiani, F., & Sperduti, A. (2003). Discretizing continuous attributes in AdaBoost for text categorization. *Lecture Notes in Computer Science*, *2633*(1), 320–334. DOI: 10.1007/3-540-36618-0_23

Neelima, P., & Reddy, A. M. R. (2020). An efficient load balancing system using adaptive dragonfly algorithm in cloud computing. In *Cluster Computing*. Springer.

Ng, M. K.-P., Yuan, Q., Yan, L., & Sun, J. (2017). An adaptive weighted tensor completion method for the recovery of remote sensing images with missing data. IEEE Transactions on Geoscience and Remote Sensing: A Publication of the IEEE Geoscience and Remote Sensing Society, 55(6), 3367–3381.

Nguyen, H., & Huynh, T. T. (2020). Real-time big data stream processing in cloud environments. *Future Generation Computer Systems*, *106*(1), 385–393.

Nisha, G., & Megala, J. (2014). Wireless Sensor Network Based Automated Irrigation and Crop Field Monitoring System". Sixth International Conference on Advanced Computing (IcoAC), 179(12), 105782. DOI: 10.1109/ICoAC.2014.7229707

Nomula, V. K. (2024). Imperative of standards and interoperability in modern medicine. *FMDB Transactions on Sustainable Health Science Letters*, *2*(1), 31–40. DOI: 10.69888/FTSHSL.2024.000170

Nomula, V. K., Steffi, R., & Shynu, T. (2023). Examining the Far-Reaching Consequences of Advancing Trends in Electrical, Electronics, and Communications Technologies in Diverse Sectors. *FMDB Transactions on Sustainable Energy Sequence*, *1*(1), 27–37.

Novovicova, J., & Malik, A. (2004). Feature selection using improved mutual information for text classification. *SSPR & SPR*, *3138*(4), 1010–1017.

Nwabuokei, I., Ghouse, M., Chen, W., Kollannur, E. T., Li, H., & Bin Sulaiman, R. (2023). Quantifying the Influence of Population on Carbon Emissions: A Comparative Study of Developed versus Developing Countries Using Machine Learning. *FMDB Transactions on Sustainable Energy Sequence*, *1*(2), 71–82.

Obeta, U., Deko, D., & Mantu, E. (2024). Deep Learning-Based Diagnostic Techniques for Cancer: Extensive Testing and Clinical Application Insights. *AVE Trends In Intelligent Health Letters*, *1*(1), 28–37.

Odoemena, O. F., & Elufidodo, G. A. (2024). Machine learning-based cardiovascular disease detection and intelligent healthcare workflow automation. *FMDB Transactions on Sustainable Health Science Letters*, *2*(2), 81–93. DOI: 10.69888/FTSHSL.2024.000174

Ogedengbe, M. T., & Agana, M. A. (2017). New Fuzzy Techniques for Real-Time Task Scheduling on Multiprocessor Systems. *International Journal of Computer Trends and Technology*, *47*(3), 189–196. DOI: 10.14445/22312803/IJCTT-V47P129

Pandey, A. K., Iqbal, R., Amin, S., Maniak, T., Palade, V., & Karyotis, C. (2021). Deep neural networks-based approach for pothole detection. 2021 4th International Conference on Signal Processing and Information Security (ICSPIS), Dubai, United Arab Emirates (UAE).

Panyaram, S. (2024). Optimization strategies for efficient charging station deployment in urban and rural networks. *FMDB Transactions on Sustainable Environmental Sciences*, *1*(2), 69–80. DOI: 10.69888/FTSESS.2024.000245

Panyaram, S. (2024). Utilizing quantum computing to enhance artificial intelligence in healthcare for predictive analytics and personalized medicine. *FMDB Transactions on Sustainable Computing Systems*, *2*(1), 22–31. DOI: 10.69888/FTSCS.2024.000194

Paramasivan, P., Rajest, S. S., Chinnusamy, K., Regin, R., & John Joseph, F. J. (2024). *Cross-Industry AI Applications*. Advances in Computational Intelligence and Robotics. IGI., DOI: 10.4018/979-8-3693-5951-8

Paulson, A. (2020a). *AI Based Indigenous Medicinal Plant Identification" 2020 Advanced Computing and Communication Technologies for High Performance Applications*. ACCTHPA.

Peppers, N., Alexakis, T., Adamopoulou, E., & Demestichas, K. (2021). Driving behavior analysis using machine and deep learning methods for continuous streams of vehicular data. *Sensors (Basel)*, *21*(14), 4704. DOI: 10.3390/s21144704 PMID: 34300447

Peralta-López, J.-E., Morales-Viscaya, J.-A., Lázaro-Mata, D., Villaseñor-Aguilar, M.-J., Prado-Olivarez, J., Pérez-Pinal, F.-J., Padilla-Medina, J.-A., Martínez-Nolasco, J.-J., & Barranco-Gutiérrez, A.-I. (2023). Speed bump and pothole detection using deep neural network with images captured through ZED camera. *Applied Sciences (Basel, Switzerland)*, *13*(14), 8349. DOI: 10.3390/app13148349

Pereira, C. H. T., & Silva, M. E. (2023). Fostering a transition to inclusive sustainability through shared urban mobility. *Research in Transportation Business & Management*, *51*(12), 101045. DOI: 10.1016/j.rtbm.2023.101045

Pham, X.-Q., Man, N. D., Tri, N. D. T., Thai, N. Q., & Huh, E.-N. (2017). A cost- and performance-effective approach for task scheduling based on collaboration between cloud and fog computing. *International Journal of Distributed Sensor Networks*, *13*(11), 1–16. DOI: 10.1177/1550147717742073

Pierre, T. J., Tao, C., Vénant, K., & Erneste, B. (2024). Speed management blueprint: Conception of an IoT-based electric vehicle speed limiter monitoring system for Kigali city vehicles. *FMDB Transactions on Sustainable Energy Sequence*, *2*(1), 33–48. DOI: 10.69888/FTSES.2024.000190

Ping, P., Yang, X., & Gao, Z. (2020). A deep learning approach for street pothole detection. *2020 IEEE Sixth International Conference on Big Data Computing Service and Applications (BigDataService)*, Oxford, United Kingdom. DOI: 10.1109/BigDataService49289.2020.00039

Pitafi, S., Anwar, T., & Sharif, Z. (2023). A taxonomy of machine learning clustering algorithms, challenges, and future realms. *Applied Sciences (Basel, Switzerland)*, *13*(6), 3529. DOI: 10.3390/app13063529

Pranav, R. P., Prawin, R. P., Paramasivan, P., Shynu, T., & Subhashni, R. (2024). IoT-SecNet: A trust-based framework for enhancing security in IoT communications and network layer protocols. *FMDB Transactions on Sustainable Computing Systems*, *2*(2), 96–106. DOI: 10.69888/FTSCS.2024.000201

Pranav, R. P., Prawin, R. P., Subhashni, R., & Das, S. R. (2023). Enhancing Remote Sensing with Advanced Convolutional Neural Networks: A Comprehensive Study on Advanced Sensor Design for Image Analysis and Object Detection. *FMDB Transactions on Sustainable Computer Letters*, *1*(4), 255–266.

Priscila, S. S., Rajest, S. S., Tadiboina, S. N., Regin, R., & András, S. (2023). Analysis of Machine Learning and Deep Learning Methods for Superstore Sales Prediction. *FMDB Transactions on Sustainable Computer Letters*, *1*(1), 1–11.

Pulivarthy, P. (2024). Optimizing large-scale distributed data systems using intelligent load balancing algorithms. *AVE Trends in Intelligent Computing Systems*, *1*(4), 219–230.

Pulivarthy, P. (2024). Research on Oracle database performance optimization in IT-based university educational management system. *FMDB Transactions on Sustainable Computing Systems*, *2*(2), 84–95. DOI: 10.69888/FTSCS.2024.000200

Qiang, W., Xiaolong, W., & Yi, G. (2005). A study of semi-discrete matrix decomposition for LSI in automated text categorization. *Lecture Notes in Computer Science*, *3248*(1), 606–615. DOI: 10.1007/978-3-540-30211-7_64

Qi, L., Song, J., Chen, M., Zhang, M., Zou, Q., & Wan, C. (2024). Mining and clustering techniques for load operation characteristics of the Internet of Things. *2024 International Conference on Intelligent Algorithms for Computational Intelligence Systems (IACIS)*, Karnataka, India. DOI: 10.1109/IACIS61494.2024.10721623

Qtaish, A., Braik, M., Albashish, D., Alshammari, M. T., Alreshidi, A., & Alreshidi, E. J. (2024). Optimization of K-means clustering method using hybrid capuchin search algorithm. *The Journal of Supercomputing*, *80*(7), 1728–1787. DOI: 10.1007/s11227-023-05540-5

Rahman, M., Rahim, M. A., Rahman, M. M., Moustafa, N., Razzak, I., Ahmad, T., & Patwary, M. N. (2022). A secure and intelligent framework for vehicle health monitoring exploiting big-data analytics. *IEEE Transactions on Intelligent Transportation Systems*, *23*(10), 19727–19742. DOI: 10.1109/TITS.2021.3138255

Rajest, S. S., Moccia, S., Chinnusamy, K., Singh, B., & Regin, R. (Eds.). (2023). Advances in Educational Technologies and Instructional Design *Handbook of research on learning in language classrooms through ICT-based digital technology*., DOI: 10.4018/978-1-6684-6682-7

Rajest, S. S., Moccia, S., Singh, B., Regin, R., & Jeganathan, J. (Eds.). (2024, August 30). Advances in Computational Intelligence and Robotics *Optimizing intelligent systems for cross-industry application*., DOI: 10.4018/979-8-3693-8659-0

Rajest, S. S., Moccia, S., Singh, B., Regin, R., & Jeganathan, J. (Eds.). (2024, August 30). Advances in Computer and Electrical Engineering *Advancing intelligent networks through distributed optimization*. IGI Global. DOI: 10.4018/979-8-3693-3739-4

Rajest, S. S., Singh, B. J., Obaid, A., Regin, R., & Chinnusamy, K. (2023a). *Recent developments in machine and human intelligence*. Advances in Computational Intelligence and Robotics. IGI Global., DOI: 10.4018/978-1-6684-9189-8

Raj, M. A., Mishra, A., & Forest, G. A. (2024). Predictive Analytics for Employee Attrition: Leveraging Machine Learning for Strategic Human Resources Management. *AVE Trends in Intelligent Technoprise Letters*, *1*(1), 13–29.

Raj, M. A., Thinesh, M. A., Varmann, S. S. M., Pothu, A. R., & Paramasivan, P. (2024). Ensemble-based phishing website detection using Extra Trees classifier. *AVE Trends in Intelligent Computing Systems*, *1*(3), 142–156.

Ramgirkar, A., & Talhar, J. (2024). Advanced intelligent systems for quantitative analysis of crop production and efficiency in Maharashtra. *FMDB Transactions on Sustainable Computing Systems*, *2*(1), 1–12. DOI: 10.69888/FTSCS.2024.000192

Rebekah, D. R. (2015). Handling Missing Values in Longitudinal panel data with multiple imputation. *Journal of Marriage and Family*, *77*(1), 277–294. DOI: 10.1111/jomf.12144 PMID: 26113748

Regin, R., T, S., George, S. R., Bhattacharya, M., Datta, D., & Priscila, S. S. (2023). Development of predictive model of diabetic using supervised machine learning classification algorithm of ensemble voting. *International Journal of Bioinformatics Research and Applications*, *19*(3), 151–169. DOI: 10.1504/IJBRA.2023.10057044

Ret-Elba, R. (2024). ReT-ELBa: A Novel Algorithm for Efficient Load Balancing in Cloud Computing", Yusif Rashid and Callistus Ireneous Nakpih. *Asian Journal of Research in Computer Science*, *17*(5), 56–64. DOI: 10.9734/ajrcos/2024/v17i5438

Rose, D., Vijayakumar, K., Kirubakaran, D., Pugalenthi, R., & Balayaswantasaichowdary, G. (2023). Neural Machine Translation Using Attention. *2023 International Conference on Artificial Intelligence and Knowledge Discovery in Concurrent Engineering (ICECONF)*, Chennai, India.

Saad, W., Bennis, M., & Chen, M. (2019). A vision of 6G wireless systems: Applications, trends, technologies, and open research problems. *IEEE Network*, *34*(3), 134–142. DOI: 10.1109/MNET.001.1900287

Said, F. B., & Tripathi, S. (2023). Epistemology of Digital Journalism Shift in South Global Nations: A Bibliometric Analysis. *FMDB Transactions on Sustainable Technoprise Letters*, *1*(1), 47–60.

Sajini, S., Reddi, L. T., Regin, R., & Rajest, S. S. (2023). A Comparative Analysis of Routing Protocols for Efficient Data Transmission in Vehicular Ad Hoc Networks (VANETs). *FMDB Transactions on Sustainable Computing Systems*, *1*(1), 1–10.

Saleh, M., Mustapha, Z. B., & Ndirmbitah, B. K. (2024). Empirical analysis of digital marketing on the purchasing habit of conservative digital users of common social media. *FMDB Transactions on Sustainable Technoprise Letters*, *2*(1), 31–41. DOI: 10.69888/FTSTPL.2024.000228

Samant, S. S., Bhanu Murthy, N. L., & Malapati, A. (2019). Improving term weighting schemes for short text classification in vector space model. *IEEE Access : Practical Innovations, Open Solutions*, *7*(11), 166578–166592. DOI: 10.1109/ACCESS.2019.2953918

Santhosh, S., Krishna, B., Al-Amin, M., & Pradeep, V. (2023). Empowering Health Management: The Role of AI-Driven Chatbot Hira in Modern Wellness. *FMDB Transactions on Sustainable Technoprise Letters*, *1*(4), 204–222.

Santos, M. S., Pereira, R. C., Costa, A. F., Soares, J. P., Santos, J., & Abreu, P. H. (2016). Generating synthetic missing data: A review by missing mechanism. *IEEE Access : Practical Innovations, Open Solutions*, *7*(1), 11651–11667.

Sarker, I. H. (2022). Machine learning for intelligent data analysis and automation in cybersecurity: Current and future prospects. *Annals of Data Science*, *10*(6), 1473–1498. DOI: 10.1007/s40745-022-00444-2

Saurabh, S., Jain, P., Agarwal, M., & Ram, O. S. (2021). Applications of Machine Learning in VLSI Design. In *VLSI and Hardware Implementations Using Modern Machine Learning Methods* (pp. 125–139). CRC Press. DOI: 10.1201/9781003201038-7

Savita, K., Kumar, N., & Siwch, A. (2024). Fuzzy Clustering is based on a distance metric under an intuitionistic fuzzy environment. *Granular Computing*, *9*(1), 9–13. DOI: 10.1007/s41066-023-00446-2

Saxena, D., & Chaudhary, S. (2023). Predicting Brain Diseases from FMRI-Functional Magnetic Resonance Imaging with Machine Learning Techniques for Early Diagnosis and Treatment. *FMDB Transactions on Sustainable Computer Letters*, *1*(1), 33–48.

Saxena, R. R., Sujith, S., & Nelavala, R. (2023). MuscleDrive: A Proof of Concept Describing the Electromyographic Navigation of a Vehicle. *FMDB Transactions on Sustainable Health Science Letters*, *1*(2), 107–117.

Sayedelahl, M. A. (2024). Enabling Intelligent Traffic Systems: A Deep Learning Method for Accurate Arabic License Plate Recognition. *FMDB Transactions on Sustainable Intelligent Networks*, *1*(1), 40–55. DOI: 10.69888/FTSIN.2024.000156

Sayedelahl, M. A., & Farouk, R. M. (2024). Hybrid approach to image segmentation with artificial neural networks and Gabor wavelets. *AVE Trends in Intelligent Computing Systems*, *1*(2), 77–90.

Schafer, J. L., & Olsen, M. K. (2010). Multiple imputation for multivariate missing-data problems: A data analyst's perceptive. *Multivariate Behavioral Research*, *33*(4), 545–571. DOI: 10.1207/s15327906mbr3304_5 PMID: 26753828

Schneider, K.-M. (2005). Techniques for improving the performance of naive Bayes for text classification. In Computational Linguistics and Intelligent Text Processing, Springer Berlin Heidelberg. Lecture Notes in Computer Science, St. Petersburg, Russia. DOI: 10.1007/978-3-540-30586-6_76

Schulz-Mönninghoff, M., Neidhardt, M., & Niero, M. (2023). What is the contribution of different business processes to material circularity at company-level? A case study for electric vehicle batteries. *Journal of Cleaner Production*, *382*(1), 135232. DOI: 10.1016/j.jclepro.2022.135232

Sebastiani, F. (2002). Machine learning in automated text categorization. *ACM Computing Surveys*, *34*(1), 1–47. DOI: 10.1145/505282.505283

Sebastian, J. E., Babu, J., & Ashifa, K. M. (2024). Family resilience during COVID-19: A study of adaptation and well-being among social work students. *AVE Trends in Intelligent Social Letters*, *1*(2), 93–103.

Sengupta, S., Datta, D., Rajest, S. S., Paramasivan, P., Shynu, T., & Regin, R. (2023). Development of rough-TOPSIS algorithm as hybrid MCDM and its implementation to predict diabetes. *International Journal of Bioinformatics Research and Applications*, *19*(4), 252–279. DOI: 10.1504/IJBRA.2023.135363

Ser, D., Bilbao, J., Lana, M. N., Muhammad, I., & Camacho, K. (2022). Efficient fake news detection using bagging ensembles of bidirectional echo state networks. In *2022 International Joint Conference on Neural Networks (IJCNN)* (pp. 1–7), Padua, Italy.

Shafi, M., Molisch, A. F., Smith, P. J., Haustein, T., Zhu, P., De Silva, P., Tufvesson, F., Benjebbour, A., & Wunder, G. (2017). 5G: A tutorial overview of standards, trials, challenges, deployment, and practice. *IEEE Journal on Selected Areas in Communications*, *35*(6), 1201–1221. DOI: 10.1109/JSAC.2017.2692307

Shahid, N.A.M., Islam, M., Mansoor Alam, M. M., & Suud, A. S. (2020). A Comprehensive Study of Load Balancing Approaches in the Cloud Computing Environment and a Novel Fault Tolerance Approach". 8(7), 99.

Shakya, R. K., & Gokhale, A. (2020). Real-time big data analytics architecture for edge computing environments. *IEEE Internet of Things Journal*, *7*(9), 8955–8965.

Shanahan, J. G., & Roma, N. (2003). Improving SVM text classification performance through threshold adjustment. In Machine Learning: ECML 2003, Springer Berlin Heidelberg. Lecture Notes in Computer Science, Barcelona, Spain. DOI: 10.1007/978-3-540-39857-8_33

Sharma, A. K., Upreti, K., & Vargis, B. (2020). *Experimental performance analysis of load balancing of tasks using honey bee inspired algorithm for resource allocation in cloud environment*. Elsevier. DOI: 10.1016/j.matpr.2020.09.359

Shen, Y., & Ke, J. (2021). Representative region-based active learning for histological classification of colorectal cancer. In 2021 IEEE 18th International Symposium on Biomedical Imaging (ISBI), Nice, France. DOI: 10.1109/ISBI48211.2021.9433931

Shen, Y., & Ke, J. (2020). A deformable CRF model for histopathology whole-slide image classification. In *Medical Image Computing and Computer Assisted Intervention – MICCAI*. Springer International Publishing. DOI: 10.1007/978-3-030-59722-1_48

Shilesh, D. M., Linson, L., Babu, J., & Ashifa, K. M. (2024). Exploring the impact of social media on adolescent food habits and dietary choices. *AVE Trends In Intelligent Social Letters, 1*(3), 148–156.

Shunmugathammal, M., Christopher Columbus, C., & Anand, S. (2020). A novel B* tree crossover-based simulated annealing algorithm for combinatorial optimization in VLSI fixed-outline floorplans. *Circuits, Systems, and Signal Processing, 39*(2), 900–918. DOI: 10.1007/s00034-019-01054-9

Shunmugathammal, M., Columbus, C. C., & Anand, S. (2020). nature-inspired optimization algorithm for VLSI fixed-outline floorplanning. *Analog Integrated Circuits and Signal Processing, 103*(2), 173–186. DOI: 10.1007/s10470-020-01598-w

Shuyang, J., & Yaming, Z. (2023). Multiple investment subjects financing contract allocation and technological innovation of new energy automobile enterprises. *Enterprise Economics, 15*(9), 7144.

Silvia Priscila, S., Soji, E. S., Hossó, N., Paramasivan, P., & Suman Rajest, S. (2023). Digital Realms and Mental Health: Examining the Influence of Online Learning Systems on Students. *FMDB Transactions on Sustainable Techno Learning, 1*(3), 156–164.

Singh, R., Preet Pal, P., & Kumar, B. (2009). Performance analysis of 32-bit array multiplier with a carry save adder and with a carry-look-ahead adder. *International Journal of Recent Trends in Engineering, 2*(6), 83.

Singh, S., Rajest, S. S., Hadoussa, S., Obaid, A. J., & Regin, R. (2023). *Data-Driven Intelligent Business Sustainability*. Advances in Business Information Systems and Analytics. IGI Global., DOI: 10.4018/979-8-3693-0049-7

Singh, S., Rajest, S. S., Hadoussa, S., Obaid, A. J., & Regin, R. (Eds.). (2023). Advances in Business Information Systems and Analytics *Data-driven decision making for long-term business success*. IGI Global., DOI: 10.4018/979-8-3693-2193-5

Sivapriya, G. B. V., Ganesh, U. G., Pradeeshwar, V., Dharshini, M., & Al-Amin, M. (2023). Crime Prediction and Analysis Using Data Mining and Machine Learning: A Simple Approach that Helps Predictive Policing. *FMDB Transactions on Sustainable Computer Letters*, *1*(2), 64–75.

Sohlot, J., Teotia, P., Govinda, K., Rangineni, S., & Paramasivan, P. (2023). A Hybrid Approach on Fertilizer Resource Optimization in Agriculture Using Opposition-Based Harmony Search with Manta Ray Foraging Optimization. *FMDB Transactions on Sustainable Computing Systems*, *1*(1), 44–53.

Soucy, P., & Mineau, G. (2003). Feature selection strategies for text categorization. *Lecture Notes in Computer Science*, *2671*(6), 505–509. DOI: 10.1007/3-540-44886-1_41

Sreenu, K., & Sreelatha, M. (2017). W-Scheduler: Whale optimization for task scheduling in cloud computing. *Cluster Computing*, *22*(6), 1–12.

Stavrinides, G. L., & Karatza, H. (2018). *A hybrid approach to scheduling real-time IoT workflows in fog and cloud environments* (Vol. 78). Springer.

Suganthi, M., & Sathiaseelan, J. G. R. (2023). Image Denoising and Feature Extraction Techniques Applied to X-Ray Seed Images for Purity Analysis. *FMDB Transactions on Sustainable Health Science Letters*, *1*(1), 41–53.

Sulaiman, R. B., Aljaidi, M., Alsuwaylimi, A. A., Butt, U., Talukder, M. S. H., Alam, S. S., Farhan, M., Das, S. R., & Alam, M. W. (2024). Enhancing security in digital payments: A comparative evaluation of machine learning models for credit card fraud detection. *FMDB Transactions on Sustainable Computer Letters*, *2*(2), 63–84. DOI: 10.69888/FTSCL.2024.000182

Sundararajan, V., Steffi, R., & Shynu, T. (2023). Data Fusion Strategies for Collaborative Multi-Sensor Systems: Achieving Enhanced Observational Accuracy and Resilience. *FMDB Transactions on Sustainable Computing Systems*, *1*(3), 112–123.

Sun, T.-W. (2020). End-to-end speech emotion recognition with gender information. *IEEE Access : Practical Innovations, Open Solutions*, *20*(2), 1–15. DOI: 10.1109/ACCESS.2020.2994628

Suraj, D., Dinesh, S., Balaji, R., Deepika, P., & Ajila, F. (2023). Deciphering Product Review Sentiments Using BERT and TensorFlow. *FMDB Transactions on Sustainable Computing Systems*, *1*(2), 77–88.

Taj, I., & Zaman, N. (2022). Towards Industrial Revolution 5.0 and explainable artificial intelligence: Challenges and opportunities. *International Journal of Computing and Digital Systems*, *12*(1), 285–310. DOI: 10.12785/ijcds/120124

Tang, Y.-P., Wei, X.-S., Zhao, B., & Huang, S.-J. (2023). QBox: Partial transfer learning with active querying for object detection. *IEEE Transactions on Neural Networks and Learning Systems*, *34*(6), 3058–3070. DOI: 10.1109/TNNLS.2021.3111621 PMID: 34570711

Tareq, W. Z. T., & Davud, M. (2024). Classification and Clustering. In *Decision-Making Models*. Elsevier. DOI: 10.1016/B978-0-443-16147-6.00024-4

Tatar, A., de Amorim, M. D., Fdida, S., & Antoniadis, P. (2014). A survey on predicting the popularity of web content. *Journal of Internet Services and Applications*, *5*(1), 1–20. DOI: 10.1186/s13174-014-0008-y

Thanka, M. R., Maheswari, P., & Edwin, E. B. (2019). An improved efficient: Artificial bee colony algorithm for security and QoS aware scheduling in cloud computing environment. *Cluster Computing*, *22*(5), 10905–10913. DOI: 10.1007/s10586-017-1223-7

Thirunagalingam, A. (2024). Bias detection and mitigation in data pipelines: Ensuring fairness and accuracy in machine learning. *AVE Trends in Intelligent Computing Systems*, *1*(2), 116–127.

Tim, P., Morris, I. R., & White, P. (2014). Tuning multiple imputation by predictive mean matching and local residual draws. *BMC Medical Research Methodology*, *5*(6), 1–13.

Tin, H. H. K., Thu, S., & Maung, K. K. (2024). A Systematic Review of Rice Husk Gasifiers: Technology, Performance, and Sustainability. *FMDB Transactions on Sustainable Environmental Sciences*, *1*(1), 31–40. DOI: 10.69888/FTSESS.2024.000146

Tripathi, S. (2023). Breaking News or Breaking Trust? The Impact of Credibility Menace on Indian Media. *FMDB Transactions on Sustainable Social Sciences Letters*, *1*(4), 189–197.

Troiano, M., Nobile, E., Grignaffini, F., Mangini, F., Mastrogiuseppe, M., Conati Barbaro, C., & Frezza, F. (2024). A comparative analysis of machine learning algorithms for identifying cultural and technological groups in archaeological datasets through clustering analysis of homogeneous data. *Electronics (Basel)*, *13*(14), 2752. DOI: 10.3390/electronics13142752

Tronnebati, I., & Jawab, F. (2023). Green and Sustainable Supply Chain Management: A Comparative Literature Review. *Jjmie*, *17*(1), 115–126. DOI: 10.59038/jjmie/170109

Trung Nguyen Quoc, V. T. (2020). Medicinal Plant identification in the wild by using CNN" 2020 International Conference on Information and Communication Technology Convergence (ICTC). 21–23, Jeju, Korea (South).

Tschiatschek, S., Mutsam, N., & Pernkopf, F. (2012). Handling missing features in maximum margin Bayesian network classifiers. *2012 IEEE International Workshop on Machine Learning for Signal Processing*. IEEE, Santander, Spain. DOI: 10.1109/MLSP.2012.6349804

Uddin, M. T., Patwary, M. J. A., Ahsan, T., & Alam, M. S. (2016). Predicting the popularity of online news from content metadata. *2016 International Conference on Innovations in Science, Engineering and Technology (ICISET)*, Dhaka, Bangladesh, 1-5. DOI: 10.1109/ICISET.2016.7856498

Ulle, R. S., & Yogananthan, S. (2024). Unmasking fake opinions through behavioral analysis and machine learning: Identifying genuine users vs. fraudulent actors. *FMDB Transactions on Sustainable Management Letters*, *2*(2), 51–64. DOI: 10.69888/FTSML.2024.000235

Usman, M., & Ullah, A. (2024). Blockchain Technology Implementation in Libraries: An Overview of Potential Benefits and Challenges. *AVE Trends In Intelligent Computing Systems*, *1*(1), 42–53.

Vahidi, J., & Rahmati, M. (2019). Optimization of Resource Allocation in Cloud Computing by Grasshopper Optimization Algorithm". In *5th Conference on Knowledge-Based Engineering and InnovatioN*, Tehean, Iran. DOI: 10.1109/KBEI.2019.8735098

Vashishtha, E., & Dhawan, G. (2023). Comparison of Baldrige Criteria of Strategy Planning and Harrison Text. *FMDB Transactions on Sustainable Management Letters*, *1*(1), 22–31.

Venkateswaran, P. S., Dharshini, S. D., Kumar, S. K., Lakshmi, D., Balan, D., & Sachani, D. K. (2024). A Study on Market Share Analysis of Select Food Products: Identifying Key Drivers and Barriers to Growth. *AVE Trends In Intelligent Social Letters*, *1*(1), 1–12.

Venkateswaran, P. S., Singh, S., Paramasivan, P., Rajest, S. S., Lourens, M. E., & Regin, R. (2023). A Study on The Influence of Quality of Service on Customer Satisfaction Towards Hotel Industry. *FMDB Transactions on Sustainable Social Sciences Letters*, *1*(1), 1–11.

Venkateswaran, P. S., Sriramkumar, M., Vaddy, R. K., Kotagiri, A., Rajest, S. S., & Regin, R. (2024). Applications of Artificial Intelligence and Robots in Service Industries. In *Advances in Computer and Electrical Engineering* (pp. 61–80). IGI Global.

Venugopalan, J., Chanani, N., Maher, K., & Wang, M. D. (2019). Novel data imputation for multiple types of missing data in intensive care units. *IEEE Journal of Biomedical and Health Informatics*, *23*(3), 1243–1250. DOI: 10.1109/JBHI.2018.2883606 PMID: 30998482

Vesin, A., Azoulay, E., Ruckly, S., Vignoud, L., Rusinovà, K., Benoit, D., Soares, M., Azeivedo-Maia, P., Abroug, F., Benbenishty, J., & Timsit, J. F. (2013). Reporting and handling missing values in clinical studies in intensive care units. *Intensive Care Medicine*, *39*(8), 1396–1404. DOI: 10.1007/s00134-013-2949-1 PMID: 23685609

Vijayakumar, S., & Rosario, J. N. (2011). Preliminary Design for Crop Monitoring Involving Water and Fertilizer Conservation Using Wireless Sensor Networks. In *Communication Software and Networks (ICCSN)*. IEEE. DOI: 10.1109/ICCSN.2011.6014979

Vijayan, S. (2020a). Fine tuned VGG19 convolutional neural network architecture for diabetic retinopathy diagnosis. *Indian Journal of Computer Science and Engineering*, *11*(5), 615–622. DOI: 10.21817/indjcse/2020/v11i5/201105266

Vijayan, T., & Karthik, B. (2020). Trainable WEKA Segmentation of Retinal Fundus Images for Global Eye Disease Diagnosis Application. *International Journal of Emerging Trends in Engineering Research*, *8*(9), 5750–5754. DOI: 10.30534/ijeter/2020/136892020

Vijayan, T., Sangeetha, M., & Karthik, B. (2020). Efficient Analysis of Diabetic Retinopathy on Retinal Fundus Images using Deep Learning Techniques with Inception V3 Architecture. *Journal of Green Engineering*, *10*(10), 9615–9625.

Waghmode, T., & Bankat, M. (2023). Adaptive Load Balancing In Cloud Computing Environment", Intelligent Systems And Applications In Engineering. *IJISAE, 11*(7), 302–314.

Wajgi, D. W., & Tembhurne, J. V. (2023). Correction: Localization in wireless and multimedia sensor networks using clustering techniques. *Multimedia Tools and Applications, 83*(7), 6881.

Wali, G. (2024). Evaluating centralized and decentralized maintenance strategies for improved operational efficiency. *AVE Trends in Intelligent Technoprise Letters, 1*(2), 91–99.

Wang, J., Li, Y., Shan, J., Bao, J., Zong, C., & Zhao, L. (2019). Large-scale text classification using scope-based convolutional neural network: A deep learning approach. *IEEE Access : Practical Innovations, Open Solutions, 7*(11), 171548–171558. DOI: 10.1109/ACCESS.2019.2955924

Wang, J., Wu, Y., Huang, X., Zhang, C., & Nie, F. (2024). Projected fuzzy c-means clustering algorithm with instance penalty. *Expert Systems with Applications, 255*(12), 124563. DOI: 10.1016/j.eswa.2024.124563

Wang, L., Ma, Y., & Zhang, Z. (2020). A scalable real-time data processing pipeline for big data applications. *IEEE Transactions on Big Data, 6*(3), 506–517.

White, I. R., & Royston, P. (2009). Imputing missing covariate values for the Cox model: Imputing Missing Covariate Values for The Cox Model. *Statistics in Medicine, 28*(15), 1982–1998. DOI: 10.1002/sim.3618 PMID: 19452569

Wong, S. D., Shaheen, S. A., Martin, E., & Uyeki, R. (2023). Do incentives make a difference? Understanding smart charging program adoption for electric vehicles. *Transportation Research Part C, Emerging Technologies, 151*(6), 104123. DOI: 10.1016/j.trc.2023.104123

Wu, C., Jia, Y., & Barnes, D. (2023). Criteria system construction for sustainable supplier selection: A product-category-oriented intelligent model. *Applied Soft Computing, 145*(9), 110586. DOI: 10.1016/j.asoc.2023.110586

Xiao, L. (2010). The Realization of Precision Agriculture Monitoring System Based on Wireless Sensor Network. *2010 International Conference on Computer and Communication Technologies in Agriculture Engineering*, 3(7), 89–92.

Xu, X., Xia, L., Zhang, Q., Wu, S., Wu, M., & Liu, H. (2020). The ability of different imputation methods for missing values in mental measurement questionnaires. *BMC Medical Research Methodology, 20*(2), 1–9. DOI: 10.1186/s12874-020-00932-0 PMID: 32103723

Yadav, C., & Gupta, Y. K. (2019). Cost Effective Ant Colony Optimization in Cloud Computing. *International Journal of Innovative Technology and Exploring Engineering*, *8*(10), 3016–3020. DOI: 10.35940/ijitee.J9460.0881019

Yang, Y., Zhang, J., & Kisiel, B. (2003). *A scalability analysis of classifiers in text categorization*. DOI: 10.1145/860435.860455

Yaseen, T., Valentyn, A., & Tolpekin, A. (2012). Application of Expectation Maximization algorithm to estimate missing values in Gaussian Bayesian Network modeling for forest growth. *IEEE Transactions on Geoscience and Remote Sensing*, *50*(5), 1821–1831. DOI: 10.1109/TGRS.2011.2168823

Yoo, D., & Kweon, I. S. (2019). Learning loss for active learning. In *2019 IEEE/CVF Conference on Computer Vision and Pattern Recognition*, Long Beach, California, USA.

Yu, B., Zheng, Z., Cai, M., Pedrycz, W., & Ding, W. (2024). FRCM: A fuzzy rough c-means clustering method. Fuzzy Sets and Systems. *An International Journal in Information Science and Engineering*, *480*(3), 108860.

Yuqiang, G., Zishuai, W., & Yu, Z. (2023). How can Big Data application curb the maturity mismatch of enterprise investment and financing-Resource effect and information effect. Financial Forum, 75(11), 102351.

Yu, Z., Liu, Y., Xie, G., Li, R., Liu, S., & Yang, L. T. (2023). TCE-IDS: Time interval conditional entropy-based intrusion detection system for automotive controller area networks. *IEEE Transactions on Industrial Informatics*, *19*(2), 1185–1195. DOI: 10.1109/TII.2022.3202539

Zaharia, M. A., Das, T., & Crankshaw, D. (2020). End-to-end real-time analytics with Apache Spark. *Journal of Cloud Computing (Heidelberg, Germany)*, *9*(1), 1–16.

Zanardo, E. (2024). Chronostamp: A general-purpose run-time for data-flow computing in a distributed environment. *AVE Trends in Intelligent Computing Systems*, *1*(2), 106–115.

Zhang, W., Zhu, L., Hallinan, J., Zhang, S., Makmur, A., Cai, Q., & Ooi, B. C. (2022). BoostMIS: Boosting medical image semi-supervised learning with adaptive pseudo labeling and informative active annotation. In *2022 IEEE/CVF Conference on Computer Vision and Pattern Recognition (CVPR)*, New Orleans, Louisiana, United States. DOI: 10.1109/CVPR52688.2022.02001

Zhang, Y., & Liu, Y. (2009). Data imputation using least squares support vector machines in urban arterial streets. *IEEE Signal Processing Letters*, *16*(5), 414–417. DOI: 10.1109/LSP.2009.2016451

Zhang, Z., Xiao, Y., Ma, Z., Xiao, M., Ding, Z., Lei, X., Karagiannidis, G. K., & Fan, P. (2019). 6G wireless networks: Vision, requirements, architecture, and key technologies. *IEEE Vehicular Technology Magazine*, *14*(3), 28–41. DOI: 10.1109/MVT.2019.2921208

Zhao, W., Zhang, G., Yuan, G., Liu, J., Shan, H., & Zhang, S. (2020). The study on the text classification for financial news based on partial information. *IEEE Access : Practical Innovations, Open Solutions*, *8*(5), 100426–100437. DOI: 10.1109/ACCESS.2020.2997969

Zhao, Y., & Liu, S.-J. (2019). Active sampling for open-set classification without initial annotation. *Proceedings of the AAAI Conference on Artificial Intelligence*, *33*(1), 4416–4423. DOI: 10.1609/aaai.v33i01.33014416

Zhou, B., Lu, B., & Saeidlou, S. (2022). A hybrid clustering method based on several diverse basic Clustering and meta-clustering aggregation techniques. *Cybernetics and Systems*, *55*(1), 203–229. DOI: 10.1080/01969722.2022.2110682

Zhuang, W.-Y., Junior, M. C., Cheong, P., & Tam, K.-W. (2011). Flood Monitoring of Distribution Substation in Low-Lying Areas Using Wireless Sensor Network". In *Proceedings of 2011 International Conference on System Science and Engineering*, Maco, China. DOI: 10.1109/ICSSE.2011.5961974

Zhu, X., Zhang, S., Jin, Z., Zhang, Z., & Xu, Z. (2011). Missing value estimation for mixed-attribute data sets. *IEEE Transactions on Knowledge and Data Engineering*, *23*(1), 110–121. DOI: 10.1109/TKDE.2010.99

About The Contributors

Ferdin Joe John Joseph is currently an Assistant Professor with the faculty of information technology, Thai Nichi Institute of technology Bangkok. He graduated his bachelor and masters degrees in computer science and engineering from Anna University Chennai during 2009 and 2011 respectively. He got his PhD in Computer Science and Information Systems from the National Institute of Development Administration Bangkok during 2015. His area of research includes deep learning, IoT and Blockchain technology. He has nearly a decade experience in teaching. He has published in peer reviewed international conferences and journals. He is certified as the "Most Valuable Professional" (MVP) with Alibaba Cloud since 2021. He is teaching as per academic curriculum to students, recognizing, nurturing the creative potential of each student. Teach students using a systematic instructional methodology comprising lecture plans (following the credit allotted to each subject), discussion groups, seminars, case studies, field assignments, and independent and/or group projects. Recently, he has been the technique program committee, the technique reviews, and the track chair for international conferences published by Springer Series. He is serving in the editor in chief, the editorial board of international journals, and he authored/edited different books and filed so many Patents. Finally, he is a member of ISTE, IET, Etc…

Karthikeyan Chinnusamy, Sr Principal with more than 25 years of experience in IT, Product Dev, R&D and Education fields. Fellow IETE, Fellow IE, Sr Member IEEE,Sr Member ACM, Project management Institute (PMI), Reviewer, Editorial Board Member of R&D Journals. Board Member & Program Director SF DAMA. SME in Data Governance, GDPR, HIPAA Compliance, Data Management, Data Architecture, Master Data, Data Quality, AI/ML, Analytics and reporting in Payment processing, Customer, Finance, CRM and License domains. Mentor in SFDC Mig, Data.com, ERP, Architecture, R&D, Embedded systems, VLSI,Adv Information processing. I am also reviewer for IEEE Silicon Valley Sr Member Elevation and Speaker, Volunteer for SFBay ACM. Reviewer of Journals in Springer Nature.

Joseph Jeganathan earned his Ph.D. in Psychiatric Nursing from Rajiv Gandhi University of Health Sciences, National Consortium for Ph.D. Nursing, (Indian Nursing Council), Bangalore, Karnataka, India in 2019. He completed his Postgraduate studies at the National Institute of Mental Health and Neurosciences, Bangalore, Karnataka, India 2011. He is working as an assistant professor in the Mental Health Nursing Department at the University of Bahrain, Kingdom of Bahrain. He has more than 16 years of Undergraduate and Postgraduate teaching experience. He has worked as a Professor at SGT University, Gurugram, Dept. of Nursing, IES University, Bhopal; Associate Professor Akal College of Nursing, Eternal University, Baru Sahib, India; and also worked as a teaching faculty in various nursing colleges in India and Nepal. Dr. Joseph Jeganathan has published many research articles in National and international Nursing Journals. His areas of research interest are Adolescent mental health, Life skills training, and Substance use disorders.

Ahmed J. Obaid, is a full assistant professor at the Department of Computer Science, Faculty of Computer Science and Mathematics, University of Kufa, He received his BSC in Information Systems (IS) in 2005, from faculty of computer science, University of Anbar in 2005. M.Tech in Computer Science and Engineering from SIT, JNTUH, India in 2012, and PhD in Web Mining and Data Mining from University of Babylon in 2017. His main line of research is Web mining Techniques and Application, Image processing in the Web Platforms, Image processing, Genetic Algorithm and information theory. Ahmed J. Obaid, is an Associated Editor in Brazilian Journal of Operations & Production Management (ESCI), Guest Editor in KEM (Key Engineering Material, Scopus) Journal, Guest Editor of MAICT-19 and ICMAICT-20 issues in IOP journal of Physics, Scopus indexed proceeding. Guest Editor in JESTEC journal (Scopus, WOS) Journal, Managing Editor in American Journal of Business and Operations Research (AJBOR), USA. Associate Editor in IJAST Scopus Journal. Ahmed J. Obaid also Reviewer in many Scopus Journals (Scientific publication, Taylor and Francis, ESTA, and many others). He is leader of ICPAS, MAICT-19, MAICT-20, IHICPS, IICPS Conferences. Ahmed J. Obaid has supervised several final projects of Bachelor and Master in His main line of work. He has edited Some books, such as Advance Material Science and Engineering (ISBN: 9783035736779, Scientific.net publisher), Computational Intelligence Techniques for Combating COVID-19, A Fusion of Artificial Intelligence and Internet of Things for Emerging Cyber Systems. He has authored and co-authored several scientific publications in journals and conferences and is a frequent reviewer of international journals and international conferences.

S. Suman Rajest is the Dean of Research and Development (R&D) and International Student Affairs (ISA) at Dhaanish Ahmed College of Engineering, Chennai, Tamil Nadu, India. He is an Editor in Chief of the International Journal of Human Computing Studies and The International Journal of Social Sciences World, He is the Chief Executive Editor of the International Journal of Advanced Engineering Research and Science, International Journal of Advanced Engineering, Management and Science, The International Journal of Health and Medicines, The International Journal of Management Economy and Accounting Fields and The International Journal of Technology Information and Computer and also he is an Editorial Board Member in International Journal of Management in Education, Scopus, Inderscience, EAI Endorsed Transactions on e-Learning, and Bulletin of the Karaganda university Pedagogy series. He is also a Book Series Editor at IGI Global Publisher, Springer, etc. All of his writing, including his research, involves elements of creative nonfiction in the Human Computing learning system. He is also interested in creative writing and digital media, Learning, AI, student health learning, etc. He has published 400 papers in peer-reviewed international journals. He has authored and co-authored several scientific book publications in journals and conferences and is a frequent reviewer of international journals and conferences. He also reviews Inderscience, EAI Journals, IGI Global, Science Publications, etc.

***

Pandi Maharajan.M currently working as an Associate Professor in the Department of Electronics and Communication Engineering at Dhaanish Ahmed College of Engineering, Chennai, Tamil Nadu, India. He obtained his Ph. D in ANNA University (2020), Chennai. He completed his M.E in Sethu Institute of Technology, (2011), Virudhunagar. He completed his BE in Mohamed Sathak Engineering College (2007), Ramanathapuram. He has published more than 9 Scopus indexed journals and 3 SCIE journals in his field. He has published 4 patents in his field. He has presented papers in 14 International conferences. He has more than 14.10 years of teaching experience. His area of interest is Special Electrical Machines, Power Converter Design, E-vehicle & Renewable Energy and its applications

M. Sakthivanitha is currently working as Assistant Professor in the Department of Computer Application,Vels institute of Science Technology and Advanced Studies(VISTAS),Chennai,India.Her experience includes,as a teaching faculty for more than Seven Years in various institutions.Her research area includes Data Mining,Internet of Things,Network Security.

Satyanarayana Naga V. Kanuboyina presently working as an assistant professor in Department of Electronics and Communication Engineering, S.R.K.R. Engineering College, Bhimavaram, A.P, India. he has PhD from Annamalai University. His current research interests ML, AI, include Image processing, Signal processing, and Internet of things.

T. Vijayan is working as a associate Professor, Department of Electronics and Communication Engineering, Bharath Institute of Higher Education and Research, Chennai. His current research interests include artificial intelligence, machine learning, soft computing, digital image processing, signal processing and communication systems. He is a member of IEEE, and IAENG.

Index

www.ingramcontent.com/pod-product-compliance
Lightning Source LLC
LaVergne TN
LVHW081350300926
849161LV00008B/2114